This companion serves both as an introduction for the interested reader and as a source of the best recent scholarship on the author and his works. In addition to analyzing his major texts, these chapters provide insight into Hemingway's relationship with gender history, journalism, fame, and the political climate of the 1930s. The essays are framed by an introductory chapter on Hemingway and the costs of fame and an invaluable conclusion providing an overview of Hemingway scholarship from its beginnings to the present. Students will find the selected bibliography a useful guide to future research.

THE CAMBRIDGE
COMPANION TO
HEMINGWAY

Cambridge Companions to Literature

Continued on page following Index

THE CAMBRIDGE
COMPANION TO
HEMINGWAY

EDITED BY
SCOTT DONALDSON

College of William and Mary

CAMBRIDGE
UNIVERSITY PRESS

PUBLISHED BY THE PRESS SYNDICATE OF THE UNIVERSITY OF CAMBRIDGE
The Pitt Building, Trumpington Street, Cambridge CB2 1RP, United Kingdom

CAMBRIDGE UNIVERSITY PRESS
The Edinburgh Building, Cambridge CB2 2RU, UK   http: //www.cup.cam.ac.uk
40 West 20th Street, New York, NY 10011-4211, USA   http: //www.cup.org
10 Stamford Road, Oakleigh, Melbourne 3166, Australia

First published 1996
Reprinted 1997, 1998

Printed in the United States of America

Typeset in Sabon

A catalogue record for this book is available from the British Library

Library of Congress Cataloguing-in-Publication Data is available

ISBN 0-521-45479-4 hardback
ISBN 0-521-45574-X paperback

CONTENTS

CONTRIBUTORS

ELIZABETH DEWBERRY, Assistant Professor of English at Ohio State University, is a novelist as well as a critic. Her first two novels were *Many Things Have Happened Since He Died* (Doubleday, 1990) and *Break the Heart of Me* (Doubleday, 1994).

SCOTT DONALDSON is Louise G.T. Cooley Professor of English, Emeritus, at the College of William and Mary. He is the author of *By Force of Will: The Life and Art of Ernest Hemingway (Viking Press, 1977)*, and of a number of articles on Hemingway. He has also written biographies of Winfield Townley Scott, F. Scott Fitzgerald, John Cheever, and Archibald MacLeish.

SUSAN F. BEEGEL, University of Idaho, edits *The Hemingway Review*. She is the author of *Hemingway's Craft of Omission: Four Manuscript Examples* (UMI Research Press, 1988) and editor of *Hemingway's Neglected Short Fiction: New Perspectives* (University of Alabama Press, 1992).

ROBERT E. FLEMING is Professor of English and Associate Dean at the University of New Mexico. Among his publications are reference guides to James Weldon Johnson, Arna Wendell Bontemps, and Sinclair Lewis, and several articles on Hemingway's stories and *The Garden of Eden,* in addition to *The Face in the Mirror: Hemingway's Writers* (University of Alabama Press, 1994).

ALLEN JOSEPHS, Professor of Spanish at the University of West Florida, is author of *White Wall of Spain: The Mysteries of Andalusian Culture* (Iowa State University Press, 1983), and of several other books and articles on Spanish life and literature. His most recent book is *For Whom The Bell Tolls: Ernest Hemingway's Undiscovered Country* (Twayne, 1994).

J. GERALD KENNEDY, Professor of English at Louisiana State University, has written *Poe, Death, and the Life of Writing* (Yale University Press, 1987), and *Imagining Paris: Exile Writing and American Identity* (Yale University Press, 1993). He also edited *Modern American Short Story Se-*

quences: Composite Fictions and Fictive Communities (Cambridge University Press, 1995).

KENETH KINNAMON, Professor of English at the University of Arkansas, has edited and written several books on African-American writers, including *James Baldwin: A Collection of Critical Essays* (Prentice-Hall, 1974) and *The Emergence of Richard Wright: A Study in Literature and Society* (University of Illinois Press, 1972), as well as several articles on Hemingway.

JAMES NAGEL, J. O. Eidson Distinguished Professor of American Literature at the University of Georgia, edited *Ernest Hemingway: The Writer in Context* (University of Wisconsin Press, 1984), and with Henry S. Villard wrote *Hemingway in Love and War: The Lost Diary of Agnes von Kurowsky* (Northeastern University Press, 1989), in addition to other books on American writers from Crane to Hemingway.

MICHAEL REYNOLDS, Professor of English and Associate Dean at North Carolina State University, is writing a multi-volume literary biography of Hemingway, the first three volumes of which are *The Young Hemingway* (Basil Blackwell, 1986), *Hemingway: The Paris Years* (Basil Blackwell, 1989), and *Hemingway: The American Homecoming* (Basil Blackwell, 1992). Among his other publications on this subject are *Hemingway's First War: The Making of A Farewell to Arms* (Princeton University Press, 1976), and *Hemingway's Reading: 1910–1940* (Princeton University Press, 1981).

RENA SANDERSON, Assistant Professor of English at Boise State University, edited *Blowing the Bridge: Essays on Hemingway and For Whom the Bell Tolls* (Greenwood Press, 1992). She is book review editor for the *Rocky Mountain Review.*

PAUL SMITH, who is James J. Goodwin Professor of English, Emeritus, at Trinity College, was the founding president of the Hemingway Society. Through his work with the manuscripts at the John F. Kennedy Library in Boston, he has established himself as the leading authority on Hemingway's short fiction, culminating in his *Reader's Guide to the Short Stories of Ernest Hemingway* (G. K. Hall, 1989).

THOMAS STRYCHACZ, Assistant Professor of English at Mills College, is the author of *Modernism, Mass Culture, and Professionalism* (Cambridge University Press, 1993) and of several articles on Hemingway.

BICKFORD SYLVESTER, Associate Professor of English at the University of British Columbia, has written widely on Hemingway's stories and novels, paying scrupulous attention to the connotations and implications of the language.

CHRONOLOGY

1899   Ernest Miller Hemingway is born in Oak Park, Illinois, a suburb of Chicago, the second child of Dr. Clarence Edmonds Hemingway and Grace Hall Hemingway, a talented singer and music teacher.

1900   Goes with his family to their summer cottage called Windemere in northern Michigan, where he was to learn fishing and hunting and the lessons of nature from his father, a devoted outdoorsman.

1905   Enters first grade in same class with year-older sister Marcelline.

1913   Attends Oak Park and River Forest high school, where he distinguishes himself as an aspiring journalist/writer.

1917   Graduates from high school in June, takes job as cub reporter on the *Kansas City Star* in October.

1918   On May 23 sails to Europe to assume duties as Red Cross ambulance driver in Italy; badly wounded in Fossalta July 8 while distributing chocolate and cigarettes to troops; meets and falls in love with nurse Agnes von Kurowsky while recuperating in Milan.

1919   Returns to the United States, rejected by Agnes as too young.

1920   Quarrels with mother, who banishes him from Windemere shortly after his twenty-first birthday.

1921   Marries Hadley Richardson September 3; provided with letters of introduction from Sherwood Anderson, the newlyweds leave for Paris after Thanksgiving, where Hemingway writes dispatches for the *Toronto Star* and begins to hone a distinctive American prose style.

1922   In Paris meets expatriates Ezra Pound – "he's teaching me to write," Hemingway reported, "and I'm teaching him to box" – and Gertrude Stein, who reads a fragment of his novel-in-progress and advises him to "Begin over again and concentrate."

In December Hadley takes the train to Lausanne where he is on assignment and en route loses a valise containing the manuscripts of all of Ernest's unpublished fiction.

1923   Goes to Spain for the bullfights at Pamplona; briefly returns to Toronto for the birth of his son John Hadley (Bumby) in October; publishes *Three Stories and Ten Poems* in limited edition.

1924   Assists Ford Madox Ford in editing the *transatlantic review,* which prints "Indian Camp" and other early stories; brings out slim *in our time* volume.

1925   *In Our Time* appears, containing several stories set in Michigan about the maturation of a semiautobiographical character named Nick Adams and concluding with "Big Two-Hearted River"; in May meets and befriends the somewhat older and more established writer F. Scott Fitzgerald.

1926   Fitzgerald sends him to Scribner's and editor Maxwell Perkins for a career-long association, beginning with *The Torrents of Spring,* a satiric attack on Anderson, and *The Sun Also Rises,* his famous novel about expatriate life in Paris and Pamplona.

1927   Publishes *Men without Women,* a story collection including "Hills Like White Elephants" and "The Killers"; divorced by Hadley, marries Pauline Pfeiffer.

1928   Leaves Paris, moves to Key West; son Patrick born; Dr. Hemingway kills himself with a .32 revolver.

1929   *A Farewell to Arms* – a novel of love and war in Italy during World War I – published in September to good reviews and sales, despite Boston censorship of the serialized version in *Scribner's* magazine.

1930   Breaks arm in auto accident near Billings, Montana, one in a series of many injuries to his arms, legs, and head.

1931   Son Gregory Hancock born.

1932   Brings out his book on bullfighting, *Death in the Afternoon.*

1933   Publishes *Winner Take Nothing,* a book of stories including "A Clean, Well-Lighted Place"; goes on safari to Africa, the setting for his two long stories "The Snows of Kilimanjaro" and "The Short Happy Life of Francis Macomber" (both published in 1936).

1935   *Green Hills of Africa,* an account of adventures on safari.

1937   Serves as war correspondent during Spanish civil war; works on propaganda film *The Spanish Earth;* contributes funds to the

Loyalist cause; publishes *To Have and Have Not*, his most overtly political novel.

1938   Publishes *The Fifth Column and the First Forty-nine Stories*, comprising a play about the war in Spain and his stories to date.

1939   Separates from Pauline; moves to Finca Vigia, a house hear Havana, Cuba.

1940   Marries writer Martha Gellhorn; publishes *For Whom the Bell Tolls*, his best-selling novel about a band of guerrillas during the war in Spain.

1942   Outfits his boat the *Pilar* to hunt down German submarines in the Caribbean; none found.

1944   As correspondent, observes D-day and attaches himself to the 22nd Regiment, 4th Infantry Division for operations leading to the liberation of Paris and the battle of Hürtgenwald; begins relationship with newswoman Mary Welsh.

1945   Divorced by Martha in December.

1946   Marries Mary in March; they live in Cuba and in Ketchum, Idaho.

1950   Publishes *Across the River and into the Trees*, a novel about a December–May romance widely attacked by critics.

1952   *The Old Man and the Sea*, his short book about the trials of the Cuban fisherman Santiago, printed in its entirety in a single issue of *Life* magazine.

1953   Returns to Africa for safari with Mary.

1954   In January, severely injured by two successive plane crashes in Africa, reported dead in some erroneous accounts; awarded the Nobel Prize for literature.

1959   In declining health, follows the Ordoñez–Dominguín bullfights and observes his sixtieth birthday in Spain.

1961   Undergoes shock treatment for depression; on July 2, kills himself with shotgun; buried in Sun Valley, Idaho.

1964   *A Moveable Feast* is published, with vivid and sometimes abusive sketches of people Hemingway knew in Paris during the 1920s such as Stein and Fitzgerald.

1970   *Islands in the Stream*, a semiautobiographical novel about the painter Thomas Hudson and his family relationships.

1972   *The Nick Adams Stories*, gathering in one volume all of the fiction about Nick, including several previously unpublished stories and fragments.

1981   *Ernest Hemingway: Selected Letters,* edited by Carlos Baker, containing some of the most interesting of Hemingway's vast correspondence.

1985   *The Dangerous Summer,* an account of the Ordoñez–Dominguín bullfight rivalry; *Dateline Toronto: The Complete Toronto Star Dispatches,* bringing together the journalistic work Hemingway did during the apprenticeship years 1920–24.

1986   *The Garden of Eden,* a substantially cut and rearranged version of the manuscript Hemingway left behind, recounting love affairs involving two women and one man, and causing many to revise their opinions about the writer's macho image.

1987   *The Complete Short Stories of Ernest Hemingway,* assembling the first forty-nine stories and a number of other, previously uncollected ones.

I

SCOTT DONALDSON

Introduction:
Hemingway and Fame

A full generation after his death Ernest Hemingway remains one of the most famous American writers. Even those who have never read a word he has written, in school or college or on their own, are aware of his presence in the world of celebrity – a rugged macho figure called Papa with a signature white beard. The outpouring of recognition and praise that followed his suicide on the morning of July 2, 1961, nearly obliterated the boundaries of space and time. Hemingway's passing was memorialized by the Kremlin and the White House, in the Vatican and the bullrings of Spain. "It is almost," the *Louisville Courier-Journal* editorialized, "as though the Twentieth Century itself has come to a sudden, violent, and premature end" (Raeburn 168). Manifestly, at the time of his death he had become to the general public something more – or less – than a writer of stories and novels. He had become a legendary figure, and seems fated to remain one. Critics and college professors lament this state of affairs. The spurious anecdotes and half-baked biographies and Key West contests for Hemingway look-alikes only serve to draw attention away from his work, they assert, so that the great unwashed public will not take him seriously. This is a danger, all right, the same danger that faced the other most celebrated of American writers, Mark Twain. Twain wore a white suit and a mustache, took his comedy act on the road, and otherwise made himself so conspicuous as to be widely thought of in his own time as a mere entertainer. Twain has survived his celebrity, as will Hemingway, and for the same reason: They wrote some wonderful books. But both writers have been admitted to the canon *despite* the off-putting aroma of publicity that surrounds them. So certain questions impose themselves. Why was Hemingway, like Twain, inclined to present himself – or some versions of himself – to public view? Knowing the risks, as he certainly did, why did he take the chance? Was there something in the water he drank or the air he breathed growing up in Oak Park, Illinois, which drove him to seek not only accomplishment but fame?

Like most middle-class American boys at the turn of the century, young Ernest Hemingway was brought up on the tales of Horatio Alger, in which worthy, healthy-minded, and hard-working lads rapidly ascended the ladder of success. Atop that ladder lay riches and recognition, and in Alger's unvarying formulation the message was clear that these rewards were within the reach of every youth willing to apply himself. In these books written to edify and instruct American boys, success was the goal to strive for, and success was to be measured by rising above the station one was born into, or, to put it more baldly, by doing better than one's father. If your father was a butcher, you should own the meat market; if he sold shoes, you should manufacture them. The trouble was that this process of outdoing one's forebear, generation after generation, was simply impossible. Only in a society of consistently rising expectations, like that of nineteenth-century America, could it have taken hold as an ideal to be sought, and only in a society determined to cling to outmoded values could it have continued to exert its power in the following century. In France, for example, the fundamental dignity of remaining within one's native station found expression in derogatory terms for those who strained to rise to a higher position. Consider how powerfully parvenu and nouveau riche contrast with the American "self-made man" (Cawelti 2).

The usual standard of measuring success in America was, of course, the accumulation of money. But you had to *make* the money; it was not enough to inherit it or to have it descend from the skies. And others had to take notice – particularly in the other-directed society of the twentieth century, recognition was an essential ingredient in the stewpot of success. (No wonder that the culture descended to ostentatious displays of wealth, or in the parlance of Marx and Veblen, to commodity fetishism and conspicuous consumption.) For a writer or an artist, in fact, external recognition in quantity – fame, to give it a title – could take the place of money, or nearly so.[1] Hemingway's own case is interesting in this respect. As an apprentice writer in Paris, in the mid-1920s, he vigorously repudiated what he regarded as his friend F. Scott Fitzgerald's obsession with how much he was paid for his stories. Yet later in his life, he demanded compensation for his own magazine work that was at least slightly higher than anyone else got. His attitude toward money changed as his career wore on. But so did his attitude toward fame, and it was fame that drove him.

In his 1967 book *Making It*, Norman Podhoretz presented a confessional, and to many a shocking, disquisition on his own pursuit of recognition. From his first appearances with critical articles in *Commentary*, what Podhoretz wanted was "to see my name in print, to be praised, and above all

to attract attention." Many who have started out in journalism, like Hemingway, have felt much the same. Getting paid was important, but bylines were
even better. When Podhoretz was asked by his Columbia mentor Lionel
Trilling what kind of power he sought – money, fame, professional emi-
nence, social position – he replied immediately that it was fame he was
after: He wanted to be a famous critic, and he expected that everything else
would flow from that. Any intelligent person could walk into a room and
tell the generals from the lieutenants, and the lieutenants from the privates,
Podhoretz wrote, and he wanted to be a general (Podhoretz 96, 146, 335).
As Milton put it,

> Fame is the spur that the clear spirit doth raise
> (That last infirmity of Noble mind)
> To scorn delights and live laborious dayes.

Making It caused something of an uproar in literary circles, not so much
because its author wrote about his own ambitions but because he did so
with such unabashed openness. As he observed, there was a nagging contradiction in the American ideal of success that did not present a problem to
the Puritan poet. On the one hand, you had to get ahead; on the other hand,
you were not supposed to try too hard to do so, and certainly not supposed
to make a public disclosure of your "laborious dayes." But Podhoretz tried
hard and told all, and so offended those academic overseers who agreed
with William James that "the exclusive worship of the bitch-goddess success [was] our national disease," who were inclined like his professors at
Columbia to equate *successful* with *corrupt,* who felt that ambition had
replaced lust as the "dirty little secret" festering in the American soul. Envy
flourished in this environment, where excessive public recognition of someone else's work was taken as evidence that he or she must have pandered
after the bitch-goddess (Podhoretz xi–xvii, 61, 265). In such a climate it was
imperative to keep a low profile. Win the election, but don't let your cam-
paigning show. Publish if you must, but don't sell, and above all don't
advertise. Young John Cheever used to daydream about future rewards for
his writing. Thank you very much, he would say, but no thank you: I
couldn't possibly accept.

This reticence about public renown may owe something to the paradox at
the heart of the Protestant ethic. Capitalism demands that we struggle
against each other in an often brutal contest of individual wills. But Christian morality dictates that we treat one another with compassion and generosity. Hence, many of those who achieve substantial gains are tormented by
guilt – a malady relieved to some degree by the gospel of wealth's rationale

that we must first get in order to be able to give, that to be of service to others we must be financially capable of serving. Most writers, however – even most truly great writers – do not make enough money to be overly troubled by this particular contradiction. For them, the egalitarian strain in American culture exerts a powerful restraint against excessive acclaim. Our political heroes are those who manage to do great things while looking and acting very much like the rest of us: honest George, homely Abe, and rough-riding Teddy, to name three of the four iconic figures chiseled into Mount Rushmore. (Teddy Roosevelt, not incidentally, was *the* political figure most admired during Hemingway's boyhood in Oak Park.) So, too, we tend to ask our artists to minimize rather than insist upon their difference from the common folk. Walt Whitman, who understood this anomaly, repeatedly proclaimed his involvement in humankind while at the same time trumpeting his individuality.

> I celebrate myself, and sing myself,
> And what I assume you shall assume,
> For every atom belonging to me as good belongs to you.

Whitman wrote as if to obliterate all distinctions among persons. "No other country," Leo Braudy comments in his first-rate *The Frenzy of Renown: Fame and Its History* (1986), "so enforces the character-wrenching need to be assertive but polite, prideful but humble, unique but familiar, the great star and the kid next door" (11).

Over the centuries fame has had a significantly better press than money as a measurement of success. Fame harms no one else, the argument goes, while money is often acquired through ill treatment of others. In addition, money is a yardstick of materialism; fame, of accomplishment (Podhoretz 245). Yet it is also clear that fame in the twentieth century has had "a baroquely warping effect" on the lives of those engaged in its pursuit (Braudy 12). To a considerable degree, this debilitating effect is owing to the devaluation of fame by its exploitation in the mass media. Often, if not universally, famous people have shrunk into celebrities under the klieg lights of publicity. What they have achieved is forgotten, while their private lives undergo such intense scrutiny that finally only revelation of the most intimate details about them will satisfy their curious audience.

"Two centuries ago," Daniel J. Boorstin lamented in his 1962 diatribe against the culture of celebrity, "when a great man appeared, people looked for God's purpose in him; today we look for his press agent." Fame and greatness were never precisely synonymous, he acknowledged, but with the proliferation of the mass media into every corner of modern life and the development of image makers, the distance between the hero (who had achieved something of importance) and the celebrity (whom Boorstin defined as "a person who is known for his well-knownness") had widened enormously. "The hero created himself; the celebrity is created by the media," he concluded, with the switch in tenses conveying his conviction that nowadays there were no heroes, only celebrities (Boorstin 45–61). Even those who began as genuine heroes were degraded into celebrities by the media's relentless exploration of their private lives. A major case in point for Boorstin was Charles Lindbergh, the Lone Eagle who boldly and with professional skill flew solo across the Atlantic in 1927. Lindbergh's act of individual courage and daring qualified him as an authentic hero. It also subjected his most private thoughts and actions to relentless public examination. The media left no corner of Lindy's personal life unexposed, and finally this scrutiny had deadly consequences when the much-publicized first child of Lindy's marriage to Anne Morrow was kidnapped and killed.

Braudy draws lines of comparison between Lindbergh and Hemingway as midwestern lads, approximate contemporaries, and self-made men who achieved international fame through mastery of a professional craft. In Braudy's judgment, fame has always given and taken away. "In part it celebrates uniqueness, and in part it requires that uniqueness be exemplary and reproducible" (Braudy 5). The reproduction can take shape as an article of clothing, like Davy Crockett's coonskin cap, or a gesture, like Winston Churchill's V for Victory, or a physical signature, like Hemingway's beard – but every reproduced imprint tends to devalue the original edition. In another such exchange, we pursue fame as a means of escaping drab anonymity, but upon gaining that objective find ourselves trapped by the gaze others fix upon us.

This was precisely the case with Lindbergh, as Braudy points out. Initially eager for admiration, he later found it impossible to withdraw from public attention. He could conquer distance in flight, but could not outrace the gossip his fame engendered. Ernest Hemingway, Braudy suggests, "could almost be considered Lindbergh's wiser older brother," but only almost, for he was to emerge as "the prime case of someone fatally caught between his genius and its publicity." Toward the end of his life, the image of Papa Hemingway outdoors, fishing or hunting or at war, had come to supplant that of the dedicated artist at his desk. In the consciousness of most people, he existed less as a great storyteller and prose stylist than as a rugged, no-nonsense type with a prodigious appetite for eating and drinking, brawling and defying death. The image – Papa with beard and shotgun, say – was so deeply imprinted that the person behind it disappeared into the shadows.

Certain Indian tribes resist having their photographs taken, on the theory that some part of themselves will vanish with each snap of the shutter. From the middle of the twentieth century on, this policy has come to seem more sensible than superstitious (Braudy 22–27, 544–47).

In his book-length study of the subject, John Raeburn emphasizes two basic points about Hemingway's fame. First, Hemingway became the most public of all American writers. During his lifetime, both slick magazines appealing to the college-educated and pulp publications aimed at blue-collar workers kept their readers regularly informed about Hemingway, while syndicated newspaper columnists reported on his travels and opinions. Then, within eight years following his death, seven biographies appeared. Scanning through this outpouring of prose, much of it inaccurate and badly written, made it clear to Raeburn that it was Hemingway's *personality* that generated most of this interest. The media concentrated on him as a sportsman or warrior, not as a writer, for there wasn't much glamor in the drudgery of darkening paper with words. Raeburn's second and somewhat judgmental point is that what happened was Hemingway's own fault. "Far from being either the unwitting or the unwilling recipient of this personal attention as he liked to intimate he was, [he] was the architect of his public reputation." In good part, his advertisements for himself took the form of nonfiction, much of it written during the 1930s (Raeburn 2, 6–7). Even during his Paris years of the early 1920s, when he was very little known across the Atlantic, Hemingway radiated a kind of charisma that made people talk about him. But in that decade, he was far less openly engaged in the building of a reputation – and much more insistent upon devotion to his craft – than later in his career. One useful way of measuring this difference is to compare two profiles of him published in the *New Yorker:* Dorothy Parker's "The Artist's Reward" of November 30, 1929, and Lillian Ross's "How Do You Like It Now, Gentlemen?" of May 13, 1950.

Parker was obviously smitten with Hemingway, whom she had met through their mutual friends Gerald and Sara Murphy. Her profile, which ran to less than three pages in the *New Yorker,* presented an adoring portrait of the author who had just published his second novel, *A Farewell to Arms.* She raves both about Hemingway's person and about his achievement. "He certainly *is* attractive," Parker assures her female readers, " . . . even better than his photographs." Not only that, but to her mind he ranked as "far and away the first American artist" – at thirty years of age! A great many falsehoods had been circulated about Hemingway, she points out: "Probably of no other living man has so much tripe been penned and spoken."

Parker humorously recounts some of the wild rumors about his toughness and athleticism, concluding with a passage reminiscent of Gatsby. "About all that remains to be said is that he is the Lost Dauphin, that he was shot as a German spy, and that he is actually a woman, masquerading in man's clothes" (Parker 28).[2]

Having warned the reader about apocryphal tales, Parker proceeds to contribute a few of her own. In his youth, she writes, Hemingway left home to become a prizefighter. Then he served in the Italian army, where he suffered seven major wounds, acquired an aluminum kneecap, and "received medals." Such reports are either inventions, like the one about boxing, or distortions, like the inflated account of his wartime service in a Red Cross ambulance unit. Parker did not have much to work with, for Hemingway was apparently loath to provide the facts of his life – "I can find out nothing about his education," she sadly reports – and at the same time willing to encourage tales of his prowess in the ring or on the battlefield. She simply put down what he saw fit to tell her or others about himself, including the legend (in fact, Hemingway was never so poor as he claimed to be) that his art derived from "the kind of poverty you don't believe – the kind of which actual hunger is the attendant." Now, though, she reports, he does his writing "mostly in bed," like a latter-day Proust (Parker 28–29).

Parker's description of Hemingway's personality is more accurate where she can rely on her own powers of observation. She comments on his abundant energy and "a capacity for enjoyment so vast . . . that he can take you to a bicycle-race, and make it raise your hair." She acknowledges his extraordinary sensitivity to criticism, supplying a few examples of the wrong-headed commentary that had greeted his early work. She detects beneath his manly exterior "an immense, ill-advised, and indiscriminate tenderness." And in calling particular attention to his bravery and unwillingness to compromise, she prints for the first time his definition of "guts" as "grace under pressure" – a phrase that became a famous ingredient of his legend. Throughout Parker insists on Hemingway's integrity as a dedicated and hard-working writer. "He works like hell, and through it," she observed. He rewrote the ending of A Farewell to Arms seventy times, she cites as evidence, and in fact more than thirty variant endings have been unearthed among his working drafts. The Hemingway who emerges from her pastiche of half-truths, inaccuracies, and admiring descriptions is well on his way to becoming a public figure, someone "people want to hear things about." But her 1929 profile never loses sight of the fact that it is his art that makes him worth writing about (Parker 30–31).

With Lillian Ross's far longer and very different piece twenty-one years later, the situation had changed drastically: Now Hemingway has become a star who commands center stage throughout. Unlike Parker, who occasionally delivered witty asides, Ross keeps herself at a distance throughout and lets her protagonist perform. Her intention, as she outlined it in her 1964 collection *Reporting,* was "to describe as precisely as possible how Hemingway, who had the nerve to be like nobody else on earth, looked and sounded when he was in action, talking, between work periods – to give a picture of the man as he was, in his uniqueness and with his vitality and his enormous spirit of fun intact" (Ross 189). The trouble was that in her account he looked and sounded boorish to others and egocentric about himself. She liked Hemingway enormously, Ross maintained, yet for many readers her profile remains the most damaging document about him ever published.

Part of the problem may have been that she caught the author off guard, during a two-day trip to New York immediately after completing the manuscript of *Across the River and into the Trees.* With that major project behind him (and it had been ten years between novels), Hemingway was very much on holiday and understandably proud of the new book he was bringing along for delivery to his publisher. Ross met the author and his wife Mary at the airport, where he was maintaining a bearish grip on his seatmate during the flight from Cuba, a wiry little fellow who had been coerced into reading the manuscript en route. "He read book all way up on plane," Hemingway said in an Indian patois stripped of articles. "He liked book, I think." "Whew!" said the seatmate (Ross 195).

Whew! pretty well describes the frenetic activities of the next two days, which included visits to Abercrombie and Fitch and the Metropolitan Museum of Art, meetings with Marlene Dietrich, Charles Scribner, and son Patrick, and an enormous amount of drinking. Readers of Hemingway's books are sometimes incredulous about the quantities of liquor his characters consume, but on the basis of Ross's profile can feel sure that his fiction does not exaggerate from the life. Liberated from the grind of finishing his book and subject to what he calls "the irresponsibility that comes in after the terrible responsibility of writing," Hemingway commences his drinking immediately with double bourbons at the airport cocktail lounge. At his hotel room in town, two champagne buckets are pressed into use to keep the wine cold for consumption at all hours, including early morning. During his tour of the Metropolitan, he takes long pulls from a silver flask. It's as daunting as Bill Gorton's drinking in Paris, or Jake Barnes's in Madrid in *The Sun Also Rises.*

In the most memorable passages of Ross's portrait, Hemingway compares his own writing to that of great figures from the past, employing metaphors from the world of sport. A novelist is like a starting pitcher with no relievers in the bullpen, he remarks. "Novelist has to go the full nine, even if it kills him." During his Paris years, he said, he had perfected his pitching skills by reading such French masters as "Mr. Flaubert, who always threw them perfectly straight, hard, high, and inside . . . Mr. Baudelaire, that I learned my knuckle ball from, and Mr. Rimbaud, who never threw a fast ball in his life." Then, in a burst of braggadocio, Hemingway used boxing, not base-ball, to lay claim to his place in the company of the great. "I started out very quiet and I beat Mr. Turgenev. Then I trained hard and I beat Mr. de Maupassant. I've fought two draws with Mr. Stendhal, and I think I had an edge in the last one. But nobody's going to get me in any ring with Mr. Tolstoy unless I'm crazy or I keep getting better." On two other occasions, he goes out of his way to denigrate a more recently deceased rival, F. Scott Fitzgerald, for his lack of knowledge of prizefighting and football. And when he signs a contract for Charles Scribner's Sons, he declares himself ready to fight any present-day competition. "Never ran as no genius, but I'll defend the title again against all the good young new ones" (Ross 196, 202, 208–9, 212).

The Hemingway Lillian Ross tracked around New York in 1949 was very different from the one Dorothy Parker had met in Europe twenty years earlier. Parker judged him "the first American artist" in the earlier profile, while in Ross's report it is Hemingway who announces his preeminence. Instead of insisting on the dignity of the calling, as he had in 1929, the now-bearded Papa called the roll of the great, placing himself at the forefront. The admirable, dedicated, and hard-working young man who, Parker tells us, was reluctant to talk about his past, had apparently deteriorated into something of a buffoon, whose talk and actions smacked of grandiosity. He was indeed on holiday at the time, and probably poking fun at himself as well as everyone else, but it is hard to detect self-parody in the absence of any guiding commentary to that effect from Ross, who maintained a pos-ture of strict objectivity throughout. In giving only the facts, she may have done her subject a real disservice. Certainly the piece reads as if he is just as serious when proclaiming himself victorious over Flaubert and Stendhal as when instructing his son Patrick about paintings in the Metropolitan.

What seems clear is that Hemingway was determined to distance himself from the conventional image of the aesthete as an effete and asexual crea-ture, just as he had done, fictionally, with the early story "Mr. and Mrs. Elliot." He was no innocent victim of the press; he knew precisely why Ross was at his elbow and what kind of reporting she did (a few years earlier, she had written a profile of his friend Sidney Franklin, the bullfighter from

Brooklyn, for which he was an interviewee). In his youth, as an aspiring writer in Chicago, he had railed against other would-be artists who talked endlessly of "art, art, art." To take the curse of dilettantism off his own remarks on the topic for Ross, he couched them in the jargon of the sports pages. If possible, Hemingway wanted it both ways – he wanted to be recognized for his fiction and at the same time to be regarded as a rugged, manly fellow. So he emerged from the second *New Yorker* profile not merely as "one of the roughs" (like Whitman) but as the roughest of all, a man who wrestled bears, spoke pidgin English, and by the way also wrote some of the most enduring stories and novels of his time.

The sensitive tough guy has become a cliché in films – John Garfield made a career out of it – and Hemingway was cast in that part at least as early as 1933, when a William Steig cartoon in *Vanity Fair* depicted him with a rose in his hairy, tattooed fist. It was the fist and not the rose that he chose to emphasize in his public appearances and comments. Significantly, in Malcolm Cowley's "A Portrait of Mr. Papa" for *Life* magazine the year before Ross's *New Yorker* profile, Hemingway asked for one important change in the original copy. Cowley had written that in high school Hemingway "was a literary boy, not a sports boy." This was accurate enough, but Hemingway wanted the passage cut, and so it was (Raeburn 132). He understood and accepted his public role, but it involved at least two dangers: first, that he would, like many actors, become so stereotyped in the public mind as to be uncastable in other roles; second, that he would become so integrated into the part as to give up any distinct identity. In Ross's 1950 article, Hemingway appears to be falling victim to both dangers.

As Braudy accurately observes, Hemingway "seemed to carry the burden of early success fairly well" (543). He had the good fortune not to be overwhelmed by popular or critical attention at the beginning of his career. In 1924 he wrote to Ezra Pound from Spain about the recognition accorded young bullfighters, the "ovations, Alcoholism, being pointed out on the street, general respect and the other things Literary guys have to wait until they are 89 years old to get" (*SL* 119). He did not have to wait that long. His expatriate pamphlets *Three Stories and Ten Poems* (1923) and *in our time* (1924) caught the canny eye of Edmund Wilson, whose joint review in the *Dial* Hemingway praised for being "cool and clear minded and decent and impersonal and sympathetic" and above all concentrated on the work itself. "Christ how I hate this terrible personal stuff," he added (*SL* 129). Not until he was thirty and the best-selling and controversial *A Farewell to Arms* came out to a mingled chorus of praise and outrage for its straightforward language and frank depiction of a love affair out of wedlock did he begin to generate *New Yorker* articles and other public explorations of his personality.

The brouhaha about *Farewell* may have had the same kind of effect on Hemingway that publication of *The Naked and the Dead* did on Norman Mailer in 1948 (though Mailer was only twenty-four, not thirty, when his novel of World War II was published). "[F]rom now on," the younger writer observed, "people who knew me would never be able to react to me . . . for myself alone. . . . I was a node in a new electronic landscape of celebrity, personality, and status." The experience, Mailer confessed, blasted him "a considerable distance away from dead center" (92), and undoubtedly contributed to his cultivation of a persona designed to satisfy the demands of public curiosity while protecting himself against them. In discussing the biographical treatment of Sylvia Plath, who, like Hemingway, committed suicide, Janet Malcolm points out the psychic costs writers characteristically pay. "Poets and novelists and playwrights make themselves, against terrible resistances, give over what the rest of us keep safely locked within our hearts" (109). Having so bared themselves in their art, they often create a shielding public persona for purposes of self-preservation.

Working in collaboration with the mass media. Hemingway shaped his own public image, largely in his nonfiction of the 1930s, which included *Death in the Afternoon, Green Hills of Africa,* a series of articles for *Esquire* on sports, politics, and art, and correspondence from Spain during the Spanish civil war. As Raeburn observes, whether the subject was bullfighting, big-game hunting, or the battle for Madrid, Hemingway was actually writing about himself. Taken together, these works "were sketches toward an autobiography" – the autobiography of the personality he chose to present to the public (15). That complicated personality, as Raeburn analyzes it, consisted of no fewer than nine roles: the sportsman, the "tough and virile" manly man, the exposer of sham, the arbiter of taste, the world traveler, the bon vivant, the insider, the stoic veteran, and finally and most important, the heroic artist (39–43). But the image that stuck could be reduced to that of the tough guy who also happened, incredibly, to be a literary genius, the man of action eager to test his courage against great beasts and the weapons of war oddly merged with a literary artist who shaped a new prose style for the century. By the end of World War II, during which he served as war correspondent for *Collier's* and uncommissioned leader of his own band of irregulars in France, that persona had taken a strong hold on the American consciousness. And of course it was the first half of the combination – the sportsman-warrior rather than the heroic artist – whose activities were most widely reported on and talked about. Over time Hemingway became a celebrity rather than a famous writer, and if he was not only willing but complicit in the formation of that celebrity's image, he eventually found that carrying that persona around with him could be psychologically and even physically troubling.

In 1952 a young scholar named Philip Young brought out his *Ernest Hemingway,* a book that Hemingway tried to stop before publication and disparaged afterwards. While his volume was ostensibly a critical study of the fiction, Young relied upon the Freudian concept of "repetition compulsion" to explain the extraordinary pattern of wounds suffered by Hemingway protagonists. According to Young's argument, this pattern had its origin in Hemingway's serious wounding in Italy during World War I. His traumatic reaction to that wound led not only to nightmares but to a compulsion to relive the terrible experience. This theory, Young argued, not only explained the psychological makeup of Hemingway's heroes but also provided a rationale for his own repeated confrontations with danger and the many mutilating wounds – to arms and legs and head – that he suffered as a consequence. Young's volume attempted to penetrate to the innermost recesses not only of Hemingway's characters but also of the author who created them. If this was not biography, it certainly represented an invasion of Hemingway's privacy, and though he railed against critics taking such liberties during his lifetime, he had long before opened the gates and was hardly in a position to close them to intruders. Interestingly, Young's hypothesis suggests that the public Hemingway, the macho figure who repeatedly sought occasions to demonstrate his grace under pressure, did so not because he wanted to cultivate such an image but because he couldn't help it. Young's book made him out to be "crazy," Hemingway complained (Raeburn 139–41).

Hemingway's most widely reported brush with death occurred in January 1954, when he and his wife Mary, on safari in Africa, survived two plane crashes in two days. When the wreckage of the first crash was sighted, word went out that he had been killed, so that Hemingway had the pleasure of reading his own obituaries. "My luck, she is still good," he told interviewers afterwards, but actually the two crack-ups took a severe toll. In addition to a "full-scale concussion, his injuries included a ruptured liver, spleen, and kidney, temporary loss of vision in the left eye, loss of hearing in the left ear, a crushed vertebra, a sprained right arm and shoulder, a sprained left leg, paralysis of the sphincter, and first degree burns on his face, arms, and head" (Baker, *Life Story* 522). Carlos Baker, his official biographer, believed that these were the most drastic injuries of the many Hemingway suffered, and that he never really recovered from them.

In the immediate aftermath of the accidents, the process of recuperation called for rest and quiet, but these were difficult for a celebrated man of action like Hemingway to secure. Still quite weak a few months later, he was driving through the Italian Alps with companion (and unofficial biographer) A. E. Hotchner when the consequences of his international fame were vividly brought him to him. They stopped to buy a bottle of Scotch in the Alpine town of Cuneo, and Hemingway was recognized in the liquor store. Soon a crowd surrounded him, demanding that he autograph not only his own books (the local bookstore was next door) but everything in English "from *Of Human Bondage* to *Casserole Cookery.*" Then the crowd turned into a mob, pushing against Hemingway and effectively preventing him from making his way back to the car. A small detachment of soldiers was required to liberate him from the crush. Badly shaken, he shaved off his beard the following day in hopes of avoiding further violent displays of admiration from strangers (Hotchner 115–16).

A few months later, he was back in the news as winner of the 1954 Nobel Prize for literature, but still in poor health and unable to attend the ceremony. Instead he sent a statement about the loneliness of the writer and how he "should always try for something that has never been done or that others have tried and failed." With luck, success might follow, but only if the writer was willing – like Santiago in *The Old Man and the Sea* – to be "driven far out past where he can go, out to where no one can help him." Then he concluded his brief statement. "A writer," he observed, "should write what he has to say and not speak it" (Baker, *Life Story* 528–29). As prose, Hemingway's eloquent Nobel acceptance speech reads like some of his earliest fiction, where he managed by legerdemain to communicate complicated emotions in the simplest of English words. And by urging upon his worldwide audience the lonely and courageous and terribly difficult task confronting the writer, he called up yet again the image of the artist as hero.

Lillian Ross, in a kind of apologia written after Hemingway's death in 1961, judged him to have been just such an artist. When at work, she commented, "he was heroically and uncorruptedly and uncompromisingly occupied day after day with writing as hard as he could." And when he couldn't write, she added, he lived his life to the full and generously made "his private experience public, so that everybody else could also have a wonderful time." This observation, which served to place Hemingway's "gin-crazed Indian" of her *New Yorker* profile in a more flattering light, was probably intended to make amends, but it oversimplified the motives behind his public image (Ross 191; Hotchner 117). Hemingway's presentation of himself may have owed something to altruism, but he may also have adopted his image to gain approval and attention, to prevent raids on his psyche, to prove himself against the most demanding tests, or for all these reasons. He was, as Baker and all subsequent biographers have concluded, an extremely complex man whose actions could not conveniently be ascribed to single causes.

Why did Hemingway kill himself? students invariably ask, but this is precisely the kind of question that does not lend itself to any one answer. He was deeply depressed; he had paranoid tendencies that may have been projected from self-hatred; his body was deteriorating and his energy and strength were ebbing away; he could not write as he once had. There were those who argued after his death that he had long before lost his touch, that he peaked early and went downhill from 1930 on. For a long time his celebrity kept people from noticing the decline, Dwight Macdonald observed in a retrospective piece that made satiric use of the author's public image, but finally Hemingway himself realized he could no longer defend his title: "the position is outflanked the lion can't be stopped the sword won't go into the bull's neck the great fish is breaking the line and it is the fifteenth round and the champion looks bad" (Raeburn 171). From the distance of yet another generation, that argument has some validity. Hemingway *did* do his best work in the 1920s, though he wrote important and valuable books for thirty years thereafter. Like all American authors, he confronted the problem of encore. How was he supposed to surpass the wonderful stories of the Paris years, and such novels as *The Sun Also Rises* and *A Farewell to Arms?* But his celebrity exacerbated the difficulty, as the general public concentrated its gaze on the exploits of his private life and could only occasionally be roused to acknowledge – as by an entire issue of *Life* containing *The Old Man and the Sea* or by the granting of a Nobel Prize in Sweden – that the Papa Hemingway they knew was an artist as well. As Braudy points out, "[t]he media-soaked years after World War Two spawned a whole tribe of artistic suicides, many of whom had discovered how hard it was to retain their personal integrity, when interest in their work played a weak second to fascination with their private lives and whether they would be able to repeat their past performances." In addition to Hemingway, he cites Sylvia Plath and Anne Sexton, Ross Lockridge Jr. and Thomas Heggen. Suicide offered all of these American writers a "final act of cohesion . . . in a world where the false and the true [were] hard to tell apart," Braudy writes, but Hemingway was far more famous, and hence far more subject to "a fragmentation of self and public image" than the others (28). One of the things that caused him to take his life may well have been the disparity between his universal fame and his fading powers. Even after death, Hemingway has been haunted by the afterglow of publicity. But books like this one stand as evidence that his reputation will outlive the ongoing burden of celebrity and that his achievement ranks him among the great writers of the century.

NOTES

1. For much of this discussion of the nature of success in America, I am indebted to Richard M. Huber, *The American Idea of Success* (New York: McGraw-Hill, 1971), particularly the opening chapter.

2. More than two decades later, one of Hemingway's sons was arrested for transvestism.

WORKS CITED

Baker, Carlos. *Ernest Hemingway: A Life Story.* New York: Charles Scribner's Sons, 1969.

———, ed. *Ernest Hemingway: Selected Letters, 1917–1961.* New York: Charles Scribner's Sons, 1981.

Boorstin, Daniel J. *The Image.* New York: Atheneum, 1962.

Braudy, Leo. *The Frenzy of Renown: Fame and Its History.* New York: Oxford University Press, 1986.

Cawelti, John G. *Apostles of the Self-Made Man.* Chicago: University of Chicago Press, 1965.

DeMott, Benjamin. "Archibald MacLeish." *Writers at Work,* 5th series. New York: Viking, 1981.

Hotchner, A. E. *Papa Hemingway: A Personal Memoir.* New York: Random House, 1966.

Huber, Richard M. *The American Idea of Success.* New York: McGraw-Hill, 1971.

Mailer, Norman. *Advertisements for Myself.* New York: Putnam, 1959.

Malcolm, Janet. "The Silent Woman." *New Yorker* (August 23 and 30, 1993).

Parker, Dorothy. "The Artist's Reward." *New Yorker* (November 30, 1929): 28–31.

Podhoretz, Norman. *Making It.* New York: Random House, 1967.

Raeburn, John. *Fame Became of Him: Hemingway as Public Writer.* Bloomington: Indiana University Press, 1984.

Ross, Lillian. "Portrait of Hemingway." *Reporting.* New York: Simon and Schuster, 1964.

Young, Philip. *Ernest Hemingway: A Reconsideration.* University Park: Pennsylvania State University Press, 1966.

2

ELIZABETH DEWBERRY

Hemingway's Journalism and the Realist Dilemma

In November 1923, after having written for his high school newspaper, trained as a cub reporter for the *Kansas City Star,* and worked as a correspondent for the *Toronto Star* on and off from 1920, Hemingway wrote to Gertrude Stein, "I am going to chuck journalism I think. You ruined me as a journalist last winter" (*SL* 101). Yet Hemingway stayed with the *Toronto Star* until September 1924, and he continued to write for newspapers and magazines at intervals throughout his career, covering the Spanish civil war for the North American Newspaper Alliance in 1937 and 1938, the tension in the Orient for *PM* in 1941, and World War II in England and France for *Collier's* in 1944, as well as writing intermittently for *Esquire, Look,* and *Life,* among other publications, until as late as 1960, all the while producing short stories, novels, and other books and essays of creative nonfiction as well.

Although Hemingway often complained that journalism robbed him of the juices he needed to write fiction, there is evidence that moving among journalism, creative nonfiction, and fiction stimulated all his writing, that his work in each genre informed and enriched his experience in the others. In this essay I will examine the journalism Hemingway produced at intervals throughout his life, focusing on the significance of the choices this writer of realist fiction made when he found himself reporting real life and on how these choices in turn inform his fiction. I demonstrate that throughout his career Hemingway tends to blur distinctions between fiction and nonfiction as well as between the concrete and imagined realities they purport to represent. I argue that he does so, not usually in the cleverly self-conscious way he does in *The Torrents of Spring,* but consistently and purposefully, as part of a lifelong investigation into the nature of reality and the relationship among reality, representation, and language. I suggest that throughout his work, Hemingway reveals a fluid but persistent skepticism regarding the assumption on which both journalism and literary realism have traditionally based their claims to "truth" – that reality can be accurately represented.

I begin by focusing on what Hemingway wrote specifically for newspapers early in his career, reasoning that newspaper journalism generally concerns itself more with conveying everyday reality than does either creative nonfiction or fiction and that it therefore most directly communicates Hemingway's concept of the possibility of representing that reality in or through language. I then explore several ways Hemingway uses in his early fiction what he learned as a journalist, focusing mostly on techniques and material that first appeared in the journalism and were later transformed, recontextualized, and reconstituted in the fiction. I follow with an examination of the relationship among Hemingway's later journalism, creative non-fiction, and fiction, where connections are so integral as to suggest an attempt to challenge conventional distinctions not only among the genres but also between historical and fictional realities. I conclude that throughout his work Hemingway uses the complex connections among journalism, creative nonfiction, and fiction to challenge traditional journalists' and literary realists' assumptions about the relationship among language, history, fact, and fiction.

The work Hemingway produced for *The Trapeze,* Oak Park High School's student newspaper, demonstrates that from the beginning he was capable of writing both conventional, factual journalistic articles and experimental pieces that comment on and challenge the limits of conventional journalism. Hemingway's tone in his first few pieces is serious and detached, and almost all his information is presented as verifiable fact. In an article typical of those he wrote in his first weeks as an amateur journalist, dated February 3, 1916, Hemingway opens with a sentence that communicates the standard who, what, when, and where: "Mr. David E. Goodwillie gave an excellent presentation of the employer's side of the labor problem at the Hanna Club, last Friday" (*Hemingway's Apprenticeship* 7). The article proceeds with an objective report of the meeting.

Yet by the next month, Hemingway had begun inserting his own voice and opinions into otherwise standard factual articles. In his March 9, 1916 article, for instance, Hemingway provides an account of another Hanna Club meeting, but adds a parenthetical question mark: "The usual good supper and good (?) jokes preceded the speech" (*Hemingway's Apprenticeship* 17). Later in the same article he states, "Every fellow that misses a meeting loses just so much from his life, so let' (sic.) all get out _____ etc. Fill in the blank with the conclusion of one of Brabrook's appeals for attendance" (18). Both the question mark and the blank imply Hemingway's awareness that what is reported and read as fact may be only assumption or generally accepted fiction, and they indicate his consciousness of the power of language, particularly written language, to shape people's perceptions of the world, whether accurately or inaccurately.

By November 1916 Hemingway had begun writing articles that mimicked Ring Lardner, incorporating fictitious characters and events into his journalism. Charles Fenton accurately characterizes these imitations as "an invaluable opening exercise in some of the technicalities of idiomatic prose, as well as a profitable experiment in various levels of humor, burlesque, and satire" (26). Yet they are also significant because they constitute his first experiments in fictionalized journalism and journalistic fiction. Hemingway's first Lardner imitation, for example, appropriates journalistic-sounding facts to a fictional account of a game. By employing a sportswriter's phrases and placing his article in the context of a newspaper, he sets up expectations in the reader that his work is an accurate account of a real event. Yet he immediately exposes the piece as a fiction. Dated November 24, 1916, the article reports a combination of athletic games and other activities that could only occur together in a fiction: "Wilcoxen signalled for the hit and run play but Gordon was caught at second by a perfect throw from the catcher. Hemingway went over for the first touchdown by way of the Lake Street 'L.' Colville missed goal, the ball hitting the bar and causing havoc with the free lunch" (33). The article closes with a report of Hemingway's funeral, where "A pleasant Time (sic.) was had by all" (34). This fictional obituary notice, appearing in a newspaper article with the supposedly dead person's byline and echoing newspaper society pages, provides an interesting if jejune example of Hemingway's early attempt to combine traditional elements of journalism with fiction.

In his February 16, 1917 article, "Ring Lardner, Jr., Discourses on Editorials," signed "Ernie Hemingway" (all other bylined Hemingway *Trapeze* articles identify his first name as Ernest or E.), Ernie speaks in phrases that Ernest would never use when speaking in his own voice, such as "I thot as how . . . ," "this here nation . . . ," and "I ain't ascairt . . . " (*Hemingway's Apprenticeship* 57). Hemingway was almost certainly unaware of the theoretical ramifications of having a fictional character claim authorship of the "real" Hemingway's work. Yet these attempts to cross generic boundaries between journalism and fiction mark the beginning of a career of experimentation with fictional techniques not only in nonfiction, as a method of both communicating and questioning the verifiability of the historical facts being reported, but also in fiction, as a way of revealing a text's fictionality while simultaneously creating the illusion of its representational function. Here, as in much of his work for the *Trapeze,* Hemingway's experimentation with the genre of journalistic reporting suggests the beginning of his awareness of the limitations of the genre and the inevitable fictionality of any ostensibly objective stance.

After Hemingway graduated from high school, he took a job as a cub reporter for the *Kansas City Star,* where his training played a significant role in shaping his prose. "On the *Star,*" Hemingway told George Plimpton in 1958, "you were forced to write a simple declarative sentence. This is useful to anyone" ("Interview" 27). The *Star*'s stylesheet of 110 rules began, "Use short sentences. Use short first paragraphs. Use vigorous English. Be positive, not negative." The stylesheet also contained injunctions to avoid the use of adjectives and to eliminate every superfluous word, all of which Hemingway followed more or less throughout his career as a writer, regardless of the genre in which he was writing.

Because he had more restrictions regarding style, point of view, and subject matter placed on him at the *Kansas City Star,* the few articles we know Hemingway wrote while he worked there are much less blatantly experimental than the juvenilia. Matthew J. Bruccoli's collection of the *Kansas City Star* pieces, *Ernest Hemingway, Cub Reporter,* contains no Ring Lardner imitations and no articles that overtly reveal themselves to be wholly or partly fictional. Yet many of the *Kansas City Star* pieces reveal at least as great an interest on Hemingway's part in testing the limits of the stylesheet's rules as in abiding by them. For example, characterizing a young boxer in "Kerensky, the Fighting Flea," Hemingway takes every liberty against which the *Star*'s stylesheet warns without prohibiting: "In certain cases, where 'kids' conveys just the proper shading and fits the story, it is permissible" (Rule 69). Old slang, however, is never permissible: "Slang to be enjoyable must be fresh" (Rule 3). Yet Hemingway calls the boxer a kid several times in the piece and, when explaining how "Kid" Kerensky began his pugilistic career, says, "Well, he just picked up his skill. For several years he sold papers, and you know how one thing leads to another" (*Ernest Hemingway, Cub Reporter* 17). Certainly "kid" conveys the proper shading here; whether "just picked up" and "you know how one thing leads to another" are fresh is more debatable.

As Hemingway was developing his prose style by following the rules, then pushing them to their limits, he was also testing the beliefs and assumptions that inform those rules. The Kansas code of journalistic ethics, adopted in 1910, and the "Canons of Journalism," adopted by the National Association of Newspaper Editors in 1923, both condemn inaccuracy and untruth in newspaper writing. Yet by the time Hemingway had established himself as a journalist and fiction writer, scholars of journalism had begun openly to question whether it was possible for a journalist to portray reality truthfully. In 1924 Casper S. Yost, for example, argued that "Even if [a reporter] is a witness of the circumstances leading to the [reported event], the limitations of observation, of knowledge, and of memory render absolute and complete accuracy in every detail of his narration a difficult accomplishment" (57). Leon Nelson Flint, writing in 1925, further complicates the problem by pointing out that accuracy constitutes only one aspect of truth:

> Accuracy in the news has to do with details: truth, with those larger problems of selection and proportion and perspective which determine the general impression made on the reader. Accuracy is one means towards attaining truth, but it is a comparatively elementary matter, like correct grammar, while the other essentials to truth are often so difficult as to be baffling. (50)

Certainly if, as Yost claims, any "thoughtful and experienced newspaper man" (vi) would be aware of the limitations inherent in the journalist's endeavor to communicate truth, Hemingway would, and in fact much of his early journalism and fiction addresses this issue.

"Battle of Raid Squads," for example, raises implicit questions about the journalist's ability to represent reality by presenting several contradictory "facts." The opening sentence says that two revenue officers "may die . . . as a result of a revolver battle yesterday through a case of mistaken identity" (*Ernest Hemingway, Cub Reporter* 21). Yet eleven lines later the article states, "Both [officers] will recover" (22), and five lines later Hemingway calls into question his own statement of the cause of the shooting: "While on the surface the shooting of the two government officers appeared to be a case of mistaken identity, elements of a mysterious nature which Francis M. Wilson, United States district attorney, refused to make public, crept into the case last night" (22). The remainder of the article presents without evaluation two conflicting eyewitness accounts of the story. Both stories sound credible, and both are told by government officials, presumably reliable narrators. Yet the facts of the first version contradict those of the second, indicating Hemingway's awareness that truth and accuracy are relative terms, dependent on the perspective of the speaker. This early journalism therefore remains within the tradition of journalism while implicitly questioning assumptions about the nature and function of representation on which this tradition is based.[1]

Hemingway's efforts to push journalistic representation to or past its conventional limits are also evident in his January 20, 1918 *Kansas City Star* article, "At the End of the Ambulance Run." Here he breaks down barriers between fiction and nonfiction by using a reportorial voice that assumes an objective stance but nevertheless reveals the subjective emotional core of a human situation and by creating dialogue, plots, and characters out of the facts he finds himself covering. For example, instead of stating the bare fact that the victim of a street brawl was named George Anderson, Hemingway uses emotionally charged details to emphasize the man's solitary state and to suggest what he has lost:

> No one knew who he was, but a receipt, bearing the name of George Anderson, for $10 paid on a home out in a little Nebraska town served to identify him.
> The surgeon . . . [said], "Well, George, you're not going to finish paying for that home of yours." (*Ernest Hemingway, Cub Reporter* 28)

He also develops a suggestion of typicality as he suggests that journalism and literature are based on the same kinds of human experience: "It was merely one of the many cases that come to the city dispensary from night to night . . . ; the night shift, perhaps, has a wider range of the life and death tragedy – and even comedy, of the city" (28). And in a passage that treats his subjects more like fictional characters to whose motives and feelings an author is privy than like real people, he implies a contrast between their interior responses to the situation and their observable demeanor:

> When "George" comes in on the soiled, bloody stretcher and the rags are stripped off and his naked, broken body lies on the white table in the glare of the surgeon's light, and he dangles on a little thread of life, while the physicians struggle grimly, it is all in the night's work, whether the thread snaps or whether it holds so that George can fight on and work and play. (28)

By shifting into the literary present tense and abandoning the stylesheet's injunction to use short sentences, Hemingway suggests that this story is something more than, perhaps other than, conventional reporting, and when he demonstrates that the surgeons' unemotional objectivity is a matter of professionalism rather than an indication of their inability to respond to human suffering, he is also, at least implicitly, explaining something about both the journalist's stance and the fictional style for which he would later become famous.

Hemingway's interest in the vignette as a fictional form may also have grown out of this article, which is structured as a series of six vignettes, and the one-paragraph news stories over which Pete Wellington remembers him carefully laboring (see Fenton 42). One of Hemingway's first forays into fiction, *in our time,* consists of a series of eighteen vignettes, of which twelve are one paragraph long and none is more than a few paragraphs in length. This practice is consistent with the theory Hemingway later learned from

Gertrude Stein, that paragraphs are the best means of communication for twentieth-century literature because they can be written so as "to include everything" (Stein 257). A one-paragraph news story would necessarily "include everything," or at least all the information that made the story newsworthy, and Hemingway's interest in developing this form may have been one reason that when he arrived in Paris he placed himself under the tutelage of Stein.

The best-known of Hemingway's *Kansas City Star* pieces also defies journalistic convention by using techniques more often associated with fiction than with journalism to describe a soldiers' dance on the sixth floor of a YMCA building. Entitled "Mix War, Art and Dancing," the article opens, "Outside a woman walked along the wet street-lamp lit sidewalk through the sleet and snow" (*Ernest Hemingway, Cub Reporter* 56), replacing the standard journalistic opening sentence that tells who, what, when, and where with one that creates a mood, a setting, a character, and a question in the reader's mind about what has happened and what will happen next – all elements that would be more likely to appear in the first line of a short story or novel than in a newspaper article. The focus of the article then shifts to the party inside, describing the soldiers, musicians, and "girls" at the dance. A second reference to the woman comes almost exactly in the middle of the article. It juxtaposes her with a girl at the dance, implying by omission a comparison between innocence and experience, and suggesting the extent to which the soldiers participate in both, all in a two-sentence paragraph: "A crowd of men rushed up to the girl in the red dress to plead for the next dance. Outside the woman walked along the wet lamp-lit sidewalk" (57). A third reference to the woman closes the story: "After the last car had gone, the woman walked along the wet sidewalk through the sleet and looked up at the dark windows of the sixth floor" (58). Hemingway's references to the prostitute at the beginning, middle, and end of the article show that he is learning to use the fictional technique of framing even in journalism. They demonstrate his tendencies to avoid convention, to reach toward methods that reveal more about the natures of people than facts alone can, and to communicate the significance of events through internal, rather than or in addition to external, reference, all of which will recur in his fiction.

Other concepts to which Hemingway was first exposed at the *Kansas City Star* and which he later applied to his fiction include the idea that good writing, like good bullfighting, cannot be "faked," and the writer's need for a "shit detector." The journalistic meaning of the term "to fake" a story was certainly familiar to Hemingway. Flint concludes the twelve pages of material in his subchapter "Newspaper Faking," "There is one good thing about faking – it is no secret!" (48), and he quotes H. J. Haskell, chief editorial writer for the *Kansas City Star* when Hemingway worked there: "No self-respecting newspaper can tolerate faking or misrepresentation on the part of members of its staff. Faking is precisely on a par with short weights and adulterated goods" (cited in Flint 49). Hemingway often used the same term to express a similar opinion regarding fiction writing. In *Death in the After-noon* he argues: "If they [characters] do not talk of [certain] subjects and the writer makes them talk of them he is a faker, and . . . he is spoiling his work" (191). Similarly, Yost wrote in 1924 that the good journalist must exercise "intuitive discrimination between what is important and what is not, between the essentials and the nonessentials" (70), and Hemingway later expressed his opinion that the good fiction writer does the same thing: "The most essential gift for a good writer is a built-in, shock-proof, shit detector. This is the writer's radar and all great writers have had it" ("Interview" 38). Thus, when Hemingway left the *Kansas City Star* in 1918 to join the Italian ambulance corps he took with him the lessons of a valuable apprenticeship in both journalism and fiction writing.

When he began writing feature articles for the *Toronto Star* in 1920, he created an opportunity to continue honing both crafts. He was expected to provide the paper with humor, color, and entertainment, and the *Star* gave him "virtually unlimited freedom in choosing material" (Donaldson 91). Significantly, then, the subjects about which he chose to write included the topics that would inform his fiction and nonfiction for the rest of his life: fishing, camping, eating, money, traveling, bullfighting, politics, expatriates, and war, to name a few. Even when he covered news events on assignment, his articles usually supplemented wire reports of the same stories (some of which he wrote himself under a pseudonym), an arrangement that allowed him to continue choosing which stories, and which parts of those stories, to tell. Incidentally, Hemingway's iceberg theory – that "you could omit anything if you knew that you omitted and the omitted part would strengthen the story and make people feel something more than they understood" (*AMF* 75) – may have its beginnings in his realization that he could tell stories that communicated truth about the world while leaving out the basic information that wire reports would have provided.

Throughout the *Toronto Star* dispatches, Hemingway uses dialogue, character development, complex and inventive point of view, a more conversational than reportorial narrative voice, and dramatic scene rather than or in addition to historical summary to tell his stories as he "cultivate[s] his satirical bent, writing pieces at the expense of phony would-be artists, thrill-seeking tourists, venal Frenchmen, and rude Germans" (Donaldson 91).

Hemingway sometimes seems to be using these fictional storytelling techniques in an attempt to access otherwise inaccessible historical truths, but at least as often, and sometimes in the same articles, these techniques invoke a fictionalized view of reality. His December 23, 1923 dispatch, a series of three vignettes on Christmas in Germany, Italy, and France, is an example. The story shifts in narrative voice from first to third person, in verb tense from past to present and back to past, and in tone from delight to despair, developing complex characters and conflicts in the process. The last vignette focuses on the tense dialogue between a young, newly expatriated couple eating a lonely Christmas dinner in a Paris restaurant, unwilling or unable to speak directly of their disappointment or their homesickness:

> "Do you remember turkey at home?" asks the young girl.
> "Don't talk about it," says the boy.
> They attack the potatoes, which are fried with too much grease.
> "What do you suppose they're doing at home?" says the girl.
> "I don't know," said the boy.

As they leave, Hemingway notes, "They walked out into the streets of old Paris that had known the prowling of wolves and the hunting of men and the tall old houses that had looked down on it all and were stark and unmoved by Christmas" (*Dateline: Toronto* 425–26). Here, as in much of his work for the *Star*, Hemingway's fictional techniques so thoroughly inform his journalism that they render conventional distinctions between the two genres almost superfluous. The article accomplishes what it does regardless of whether it accurately accounts for what happened on any particular evening in Paris; the truths being communicated here are universal truths, not historical ones.

Hemingway also uses these and other fictional techniques, including direct narrative comment, to call attention to the inherent subjectivity, even fictionality, of any supposedly objective report. In the process he challenges traditional beliefs about the verifiability of historical facts that exist independently of our perceptions of them. In his article on the debut presence of women at Toronto prizefights, for example, Hemingway raises questions about the reliability of the "facts" of the event as perceived and reported by both the press and eyewitnesses:

> A press agent story said there would be four hundred boxes filled with members of society attending the bouts in evening clothes. There really were about a hundred women present.
> They came ostensibly to see Georges Carpentier give a sparring exhibition. In reality they saw a series of gladiatorial combats and they smiled and applauded through it all. (*Dateline: Toronto* 30)

Similarly, in his report on a violent demonstration of "passive resistance" in the Ruhr, for example, he says, "I have heard at least fifteen different accounts of what actually happened. At least twelve of them sounded like lies" (*Dateline: Toronto* 290). And later in the same article:

> The funeral at Essen was delayed the last time because the French and German doctors could not agree on the nature of the bullet wounds. The Germans claimed eleven of the workmen were shot in the back. The French surgeon claims that five were shot in the front, five bullets entered from the side and two in the back. I do not know the claims on the two men who died since the argument started. (*Dateline: Toronto* 290)

Whether Hemingway was writing light human interest pieces or relating events of serious historical import, the *Toronto Star* articles repeatedly imply that the truth of objective reality, if it exists, is not what gets directly reported, in either the media or everyday conversation. At least one reason for this condition, the articles suggest, is that people's perceptions of external reality tend to be influenced by their internal, subjective realities – their hopes and expectations, their political agendas, or their patriotism, for example – and even a reporter who tries to put aside his own subjectivity usually has little more than the subjective perceptions of others with which to work. History, inevitably recontextualized through the acts of telling and writing, is also text, a situation that problematizes conventional distinctions between journalism and fiction, fact and imagination, and reality and perception.

At the same time he was writing for the *Toronto Star* Hemingway was also using many of the stories and techniques he acquired through his newspaper work to create his first full-length work of fiction, *In Our Time*. Most of Hemingway's contemporary readers would have recognized similarities between certain events in *In Our Time* and events reported through journalism, regardless of whether they had read Hemingway's dispatches. At least twenty-five *Toronto Star* articles are directly echoed in *In Our Time,* and the jacket and inside covers of the first *in our time* – montages of newspaper clippings about current events and trivia – served as another reminder of this connection. Bill Bird's idea of "framing each page with a border of newsprint, carefully selected to serve both as decoration and illustration" (Baker 116), of which Hemingway did not disapprove, would have stressed this relationship even more. Furthermore, although Hemingway later concurred with Ezra Pound's identification of the title's source as the English *Book of Common Prayer* (SL 378), the title certainly affirms a connection between the fiction and current events as well. These connections between *In Our Time* and journalism suggest that Hemingway is not only using language in this fiction as he learned to use it in journalism; he is also establishing a more specific relationship between journalism and *In Our Time*.

Hemingway uses journalism in *In Our Time* like clay from which to sculpt another reality while reminding his reader of the base material from which his art is created. He thus acknowledges the separate reality that exists in and is constituted by the fiction. At the same time, he raises questions about the natures of the realities that both kinds of texts create and about the relationship between a journalistic report of life and an artistic presentation of it. These issues may be clarified by comparing and contrasting the referential functions of the language of chapter 2 ("Minarets stuck up in the rain"), for example, with those of the four articles about the Thracian evacuation that Hemingway produced for the *Toronto Daily Star* before he wrote the vignette: "Tired Christians, and Hungry, Leave Thrace to Turks," October 16, 1922; "A Silent, Ghastly Procession Wends Way from Thrace," October 20, 1922; "Betrayal Preceded Defeat, Then Came Greek Revolt," November 3, 1922; and "Refugee Procession Is Scene of Horror," November 14, 1922 (*Dateline: Toronto* 226, 232 244–45, 249–52).

One difference between chapter 2 and the journalism on which it was based is that Hemingway the journalist grounds his story in history, while the narrator of chapter 2 distances his story from history, explicitly revealing almost nothing about the historical context of the evacuation. J. F. Kobler points out that while the newspaper accounts explain "who is fleeing from whom, where to, and why" (12), the fiction only vaguely hints at the site of the action. The meaning of the nonfictional evacuation is determined by its historical context; the lack of historical context in the fictional evacuation draws attention to the function of verbal and imaginal context. Thus, if chapter 2 is to have meaning, either it must create its own fictional context or its reader must supply an (imagined) historical context. When history becomes "the thing left out," a mutually exclusive dichotomy between historical and fictional realities is no longer possible.

Similarities between Hemingway's lists of the contents of the carts in the journalism and the fiction further suggest the extent to which historical and fictional realities intersect by calling attention to the linguistic status of both descriptions. In "Refugee Procession Is Scene of Horror" Hemingway describes the carts as "piled high with bedding, mirrors, furniture, pigs tied flat, mothers huddled under blankets with their babies" (*Dateline: Toronto* 251), where thirteen of sixteen words alliterate. In the fiction he writes,

"Women and kids were in the carts crouched with mattresses, mirrors, sewing machines, bundles" (21), where "and," "in," "the," "sewing," and "bundles" are the only nonalliterative words. Hemingway's language in the vignette constructs both an illusion of that which is being described and a reminder of the presence of language, while his language in the journalism functions as it often does in his juvenilia, demonstrating his interest in using conventions of fiction (or poetry) in journalism and breaking down traditional barriers between the two.

The difference between the length of the historical evacuation and that of the fictional exodus also establishes a linguistic context for the fiction that is separate from but related to the reality as reported through the journalism on which it is based. Hemingway writes for the *Toronto Daily Star,* "The main column crossing the Maritza River at Adrianople is twenty miles long. Twenty miles of carts . . . " (232); he says in the vignette, "The carts were jammed for thirty miles along the Karagatch road" (21). The difference separates the fiction from history while simultaneously reconnecting the fictional context to the historical context it recalls.

Hemingway's descriptions of a woman in labor function similarly. He closes his report for the *Daily Star:* "A husband spreads a blanket over a woman in labor in one of the carts to keep off the driving rain. She is the only person making a sound. Her little daughter looks at her in horror and begins to cry. And the procession keeps moving" (*Dateline: Toronto* 232). He also closes chapter 2 with a description of a woman in labor, but he places this woman in a more melodramatic situation by omitting her husband and having no one but her daughter help: "There was a woman having a kid with a young girl holding a blanket over her and crying. Scared sick looking at it. It rained all through the evacuation" (21). The idea of a baby being born without a father is both credible and conventionally suggestive of the kind of uprootedness and lack of protection these evacuees are experiencing, but Hemingway's description of the woman going into labor in the presence of other mothers as well as "old men and women" (21), none of whom offers any assistance, is almost too pitiful to believe. This melodramatic situation makes an abstract statement on the human condition being depicted throughout the vignette: Metaphorically, all the evacuees are in the process of generating new lives for themselves, yet "scared sick" and fatherless in those lives. By straining its own credibility to make this point, the description also reminds us of the extent to which any act of reading fiction is a willing suspension of disbelief, or a willing animation of belief in whatever alternative reality that fiction creates through its descriptions of it.

Echoes of Hemingway's journalism in his fiction therefore raise questions about the natures of fictional and historical realities and the relationship between them. For example, what does the fact that fiction can be true without accurately reproducing the world it purports to represent suggest about the nature of that which is represented or the nature of representation itself? What do the differences and similarities between the newspaper articles and the fictional vignettes that grew out of them suggest about the relationship between real life and fiction or between the representation of real life through journalism and the (re)presentation of real life through (fictional) art? The implied answers to these questions change and evolve throughout Hemingway's work, but what remains consistent is his appreciation of the complex nature of all reality and all acts of storytelling as well as his perception of the fluidity of the boundaries between nonfiction and fiction and the concrete and imagined realities they represent. Thus in *In Our Time,* as in his early journalism, Hemingway uses the relationship between history and fiction to explore the roles that reality, imagination, and language play in each.

After Hemingway left the *Star* in 1924, he took a thirteen-year hiatus from working for newspapers to devote his talents to fiction and creative nonfiction. Significantly, however, much of the best writing he produced during that period contains material whose origins can be traced to the early journalism. Hemingway first described the Paris nightlife and fiesta-time Pamplona of *The Sun Also Rises* as well as the bullfights of *The Sun Also Rises* and *Death in the Afternoon,* for example, to his *Toronto Star* readers, and the war and evacuation scenes in *A Farewell to Arms* recall his 1922 reports of the Greco-Turkish war and the Thracian evacuation. In virtually all the work produced during these years, he used insights, techniques, or approaches he first practiced in the newspapers.

By 1937, when Hemingway returned to newspaper journalism as a correspondent for the North American Newspaper Alliance (NANA) covering the Spanish civil war, he had matured both as a writer of fiction and as a man, and the world as he saw it had placed itself in greater jeopardy than Hemingway had perceived during World War I. Hemingway understood the Spanish civil war as the precursor to World War II it turned out to be, and despite his continuing skepticism regarding any journalist's ability to report reality objectively, he believed that the way to secure U.S. involvement and win the war was by presenting to the American people a convincing and compelling set of the facts. His editor at NANA, like those at the *Toronto Star,* wanted "color and drama and the personal adventures of the celebrated writer" (Watson 7), and his dispatches deliver these features, but most of the humor and ironic detachment of the earlier features is replaced by a level of seriousness and commitment to reporting the events of the war and explaining their consequences that was not usually evident in the earlier work. Propaganda, censorship, soldiers' bravado, and the turbulent conditions of war, as well as the general nature of reality, rendered the achievement of accuracy in any form difficult, but whereas in the 1920s Hemingway often seemed to enjoy playing with the elusive nature of truth, here he struggled with it both intellectually and physically, more than once risking life and limb to uncover it. Thus, although these articles continue to raise some of the same questions about truth and accuracy that the earlier work did, they do so with a new emphasis and a new sense of urgency and anxiety.

In all thirty of Hemingway's NANA dispatches, he more often posits the possibility of the existence of an at least partially knowable, objective reality than he has before, and throughout the series he takes pains to separate what is knowable from what is believable from what is neither, often emphasizing the extent to which the truth eludes policy-making officials, soldiers, other reporters, and himself. His second dispatch, for example, opens with an implied criticism of the extent to which U.S. policy was based on ignorance: "On the day on which the American State Department, following its policy of strictest neutrality, refused Sidney Franklin permission to proceed to Spain to earn his living as a war correspondent fearing he might engage in bullfighting, 12,000 Italian troops were landed at Malaga and Cadiz" ("Dispatches" 14). The story continues with information "from a most reliable source" (14) regarding the number of foreign troops stationed throughout Spain, only to admit that some Senegalese troops "have been mistaken by combatants for Italian Askaris" (15) and to state twice that the number of Germans enlisted there "cannot be ascertained" (15).

"This is a strange new kind of war," he writes in his eighth dispatch, "where you learn just as much as you are able to believe" (33). Over and over, these dispatches imply that in this war, even more so than in peace, obtaining the complete facts of objective reality, if such a thing exists, is both crucial and impossible. Although some facts are verifiable and some truths accessible, the whole truth is at best absurdly distorted and at worst dangerously unattainable – in either case, ultimately unknowable. Hemingway closely followed the Spanish civil war before and after the time he spent in Spain covering it, but as early as 1934 he had written, "No history is written honestly. You have to keep in touch with it at the time and you can depend on just as much as you have actually seen and followed" (*Byline* 181).

If the truth is difficult to pinpoint, however, its opposite does not seem to be, for throughout the dispatches Hemingway devotes a relatively large proportion of space to exposing lies and inaccuracies. For example, referring to published reports in American papers that Nationalist troops were expected to take Belchite, he says: "Such reporting would be laughable if it were not criminal lying" ("Dispatches" 59). And in a discussion of the aftermath of a particularly bloody battle in Belchite, he complains, "The P. O. U. M. troops have boasted they have never lost a foot of ground on the Aragon front, but they omitted to state that they hadn't lost a man either in six months of so-called fighting nor ever gained a yard" (50). In the same dispatch he explains that General Kleber, who led one of the offensives, "is far from being regarded in Spain as the military genius some American periodicals have tried to make him" (50). He closes his last report with a final nod at the difference between reported history and reality: "There is a year of war clearly ahead where European diplomats are trying to say it will be over in a month" (92). Thus, while in his *Toronto Star* stories he often played with the concept of the fictionality of history, here he frequently frets over the idea that what is being called history is a dangerously false fiction.

Despite his skepticism regarding contemporary history as he sees it being reported to the world, he often attempts to use recorded history to inform present reality. His eleventh dispatch, a carefully and intelligently argued assessment of the current situation in Spain, opens, "You need many past performances to study a war" (40). Referring in some detail to the American and Russian civil wars and the roles time, foreign intervention, and geography played in each, he then turns to a discussion of how those factors are similarly influencing the Spanish civil war to argue, "A belligerent with time and geography on his side has the two most precious allies" (40). In a later dispatch, following a discussion of the underestimated impact of regionalism on the course of the war, he comments, "United, there has always been sectional jealousy. Once divided, comes the pride of province, of section, of city and of district. Napoleon found this out to his defeat and two other dictators are discovering it today" (92). If reported history cannot be trusted to be accurate, these dispatches imply, neither can it be ignored.

Like all Hemingway's newspaper work, the quality of the writing in the NANA dispatches is uneven, and the stories range from more or less straight reporting of current events to highly personalized accounts that read more like fiction than conventional journalism. Also, as in his earlier journalism, many of the pieces contain strong narrative threads, dialogue, characterization, and description that set both a scene and a mood. One difference between this and Hemingway's earlier newspaper work is that here Hemingway's personal involvement with the work seems to be less about using it to figure out how to write, how to re-present the world in journalism or to present an alternate, imaginative world in fiction, than about the role stories of all kinds – real and imagined – can play in the world, not only in their capacity to communicate truth but also in their potential to create truth, to shape the world by influencing its course.

As Hemingway's work for the *Kansas City Star* and the *Toronto Star* influenced his other writing in the 1920s and 1930s and beyond, the NANA dispatches also inform his later fiction and nonfiction, most obviously *For Whom the Bell Tolls*. An accomplished fiction writer by this time, Hemingway seems much less interested in developing new methods of storytelling here than in his earlier journalism. At least one technique he employs throughout *For Whom the Bell Tolls,* that of substituting obscenities with words such as "unprintable" and "unspeakable," has its origin in the NANA dispatches. More important, it was while writing the NANA dispatches that Hemingway acquired the understanding of the war that provides the physical, intellectual, and emotional context for every character and action in *For Whom the Bell Tolls*. The impact of Spanish history, terrain, and regionalism on the war as well as its relation to the American and Russian civil wars, all first introduced in the NANA dispatches, repeatedly inform the novel, as does the skepticism about the reliability of reported history that sent Hemingway to Spain to see the war for himself in the first place.

Other work that originated in part with the NANA dispatches includes a series of propagandistic editorials written for *Ken* magazine and a documentary film called *The Spanish Earth*. *The Spanish Earth* was produced to raise money for the Loyalist cause, and *Ken* was in its conception a leftist publication interested more in opinions than objective facts. In both Hemingway wears the guise of the reporter, using facts and fact-based arguments in whatever ways best suit his purpose, that of generating support for the Loyalists and therefore changing the course of world history. If history and reality are constructs of the imagination, this work implies, then the important question is whose imagination will construct it. As he has done elsewhere, Hemingway disregards traditional boundaries between genres, but here, rather than puzzling or struggling over the concept of truth or history as a construct, he attempts to construct truth and history, both in his nonfiction and in the world.

After 1938 Hemingway never returned to newspaper reporting, although before he went to China in 1941 to write a series of essays on the tension in the Orient for *PM,* he contracted to write daily cables for that publication if war broke out while he was there. This did not happen, but the essays he wrote for *PM* at that time, like those he wrote for *Collier's* from Europe in 1944, contain his unique blend of reportage, military analysis, editorial, portraiture, description, human interest, personal anecdote, humor, and fictionalization of fact. Like his previous war reporting, the *PM* and *Collier's* essays are often structured around the tension between Hemingway's desire to get the facts right, or to make his readers think he is doing so, and his skepticism regarding that endeavor. On the Soviet ambassador's announcement during a dinner party that Russian aid to China would continue, Hemingway notes: "At the time that incident happened I did not care to write it because diplomats rarely impart bad news over the dinner table and it was possible that very different news might come out of Moscow. But since then I have heard directly from both Dr. Kung and Mme. Chiang Kai-shek that Russian aid is continuing to arrive" (*Byline* 315). And on Japanese neutrality: "Now Japan has made a neutrality pact with Soviet Russia which presumably should free her divisions in Manchuria for a southern move. But does it?" (324). The question is not answered definitively, but the remainder of the article discusses several possible reasons for both potential responses. And closing his report of the D-Day invasion of Fox Green and Easy Red beaches: "There is much that I have not written. You could write for a week and not give everyone credit for what he did on a front of 1,135 yards. Real war is never like paper war, nor do accounts of it read much the way it looks. But if you want to know how it was in an LCV(P) on D-Day when we took Fox Green beach and Easy Red beach on the sixth of June, 1944, then this is as near as I can come to it" (355). Here, as he has done since he first began reporting for the *Trapeze,* Hemingway remains within the tradition of journalism while continuing to challenge assumptions about reality on which this tradition is based. Whereas in the early work his interests seemed focused on the connection between language and perception, the extent to which one shapes the other, the later work reveals a sharper awareness of the gap between language and reality, the difficulty inherent in any attempt to represent experience in or through language.

Most of Hemingway's work is informed in some way by his journalism and the quest he began in his newspaper reports to blur traditional distinctions among journalism, creative nonfiction, and fiction. "A Natural History of the Dead" and "Che ti dice la patria," for example, were both published first as nonfiction and later as fiction, and *Across the River and into the Trees* poses as a novel while it reprises "themes, characters, situations and sometimes phrases found in the novels, stories, and nonfiction of the quarter-century before" (Stephens 300). As Robert O. Stephens points out, "Readers of his journalism and other nonfictional pieces . . . could recognize also that Hemingway drew upon ideas, passages, and situations from that body of work, which ranged from some of his earliest articles to those as late as the war reports on the invasion of Germany" (300). *Green Hills of Africa,* also a novel, more or less, was written, Hemingway claimed in the foreword, "to see whether the shape of a country and the pattern of a month's action can, if truly presented, compete with a work of the imagination." Similarly, *A Moveable Feast* opens with a preface detailing what has been left out and implying the extent to which this book of nonfiction has not even aimed for accuracy. The preface concludes, "If the reader prefers, this book may be regarded as fiction. But there is always the chance that such a book of fiction may throw some light on what has been written as fact." These and many other Hemingway works suggest that for Hemingway, the boundaries between imagined and experienced realities, and among the journalism, nonfiction, and fiction that record them, are at least somewhat fluid.

Much of the other writing Hemingway produced during his last years as well as his well-documented "mythologizing" of his own life story corroborate this idea. In a long essay published in *Look* under the title "The Christmas Gift," for example, Hemingway reports with irony and delight on reading his own obituaries after two plane crashes in Africa, discovering, in other words, that journalists from around the world had fictionalized the facts of his life, albeit unintentionally. Whether he was writing journalism, creative nonfiction, or fiction, Hemingway was first and foremost a storyteller, and the evidence that some of his journalism and other nonfiction was drawn from his imagination and that much of his fiction was drawn from reality suggests that distinctions between reality and imagination were not as important to him as communicating other kinds of truth.

In sum, similarities between Hemingway's early journalism and his early fiction not only reveal where Hemingway began to learn to write fiction; they also suggest his early interest in representing both the world and the discourses that construct it and therefore in implicitly evoking the contexts of everyday life to reveal that they are linguistically constructed. Even Hemingway's earliest journalism demonstrates his propensity to use journalism to challenge traditional assumptions about truth, accuracy, and the relationship between fact and fiction and to use fictional techniques to create a larger, and other, reality than journalism usually attempts to represent. Throughout his career Hemingway continued to use connections between journalism and fiction and between imagined and experienced realities to foreground uncertainty about our perception of historical reality. Similarly, he often used journalistic echoes in the fiction to raise questions about our perceptions of the nature of fictional reality. Thus, his work in all genres tends to draw on the relationship between journalism and fiction to raise questions about the natures of the realities both kinds of texts create, ultimately challenging traditional assumptions that history exists independently of our perceptions of it and that we can therefore report it accurately and objectively. Focusing on Hemingway's journalism and its relationship to his other writing emphasizes the extent to which all his work exposes both history and fiction as constructs of the imagination that are at least partially linguistic in nature and therefore challenges traditional realist assumptions about the relationship among fact, fiction, language, and reality.

NOTES

This article was written with the support of a grant from the Ohio State University, for which I am grateful. I am also grateful to Professor James Phelan for reading this work in progress and offering some valuable suggestions for revision. A portion of this article appeared in different form in an article I published in the spring 1992 issue of *Hemingway Review* (vol. 11, no. 2, pp. 11–18), entitled " 'Truer Than Anything True': *In Our Time* and Journalism."

1. There is some question as to whether Hemingway wrote "Battle of Raid Squads" (12), yet Bruccoli includes it in his collection of Hemingway's *Kansas City Star* journalism because "Hemingway said he was there and proudly sent a clipping of the story to his father" (21), claiming it was his. Regardless of who wrote it, Hemingway's contention that he did is instructive because it suggests what he valued in journalism or at least what interested him and because of the questions the article implicitly raises about the journalist's ability to represent reality by presenting the facts.

WORKS CITED

Baker, Carlos. *Ernest Hemingway: A Life Story.* New York: Charles Scribner's Sons, 1969.

Donaldson, Scott. "Hemingway of *The Star.*" *Ernest Hemingway: The Papers of a Writer.* Ed. Bernard Oldsey. New York: Garland, 1981, 89–107.

Fenton, Charles A. *The Apprenticeship of Ernest Hemingway: The Early Years.* New York: Farrar, Straus, and Young, 1954.

Flint, Leon Nelson. *The Conscience of the Newspaper.* New York: D. Appleton, 1925.

Hemingway, Ernest. *Byline: Ernest Hemingway.* Ed. William White. New York: Charles Scribner's Sons, 1967.

———. *Dateline: Toronto.* Ed. William White. New York: Charles Scribner's Sons, 1985.

———. *Death in the Afternoon.* New York: Charles Scribner's Sons, 1932.

———. *Ernest Hemingway's Apprenticeship: Oak Park, 1916–1917.* Ed. Matthew J. Bruccoli. Washington, D.C.: NCR Microcard Editions, 1971.

———. *Ernest Hemingway, Cub Reporter: Kansas City Star Stories.* Ed. Matthew J. Bruccoli. Pittsburgh: University of Pittsburgh Press, 1970.

———. *Green Hills of Africa.* New York: Charles Scribner's Sons, 1935.

———. "Hemingway's Spanish Civil War Dispatches." Ed. William Braasch Watson. *The Hemingway Review* 7.2 (Spring 1988): 13–92.

———. "An Interview with Ernest Hemingway (*Paris Review* Interview)." with George Plimpton. *Ernest Hemingway: Five Decades of Criticism.* Ed. Linda Welshimer Wagner. East Lansing: Michigan State University Press, 1974, 21–37.

———. *A Moveable Feast.* New York: Charles Scribner's Sons, 1964.

———. *Ernest Hemingway: Selected Letters, 1917–1961.* Ed. Carlos Baker. New York: Charles Scribner's Sons, 1981.

Kobler, J. F. *Ernest Hemingway: Journalist and Artist.* Ann Arbor, Mich.: UMI Research Press, 1985.

Stein, Gertrude. "The Gradual Making of the Making of Americans." *Selected Writings of Gertrude Stein.* Ed. Carl Van Vechten. New York: Vintage, 1945, 1972, 239–58.

Stephens, Robert O. *Hemingway's Nonfiction: The Public Voice.* Chapel Hill: University of North Carolina Press, 1968.

Watson, William Braasch. "Hemingway's Spanish Civil War Dispatches: Introduction." *The Hemingway Review* 7.2 (Spring 1988): 4–13.

Yost, Casper S. *The Principles of Journalism.* New York: D. Appleton, 1924.

3

PAUL SMITH

1924:
Hemingway's Luggage
and the Miraculous Year

For someone who traveled as long and far as Ernest Hemingway did, it is little wonder that his luggage – a trunk stored in the family attic, a valise stolen at a railway station, another trunk left for decades at a hotel – might become metaphors for his life; and it is less wonder that their contents, known or suspected, would be curiously examined at the borders of Hemingway criticism. I will inspect two of them here: the trunk holding boxes of early papers stored in Oak Park just before Ernest and Hadley sailed for Paris in December 1921, and the valise of manuscripts stolen from Hadley at the Gare de Lyon as she was on her way to join Ernest in Lausanne in December 1922.

The first set of Chicago manuscripts was returned to Hemingway by several editors of popular magazines as not worth publishing; and the second set, not worth stealing, was probably dropped into a Paris sewer by a disgruntled thief. By 1924 both the rejection of the first and the theft of the second variously informed the composition of *In Our Time,* and those erstwhile losses became early instances of Hemingway's long-standing luck.

THE CHICAGO TRUNK – 1919–21

In late November 1921 Ernest packed his papers in cartons for storage in a trunk at his boyhood home. Two years later his father shipped them to Toronto, where Ernest and Hadley had returned for the birth of their son John. One had been marked "private papers," another, "old papers"; Clarence wondered whether he should send along Ernest's "boyhood papers and War togs."[1] It is likely that the boyhood papers were his high school stories and journalism and that the private papers included letters from his once beloved Agnes von Kurowsky, but what made up those old papers is of more interest here.

From the late fall of 1918 to the fall of 1921, Hemingway wrote some thirteen stories or sketches; he sent most of the finished ones to magazines, like the *Saturday Evening Post,* and, as he recalled,

> The Saturday Evening Post did not buy them nor did any other magazine and I doubt if worse stories were ever written. . . . After Christmas when I was still writing for the Saturday Evening Post and had $20 left of my savings, I was promised a job at the pump factory . . . and looked forward to laying off writing for the magazines for a time. (KL/EH 820)[2]

However easy it was in later years for him to call these stories the worst ever written, in the winter of 1921 he might have found it hard to mark their box "old" papers.

Most of what he had written during those two years was in his Chicago style, a brash and savvy manner that flaunts his intimacy with an exotic realm before a proper hometown audience, while it beckons them toward it with metaphors they would appreciate.[3] "The Mercenaries" of late 1919 opens with the sentence: "If you are honestly curious about pearl fishing conditions in the Marquesas, the possibility of employment on the projected Trans Gobi Railway, or the potentialities of any of the hot tamale republics, go to the Cafe Cambrinus on Wabash Avenue in Chicago."[4] The narrator knows the underworld of Wabash Avenue and, later in the tale, mimics the stereotypical language of Italian gangsters and French mercenaries. An inside witness, he enters the café "armed with a smile from Cambrinus himself," for he has passed the proprietor's "famous camel-needle's eye gymkhana" for entry. But had he uttered the Britishism "gymkhana" or alluded to the Gospels at the café door, Cambrinus's smile would have faded and the narrator would have found himself on the sidewalk. No, the metaphor is meant for the readers following him – if not his Oak Park parents, then his English teachers who would have raised his grade for the precocious metaphor.

Of course, there is little new in this attitude: Sportswriters like Ring Lardner took the same stance, and by 1920 Hemingway had read enough of Joseph Conrad's narratives-within-narratives to recommend him as "the king" to a friend.[5] Wherever he learned it, Hemingway had adopted a style and a voice that would center on the events and characters of an exotic locale and social class and then record them in a language that catered to an audience from another class and neighborhood, and so work both Chicago's Wabash and Oak Park's Kenilworth avenues.

Nor were all those stories the worst ever written, for among them were the "Crossroads" sketches. Michael Reynolds has chronicled their inception in letters to Hemingway from Bill Smith, his childhood friend and later literary confidant, suggesting that together they might imitate and better the popular sketches of E. W. Howe running in the Post as "The Anthology of Another Town" ("Introduction" 4–6). Smith offered anecdotes with scraps of dialogue and Hemingway wrote eight sketches titled "Crossroads: An Anthology." The sketches follow Howe's model: a character's name for a title; an opening sentence repeating the name and citing a seemingly innocent but enticing fact; then a brief and homespun narrative, dramatic only in its implications; and finally a summary remark from the laconic narrator or a character alluding to the opening sentence. "Pauline Snow" is an example:

> Pauline Snow was the only beautiful girl we ever had out at the Bay. She was like an Easter lily coming up straight and lithe and beautiful out of a dung heap. When her father and mother died she came to live with the Blodgetts. Then Art Simons started to come around to the Blodgetts in the evenings.
>
> Art couldn't come to most places at the Bay, but old Blodgett liked to have him around. . . . Art would go out to the stable with Blodgett when he was doing the chores and tell him stories, looking around first to see that no one would overhear.

Art is a bounder, as they would say in those days, but old Blodgett thought "he brightened up the place," and he told Pauline that Art was the "only regular fellow around the Bay." She was "frightened at first of Art, with his thick blunt fingers," but Blodgett persuaded her to walk out with him. On one of these walks she admired the sunset along the hills toward Charlevoix, and Art replied, "We didn't come here to talk about sunsets, kiddo! . . . and then put his arm around her."

The story ends in the next paragraph when "some of the neighbors made a complaint, and they sent Pauline away to correction school down at Coldwater. Art was away for awhile, and then came back and married one of the Jenkins girls" (Griffin 124).

Nothing here in these sketches of a killer's capture in the saloon at Chicago's Ninth and Grand ("The Ash Heel's Tendon") or a soldier of fortune's shoot-out at Taormina when his lover's husband unexpectedly returns ("The Mercenaries"). There is only Pauline Snow, an orphan girl with a beautiful face, and the complaining neighbors. Other sketches give us Old Man Hurd, a pig farmer with "a face that looks indecent," and his wife, who is puzzled to recall she knew that before they married; or Ed Paige, a lumberman who lasted six rounds against a titled champion at a burlesque show; or Bob White, a veteran who landed in France three days before the Armistice and came home to tell all about the war at the Odd Fellows Lodge.

One could argue that these twice-told tales of Hortons Bay demanded a new style to fit the form Hemingway had improvised from E. W. Howe's model. But there is that odd simile likening Pauline to an "Easter lily coming up straight and lithe and beautiful out of a dung heap" – odd, not because it dramatizes the narrator's perception of Pauline, but because it reveals at the outset the implication these narratives ordinarily disclose with the last line: Whatever she was, Art and the Blodgetts and all their neighbors were, to put it politely, dung. When the narrator succumbs to this simile, close to that "camel-needle's eye gymkhana" of "The Mercenaries," he speaks, for a moment, over the heads of the local listeners assumed in the rest of the narrative to a more distant audience of sophisticated readers.

The simile is revealing because it is an early instance of Hemingway facing at once all the complex relationships among the vistas and limits of his subject (the unsung annals of the Bayites), the audience he would address and so create (locals at the general store), and the narrator's role that best mediates between that subject and audience.

Moreover, Hemingway's response to that complexity offers an early example of one of three formulas for fiction Gerry Brenner has traced in over thirty stories from the high school tale "Sepi Jingan" of 1916 to "The Short Happy Life of Francis Macomber" of 1936, near the end of Hemingway's career in short fiction. The conclusion of "Pauline Snow" depends on the strategy Brenner calls "the lexical riddle," in which an "unarticulated or ambiguous" word leads readers to "stew over the missing or ambiguous term [so] that once they discover it or its meaning, they will feel they have solved the story" – but sometimes too soon, for the quick solution of the riddle may distract readers from asking more significant questions with more complex answers (161).[6]

In this sketch the rather simple riddle lies in the neighbor's "complaint": What was it about and to whom was it made? The likely answer is that Pauline became pregnant by Art, and the neighbors complained to the Blodgetts. To leave it at that, however, is to miss the fact that the sketch might have been titled "Old Blodgett": It was he who welcomed Art to his stable and laughed at his racy stories until his "face was red as a turkey's wattles"; and when Pauline seemed frightened of Art, it was Blodgett who "made fun of her" and said, "Be a sport, Pauline!" That much should make us wonder what motives impelled this man, reliving Art's stories while he shoveled dung, to pander for his friend.

By far the best of Hemingway's apprentice fiction, the "Crossroads" sketches come closest to the style and narrative strategies of the *In Our Time* stories; and yet he left them at home in that carton of "old papers" when he sailed for France in December 1921. What he did pack for Paris was, it is assumed, the beginning of a novel, possibly some war stories set on the Italian front, and a sheaf of poems.[7]

The one manuscript he certainly took with him was an early draft of "Up in Michigan," the first story he completed in Paris, and for which "Pauline Snow" offered a preliminary sketch. Like the orphaned Pauline, Liz Coates – whose parents are never mentioned – works as a maid for the Smiths; and, if not beautiful, she is neat and jolly in Jim Gilmore's eyes. On his return from a hunting trip, and after a big dinner and the bottom of a jug of whiskey, he approaches her in the kitchen and takes her breasts in his big hands; then they walk down to the dock, where he rapes her. Liz is as frightened of the event as Pauline is of Art's manner, but at the end she covers the sleeping Jim with her coat. The story ends with a "cold mist . . . coming up through the woods from the bay" (*SS* 86).

She is not sent downstate as was Pauline. In the draft Hemingway took to Paris, he had another beginning and ending in mind that followed the "Crossroads" model: It begins with the sentences, "Wesley Dilworth got the dimple on his chin from his mother. . . . Jim Dilworth married her when he came to Hortons Bay"; and it ends with Liz in bed, feeling "ashamed and sick" and waking in the dark to wonder 'What if I have a baby?' " (KL/EH 800, 801). Hemingway's intention in this manuscript was to answer Liz's question and return to the teasing first sentence: She will marry Jim and give birth to Wesley, dimple and all. With that frame enclosing a narrative of the hunter returning to the hearth-keeper as if to claim her as a reward for his kill, Hemingway moves further inside the narrative to Liz's sentimental expectations and the cold reality of her rape. Once again, he speaks, for a moment, to two audiences: a popular audience charmed by Wesley's dimple, and another familiar with the lives lived in Horton's Bay in the 1880s.

That Hemingway, in the late fall of 1921, drew on the "Pauline Snow" sketch for this early manuscript of "Up in Michigan" argues that he had begun to reread his apprentice fiction, deciding what to leave and what to take, in anticipation of Paris and the literary likes of Gertrude Stein and Ezra Pound. Stein found "Up in Michigan" *inaccrochable* (unfit for public display) – another lucky judgment for Hemingway, for on the strength of it he kept the manuscript in a drawer apart from all the others Hadley gathered up for the trip to Lausanne in 1922 (*AMF* 18).

THE STOLEN VALISE – DECEMBER 2, 1922

The theft of the valise became, like most of Hemingway's recollections, a good story: one that could be read in at least two ways and, in later days, would include another lexical riddle. As Hemingway recalled it in *A Moveable Feast*, Hadley was so grief-stricken she could not tell him what happened when he met her in Lausanne. He tried to console her, had a friend cover his reporting at the Lausanne conference, and took the next train to Paris. Arriving that afternoon in Paris, he confirmed that she had packed all the "originals, the typescripts, and the carbons . . . in manila folders"; and then, as he wrote some thirty-five years later, he thought of "what I did in the night after I let myself into the flat and found it was true" (74–75).

The answers to the riddle, "what I did in the night," range from the lurid fiction implied in *A Moveable Feast* (a drunken or vengeful night with a whore) to the empirical facts of biography (nothing). James Mellow argues that Hemingway did not return to Paris until some six weeks later. Rather, Lincoln Steffens and Guy Hickok, who were returning to Paris, agreed to ask about the lost luggage at the Gare de Lyon, while he, Hadley, and "Chink" Dorman-Smith spent the holidays skiing on the slopes above Chamby and shopping in the streets of Montreux (209).[8]

In his earliest reference to the incident, a letter to Ezra Pound of January 23, 1923, he assumed that Pound had heard of "the loss of my Juvenilia," reported that "last week" (in mid-January) he had returned to Paris to discover that "Hadley had made the job complete," and mentioned that he had worked "3 years on the damn stuff. Some like that Paris 1922 I fancied" (*SL* 77). Yet most, if not all, of that three years' work would have included the thirteen sketches and stories safely in the Chicago trunk, and the six "Paris 1922" sentences were either not lost or were soon rewritten (Baker, *Life Story* 90–91).

From then on, largely through the evidence of Hemingway's letters in the 1950s, the inventory of the lost prose grew to include some "good stories about Kansas City" (Meyers 68); two "short stories set on the Italian front" (Reynolds, *Young Hemingway* 259); the novel he had "begun" became the novel he had "written" (Mellow 210; *AMF* 75).[9]

For some, that inventory of stolen manuscripts may account for Hemingway's remarkable burst of creativity in the early months of 1924. Earlier, Ezra Pound had answered Hemingway's news of the loss with the cold comfort that all he had really lost was "the *time* it will . . . take you . . . to rewrite the parts you can remember. . . . If the middle, i.e., *FORM,* of a story is right one ought to be able to reassemble it from memory. . . . If the thing wobbles and won't reform then it . . . never *wd.* have been *right*" (KL/EH, EP/EH, January 27, 1923).

If Hemingway took this advice, then it is possible that some of the *In Our Time* stories were recollections of the stolen manuscripts. But with no manuscripts as evidence, this is only a speculation, and one that seriously overlooks both the saved stories and the fiction of 1923. "Up in Michigan," finished in early 1922, was shelved because Stein disapproved of it – a nice irony; and "My Old Man," from that summer, was in the mail to editors. In early 1923 Hemingway wrote the first six *in our time* sketches, published in March; then "Out of Season" in April, published with the two saved stories in August in *Three Stories and Ten Poems;* and finally another twelve of the *in our time* sketches between May and August, to complete the eighteen that were in galleys by December. All this – and over fifty *Toronto Star* articles – within a year after the loss of the manuscripts when, as he later remembered, "I did not think I could write any more" (*AMF* 74).

THE MIRACULOUS YEAR – 1924

The year 1924 was miraculous, or at least its first quarter was. From February through April Hemingway wrote – at times easily, it seems – eight of the *In Our Time* stories: "Indian Camp," "Cat in the Rain," "The End of Something," "The Three-Day Blow," "The Doctor and the Doctor's Wife," "Soldier's Home," "Mr. and Mrs. Elliot," and "Cross-Country Snow." By early May, Hemingway could add the *Three Stories* of 1923 and two of the 1924 *in our time* sketches, "A Very Short Story" and "The Revolutionist," to make thirteen and one to go. But that one, "Big Two-Hearted River," was difficult to write: It took three months to mid-August to complete with its first ending (published in 1972 as "On Writing" [*NAS* 233–41]) and another three to mid-November to realize that the story demanded another ending. That late revision was, if not another kind of miracle, a very lucky move.[10]

In many ways "Big Two-Hearted River" dominates *In Our Time:* The last story in the collection, it was Hemingway's attempt to match "The Dead," the last in James Joyce's *Dubliners;* and the stories that precede it, like those in Joyce's collection, seem to play to the last one's strength.

From here on, with the last story exemplifying the achievement of *In Our Time,* I will consider the way in which Hemingway discovered a "scenic" pattern in the earlier "Out of Season" and "Cat in the Rain"; then was led back to that pattern as he perfected his prose style in his last story; and, finally, how his penchant for a two-part story, or perhaps two opening chapters of a novel, brought him within an ace of diminishing the brilliant achievement of both "Big Two-Hearted River" and *In Our Time.* What he wrote in the early spring with such seeming facility is, I think, no more a mark of his singular gift than the laborious revision of that story's last nine pages in the late fall of 1924.

Scenic Pattern in "Out of Season" and "Cat in the Rain"

One of the most curious remarks in Hemingway's letters is one to F. Scott Fitzgerald in late December 1925; there he graded the stories of *In Our Time* this way: "Grade I (Big 2 Hearted. Indian Camp. 1st ¶ and last ¶ of Out of Season. Soldier's Home)" (*SL* 180). Why did he rank two paragraphs of his 1923 story just below the brilliant stories that began and ended *In Our Time* and just above "Soldier's Home"? My guess is that he had looked again at "Out of Season" and recalled Ezra Pound's remark about the middle, the form, of a fiction, and that he wanted to call Fitzgerald's attention to some structural feature of the story.

The manuscript of "Out of Season" demonstrates that Hemingway took particular care to link, not the first and last paragraphs of the story – he was as cavalier about what constituted a paragraph as he was about spelling – but its introduction and conclusion. In the introduction, the young couple's fishing guide, Peduzzi, gets drunk on four lire, drinks three grappas (Hemingway first wrote "two grappas" and then changed it to three), and promises the young gentleman a fine day of fishing. In its conclusion, the guide is paid off with another four lire, although he asked for five; empties a bottle of marsala with three swigs; and repeats his earlier promises word for word. Those thematic repetitions in the story's introduction and conclusion direct our attention to the formal pattern of the story's action, alternating two and three characters in separate scenes: *A:* the introduction, with Peduzzi and the husband; *B:* their walk with the young man's wife to the Concordia Hotel; *C:* the couple's smoldering conversation alone in the hotel; *B* (again): their walk with Peduzzi to the river; and *A* (again): the concluding dialogue between Peduzzi and the husband. Because it is among the simplest of fictional patterns – {A [B (C) B] A} is a way to sketch it – we may overlook it at first; but noticing it turns our attention to the story's center and what Carlos Baker first recognized as the tale's "metaphorical confluence of emotional atmospheres" (*Life Story* 109). That metaphor joining the inner emotional lives of the benighted American couple with the dismal weather and the illegal fishing out of season is one Hemingway discovered as he wrote and revised: In the Concordia Hotel, the husband says to his wife, "I'm sorry you feel so rotten"; and when they walk to the river, Hemingway added the husband's remark in the manuscript, "It's a rotten day," and later, "We aren't going to have any fun anyway" (*SS* 175, 177; KL/EH 644, p. 4).

All this may seem to slight Hemingway's later account of writing the story and discovering his "new theory": "[T]hat you could omit anything . . . if the omitted part would strengthen the story and make people feel something more than they understood" (*AMF* 75). But aside from the fact that there is no evidence to prove, and much to disprove, the "omission" of Peduzzi's suicide, the event Hemingway said had occasioned the discovery of the "theory," it was neither new to Hemingway nor a theory to anyone else.[11] The three formulas Gerry Brenner isolated in Hemingway's fiction are strategies founded on the simple idea that a reader's discovery of an implication is often more persuasive than an author's statement – a notion that Hemingway first experimented with in the stories he wrote in high school, where he, like the rest of us, must have heard it first.

A more probable account of the story's genesis would begin with Ezra Pound's advice on the centrality of form in his letter of January 1923, advice which – knowing Pound – he would have repeated during the Hemingways' visit two weeks later in Rapallo. During that February, Hemingway read Pound's copy of T. S. Eliot's *The Waste Land* and wrote four pages of random notes that led a year later to the writing of "Cat in the Rain."

That story, which might well have been the first written in the early months of 1924, shares with "Out of Season" a profound influence from Eliot's poem, and, more to the point here, a nearly identical scenic pattern. Like the earlier story, "Cat in the Rain" rests on a pattern of five scenes with different sets of characters: *A:* A couple in a hotel room, from which the wife sees a cat in the rain; *B:* her descent to the lobby, passing the police padrone; *C:* her unsuccessful search for the cat in the square with the maid; *B* (again): her return past the padrone at his desk; and *A:* (again): her return to the room and her husband. "Cat in the Rain" differs from "Out of Season" in beginning with a paragraph describing the rain-swept square, and in ending with a brief ironic twist when the maid enters the room with a gift from the padrone, a male tortoise-shell cat, as sterile an animal as the spawning trout are fecund in "Out of Season."

Beginning with the story of another spiritless couple, not by accident named "Mr. and Mrs. Elliot," "Cat in the Rain" and "Out of Season," followed by "Cross-Country Snow," make a set of four stories, the ninth through the twelfth of *In Our Time,* often considered with "A Canary for One" and "Hills Like White Elephants" (written later) as Hemingway's "marriage tales." Whether these stories reflect Hemingway's own marriage seems of less moment than that the subject of marriage inspired his return to fiction in 1923, is at the center of four stories, and is at least tangential in another four, written in early 1924: "The Doctor and the Doctor's Wife,"

"The End of Something," "The Three-Day Blow," and "Soldier's Home" – these eight alone might have made up a unified collection.

The Perfection of Style in "Big Two-Hearted River"

The most persistent misconception of Hemingway's style is that it was attained through a process of deletion. From Carlos Baker on, most critics have assumed that Hemingway "always wrote slowly and revised carefully, cutting, editing, substituting, and experimenting with syntax to see what a sentence could most economically carry, and then throwing out all that could be spared" (*Writer as Artist* 71–72). A natural assumption, yet it is founded on a metaphor from physical exercise: Any lean and frugal style must once have been fat and prodigal, and has now achieved its trim economy through the exercise of deletion. But the manuscripts demonstrate that Hemingway's sentences more often began life as scrawny little things, and then grew to their proper size through a process of accretion.

Consider a crucial scene in "Big Two-Hearted River," when Nick Adams stands on the bridge at Seney and first sees the trout in the stream below. Hemingway first wrote (deletions are enclosed by [], additions by ⟨⟩):

> It had been years since he had seen trout. As he watched a big trout shot up stream in a long angle burst through the surface of the water and [then] ⟨curved in the air to re-enter the water and then under the surface of the fast water again⟩ seemed to float back down stream with the current to its post under the bridge. Nick's heart tightened as the trout moved. He felt all the old thrill. This remained at any rate. (KL/EH 274, pp. 3–4)

This first thin draft reads like hurried notes for a later sketch. It tells us that after some years, Nick watches a big trout leap and then return to its post under the bridge. Nick's heart tightens; he feels the "old thrill," and in a self-pitying mood, consoles himself that this much is left him.

Later Hemingway rewrote that passage (the changes from the first draft are underlined):

> It was a long time since Nick had looked into a stream and seen trout. They were very satisfactory. As the shadow of the kingfisher moved up the stream a big trout shot up stream in a long angle, only his shadow marking the [shadow] ⟨angle⟩, then lost his shadow as he came through the surface of the water, caught the sun, and then as he went back into the [water] ⟨stream⟩ under the surface his shadow seemed to float [back] down the stream with the current, unresisting, to his post under the bridge where he tightened, facing up stream.
>
> Nick's heart tightened as the trout moved. He felt all the old [thrill. This remained] ⟨feeling⟩. (KL/EH 274, pp. 2–3, insert)

I imagine that when Hemingway returned to the first version, he saw a clear signal to revise; like any fisherman, he would recall that, with the sun overhead, all one can see of a brown, speckled trout is its shadow on the gravel streambed. But the first shadow cast is that of the kingfisher, a powerful and fierce bird of the air and the water, as it flies upstream. Only after the kingfisher leaves does the trout make its brilliant leap into the deadly air to catch the sun.

Hemingway would have seen, too, that the progression of the first draft is dominantly linear and temporal – this happened, then this, and then this – with only one spatial metaphor, the trout's leap "in a long angle"; for he then merged that metaphor with the trout's "shadow marking the angle." The image of that shadow marking the angle becomes one of the set of triangulated lines connecting the great fish, the kingfisher waiting for the kill, and the passive, witnessing fisherman, Nick. Hemingway's recognition of this emerging pattern is marked again by a second change: In the first draft, "Nick's heart tightened *as* the trout moved"; but in the revision, *first* the trout "tightened, facing up stream," and *then* Nick's heart tightened, as he angles with his eyes.

Two-Part Stories before "Big Two-Hearted River"

When Hemingway returned the signed contract for *In Our Time* to his publisher the last day of March 1925, he assured him that the book "will be praised by highbrows and can be read by lowbrows" (*SL* 155). That distinction between two markets for his book suggests Hemingway's own low-brow way of admitting to the highbrow distinction between two implied audiences in several of its stories.

Like "Big Two-Hearted River," "The End of Something" and "The Three-Day Blow" strike some readers as two chapters of an incipient novel. "Indian Camp" was first conceived with two distinct parts: the first part, manuscript pages 1–8, was published in 1972 as "Three Shots" (*NAS* 13–15); the second, "Indian Camp," as we have it in *In Our Time*.

Taken together, "The End of Something" and "The Three-Day Blow" seem like an adolescent version of the two parts of "Big Two-Hearted River" with its original conclusion, "On Writing." "The End of Something" begins with two paragraphs describing the ruins of the old mill and the history and environs of Hortons Bay as the setting for the end of Nick's affair with Marjorie. So, too, the first paragraph of part 1 of "Big Two-Hearted River" begins with the history of the once-lively town of Seney with its thirteen saloons and Mansion House Hotel, now burned to the ground.

Each story then follows its characters as they arrive at a fishing spot and prepare a meal, and both end with a revelation of Nick's troubled emotions.

Like part 2 with "On Writing," "The Three-Day Blow" opens on another day, reintroduces Nick's boyhood companion Bill, and as they drink themselves into profundity, follows their random discussion of baseball, books, and marriage. The critical pronouncements of these boys on a binge – Walpole's *Fortitude* is a "real book," "Chesterton's a classic," and the naked sword between two sleeping lovers is not a "practical" guarantee of chastity but a "symbol" (*SS* 118) – are close to Nick's more sober judgments alone on the river in "On Writing" – *The Enormous Room* "was one of the great books," "Joyce was so damn romantic and intellectual about" Daedalus, and "writing about anything actual was bad" (*NAS* 237–39).

"The End of Something" dramatized the conflict between what Marjorie and Bill represent in Nick's consciousness. At the end of "The Three-Day Blow," with its talk of books and baseball now drowned in drink, that conflict is manifested both in Bill's virulent condemnation of marriage, Marjorie, and her family and in Nick's own sobering silence. The "liquor had all died out of him and he was alone," and the subject "was no longer so tragic" (*SS* 123, 125). Having confronted something that once seemed tragic, Nick finds some comfort in the thought that "he could always go into town Saturday night" (*SS* 125).

The story seems to predict the dilemma Hemingway faced five months later as he tried first to end "Big Two-Hearted River" with "On Writing" and delayed – from August to November – the necessary ending of Nick's day on the river when he faces the impenetrable swamp. Nick recognizes for the moment that "in the fast deep water, in the half-light the fishing would be tragic," but then, again, he finds solace in "the days coming when he could fish the swamp" (*SS* 231–32).

"Three Shots" is the publisher's title for the first eight pages of the original "Indian Camp" manuscript. The two typescripts of the story indicate that for at least two months, and for some time after it was published as "Work in Progress" in the April *Transatlantic Review,* Hemingway was still thinking of those eight pages either as a part of "Indian Camp" or possibly as its companion story.

It opens on the night of "Indian Camp" as Nick recalls the previous night. Nick's father and uncle had told him to fire three shots in case of an emergency and then left him alone in a tent while they were out fishing. He remembered a hymn sung in church a few weeks before that had made him realize for the first time he would die someday; and with that fearful recollection and some strange noises in the woods, he fired the three shots. His uncle resented the interruption, but his father consoled the young boy. While undressing on the next night, he hears a boat being drawn up on the beach, and his father calls him to go with him to the Indian camp.

"Three Shots" is most often cited to interpret the unexpected ending of "Indian Camp." Through a brutal night, Nick watches as his father, a doctor, performs a cesarean section on an Indian woman with a jackknife and no anesthetic; when his father delivers the child and turns to the Indian husband on the upper bunk, they see that he had slit his throat during the birth. The story ends as they return to their fishing camp: "Nick trailed his hand in the water. It felt warm in the sharp chill of the morning. In the early morning on the lake sitting in the stern with his father rowing, he felt quite sure that he would never die" (SS 95).

Interpretations derived from "Three Shots" often ignore Hemingway's reasons, however belated, to cut the original beginning. With "Three Shots," Nick's feeling "quite sure that he would never die" becomes little more than a boy's momentary denial of fears suddenly brought home in a suburban white world with a memory of a Christian hymn – a brief and ironic sublimation of the primal events he has witnessed. Without "Three Shots," Nick's final perception turns us back to the story to discover its analogues with initiation rituals and, beyond them, with universal patterns that confirm the validity, indeed the necessity, of Nick's conviction he will never die. That Nick will die someday is true but trivial. What is both true and profound is his indisputable sense that this night journey to witness the mysterious unity of birth and death, for all its brutality, is a consolation natural to these woods and native to these Indians. As a young boy, of course, he cannot express it; he can only feel it, as his hand feels at once the warm lakewater and the chill of the morning.

The two parts of the story in its original manuscript derive from two virtual worlds and their cultures: "Three Shots" presents an adolescent world and white culture in which a boy may be terrified by a line from a hymn, "Some day the silver cord will break," then find respite from the fear of death by reading *Robinson Crusoe,* or be comforted by his father's reassuring explanations of the sounds in the night (NAS 14–15). But "Indian Camp" guides a young boy and his father into another world – and an otherworld – where a boy has no comforting novel or his father's consoling wisdom to allay the fear of death, and his father himself has none of his instruments or opiates to ease the pain of birth.

Each representation of these two worlds suggests a different audience:

With "Three Shots" Hemingway implies a conventional and popular audience, even one of younger readers and their approving parents, like his own, who subscribed to the *St. Nicholas* magazine for boys and were assured by stories that would calm the fears of adolescents, if *Robinson Crusoe* did not. With "Indian Camp" alone, he creates an audience who will follow Nick and his father into a mysterious realm, divested of the commonplace answers and ordinary devices of their culture, to be initiated, like them, in a primal experience to a radical truth.

The Two Endings of "Big Two-Hearted River"

At the end of part 1 of "Big Two-Hearted River," Nick's concentration on making camp and dinner is invaded when he recalls fishing with his friend Hopkins and arguing over whether to boil or to steep coffee on a campfire. That recollection is a rare instance of Nick's failure to leave behind "the need for thinking, the need to write" (*SS* 210); yet it reveals why Nick has deliberately carried a too heavy pack farther than was necessary: He knew that if he tired his body enough on a longer trek, his mind "could choke" memories like this when he went to sleep. Nor has Nick left behind all vestiges of his "need to write": He recognizes the memory of Hopkins and the "bitter coffee" as if it were a rough sketch with a "good ending to [an ironic] story" (*SS* 218). That unexpected episode in a story of a writer who so calculates his acts to avoid writing is a prelude of sorts to the story's first ending. Among the obvious contrasts between the two endings – "On Writing" is discursive, random, and contentious as it looks back to the past; the final version is dramatic, ordered, and resigned as it contemplates the present – the differences between the virtual worlds of the two, and necessarily between their fictive audiences, are salient.

"On Writing" begins after Nick lands his first good trout (*SS* 228). From then on, his thoughts and memories follow, for the most part, a sequence of opposites: the act of fishing / books on fishing; marriage / male friendship; summers at Walloon Lake / summers in Spain; bullfighting / bullfight reporting; writing from imagination / writing from actuality; original art, like Cézanne's / "tricks" in writing, like Joyce's; a few good writers / many bad ones, and so on. Nick's reveries end when he turns to the scene before him, and "knew just how Cézanne would do this stretch of river"; with that perception, he "waded" across the stream, moving in the picture." It is a brilliant moment in which the "cold and actual" water in the landscape of the stream merges with a landscape painting as Cézanne would have done it.

Hemingway easily could have ended the story here, but he labored on, twice marking the manuscript as finished, until Nick starts back to his camp "holding something in his head" (*NAS* 241). That earlier moment is rare in the monologue's long, complex, and allusive mosaic of recollections. Its confidential style seldom admits the sort of discovery Hemingway made in the paragraph on the trout at the bridge, and that may be the result of a rhetorical stance that invites its implied audience to enter the artistic world of Paris.

I find that stance reminiscent of Hemingway's apprentice fiction, as in "The Mercenaries." When Nick recalls Cézanne's paintings in "On Writing" – "He could see the Cézannes. The portrait at Gertrude Stein's. She would know if he ever got things right. The two good ones at the Luxembourg, the ones he'd seen every day at the loan exhibit at Bernheim's" (*NAS* 229–40) – I hear an echo of that voice in "The Mercenaries," sounding like this: "If you are honestly curious about the Cézannes at Stein's in the Rue de Fleurus, the possibility of seeing the two good ones in the Musée du Luxembourg, or the potentialities of loan exhibits at Bernheim's on the Boulevard de la Madelaine, go to the Café des Amateurs on Rue Descartes in Paris." Of course there are differences between the two voices, one from 1919 and the other from 1924, but they presuppose a similar audience, one as interested in the "pearl fishing conditions in the Marquesas" as the other is with "the two good [Cézannes] at the Luxembourg." Moreover, in "On Writing" there are some twenty occurrences of the second-person pronoun in this monologue, all but a few of which arise with the subject of writing, when Nick, in a rather tendentious manner, seems to instruct us on the art of fiction.[12] (That manner might well have recommended the title "On Writing" to its editors in 1972, as if they had discovered an unpublished essay by Cicero or Francis Bacon.)

"On Writing" is centered in the literary world of Paris in 1924, but it gathers in memories of that summer's bullfights in Spain and of earlier summers in Michigan. The rest of the story is centered on the river in Michigan's Upper Peninsula, with only the recollection of Hopkins reaching as far as Chicago. Although each purview has its own arcana, an elliptical reference – "Against this age, skyscraper primitives" (*NAS* 239) – is not addressed so much to insiders, like the Paris literati, as it is to outsiders unfamiliar with the literary scene of the early 1920s or references to Maxwell Bodenheim's *Against This Age* or Gorham Munson's phrase "skyscraper primitives."[13] However, in the perspective of the story the function of a "double tapered fly line" and the procedure for pitching a tent are manifested immediately as Nick threads the line and stakes out his tent (*SS* 214–15, 223). To know the first world requires an encyclopedia, an atlas, and some Spanish; to know the second, a school dictionary and a Michigan road map will do.

In mid-November 1924 Hemingway wrote to Robert McAlmon about the conclusion of the original manuscript: "I got a hell of a shock when I realized how bad it was and that shocked me back into the river again and I have finished it off the way it ought to have been all along. Just the straight fishing" (*SL* 133). Now Hemingway was holding in his head what Nick held in his when he returned to camp to write.

Later, in *A Moveable Feast*, Hemingway recalled that during his apprenticeship in Paris he had learned "something from the painting of Cézanne that made writing simple true sentences far from enough to make my stories have the dimensions that I was trying to put in them" (13). Whether he learned it from Cézanne or not, the revisions of the paragraph on the trout at the bridge would have confirmed his sense of those necessary scenic dimensions within the story's world of air and water and earth, the domains of the kingfisher, the fish, and the fisherman. Here, only natural law, instinct, the sun's course from dawn to dusk, and the weather determine the world; and for Nick, in his brief time, the fisherman's lore and rituals – always the rituals – both govern and test his character and conduct.

As he fished downstream, Nick tested the limits of the tension his heart could bear with varying tensions on his gut leader: One small trout is released, a large one broke the leader, then he landed the "one good trout" – and the story went awry. Hemingway returned to that moment on the river when the noonday sun drives the fish to cooler waters, and he returns Nick to be tested further with more difficult casts among overhanging branches and sunken logs, losing one trout and landing a second. Having discovered the limits of his emotions in the practice of his skill, he knows himself enough to turn away from the dark swamp where the "fishing would be tragic," but not before he performs one last act.

Earlier that morning he had seen a mink enter the swamp (*SS* 221), and now when he cleans the fish, he tosses "the offal ashore for the minks to find" (*SS* 231). Nick's gesture has the resonance of a ritual offering, here to the totemic animal of the swamp and to its cedared and inviolable domain.

And I imagine Hemingway, as he wrote that passage, seeing it for a moment as his own offering to the story that waited for him to recall the way it ought to have been all along. Years later in *A Moveable Feast* he remembered writing it in a Paris café: "When I stopped writing I did not want to leave the river where I could see the trout in the pool. . . . But in the morning the river would be there" (76).

NOTES

1. Clarence Hemingway to Hadley and Ernest, September 22 and 25, 1923, cited by Michael Reynolds from the Hemingway collection of the Humanities Research Center of the University of Texas (*Young Hemingway* 259). My thanks to him for copies of the letters. Hemingway had apparently asked his father to return the trunk with its papers, but it is unlikely that he lugged *all* these letters, papers, and manuscripts back to Paris.

2. (KL/EH with an item number) indicates a file of materials in the Hemingway collection of the John Fitzgerald Kennedy Library in Boston, Mass.

3. For a review of this fiction, see Smith, "Hemingway's Apprentice Fiction."

4. Griffin, *Along with Youth* 104; '"The Mercenaries" and four other Chicago stories were first published in this biography.

5. Hemingway used the byline "Ring Lardner, Jr." in his school paper; for the probable influence of Conrad, see Reynolds, *Hemingway's Reading* 112.

6. The formulas Brenner characterizes as responses to problems of knowledge do not resolve those problems as much as they place them at the center of the story, where they deceptively offer an easy understanding of a far more difficult issue. The two others are "textual perplexity," which places a character "in circumstances [that] so overwhelm him with mixed signals . . . he is struck speechless or regresses to some comforting nostrum that ill deals with the conditions at hand" (159); and "extratextual reversal," which introduces a character "whose occupation or easily labeled role calls up cultural expectations of stereotypical behavior, ones Hemingway partly honors . . . but primarily subverts" (162). The "lexical riddle," like the strategy in this sketch, "pivot[s] on a lexical crux, the unarticulated or ambiguous words abortion [in 'Hills Like White Elephants'], lesbian [in 'The Sea Change'], and corrupt [that is, homosexual, in 'A Simple Enquiry']" (161).

7. This assumption rests rather unsteadily on Hemingway's statements that *all* his manuscripts (except "My Old Man" and "Up in Michigan") were in the valise stolen from Hadley in December 1922, and on two of his letters from the mid-1920s cited by biographers (Meyers 68; and Reynolds, *Young Hemingway* 259). In 1933, Gertrude Stein recalled she "went over all the writing he had done up to that time," but notes only a novel he had begun and she "found wanting" and some poems published later (200–201). I know of no other references to fiction brought to Paris in 1921, and then stolen before Hemingway began recalling the event for Charles Fenton and Carlos Baker in 1951, and Hadley recollected them for Michael Reynolds in 1970. In the summer of 1957, Hemingway remembered the lost fiction as his "early work" and "a novel" in the manuscript of *A Moveable Feast* (74, 75; Tavernier-Courbin xix).

8. Mellow 208–10. Nor could Hemingway have lunched with Gertrude Stein on December 4, after that riddling night, as he claimed in a letter to Edmund Wilson (*SL* 105; November 23, 1923), for she was at St. Rémy (Reynolds, *Paris Years* 367, n. 1).

9. Later biographers have followed the fictional analogues of the loss of the manuscripts through the unpublished chapter of *Islands in the Stream* ("The Strange

Country"), in which the tally is "Eleven stories, a novel, and poems" (*CSS* 648); and *The Garden of Eden,* in which Catherine Bourne sets fire to David's manuscripts (Mellow 210–11).

Hadley's recollections of the contents of the valise are hopelessly contradictory. She told Baker in 1964 that it was a "knockout" and dealt with Nick Adams in Michigan (cited in Diliberto 137); but in 1970 she wrote Reynolds that "she had never read the manuscripts" of the novel, that "most of the stories were concerned with the early adventures of Nick Adams," but that if Ernest had tried to rewrite the lost stories "she never saw a completed work about . . . Nick" (cited in *Hemingway's First War* 277).

10. For the dating of Hemingway's composition of the stories, see Smith, *Reader's Guide.*

11. For the evidence contradicting the discovery of the theory of omission, see Smith, "Some Misconceptions of 'Out of Season.' "

12. By contrast, *you* occurs six times in the published version: four in the second long paragraph describing fishing on the Black River and marking the point where Hemingway began his original ending (*SS* 229), and two in sentences describing what fishing would be like in the swamp (*SS* 231). It was on the Black River that Nick fished with Hopkins (*SS* 217) and with Bill Smith (*NAS* 233).

13. Bodenheim's *Against This Age,* a volume of poems and one story much concerned with irony and aspects of language, was published by Boni and Liveright in 1923; Munson coined the term "skyscraper primitives" for New York artists and writers with a Dadaist fascination for American technology in *The New Republic* of April 1923.

WORKS CITED

Baker, Carlos. *Ernest Hemingway: A Life Story.* New York: Charles Scribner's Sons, 1969.

———. *Hemingway: The Writer as Artist.* Princeton: Princeton University Press, 1963.

Brenner, Gerry. "From 'Sepi Jingan' to 'The Mother of a Queen': Hemingway's Three Epistemologic Formulas for Short Fiction." *New Critical Approaches to the Short Stories of Ernest Hemingway.* Ed. Jackson J. Benson. Durham, N.C.: Duke University Press, 1990.

Diliberto, Gioia. *Hadley.* New York: Ticknor and Fields, 1992.

Griffin, Peter. *Along with Youth: Hemingway, The Early Years.* New York: Oxford University Press, 1985.

Hemingway, Ernest. *A Moveable Feast.* New York: Charles Scribner's Sons, 1964.

———. *The Complete Short Stories of Ernest Hemingway: The Finca Vigía Edition.* New York: Charles Scribner's Sons, 1987.

———. *The Nick Adams Stories.* New York: Charles Scribner's Sons, 1972.

———. *Ernest Hemingway: Selected Letters, 1917–1961.* Ed. Carlos Baker. New York: Charles Scribner's Sons, 1981.

———. *The Short Stories of Ernest Hemingway.* New York: Charles Scribner's Sons, 1938.

Mellow, James R. *Hemingway: A Life without Consequences.* Boston: Houghton Mifflin, 1992.

Meyers, Jeffrey. *Hemingway: A Biography.* New York: Harper and Row, 1985.

Reynolds, Michael S. *Hemingway's First War: The Making of* A Farewell to Arms. Princeton: Princeton University Press, 1976.

_____. *Hemingway's Reading 1910–1940: An Inventory.* Princeton: Princeton University Press, 1981.

_____. *Hemingway: The Paris Years.* Oxford: Basil Blackwell, 1989.

_____. "Introduction: Looking Backward." *Critical Essays on Ernest Hemingway's* In Our Time. Ed. Michael S. Reynolds. Boston: G. K. Hall, 1983.

_____. *The Young Hemingway.* Oxford: Basil Blackwell, 1986.

Smith, Paul. "Hemingway's Apprentice Fiction: 1919–1921." *American Literature* 58 (December 1986): 574–88. Reprinted in *New Critical Approaches to the Short Stories of Ernest Hemingway.* Ed. Jackson J. Benson. Durham, N.C.: Duke University Press, 1990.

_____. *A Reader's Guide to the Short Stories of Ernest Hemingway.* Boston: G. K. Hall, 1989.

_____. "Some Misconceptions of 'Out of Season.' " *Critical Essays on* In Our Time. Ed. Michael S. Reynolds. Boston: G. K. Hall, 1983.

Stein, Gertrude. *Selected Writings of Gertrude Stein.* Ed. Carl Van Vechten. New York: Vintage, 1945.

Tavernier-Courbin, Jacqueline. *Ernest Hemingway's* A Moveable Feast: *The Making of a Myth.* Boston: Northeastern University Press, 1991.

4

THOMAS STRYCHACZ

In Our Time, Out of Season

If there is one central story in the bundle of whipsaw-keen narratives, terse vignettes, and fragmentary epiphanies of Ernest Hemingway's *In Our Time* (1925), it may be "Out of Season." The story probes the paradox of the book's title by asking, What does it mean to be in our time but out of season? The phrase "in our time" promises both relevance and revelation. It suggests that the book will deal with contemporary historical circumstances, perhaps record valuable collective wisdoms, and certainly stake a claim to documenting the entire epoch. Moreover, by echoing the plea in the English *Book of Common Prayer* to "Give us peace in our time, O Lord," the phrase invites a new descent of the Holy Spirit into the era following the World War I apocalypse. But "Out of Season," like all the stories of *In Our Time,* presents a world of thorough disorientation. Spiritual deadness, anomie, aimless wandering, conflict between genders and cultures, and miscommunication – these define the relationship between the expatriate American couple and their guide Peduzzi, and emerge more broadly as Hemingway's concerns in *In Our Time,* his first major inquiry into the state of the lost generation. The story suggests powerfully that we may only understand our time as the communal loss of temporal, geographical, and cultural certainties; and it focuses *In Our Time*'s often ironic and sometimes funny quests for adequate guides, codes of conduct, and manly actions in a world where the old, communal prayers seem to have lost their power.

The Americans of "Out of Season" lack both a cohesive sense of time and a language in which to express its loss. Peduzzi intends the Americans to fish before the season officially opens; the young gentleman is tardy at the beginning of the story; the Specialty of Domestic and Foreign Wines shop is "closed until two" (*IOT* 98) when Peduzzi tries to purchase marsala; and Tiny, the young wife, may herself be "past her time" – that is, pregnant.[1] Narrative chronology, too, seems oddly truncated. In the first paragraph, for instance, the statement that the "young gentleman went back into the hotel and spoke to his wife" segues directly into "He and Peduzzi started down the road." The narrative suspends the familiar logic of sequential events – the young gentleman speaking to his wife, then coming out of the hotel, then starting down the road. Momentary and fragmentary actions appear out of a continuum we can only intuit. To be out of season is to experience time as other, to see it as separate from the normal processes and aspirations of human life. Narrative gaps in time and action suggest that dissociation from commonplace logic.

If temporal dislocations characterize "our time," how much more ironic sounds the prayer to "give us peace . . . O Lord." For the intercessor – the Holy Spirit – of "Out of Season" is the war veteran Peduzzi, who tries to intercede between the warring couple but proves hilariously inept at setting things right. Though the Holy Spirit bestows the gift of tongues on Christ's disciples, Peduzzi merely confuses his charges as he speaks "[p]art of the time in d'Ampezzo dialect and sometimes in Tyrolen German dialect," and sometimes in Italian, while the "young gentleman and the wife understood nothing." Yet Peduzzi, clownish as he seems, is the one character who is not ruled entirely by disrupted chronologies. For Peduzzi, unlike the American couple, the duration of time spent does not alter the significance and value of the experience. "It is good half an hour down. It is good here, too," says Peduzzi in response to the young gentleman's baffled inquiry about why they are not moving on. And though on discovering they have no *piombo* (lead) Peduzzi's day seemed to be "going to pieces before his eyes," the bottle of marsala restores lost harmony: "It was wonderful. This was a great day, after all. A wonderful day," and the "sun shone while he drank" (100–102). The day and Peduzzi together experience rebirth along with the resurrected sun; time cycles back, reminding us of the seasonal return of life, light, sun, and spring. And perhaps the tipped bottle reminds us of the rites practiced from generation to generation to celebrate that return. Though we should not miss the irony of Peduzzi's heroic stature – "Life was opening out," he promises himself when accepting four lire from the young gentleman at the end of the story, which reminds us that to begin with "On the four lire Peduzzi had earned by spading the hotel garden he got quite drunk" – for a moment he lives in transcendent or mythic time. He experiences briefly the unchangingness of seasonal change.

Peduzzi's bumbling efforts to save the day appear painfully (though comically) representative of our time and *In Our Time,* for Hemingway, like many other modernist writers, saw the disruption of time and mythic experience as at once a pressing reality and a pertinent metaphor for the entire angst- and anomie-ridden post–World War I landscape. Like other modernists, Hemingway understood that such a drastic reshaping of temporal experience demanded new narrative strategies. T. S. Eliot put the case most strikingly, claiming that others would follow James Joyce in finding ways of "controlling, of ordering, of giving a shape and a significance to the immense panorama of futility and anarchy which is contemporary history."[2] Works like *The Waste Land* (1922) and *In Our Time* register the decay of what must once have seemed fundamental verities: religion, intimate human relationships, hierarchies of culture and class, masculine authority. New strategies of fragmentation, temporal discontinuity, and abrupt juxtaposition would be pressed into service as attempts to define and respond to a terrifyingly denatured and devitalized landscape of alienation, lostness, and emptiness. The wanderers of Hemingway's stories, out of season and beset with impotent guides like Peduzzi, are at once empty and revelatory of these profound changes.

Hemingway's stories of the lost generation arose out of historical and geographical circumstances more favorable to the production of art than Eliot's austere statement about contemporary history would have us believe. It was Hemingway's good fortune and good judgment in the early 1920s to arrive in a Paris stirred to artistic ferment by the years following World War I. James Joyce was there; and *Ulysses,* banned in the United States, was available at Sylvia Beach's famous bookstore Shakespeare and Co., whose lending library of classic and contemporary literature Hemingway was to frequent. Gertrude Stein was monumentally there, imparting her theories about writing in a studio that was a veritable gallery of the movers and shakers of modernist art – Cézanne, Picasso, Matisse. Ezra Pound passed through, drumming home his own message about ridding the English language of the verbiage that had, he argued, infected it for too long. Perhaps most important, Paris provided a culture of artistic endeavor, fostered in the thriving Parisian café scene and pursued by the geniuses and pretenders to genius inhabiting the studios of the Left Bank.

In Paris, Ernest Hemingway, buoyed by the strong dollar into a kind of genteel bohemianism, began the apprenticeship that would lead to his first two major works, *In Our Time* and *The Sun Also Rises* (1926). In this he was abetted by his position as foreign correspondent for the *Toronto Daily Star.* His work brought him to the heart of the action. Hemingway was on hand during the important 1922 Economic Conference at Genoa and the Greco-Turkish war (also in 1922), as Europe, still riven by political turmoil, shook itself into new configurations. But his travels, both on and off the job, also took him to countries like Spain where ancient cultures remained, evoking nostalgia in him for old codes and rituals that seemed still wedded to the natural, seasonal cycles of death and regeneration. Equally important, journalism via the expensive transatlantic cables enforced a particular style. "Cabelese" demanded a new rhetorical economy based on the maximum of information compressed into a minimum of space. What governed the writer was accuracy, elision, and the pressure to select the one truly descriptive image – to put down, as Hemingway wrote in 1932, "what really happened in action; what the actual things were which produced the emotion that you experienced" (*DIA* 2). In his Parisian encounters with Hemingway, Pound had only to reinforce techniques that were already second nature to the younger writer.

The most immediate impetus for Hemingway's literary work was William Bird, who in 1922 purchased a small printing press in Paris and decided (at the prodding of Ezra Pound) to publish a six-volume "inquest" into the contemporary state of English prose. Bird's contributors included Pound, Ford Madox Ford, William Carlos Williams – and Ernest Hemingway, who seemingly had precious little to offer beyond Pound's recommendation and his own ambition.[3] Hemingway set to work regardless, and in early 1924 Bill Bird's Three Mountain Press published eighteen short vignettes under the title *in our time,* which would be incorporated into the longer work *In Our Time* the following year.[4]

Drawn from conversation, newspaper reports, and personal experience, the original vignettes anatomized war, bullfighting, and crime with the tautness and compression of an imagist poem. "The apparition of these facts in the crowd; / Petals on a wet, black bough" Pound had written in 1913, throwing a few words like a gauntlet into the face of the poetry-loving public, and Hemingway's terse, tight-lipped, tightly wound fragments are equally extraordinary in their dramatic intensity. They are Joycean epiphanies without an enclosing narrative; or, perhaps, epiphanic moments revealing patterns so archetypal that they need not even be spoken. Hence chapter 3 of *In Our Time:* "We were in a garden at Mons. Young Buckley came in with his patrol from across the river. The first German I saw climbed up over the garden wall. We waited till he got one leg over and then potted him. He had so much equipment on and looked awfully surprised and fell down into the garden. Then three more came over further down the wall. We shot them. They all came just like that" (29). The anonymous voice speaks casually, almost coldly. The horror is that it all sounds so commonplace. The narrator registers the only human attribute of the German (he "looked awfully surprised") with a kind of dull bemusement. For the rest, we infer slaughters so frequent that either the narrator has become dehumanized or else uses a dehumanized language as a buttress against the inhuman. The first German appears and tumbles like a marionette. The Germans are not killed but "potted" like so many ducks; all are stripped of individuality as they "all came just like that." Appropriately, the narrator's images repeat with the fixedness of nightmare: "in a garden," "over the garden wall," "down into the garden," "down the wall."

The narrator speaks so dispassionately that it is easy to miss the odd warping of logical sequence. We expect that characters, observations, and events will be salient to the narrative. We expect, in other words, that young Buckley coming in with his patrol will relate somehow to the first German seen; that the German having so much equipment on will relate to his looking awfully surprised. Yet the appearance of the first German seems random; the fact that the sentences are juxtaposed seems not to signify any causal or chronological relationship. (And is this the first German over the garden wall, or the first the narrator has seen?) Similarly, the connectives in "He had so much equipment on *and* looked awfully surprised *and* fell down into the garden" (emphasis added) mask a deeper sense of disconnection. Three separate observations are wrenched together into a mere illusion of coherence; "and" becomes a last desperate attempt to hold together a chaos of impressions. The vignette conveys the casual logic of the killing fields while revealing the misfirings of a mind under extreme pressure.

The vignette also reveals language under extreme pressure, and does so in ways that should revise stereotypes of Hemingway's work. Hemingway is rightly seen as the master of the simple declarative sentence, pursuing "what really happened in action" in a direct, hard-boiled style so that writing reproduces the action or event in all its completeness. Hemingway himself fostered this theory about his writing, though even for him the presentation of action was clearly twofold: an action was to be represented as truly as possible, but the totality of actions within a story was to be incomplete, for the author must select out of a continuum the smallest number of precise details in order for the reader, when viewing the ensemble, to intuit the entire narrative. Hemingway later said that his style was fashioned on the "principle of the iceberg," for "seven eighths of it [is] under water for every part that shows."[5]

But his early experimental work, as this vignette shows, is still more complex. We may indeed guess at more than the vignette actually says – from his use of words like "awfully" and "potted" we guess the narrator is British; he is older than and probably the superior of young Buckley; he may be exercising incredible self-control in the face of unspeakable horror. But the vignette does not present an event, in the sense of a clearly defined action or sequence of actions, and its style is characterized more by narrative discontinuities than by the controlled, graceful, action-driven prose for which Hemingway is famous. In his early work in particular, Hemingway stood ready to sacrifice the logic of traditional narrative and rhetorical modes in order to present the incoherence and incompleteness of action. As though in recognition of this impulse toward incoherence, "On the Quai at Smyrna," which Hemingway added as a new introduction to the collection in 1930, seems deliberately designed to confuse the reader. The piece begins: "The strange thing was, he said, how they screamed every night at midnight. I do not know why they screamed at that time. We were in the harbor and they were all on the pier and at midnight they started screaming." Immediately we lose our bearings amid a profusion of pronouns. Who are "they" and who are "we," and what is the connection between the speaker and the "we" in the harbor, or between the speaker and the silent listener, who is apparently known to the speaker and the events he describes ("You remember the harbor?"). As the piece unfolds, we begin to realize that the speaker is describing the evacuation of refugees from Smyrna during the Greco-Turkish war. But the piece gives rise to a more narrative questions and doubts (such as why the refugees scream at midnight) than it answers. Like the vignette in the garden at Mons, "On the Quai at Smyrna" explores not the clarity but the terror of events that rupture the boundary of what is rational and comfortably known.

In late 1924 and early 1925, driven by a creative flowering to compose the best short stories of his career, Hemingway began to envisage a new role for the vignettes. Interspersed between the short stories, the vignettes allowed Hemingway to exploit a typically modernist aesthetic of fragmentation and juxtaposition. The rapid-fire exchange of story and interchapter in the new *In Our Time*, sometimes working by complementary meanings and sometimes by ironic counterpoint, drew on the collage technique of Pablo Picasso and Georges Braque, the film montage of Sergei Eisenstein, the poetics of Pound and Eliot, and the narrative experiments of Joyce. As the work unfolds, the reader comes under increasing pressure to make sense of the crosscutting of scenes and characters, abrupt transformations of narrative voice and perspective, and sudden shifts in geographical and temporal location.

As unstructured as it might appear, *In Our Time* seems a cohesive if not necessarily unified work. The first five stories, interspersed with vignettes about war, form a relatively homogeneous section that deals with the slow maturing of Nick Adams. These stories are all set in Michigan and move chronologically through Nick's boyhood and early manhood in the years before the war. Chapter 6, following "The Battler," marks a crucial turning point: Nick becomes the subject of a vignette for the first time, subsequently disappearing from the collection until near its end; and his wounding signals an entry into the more disorienting postwar world of the second half of *In Our Time*. Three short stories, "A Very Short Story," "Soldier's Home," and "The Revolutionist," deal with the aftermath of the war, the first two concerning American soldiers returning home, and the latter (set in Italy) providing a bridge to the ensuing five stories about expatriate Americans in Europe – a sequence that reintroduces Nick Adams in "Cross-Country Snow," but breaks away to "My Old Man" before returning to Nick and Michigan in the spectacular finale, "Big Two-Hearted River." In the meantime, two pieces on crime bracket the second major thematic block of vignettes – the bullfighting sequence in chapters 9 through 14 – before the collection concludes, in L'Envoi, with the Greek king who longs for America. The reach of these stories and vignettes is thus deliberately transcultural in order to effect Hemingway's goal of examining the perilous state of Western culture. The stories shift from the United States to Europe and back to the States, while the story/vignette technique in the early part of the book constantly shifts our perspective between Michigan and the Great War. Loosely speaking, too, *In Our Time* moves from the prewar to the postwar period and from youth to disillusioned maturity, though the vignettes between the young Nick Adams stories foreshadow the war to come.

Of the five Nick Adams stories that begin *In Our Time*, "Indian Camp" is the most remarkable, treating with extraordinary delicacy the cultural, familial, and gender conflicts so central to the collection. Appropriately, the story concerns origins: not only birth, and not only Nick's untimely initiation into an adult world of blood and death, but the origins of a bitter racial conflict between Native and white American. The first scene of the story opens on what we soon know to be a doctor's humanitarian mission: "At the lake shore there was another rowboat drawn up. The two Indians stood waiting." Yet immediately it presents an archetypal moment of a different sort. Boats beached, Indians waiting, whites debarking: The scene of whites arriving in the New World or encountering tribes within the New World is strong in racial memories, pictured over the centuries in scores of illustrations and books. The similarities continue, for the narrative reenacts a subsequent history of dispossession, annexation, betrayal, and death. To the doctor and Uncle George, the mercy mission affords the opportunity for revisiting a form of Manifest Destiny upon the Indian camp. They play the role of the Great White Father, bringing to birth a child/nation supposedly deficient in civilized attributes. Uncle George even "gave both the Indians cigars," thus usurping the role traditionally accorded the father (as well as iterating a long history of territories purchased by means of trinkets and other cheap gifts). Still more effectively, as the doctor deploys his medical expertise in the cabin he implies by contrast the Native Americans' ignorance of hygiene and medical procedure. His actions and words suggest their general cultural incompetence – a reading supported by the feeling of distanced superiority he shows (or at least affects) when the woman screams: "Her screams are not important. I don't hear them because they are not important." What is important, apparently, is to preserve the history of this cultural and racial domination, for the doctor proceeds to sketch out the narrative he wishes to write: "That's one for the medical journal, George. . . . Doing a Caesarian with a jack-knife and sewing it up with nine-foot, tapered gut leaders" (16–18).

The Indian father's suicide suggests that other interpretations of "Indian Camp" might be more pertinent than the doctor's fantasy. Immobilized because of an ax wound, the father must bear witness to the white doctor's presumption of cultural superiority. The father's cultural role has been jeopardized in several ways. First, he is helpless to "father" the child in the sense of bringing it to life and consciousness. The doctor symbolically usurps that role. Second, he has lost control of his own space (the cabin). It is transformed into an operating theater in which the "great man" (as Uncle George somewhat sarcastically labels Nick's father) becomes the star performer, frequently inviting Nick to "see" and "watch" his skill (17–18). Third, and most interesting, it appears that the Indian father must participate in a ritual that his culture designates female. When Nick and his father arrive at the pregnant woman's cabin, we are told that the "men had moved off up the road to sit in the dark and smoke out of range of the noise she made" while "All the old women in the camp had been helping her" (16). Smoking (a pipe) seems an attempt on the part of the father to align himself with the "men" up the road, but his posture (he lies in the other bunk with a cut that prefigures his wife's) physically aligns him with his wife. The father's presence is thus doubly problematic: helpless to escape, he symbolically occupies a female role while prevented by gender from trying to help. The doctor, on his part, not only transgresses an age-old custom (and possesses a knowledge of the woman's sexuality previously appropriate only to the husband and the "old women"), but gives rise to the suspicion that the old customs are no longer valid and powerful anyway.

The relationships of power played out in the cabin are further complicated by the doubled father–son relationships in the story – for the newborn child, a boy, completes the analogy to Nick and his father. But the analogy is oddly skewed. The Indian father who, according to Nick's father, "couldn't stand things" (19), hides his face by rolling over against the wall. And it is Nick whose actions correspond: "He was looking away so as not to see what his father was doing"; "'Nick did not watch" (17). Deprived of father-hood and manhood, the Indian father plays the inappropriate role of son to the usurping white father. The relationship between Nick and his father thus represents and articulates the unvoiced relationship between the doctor and the Indian father. The doctor revels in emphasizing the inequality of that relationship, pressuring Nick to accept his authority. When Nick answers "I know" to the revelation that "This lady is going to have a baby, Nick," for instance, his father replies, "You don't know. . . . Listen to me." Later, the doctor refers to the details of the operation ("See, it's a boy, Nick"; "'There. That gets it"; "'You can watch this or not, Nick, just as you like") in direct proportion to Nick's unwillingness to watch (16–17). Nick's father is not inviting him to undergo a bloody initiation into a frightening adult world so much as reminding Nick (and, as a corollary, the Indian father) of the toughness and ability to "face" the adult world that the boy clearly lacks.

Nick, for his part, obediently slips into the role of child to a seemingly all-powerful father figure. The first time Nick addresses his father, for instance, he calls him "Dad"; in the cabin, as the woman starts screaming, Nick begins to use the term appropriate to younger children: "Daddy." It is thus not surprising that his father's terrifyingly incomplete answers to Nick's questions about birth, death, and suicide ("I don't know," "It all depends") leave Nick oddly content, for Nick does not want answers but the security of asking questions of an authority figure. Nick's epiphany (that he will never die) is thus appropriate not to the ordeals he has just experienced but to the strengthening of a hierarchical father–son relationship, enforced on the one side, given freely on the other. The very syntax of the last sentence, "In the early morning on the lake sitting in the stern of the boat with his father rowing, he felt quite sure that he would never die," suggests as much. It describes a gradual rise, from time, to space, to the relative positions of son and father, and culminates, in its syntactic heart, with "his father row-ing." Sentence and son thus both center on the father who, rowing in this paradisal scene, allows his son intimations of immortality. Or seems to. One more doubled relationship in the story, this time between father and father, should give us pause. For the rapid transformation of roles in the cabin (the doctor becoming the "great man" and surrogate father to the Indian child, the Indian father becoming, as it were, both son and wife) suggests the friable and temporary nature of those roles. Authority, it seems, is not vested in the man but in the man's role; and the role depends on how easily external factors (such as race, culture, class, medical expertise, and so on) can be brought to bear on a particular situation. If this is true, the doctor's authority is temporary and contingent rather than permanent.

"The Doctor and the Doctor's Wife," the next story in *In Our Time*, plays a satiric counterpoint to "Indian Camp" and extends Hemingway's inquiry into history, cultural relationships, and masculine authority. Structurally, the two stories have much in common. Both stories begin by a lake, though in "The Doctor and the Doctor's Wife" three Indians arrive in the doctor's garden to perform a task for him, rather than three whites arriving at the Indian camp; instead of the pregnant woman in the dark cabin, the doctor's wife lies in the cottage "with the blinds drawn"; and the story ends, like the first, with a moment of camaraderie between Nick and his father. The medical triumph the doctor wishes to write about in "Indian Camp" is transformed now into a possibly true but certainly weak excuse for his humiliating encounter with Dick Boulton: "Well, Dick owes me a lot of money for pulling his squaw through pneumonia and I guess he wanted a row so he wouldn't have to take it out in work." This time the medical journals remain "unopened" (25–26). Most important, the easy mastery the doctor demonstrated in the Indian cabin abruptly disappears during his confrontation with Dick.

Why his authority disappears is of great interest. Most obviously, the doctor backs down because he is outmatched by the superior strength of Dick Boulton. The "big man" Dick Boulton supplants the "great man" of "Indian Camp" in a story that is replete with Dick's dramatizations of his phallic power. Wielding no fewer than three axes, Dick, secure in the pertinence of his name and in his knowledge (as the doctor admits) that he bears the "tools," slights the doctor's manhood: "'Don't go off at half cock, Doc,' Dick said" (24). Dick Boulton draws attention to an impotence that Hemingway, along with many other writers of his generation, saw as endemic to a sexually frustrated white civilization overcommitted to the kind of cold-blooded technical expertise that the doctor exploited in "Indian Camp." Many looked to the (supposed) potency of other cultures and races for their experience of heroism, a true bond with nature, and sexual release – as D. H. Lawrence, for instance, used the lower-class Mellors in *Lady Chatterley's Lover* (1928) or as Hemingway seems to use Ojibway, Spanish, and later Masai cultures. Hemingway's own investment in the ideal of a potent masculinity seems evident in the heroic posture he took such pains to maintain in his own life: sportsman, big-game hunter, fisherman extraordinaire, bullfighting aficionado, and womanizer.

"The Doctor and the Doctor's Wife," however, turns out to be much more complex, for the doctor's humiliation is born originally of a moral blow to his self-esteem. Arguably the logs are "stolen," as Dick suggests. The real point is that they symbolize a centuries-old expropriation of Indian land, of which the doctor's garden, fenced off from the surrounding wilderness, is one example. Even the mark of the scaler's hammer in the log shows that it belongs to "White" and McNally, which gives rise to a double irony: The mark exposes the historic truth of Boulton's remark that "You know they're stolen as well as I do," in the sense that White has stolen from the Indian, but the immorality of the act comes home to the doctor only in the idea of a white stealing from White. Manifest Destiny – the idea that whites had a moral and God-granted right to possess the lands of peoples less civilized than they – now rebounds ironically against the doctor. In "Indian Camp," the doctor relied on the superiority of Western know-how to support a symbolic appropriation of the cabin space. In "Doctor's Wife," with the fact of appropriation suddenly evident, the moral superiority of white culture is shown to be a mere covering for an aggressive exploitation of natural resources. Tellingly, Boulton's first action with the log is to have the obscuring dirt cleaned off: "Wash it off. Clean off the sand. . . . I want to see who it belongs to" (24).

Back in the cottage, the doctor pumps shells in and out of his shotgun in a masturbatory attempt to regain his lost confidence in his manhood – first to prove that he is a "man" and, second, to demonstrate his access to the cultural and technological prowess that "won the West" for white settlers. Having put away the gun, however, the doctor's humiliations continue. Sent on an errand by his wife to find Nick, he must first apologize for slamming the screen door, unlike Dick Boulton, who deliberately leaves the gate into the woods open. But the errand does give him the opportunity to reprise the father–son relationship played so powerfully at the end of "Indian Camp." Nick's "I want to go with you" (27) allows his father to reassert an authoritative role ("His father looked down at him") in a way that is reminiscent of "Indian Camp": the son sitting/sitting in the stern, the father standing/rowing. But the likeness is only superficial. The doctor's escape into the woods merely points up his inability to confront his wife directly. Moreover, the impetus for their retreat comes from Nick, who "know[s] where there's black squirrels." Having lost the authority he possessed while rowing and steering the boat, having forfeited the privileged knowledge Nick once sought, the doctor follows the leader into the woods his child knows better than he.

The next pair of stories in *In Our Time*, "The End of Something" and "The Three-Day Blow," now featuring an adolescent Nick Adams as protagonist, transforms the concerns of the first two stories in intriguing and often amusing ways. The old lumbering town of Hortons Bay, abandoned when "there were no more logs to make lumber," reminds us of the history of lands and peoples exploited in the previous stories. And there are ominous hints of catastrophes to come, for Nick and Marjorie are trolling "where the bottom dropped off suddenly from sandy shallows to twelve feet of dark water" (31). But Hortons Bay also becomes a rather grandiose metaphor for the lugubrious finale to Nick and Marjorie's relationship as Nick strives to bring it to an end. Their first conversation is a masterpiece of adolescent disconnection:

> "There's our old ruin, Nick," Marjorie said.
> Nick, rowing, looked at the white stone in the green trees.
> "There it is," he said.
> "Can you remember when it was a mill?" Marjorie asked.
> "I can just remember," Nick said.
> "It seems more like a castle," Marjorie said.
> Nick said nothing. (32)

Marjorie self-consciously rebuilds Hortons Bay into a symbol of their relationship: The town is not desolate so long as it is *our* old ruin; Hortons Bay's once-thriving life can always be remembered. Nick, trying to live in the prosaic moment, merely registers its existence ("There it is") and can "just remember" a time when the ruin possessed communal life. Determinedly romantic, Marjorie attempts to transform the ruin into a castle, but Nick, seeing only the ruin their relationship has become, refuses to participate. Nick's next words are that the fish "aren't striking," and neither does Nick to Marjorie's conversational bait.

Nick's taciturnity sets the scene for the ensuing display of cool professionalism, precise actions, and careful control of emotion – in short, for the cultivation of appropriate codes of manly conduct in the face of chaotic, destructive forces that many have seen as the primary characteristic of Hemingway's heroes. Nick is the fishing master. Marjorie defers to him (" 'Should I let it drop?' Marjorie called back, holding the line in her hand"), and Nick treats her as an apprentice. Having caught and skinned three perch for bait to Marjorie's one, for instance, Nick appraises her work ("Nick looked at her fish") and advises: "You don't want to take the ventral fin out." So proficient is he that we may miss Hemingway's provocative critique of Nick's fumbling attempts to perform an adult masculine role. For Nick's performance arises out of the threat of being outperformed. Marjorie proves every bit as adept as Nick, rowing while "holding the line in her teeth" at one point, smartly "row[ing] up the point a little way so she would

not disturb the line," then driving the boat powerfully "way up the beach."
As Nick finally admits, Marjorie is less an apprentice than an equal: "You
know everything. That's the trouble. You know you do. . . . I've taught you
everything. You know you do. What don't you know, anyway?" (32–34).

The fact that Marjorie can match Nick's expertise, experience, and toughness threatens him precisely because the acquisition of such attributes has
traditionally been the prerogative of a male. As a consequence, "The End of
Something" subverts the "heroic" qualities usually identified in Hemingway's male characters. In particular, the story reveals Nick's heroic pose of
cool detachment to be contingent not on his authority but on a double fear
of humiliation. First, Marjorie vies with Nick to possess the role he attempts
to make his own. Second, and perhaps more worrying, Marjorie demonstrates that these manly characteristics do not automatically accrue to any
male. To be *male* is not the same as being a *man*, but what is a man if
Marjorie can possess all the requisite attributes? One might argue that Nick
in adolescent fashion is only aping the characteristics that will define the
true Hemingway hero. The example of Marjorie, however, suggests the
opposite: that there is something deeply problematic about the way masculine codes of behavior initiate boys into manhood.

"The Three-Day Blow," in which we find Nick still pondering the wisdom of breaking up with Marjorie, once again demonstrates Hemingway's
acute insights into the problems of manhood-fashioning. The story portrays
with a kind of relish the spartan but comfortable appurtenances of a world
without women, where Nick and Bill, drinking, talking about sport, hunting, fishing, writing, and women, shape a masculine paradise familiar from
dozens of boys' stories of adventure. According to Leslie Fiedler's still-
classic *Love and Death in the American Novel* (1959), such scenes are also
familiar as the primal material of American literature in books where the
male protagonist must leave behind society and the women who embody it
in order to achieve freedom and self-determination. As a consequence, male
characters in American literature remain boys, forever seeking a pristine
boyhood paradise free of the responsibility of adult, heterosexual relationships. "Once a man's married he's absolutely bitched," Bill states in succinct
praise of Nick's breaking off "that Marge business"; with Marge around, in
fact, "we wouldn't even be going fishing tomorrow" (46–47). Despite
Nick's ambivalent feelings about renewing a relationship with Marjorie, the
story provides evidence of the adolescent, macho posturings of which his
detractors accuse Hemingway, and which, not surprisingly, have been interpreted by many feminist writers as signifying a deep-rooted hostility toward
women.[6]

There is much to recommend Fiedler's account and other critiques of Hemingway's stories insofar as they accurately describe the codes that govern Nick and Bill's behavior and conversation. But the story explores the socially constructed nature of those codes and exposes their contradictions rather than representing them as the standards to which Nick and Bill should aspire. Both Nick and Bill, for instance, resist a world of consequences, though for different reasons. For Bill, the consequences of marriage are destructive and should thus be avoided; for Nick, picking up Bill's hint that he "might get back into it again," the consequences of the breakup appear suddenly reversible. "There was not anything," according to Nick, "that was irrevocable." But Nick himself has just given an example of something that is: "All of a sudden everything was over. . . . I couldn't help it. Just like when the three-day blows come now and rip all the leaves off the trees" (47–48). Nick here might simply be in the maudlin stages of incipient drunkenness, but his image conforms more closely to the world of inescapable contingencies that Hemingway depicts. The three-day blows occur in fall for a predictable length of time; they are irrevocable and consequential. They mean that "It's getting too late to go around without socks" (40) and that the "birds will lie right down in the grass with this" (49). And they inevitably limit action, for, as Bill proclaims at the end, "You can't shoot in this wind."

Unable to shoot, the pair nevertheless carry their guns when setting off to find Bill's father, determined, in spite of the storm, to conform to a masculine code of potent action. Like the shotgun in "The Doctor and the Doctor's Wife," the guns are useless but powerful reminders of a masculine power Nick and Bill hope to inherit. The guns signify not an intention to kill but a desired form of conduct. In what has come to seem the archetypal Hemingwayesque gesture of grace under pressure, Nick and Bill value their ostensible goal less than the process of trying to achieve it. Throughout, in fact, the story concerns processes of behavior: how to drink, how to use practical symbols in a narrative, how to love women, and even, as the intoxicated Nick struggles in with a beech log, how to pick up spilled apricots: "He laid the log down and picked up the pan. It had contained dried apricots, soaking in water. He carefully picked up all the apricots off the floor, some of them had gone under the stove, and put them back in the pan. He dipped some more water onto them from the pail by the table. He felt quite proud of himself. He had been thoroughly practical" (44–45). Nick sets the spilled apricots to rights using the kind of ritual thoroughness and care that seems more pertinent to the Villalta bullfighting vignette and to "Big Two-Hearted River." But his drunken lucidity (which even includes

68

a wonderfully slurred run-on sentence in "picked up all the apricots off the floor, some of them had gone under the stove") imparts an unsettlingly comic feel to these scenes of heroic action. Similarly, Nick and Bill attempt to abide by paternal codes and prohibitions even when they are blatantly ludicrous. Bill, for instance, says with regard to whisky that "There's plenty more but dad only likes me to drink what's open," because "He says opening bottles is what makes drunkards." If opening bottles really made drunkards, of course, Bill should never open another bottle. Nick, on the other hand, had thought that it was "solitary drinking that made drunkards" (43–44), a difference of opinion that is quietly suppressed in their quest for cohesive standards of conduct. For Nick and Bill, the point is not to question the appropriateness of the injunction but to internalize the appropriateness of making codes. The story persuades us that Hemingway's intent might be parodic rather than celebratory, but leaves us with at least two options: Are Nick and Bill naively and unsuccessfully trying to imitate the codes of true manhood, or, because those codes appear to govern even the most inappropriate, trivial situation, demonstrating the limitations of the codes themselves?

"The Battler" completes the first series of Nick Adams stories, and does so in a way that repeats and reconfigures key elements of previous stories. Bugs and Ad Francis's camp, for instance, directly recalls the camps of "Indian Camp" and "The End of Something" and the transgressions and separations enacted there. Once again "The Battler" evokes disputed territories, threats of humiliation, and symbolic evictions. "Who the hell asked you to butt in here?" (59) asks Ad Francis, a question the brakeman who knocks Nick off the train might also have asked. Like Dick Boulton, both Francis and the brakeman wish to transform enclosed spaces into symbolic arenas – in this case boxing rings – in which men compete to demonstrate their manhood. But Ad Francis, beaten too many times and slugged once more in the arena he hoped to control, is no Dick Boulton. A closer analogy exists between him and Nick Adams. Francis, for instance, looks "childish" at the end of the story, and both Francis and the brakeman refer to Nick as "kid"; Nick, who sees falling for the brakeman's trick as a "lousy kid thing to have done," concurs. Carrying the marks of a beating on his face, moreover, Nick is twice promised that he will share the boxer's experience: " You're going to take a beating, see?" says Francis, and though Nick "says he's never been crazy" like Francis, Bugs remarks that Nick has "got a lot coming to him." The story reveals a world of con tricks, unpredictable events, and uncontrollable violence; it also reveals the inadequacy or even inappropriateness of masculine codes of conduct that issue in Francis's confused, self-destructive courage and Nick's wavering command over his conduct. In his initial conversation with Francis, for instance, Nick first admits his lack of inner resilience, denying that he is "a tough one," then attempts to fall back on the macho role that Francis expects of him and that Nick deems appropriate to the situation: "You got to be tough" (53–62).

In this context of gender clash and cultural conflict, where bonds are severed, spaces dominated and transgressed, and male authority sought, won, and lost, the five war vignettes interspersed between the early Nick Adams stories become fiercely resonant. Reading *In Our Time* in linear fashion provides a new experience: a series of abrupt and often perplexing leaps in perspective. The vignette of the World War I kitchen corporal riding through the Champagne in chapter 1, for instance, precedes "Indian Camp"; we move then to the glimpse of the evacuation from Adrianople during the war between Greece and Turkey in chapter 2, and thence to "The Doctor and the Doctor's Wife." On closer inspection, an almost obsessively patterned set of correspondences begins to emerge. Chapter 1, where "Everybody was drunk. The whole battery was drunk going along the road in the dark," puts us in mind of the callow drinking yet to come in "The Three-Day Blow"; the storm in that story, which to Nick signifies his relationship to Marjorie, takes on ominous overtones in view of that battery "going along the road in the dark." The storm of "The Three-Day Blow" presages the political and military storms that Western culture was about to experience. In chapter 2, the events of "Indian Camp" return as the observer of the evacuation of Adrianople notes "a woman having a kid with a young girl holding a blanket over her and crying. Scared sick looking at it." Evacuations are also the order of the day in chapter 4, where the soldiers "had to fall back" during a battle, and in the two stories that precede it, for first the doctor and then Marjorie are ousted from arenas of conflict. Moreover, the scene enacted in the garden of "The Doctor and the Doctor's Wife" reminds us of the bloodier yet more sterile conflict in the "garden at Mons" (chapter 3), while the carts "jammed solid on the bridge" in chapter 2 metamorphose into the perfect barricade "jammed . . . across the bridge" in chapter 4.

Through it all, certain elemental patterns remain. There is "No end and no beginning" (21) to the carts out of Adrianople, and similarly no end to cycles of life and death: Men commit suicide; soldiers are "potted"; but babies are born to begin cycles anew, and adolescents like Nick and Bill undergo initiation rites into manhood. Everywhere people and peoples are dispossessed and territories transgressed. Everywhere cultures are in conflict: Greek against Turk, British against German, white American against Native American. Everywhere situations threaten to go awry: The battery is drunk, the baby cannot be born, the doctor's authority does not hold, relationships break, apricots spill, three-day blows strip the trees. And everywhere masculine codes of tough-minded, practical, expert action are brought to bear: A cesarean is skillfully performed, Germans are carefully "potted" over garden walls and through "an absolutely perfect barricade" (37), drinks are mixed and spilled apricots properly picked up.

War is the central metaphor of the early vignettes and stories and the common denominator of human experience, for conflicts between European cultures or between American Indians and white settlers or between men and women seem to occur as naturally and inevitably as the three-day blows. Yet the relationships between World War I and prewar events are complex and often ironic. Hence the disruption of Western cultures documented in the war vignettes allows a bittersweet perspective on Nick's struggles to come to grips with his breakup with Marjorie. Love approximates war, but Nick and Marjorie's romantic conflict also seems sweetly archaic compared to the casual slaughters that surround it. Similarly, the careful act of picking up the apricots seems heartrendingly inconsequential amid the mechanized nightmare of falling bombs and soldiers precisely "potted" over garden walls. At the same time, it is possible that actions undertaken and codes constructed in the prewar years form part of the historical circumstances that led to the Great War. The standoff in the garden between the doctor and Dick Boulton, for instance, does not merely happen to resemble the standoff between the Austro-Hungarian Empire and the Allies but may actually help explain it. The story describes a complex dynamic of humiliation and aggression emerging out of a history of territories annexed and dispossessed. Worse, the codes that dictate the doctor's behavior limit the options available to him. The doctor can either "fight like a man" or be shamed; his response to shame is to pick up the shotgun. These early stories are testimony to Hemingway's profound understanding of the workings of masculine psychology and to his caustic critique of the limitations it imposes. We should not miss the pertinence of his critique to the psychology of the men who led nations into the Great War.

In Our Time pivots on chapter 6, in which Nick is wounded on the Italian front during World War I. The vignette draws together the first part of the collection. It connects at last the previously disjunct time sequences of Nick's adolescence and of the war vignettes; it is the only vignette to focus on a character from one of the stories; and it even offers an ironic flashback to Nick's maudlin memories in "The Three-Day Blow" of talking to Marjorie "about how they would go to Italy together and the fun they would have" (47). Yet Nick's serious wound also foreshadows ensuing tales like "A

Very Short Story," "The Revolutionist," and "Soldier's Home," which document the geographical displacements and psychic woundings that follow hard upon the conclusion of World War I. "The Revolutionist," for instance, describes the wanderings of a communist youth in the year following the collapse of the Austro-Hungarian Empire. Moving from Hungary to Italy and then to Switzerland, psychically scarred by the "bad things" done to him in Hungary, the youth seems a symbolic heir to the carnage of Europe. His faith in the world revolution is both indomitable and self-deluding, for the revolution has failed in Hungary, is going "'very badly" in Italy, and the youth will be jailed in Switzerland. His goals seem equally contradictory: Believing in revolution, he wants only "to walk over the pass while the weather held good," for he "loved the mountains in the autumn" (81–82). Possibly he is a Christ figure, a postwar Son of Man having nowhere to lay his head, jailed and tormented for his beliefs, yet still proclaiming his faith in revolutionizing the world. If so, his pilgrimage to Sion, Switzerland (but with a play on Zion, the Holy City, or heaven), where he is jailed, seems a remarkably dispiriting one.

"A Very Short Story" and "Soldier's Home" complement this tale of rootlessness by describing ironic returns to the United States. "A Very Short Story" is a brief account of Hemingway's personal experience in Italy where, in the hospital after his 1918 wounding near the front, he and nurse Agnes von Kurowsky had a relationship that she soon brought to an end. The story progresses through odd shifts of tone. Early on, the protagonist typically exercises great self-control, going under the anesthetic "holding tight on to himself" so that he would not "blab . . . during the silly, talky time" (65). Later, after praying in the Duomo, the couple wish to get married "to make it so they could not lose it [their love]." Thereafter, the story's serious tone dissolves into one of the most disconcertingly funny "Dear John" letters ever written: "The major of the battalion made love to Luz, and she had never known Italians before, and finally wrote to the States that theirs had been only a boy and girl affair. She was sorry, and she knew he would probably not be able to understand, but might some day forgive her, and be grateful to her, and she expected, absolutely unexpectedly, to be married in the spring" (66). That near-contradictory "she expected, absolutely unexpectedly" alone gives away the thorough insincerity of the letter. Rarely has Hemingway's technique of parataxis seemed so appropriate as in the airy insouciance of Luz's stumbling string of clichés, one added to the other in a deliberate evasion of emotional disclosure. And rarely has Hemingway's common technique of flat understatement served such good effect as in the story's bathetic climax: "A short time after he contracted gonorrhea from a sales girl in a loop department store while riding in a taxicab through Lincoln Park." The punchline is cruelly funny because it is so incommensurate with the Italian experience. The messiness of disease and the transience of relationships consummated in moving taxis replace the old ethos of appropriate behavior ("holding tight on to himself"). Luz and the protagonist lose all sense of emotional strength and connectivity; and the story, likewise, fragments into disconnected styles and emotional colorings.

Harold Krebs, in the important story "Soldier's Home," also "lost everything" on his return from the Great War, but the problems he faces Hemingway now connects to a scathing indictment of American society. Returning to small-town Oklahoma too late for a hero's welcome, Krebs finds a society addicted to lies, even to the sick fantasies of atrocity stories. Lying to ingratiate himself, moreover, merely leads Krebs to "the nausea in regard to experience that is the result of untruth or exaggeration." In particular, he loses the purity of experience encountered at moments during the war: "The times so long back when he had done the one thing, the only thing for a man to do, easily and naturally, when he might have done something else, now lost their cool, valuable quality and then were lost themselves." But Krebs has also lost the will to endure the monotonous cultural imperatives of a small-town America barely touched by the war: His father drives the "same car," and "Nothing was changed in the town except that the young girls had grown up." Like the girls who "all wore sweaters and shirt waists with round Dutch collars," the town composes "a pattern" to which his mother and father want him to conform, and to which he did conform when, in his college years, he and his fraternity brothers "all of them [wore] exactly the same height and style collar." Caught between his mother's bleak piety and his father's tawdry materialism, however, Krebs prefers a self-willed paralysis. Negatives define him: "he did not want to have to do any courting. He did not want to tell any more lies. . . . He did not want any consequences." And, telling the truth when his mother asks if he loves her, he replies "No" (70–76).

The ambiguity of "Soldier's Home" is whether Krebs acquiesces to paralysis because of his hometown's mind-deadening provincialism, or whether its provincialism affords him a way of dealing with the consequences of the war. Life goes "smoothly" (77) for Krebs when he observes (the girls, his sister's baseball game) rather than participates; he likes reading about the battles he was engaged in; he prefers to "live along without consequences" (71). But does homecoming sabotage his ability to conduct himself heroically by removing "the only thing for a man to do," which came "easily and naturally" during the war? Or does it merely allow him to express the psychic trauma that arose from that heroic conduct in the war – conduct of which he may anyway no longer be capable? His situation in the latter case would be exactly opposite to that of the soldier in the vignette that precedes "Soldier's Home," whose conduct under the bombardment of the trenches at Fossalta is decidedly unheroic, but who is able to ignore his panic-stricken promise to tell everyone about Jesus and simply act, the next night, with "the girl he went upstairs with at the Villa Rossa" (67).

Understanding Krebs' behavior depends in part on how we read Hemingway's striking stylistic performance in "Soldier's Home," for Krebs' homecoming is rendered with obsessive repetitiveness in a flat prose so neutral that it sounds almost scientifically detached. "There is a picture which shows him among his fraternity brothers," we are told in the second sentence. In the second paragraph, the phrase returns: "There is a picture which shows him on the Rhine with two German girls and another corporal. Krebs and the corporal look too big for their uniforms. The German girls are not beautiful. The Rhine does not show in the picture" (69). Though one of these sentences conveys a subjective judgment (the soldiers look too big for their uniforms), there is little sense of a subjective narrator. We do not think to question who sees or who judges. The narrative voice, like the facts it registers, possesses nothing beyond a bare existence. "There is a picture" presents an unadorned fact irrelevant to the subjective realities of Krebs' life (who took the picture? who possesses it? what were they doing on the Rhine?). Likewise, the narrative voice exists as though in a vacuum; it is omniscient, but inconsequential, in the sense that it mimics an inhuman camera eye whose only function is to record. Moreover, as the repetition of "There is a picture" already suggests, long stretches of the story fall into multiple iterations of sentences beginning "He liked" and "He did not want" or simply repeat phrases like "It was not worth it," all of which reinforces the nearly mechanical quality of the narration.

In part, the narrative voice owes a debt for its experimentalism to Gertrude Stein, whose radical experiments with repetitive rhythms Hemingway himself acknowledged as a major influence on his writing, though he later sought to dissociate himself from what he saw as Stein's rather pointless abstraction.[7] In "Soldier's Home," as so often in Hemingway, style is also placed at the service of action or psychological action – though never straightforwardly. Hence the detached narrative voice matches Krebs' emotional deadness; its distanced, reportorial tone matches his own lack of involvement with his mother, the girls, and his own future. Obsessive repetition, moreover, declares a mind locked into a few simple subjects (what he likes, what he does not want, what is not worthwhile). His mind, moving tentatively from one idea and sentence to another that virtually recapitulate the same material, might suggest a state of shellshock in which each new thought represents a venture into hazardous territory. Or, possibly, repetition suggests the constraints circumstances impose on him. The hometown girls, after all, dress to the same pattern; and Krebs, by the end of the story, has been coopted by his parents into conformity with the status quo. Style, then, might signify the banal lifestyle to which Krebs, despite his resistance, increasingly configures his time and consciousness.

"Mr. and Mrs. Elliot" begins a new group of stories that includes "Cat in the Rain," "Out of Season," "Cross-Country Snow," and "My Old Man," all focusing on the experience of expatriate Americans in Europe. Written in a satiric vein rarely encountered in previous stories, "Mr. and Mrs. Elliot" is a sometimes savage and often hilarious attack on American mores, marriage, and writers. Hemingway casts his satiric net wide. The first paragraph debunks the (supposedly) aristocratic pretensions of Southern women, for Mrs. Elliot spends her time on the boat being "quite sick" and, in a neat nursery-rhyme rhythm, "when she was sick she was sick as Southern women are sick." As expatriates, she and her husband show no regard or affinity for new cultures. Their desires are mercenary (to say they have studied at the University of Dijon) and culinary (they go to Dijon in part because "there is a diner on the train"). Quintessentially ugly tourists, they even snobbishly refuse to sit at the Rotonde café because "it is always so full of foreigners" (85–87).

Mr. Elliot is shown as sexually immature and artistically impotent.[8] He "wrote very long poems very rapidly," and if we do not supply the implied "and very badly," Hemingway's parody of stuffy, artificial writing in the story gives the game away. "He was going to bring it out in Boston and had already sent his check to, and made a contract with, a publisher" says the narrator stiltedly, showing why Elliot needs to bring his work out by way of a vanity press. And Elliot's sex life appears equally futile. Having kept himself idealistically pure for his wife, he is "disappointed" on his wedding night and soon gives up trying hard to have a baby. With the arrival of Mrs. Elliot's girlfriend, the Elliots' marriage falls apart, Mrs. Elliot and the girlfriend apparently pursuing a lesbian relationship (they "now slept together in the big mediaeval bed") while Mr. Elliot's artistic pretensions dissolve into a great deal of (presumably bad) poetry and too much white wine. And "they were all quite happy," concludes Hemingway in this jaundiced fairy tale of idealized relationships gone astray (85–88).

The vignettes that bracket "Mr. and Mrs. Elliot," chapters 9 and 10, provide an important counterpoint to Hemingway's sly satire. Appropriate counterparts for Mr. Elliot might be found in the two matadors who are "hooted" by the crowd for their poor performances and the dying, "nervously wobbly" horse of chapter 10. Chapter 9, however, has a particularly complex thematic and structural function. This story of the initiation of a "kid" into manhood begins the second major group of vignettes in *In Our Time,* a series of six bullfighting scenes that begins with acts of bravery and ends with a bullfighter's death (Maera's, in chapter 14). The "kid," the young bullfighter who follows two failed matadors into the ring and therefore must "kill five bulls because you can't have more than three matadors," recalls other youths in various postures of integrity and courage, most of whom seem callow ("The Three-Day Blow") or disoriented ("The Revolutionist," "Soldier's Home"). And the "kid" who with the last bull "couldn't get the sword in" prefaces Mr. Elliot's lugubrious sexual failures.

The "kid," however, eventually succeeds, and in a way that leads to one more vital analogy. After succeeding, the young matador "sat down in the sand and puked and they held a cape over him while the crowd hollered and threw things down into the bullring" – a moment that recalls chapter 2, where we find a "woman having a kid with a young girl holding a blanket over her and crying. Scared sick looking at it." The analogous scenes confirm that the "kid" experiences a kind of birth from youth into maturity and heighten the sense that such initiations take place amid baptisms of blood and death. What distinguishes the matador's initiation from earlier adolescent pursuits of manhood is that it takes place among codes that are as well defined as the arena itself ("you can't have more than three matadors," for instance). These codes, absent in the chaotic evacuation of Adrianople, impart to initiates the logic of ritual actions that are deeply embedded within a culture's traditions.

Mr. and Mrs. Elliot and the characters of much more somber stories like "Out of Season" and "Cat in the Rain" suffer by contrast the rootlessness and meaninglessness of a life and culture without structuring codes. "Cat in the Rain" is a powerful example. George and the "American wife" seem gripped by a deep-rooted anomie born of their aimlessness: Artists come to paint the "bright colors" and Italians come to look at the war monument, but the Americans have no apparent purpose for being there. Like the Americans in "Out of Season," this couple is unseasonably early for the tourist season; it is raining, the "motor cars were gone from the square by the war monument," and they are the "only two Americans stopping at the hotel." Tourists without tourism, the Americans are stripped of everything but the most rudimentary roles. George spends the story reading, his wife wishing for whatever she does not have. The narrator, moreover, constantly identifies them in the simplest and most generic way, labeling the woman "the American wife," "the wife," and then "the American girl," while designating George "her husband" and then, even more indifferently, "The husband" (91–92).

These epithets hint at a cultural baggage of stereotypical roles that circumscribe the characters' lives yet are not adequate to the task of expressing the characters' deepest desires and fears. This is particularly true of the "American wife," whose barely conscious feelings of entrapment and yearnings for powerful models of behavior make her one of Hemingway's most sensitive female characters. That portrait is nowhere more profound than in the rich metaphoric relationship the narrative draws between the woman and the cat. Initially the cat, which is "crouched under one of the dripping green tables . . . trying to make herself so compact that she would not be dripped on," represents the woman's own claustrophobia in the hotel room, where she stands at the window looking out. Whereas the cat wishes only to escape the rain, however, the woman wants to break through the protective shelters that confine her. Her mission to rescue the cat reveals a fantasy of escape *into* the rain. Yet, ambivalently, she wishes to rescue the cat by securing it more completely within her hotel room. After her abortive venture into the rain, in fact, the fantasy she weaves around the cat suggests a longing for a traditionally feminine and maternal role: "I want to pull my hair back tight and smooth and make a big knot at the back that I can feel. . . . I want to have a kitty to sit on my lap and purr when I stroke her." The "kitty" substitutes for what she lacks – perhaps the lack of a child and certainly the complete lack of emotional and physical contact from George. The maternal woman/"kitty" relationship thus doubles for the (conventionally) romantic one between the male lover and female object of affection. The latter roles both depend on George's ability or willingness to restore a conventional paternalism.

The point, however, is not that Hemingway maneuvers the woman back into the position of "American wife," but that none of her fantasies affords her a stable and sustaining role. Her predicament is evident in her relationship to the padrone of the hotel, which recalls and extends the tense cultural engagements of the early stories. To begin with, the wife liked the hotel keeper. She "liked the deadly serious way he received any complaints. She liked his dignity. She liked the way he wanted to serve her." After her mission to find the cat, however, the woman's reaction is more complex: "As the American girl passed the office, the padrone bowed from his desk. Something felt very small and tight inside the girl. The padrone made her feel very small and at the same time really important. She had a momentary

feeling of being of supreme importance" (93). The servant-to-queen relationship augments the girl's sense of superiority as a wealthy American
tourist. Even more ironically, the padrone assumes the conventionally romantic gestures of the lover, bowing to the woman, catering to her every
whim, and finally offering her the gift (the cat) she wanted most of all.
George instructs her "Don't get wet" (92) and halfheartedly offers to re-
trieve the cat, but it is the padrone who actually causes the woman to be
sheltered and the cat to be found. By quietly anticipating and performing
every action for her, the padrone also ensures that her experience will remain vicarious. As surrogate lover/father, he merely confirms the uselessness of her existence. Feeling "very small," the girl thus becomes child to the
protective father and realizes her "supreme importance" only within his
strict limits. The conclusion to the story, in which the woman receives her
heart's desire, is thus another brilliantly parodic fairy-tale ending. "I want a
cat. I want a cat now. If I can't have long hair or any fun, I can have a cat,"
complains the woman, only to have a cat miraculously delivered. With her
articulated wants so comprehensively assuaged, however, the ill-defined and
chaotic yearnings that the cat symbolizes remain unfulfilled. And worse: By
getting exactly what she said she wanted, the woman loses the means for
expressing metaphorically the true extent of her predicament.

The implications of "Cat in the Rain" are startling. The story, like "Out
of Season," conveys a powerful sense of people displaced from meaningful
and regenerative codes of conduct and thus, like Krebs in "Soldier's Home"
and the couple in "Out of Season," condemned to near-paralysis. But "Cat
in the Rain" does not imply that expatriation has divorced George and his
wife from sustaining patterns of behavior; it simply reveals the inadequacy
of the codes themselves. The problem the story poses is not that George, for
instance, fails to measure up to the woman's romantic fantasy of being
treated like a princess but that such culturally sanctioned roles are themselves not generative or appropriate to her desires. We see this most clearly
when, by playing dutiful hero to the woman's fantasy of being rescued, the
padrone causes her fantasy of heroic rescue to *succeed*. The woman's long-
ings, moreover, combine traditionally male and female perspectives. She
wants to be rescued, but also to be the rescuer; she refuses to let her husband
get the cat for her, preferring to experience the traditionally masculine role
of self-liberation. The fact that the padrone circumvents the woman's fragile
rebellion is less important than the fact of the rebellion, which reveals that
women, like men, harbor urges toward heroic action. The story suggests,
moreover, that identity is culturally constructed rather than biologically

ordained and that the woman's paralysis must therefore be seen within a matrix of social repression rather than as her biological destiny.

"My Old Man," "Out of Season," and "'Cross-Country Snow" complete the sequence of stories about American expatriates. Though often seen as the weakest story in the collection, "My Old Man" remains pertinent to *In Our Time*'s exploration of corrupt social systems, innocence betrayed, and its near-obsessive evocation of toppled father figures, who fail through lack of personal authority (the doctor) or because of their obedience to strict cultural regimes (Krebs' father, the Indian father). But the implications of the father's death in "My Old Man" are actually quite different. "Seems like when they get started they don't leave a guy nothing," concludes the young narrator, laying the blame on an unspecified "they" composed of corrupt owners and jockeys and in particular the unsympathetic bettors who claim that the boy's father "had it coming to him on the stuff he's pulled" (129). Yet the boy's father dies accidentally after extricating himself from the corrupt system in which he was enmeshed – and which places no obstacle to prevent him from pursuing his racing elsewhere. His death results either from a particularly virulent form of poetic justice (which leaves George Gardner, who is still throwing races, untouched) or from a kind of perverse randomness. In neither case does the father's demise relate causally to his demerits, lack of skill, or the nature of the social system. His death, inexplicable in terms of a social context and apparently unrelated to his expertise as a jockey, thus signals a departure from previous stories that have, however covertly, placed their protagonists within situations conceived in relationship to cultural and historic events.

The final two Nick Adams stories and the bullfighting vignettes can be profitably juxtaposed against "My Old Man" because they question anew the dimensions of individual power and responsibility. Matadors in the bullring, like participants in a horse race, face death at every moment, but they do so in a way that is at once more risky and less arbitrary. The elaborate rituals surrounding the encounter between matador and bull ward off the operations of random chance while emphasizing the individual's control, skill, and conduct. Because humans appear to confront death purposefully and even gracefully within the arena, actions completed successfully take on a special aura of heroism. The crowd "hollered and threw things down into the bullring" to celebrate the young matador's accession to manhood in chapter 9; but it can only roar its appreciation at the mastery Villalta displays in chapter 12, where, the matador's body synchronized to the bull's charges, natural grace, power, and control are finally wedded:

"When the bull charged he swung back firmly like an oak when the wind hits it, his legs tight together, the muleta trailing and the sword following the curve behind." Amid the sexual aridity of surrounding stories like "Mr. and Mrs. Elliot" and "Cat in the Rain," the bullfight even promises a restoration of sexual potency, for, at the moment of killing, Villalta and the bull "became one."

This extraordinary display of control in the face of imminent death seems the ultimate representation of masculine conduct, to which other characters conform in their attempts to dominate arenas of conflict or to act precisely and gracefully. Yet Villalta's display is also suspect in the sense that it is made possible by an artificially controlled environment that grants his actions their symbolic import. Villalta "standing straight" after the killing may seem the measure of manhood, but he can do so only by adhering to codes that elsewhere are shattered and thus unavailable to other men. Moreover, because the codes of the bullring enforce the demonstration of individual autonomy they also intensity the humiliation that comes with actions performed poorly. If Villalta represents the pinnacle of achievement, the bullfighting vignettes more often feature narratives of incompleted actions and shameful omissions. In chapter 9 the first matador is "hooted"; the second, gored, "yelled for his sword" but "fainted." The matador of chapter 11 readily admits "I am not really a good bullfighter," and his experience in the arena, where the "crowd shouted all the time, and threw pieces of bread down into the bullring, then cushions and leather wine bottles," echoes embarrassingly the celebratory crowds of chapters 9 and 12. In a lovely reversal of chapter 9, an angry crowd in chapter 11 cuts off the failed matador's pigtail, which a "kid" then carries off. After Villalta, the two remaining bullfighting vignettes show bullfighters surrendering to drunkenness and irresponsibility (chapter 13) and death (chapter 14). Chapter 14, which describes the death of the great bullfighter Maera, and which immediately follows the father's death and shaming in "My Old Man," brings the sequence to an ambiguous conclusion.[9] We might suppose on this evidence that few are chosen to be men – or that the rigor of the code makes it all but useless even to its inner circle of initiates.

"Cross-Country Snow" bridges the chasm between Villalta's potent display and the drunkenness of the "ignorant Mexican savage" (113) in the next vignette, and the story itself describes a similar trajectory. The story begins with one of Hemingway's purest descriptions of physical action:

> [Nick's] skis started slipping at the edge and he swooped down, hissing in
> the crystalline powder snow and seeming to float up and drop down as he

went up and down the billowing khuds. He held to his left and at the end, as
he rushed toward the fence, keeping his knees locked tight together and turning his body like tightening a screw brought his skis sharply around to the
right in a smother of snow and slowed into a loss of speed parallel to the
hillside and the wire fence. (108)

In this passage Hemingway's prose lines enacts Nick's experience with remarkable precision, the repetition of "float up and drop down . . . up and
down" making the sentence rise and sink with Nick's form, while present
participles like "hissing," "keeping," "turning," and "tightening" keep the
action tautly present until the long syllables of "snow," "slowed," "loss,"
and "speed" bring the action to a smooth halt. Like George's telemark
position, his "trailing figure coming around in a beautiful right curve," the
images of Nick's skiing constantly recall Villalta fighting with "his legs tight
together, the muleta trailing and the sword following the curve behind."
And, like bullfighting, skiing toward a wire fence with anything less than
perfect control invites disaster. This early promise, however, quickly evapo-
rates. Like Luis, who prefers to dance and drink rather than face his responsibilities as a bullfighter, George wishes that "we could just bum together
. . . and not give a damn about school or anything." But the story ends in
gloom as Nick accepts marriage, fatherhood, and a forthcoming return to
the States where the mountains are "too rocky" to ski (105–11). Like
Maera and the unnamed narrator of the following vignette, Nick grudgingly
accepts new responsibilities.

In Our Time culminates in "Big Two-Hearted River," a stunning tour de
force that concludes the longer narratives and weaves together the collection's major themes, as well as posing new questions about its coherence
and overall vision. The story, as critics have long argued, suggests the slow,
silent recuperation of the human mind from the psychic trauma of (probably) World War I. Nick's refusal to think, his steadfast determination not to
hurry, his attention to the minutiae of his camp and its natural setting – all
of this bespeaks a mind fragile with shock as it attempts to construct new
grounds for a sane existence. Battered survivor of what Eliot called the
"immense panorama of futility and anarchy which is contemporary history," Nick Adams in "Big Two-Hearted River" seems poised to restore human existence to a natural order. Unlike the disoriented fishers and guide of
"Out of Season," Nick is both professionally seasoned and "in season." He
holds out for the perfect moment to eat his hot food and captures grasshoppers for bait before the sun would make them impossibly lively; he will fish
the swamp in time and in timely fashion. And unlike the displaced expatriates of *In Our Time* Nick knows exactly where he is: He "did not need to

get his map out" for he "kept his direction by the sun" and "knew where he was from the position of the river." Oriented in and by the natural world, Nick's journey toward the "good place" of the camp possesses a spiritual dimension absent from the wanderings of characters like the revolutionist or Mr. and Mrs. Elliot (135–39). Carrying a heavy pack like Christian in John Bunyan's *The Pilgrim's Progress* and moving toward a river-baptism, Nick Adams becomes an "Everyman" figure whose function is to redeem whatever is still authentic about that ancient prayer, "give us peace in our time, O Lord." The story thus promises a new beginning and a return to origins: back to the eternal verities of nature; back to Michigan; back to a camp; and even, in a sense, back to a new Indian camp, for the Native-American overtones of the title "Big Two-Hearted River" suggests a close relationship to the land now unsullied by cultural transgressions and exploitations.

Rarely in American literature has landscape been evoked with such scrupulous detail as in "'Big Two-Hearted River," and rarely has landscape evoked human emotions so precisely or forcefully. The story opens in a "'burned-over country" where the ruined town of Seney mutely indicates earlier and greater devastations, like Hortons Bay or the "rubble" (63) of the town where Nick receives his war wound. The scorched land represents a psychic scarring that causes Nick now to "choke" (142) his mind whenever it starts to work and to displace his mental energy into pure, almost mechanical observation and action. Yet Seney's destruction also testifies to all-powerful forces of nature that elsewhere promise renewal. Though "the country was burned over and changed," Nick knows that "it did not matter," for the country "could not all be burned." The river is untouched, and the trout who "changed their positions by quick angles, only to hold steady in the fast water again" still exemplify a grace under pressure that Nick desires to emulate. Even in the scorched land, Nick discovers blackened grasshoppers now adapted to a hostile environment, living proof that natural processes of transformation lead to a country – and mind – that is "alive again" (133–36). Nick's spiritual ancestors are not only Native Americans but American Transcendentalists like Ralph Waldo Emerson and Henry David Thoreau, for whom nature is a living sacrament of an all-pervading Spirit. On the Big Two-Hearted River, the heart of nature responds to the heart of human beings.

If the river is one locus of harmony and regeneration, Nick's camp is the other. After stories of aimless wandering and psychic displacement, the camp possesses the emotional aura of a true homecoming. Inside the tent, for instance, "there was something mysterious and homelike. Nick was happy as he crawled inside the tent. . . . Now things were done. There had been this to do. Now it was done. It had been a hard trip. He was very tired. That was done. He had made his camp. He was settled. Nothing could touch him. It was a good place to camp. He was there, in the good place. He was in his home where he had made it" (139). In its repetitive, staccato rhythm, the passage captures Nick's exhaustion yet also a near-triumphant sense of finality. The "good place" recalls previous enclosed spaces – the Indian cabin, the doctor's garden, Nick and Marjorie's camp, the hotel room of "Cat in the Rain" – without reproducing their scenes of entrapment and unceasing conflict. It nourishes by providing a sense of completion ("things were done") that has been frustratingly absent in previous stories, where actions remain unfinished (the abortive fishing trip of "Out of Season"), unattainable (shooting in the wind in "The Three-Day Blow," being unable to continue skiing in "Cross-Country Snow"), violent (the deaths of Maera and the fathers in "Indian Camp" and "My Old Man"), or ironically complete (the delivery of the cat in "Cat in the Rain"). As a corollary, the camp, which is now his home "where he had made it," affords Nick an unusual experience of control over himself and his environment. (That such control is unusual, the complementary vignettes demonstrate: Maera gored by a bull; Sam Cardinella, bound and hooded, losing control of his bowels; the Greek king imprisoned in the palace grounds.) For Nick, who sleeps "curled up" (142) in the womblike tent, then emerges through the tent-flaps to "look at the morning" (145), the camp signifies a psychic and spiritual rebirth – a self-delivery that recalls and transforms the bloody cesarean of "Indian Camp."

Even in this Arcadian "good place," however, there are ominous signs that Nick's rebirth is more potential than accomplished. Hooking the first big trout makes a mockery of Nick's fantasies of control: "The reel ratcheted into a mechanical shriek as the line went out in a rush. Too fast. Nick could not check it, the line rushing out, the reel note rising as the line ran out." In the aftermath, "Nick's hand was shaky. He reeled in slowly. The thrill had been too much. He felt, vaguely, a little sick, as though it would be better to sit down" (150). The battle with the big fish graphically portrays a world of unendurable pressures and sudden breaks that change faster than Nick can adjust. It suggests the limitation of Nick's measured processes of psychic reintegration while demonstrating why they are emotionally appropriate.

Apart from this scene, the kinds of control Nick exercises over his natural environment might also give us pause. Both parts of the story, for instance, conclude in death. At the end of part 1, a "mosquito made a satisfactory hiss in the flame" as Nick holds a match under it. The incident, minor in itself, takes on ominous overtones in the context of the ensuing scene of Sam Cardinella's helpless death, and still more so in the context of the "burned-over country" with all its stored-up associations of cultural devastation. Likewise, the two gutted fish at the end of the story with "All the insides clean and compact, coming out all together" seem an odd iteration of births witnessed in earlier stories. On the one hand, Nick's killing and cleaning the male fish has a cool emotional tone very different from the bloody and terrifying female process of birth described in "Indian Camp" and chapter 1, intensifying our sense that the absence of women at the river contributes to the recuperation of a man whose freedom in "Cross-Country Snow" is about to be vanquished by Helen, a child, and domesticity. On the other hand, Nick's operation on the fish possesses an unemotional dexterity and is related in a matter-of-fact language that reminds us of the efficient killing fields of chapters 2 and 3 and of the horror-struck events of "On the Quai at Smyrna."

In "Big Two-Hearted River," the solutions to the anguish of our time are partial and fragmentary. Even as the story draws together Hemingway's elemental themes of birth and death, wandering and pilgrimage, spiritual deadness and reawakening, nature and the human being, chaos and the codes of masculine behavior that promise restorative order, it hesitates, like Nick deferring his frightening trip to the swamp, to offer easy answers. "Big Two-Hearted River" uncovers a profound and beautiful emotional resonance in the natural environment even as it discloses the depths of the psychic and existential terrors Nick can barely face. For all its promise of regeneration, the story leaves us with the conundrum of a character who, like the trout who "looked like live fish" (155) in the water even after they have been gutted, seems sentient yet not self-aware, isolated yet incomplete. As if to negate the impression that "Big Two-Hearted River" unifies and centers *In Our Time,* the collection ends instead with the seriocomic L'Envoi, which reintroduces a nursery-rhyme motif ("The king was working in the garden" echoing "The king was in his counting house") and juxtaposes it ironically against contemporary brute reality ("the great thing in this sort of an affair is not to be shot oneself"). Like Nick on the river, the king desires to find freedom in America. Though we have seen that the beauty of Nick's New World garden may be just as illusory as the king's, the rising optimism of Nick's story gives way in L'Envoi to the inversions and chaotic displacements that have characterized *In Our Time* all along: A monarch wishes to voyage to democratic America; a representative of the Greek origins of Western culture is brought low by a catastrophe that might signal its end. All is in transition. Nick, who may fish the swamp, and the king, who may go to America, end somewhere between despair and a salvation still tentatively held out.

In Our Time thus concludes with a dry reminder that its time offers little hope of fairy-tale endings, even one attempted with the anguished determination of a nearly broken Nick Adams. But the book also rejects the apocalyptic finality we might have expected. Though an epic style might have befitted this Greek king, caught like the Agamemnons and Priams of old in the aftermath of colliding empires, his story of displacement and disenfranchisement is actually common among the many stories that document the travails of the lost generation in *In Our Time*. His fate is no more auspicious than Peduzzi's in "Out of Season," who on accepting four lire from the young American feels momentarily like a "member of the Carleton Club" (103) and who also awaits (futilely) his bright tomorrow. It is fitting that Peduzzi, grimy, self-deluding, and scorned in his own village, should rise on occasion to near-heroic stature, for *In Our Time*, like Joyce's *Ulysses* (1922), concerns ordinary people who feel the reverberation of uncontrollable forces yet participate most fully in what W. B. Yeats called the "casual comedy" of life. Hemingway's work is perhaps most astonishing in its capacity to evoke within its small compass such a rich variety of human predicaments and significant but often costly achievements. And it does so with a fervor for experimental writing that never obscures but only intensifies the pathos of the work's struggling survivors, whether Peduzzi, Nick Adams, or a displaced monarch. For our own time of cultural conflicts and inadequate codes of conduct, the work has never seemed so enduring, so relevant, or, though out of its own historical season, so timely.

NOTES

1. The supposition that the wife is pregnant rests in part on her misapprehension of "Tochter" (daughter) for "Doctor" and the many references in the story to "carrying."

2. T. S. Eliot, "*Ulysses*, Order, and Myth," *Dial* 75 (1923): 480.

3. For further details, see Hugh Ford, *Published in Paris: American and British Writers, Printers, and Publishers in Paris, 1920–1939* (New York: Macmillan, 1975), pp. 97–108.

4. The book was actually composed of fifteen vignettes, L'Envoi, and two other vignettes that became "A Very Short Story" and "The Revolutionist" in *In Our Time*. The chapter numbers were given to the vignettes when incorporated into the longer work. "On the Quai at Smyrna" was added in 1930. For a full textual history of the vignettes, see E. R. Hagemann's "A Collation, with Commentary, of the Five Texts of the Chapters in Hemingway's *In Our Time*, 1923–38," *Critical Essays on Ernest Hemingway's* In Our Time, ed. Michael S. Reynolds (Boston: G. K. Hall, 1983), pp. 38–51.

5. In George Plimpton, "Ernest Hemingway," *Writers at Work: The "Paris Review" Interviews* (New York: Viking, 1963), p. 235.

6. For one of the fiercer attacks on Hemingway's alleged misogyny, see Judith Fetterley's chapter on *A Farewell to Arms* in her *The Resisting Reader: A Feminist Approach to American Fiction* (Bloomington: Indiana University Press, 1979).

7. In *A Moveable Feast,* for example, Hemingway wrote that Stein "had also discovered many truths about rhythms and the uses of words in repetition that were valid and valuable."

8. His character is sketched from Hemingway's acquaintance Chard Powers Smith with snide allusions to T. S. Eliot. See Michael Reynolds, *Hemingway: The Paris Years* (Oxford: Basil Blackwell, 1989), pp. 192–93, for more information on writers Hemingway may have used to create this character.

WORKS CITED

Eliot, T. S. "*Ulysses,* Order, and Myth." *Dial* 75 (November 1923): 480–83.

Fetterley, Judith. *The Resisting Reader: A Feminist Approach to American Fiction.* Bloomington: Indiana University Press, 1979.

Ford, Hugh. *Published in Paris: American and British Writers, Printers, and Publishers in Paris, 1920–1939.* New York: Macmillan, 1975.

Hagemann, E. R. "A Collation, with Commentary, of the Five Texts of the Chapters in Hemingway's *In Our Time.*" *Critical Essays on Hemingway's* In Our Time. Ed. Michael S. Reynolds. Boston: G. K. Hall, 1983, 38–51.

Hemingway, Ernest. *Death in the Afternoon.* New York: Charles Scribner's Sons, 1932.

———. *In Our Time.* New York: Charles Scribner's Sons, 1925.

———. *A Moveable Feast.* New York: Charles Scribner's Sons, 1964.

Plimpton, George. "Ernest Hemingway." *Writers at Work: The "Paris Review" Interviews.* Second Series. New York: Viking, 1963, 215–39.

Reynolds, Michael. *Hemingway: The Paris Years.* Oxford: Basil Blackwell, 1989.

5

JAMES NAGEL

Brett and the Other Women in *The Sun Also Rises*

Nothing was ever the same after *The Sun Also Rises*. With the appearance of his first novel on October 22, 1926, Ernest Hemingway's life was forever altered. He was no longer an aspiring young writer, no longer the "promising" writer of a slim volume of short stories, no longer a journalist who also wrote fiction. This book made him, almost instantly, an international celebrity identified with an entire generation, torn by war and grieving throughout the Roaring Twenties for their lost romantic idealism. Although he was somewhat ill-suited for the role, because he was a hard-working young writer with a wife and a son to support, he came to be regarded as the spokesman for American expatriates, those disillusioned and disaffected artists, writers, and intellectuals who spent the decade on the Left Bank in Paris. On a more subtle level, the novel also established Hemingway as one of the most brilliant stylists the United States had ever produced, and his crisp and unpretentious prose changed the nature of American writing. Newspapers and magazines produced decades later bear clear indications of the transformation in style brought about by this remarkable book. This novel also changed American life, as young people began imitating its characters and lifestyle and ingenues abandoned the flapper motif for the short hair and tight sweaters of Brett Ashley. *The Sun Also Rises* was a dramatic literary event, and its effects have not diminished over the years.

But if literary stature came early to Ernest Hemingway, there was little in his background to predict this development. He was born in Oak Park, Illinois, on July 21, 1899, to comfortable, middle-class parents who were devoutly Protestant, politically conservative, and deeply concerned about the attitudes and behavior of their oldest son. His father was a physician with a specialty in obstetrics and a passion for the outdoors, for fishing and hunting and living in the woods, which he felt to be morally instructive. His mother was devoted not to science but to culture and the arts. She had studied voice in New York, debuted at Madison Square Garden, and returned home to be a wife and mother, which she saw as her calling. She insisted that her children embrace her interests, and she saw to it that young Ernest sang in the school choir and played the cello in the orchestra, endeavors for which he seemed to lack aptitude. Indeed, during his school years in Oak Park, Ernest was unremarkable as musician, athlete, or scholar, but he did show promise as a journalist, writing for the school newspaper and literary magazine. After graduation from high school in 1917 he did not follow his classmates to college but used family influence to secure a position on the *Kansas City Star* as a cub reporter. Guided by the stylebook that had helped make the *Star* one of the leading newspapers of the day, Hemingway began the process of forming his mature style, paring away adjectives and metaphor, attempting to describe the way things are, or appear to be, in their particularity. Although he worked at this position for less than a year, it proved to be one of the transitional episodes of his life.

Another such episode arose out of his newspaper work. On the staff was Theodore Brumback, a young man who had just returned from France after a tour of duty as an ambulance driver for the American Red Cross. Because the period of service was only six months, there was a good deal of demand for volunteers, and Brumback and Hemingway decided to enlist for service in Italy. Only a few weeks after his arrival at the front, Hemingway was hit by mortar and machine-gun fire near Fossalta di Piave. Although his wounds were not life-threatening, the bullet in his right knee required surgery in a hospital in Milan, and it was here that he fell in love with a comely nurse named Agnes von Kurowsky. She saw him through his convalescence and agreed to marry him once he was established in a position back in the States. Soon after he returned home in 1919, however, she sent him a letter of rejection, ending, rather painfully, his first real romance.[1] These experiences, and this aborted romance, Hemingway would use a decade later for his first two novels, *The Sun Also Rises* and *A Farewell to Arms*.

Back in Chicago, Hemingway continued his work as a journalist, doing freelance articles for the *Toronto Star* and taking an editorial position on the *Cooperative Commonwealth* magazine. In the autumn of 1920 he met a beautiful young woman from St. Louis, Hadley Richardson, and they were married in 1921. Because Hadley had inherited a modest trust fund, they were free to travel; they moved to Paris, where Ernest continued to write for newspapers but devoted an increasing amount of his time to fiction. The rich cultural milieu of the Left Bank provided Hemingway with his literary education, and under the influence of Gertrude Stein and Ezra Pound, he began producing remarkable short stories for the "little magazines." A small volume, *Three Stories and Ten Poems*, appeared in 1923, followed a year later by two versions of *In Our Time*, containing vignettes and stories that attracted a good deal of attention. It was during this period as well that Hemingway first became interested in the bullfight, and he and Hadley enjoyed long holidays in Spain, especially at the Festival of San Fermín in Pamplona.

It was this fiesta in 1925 that provided the background for *The Sun Also Rises*. The year before everything had been wonderful – the bullfights, the fishing on the Irati, the friendships. But in 1925 there were problems. Hemingway and Hadley went to Pamplona for the fiesta with Donald Ogden Stewart, known for his wit and good spirit, and Bill Smith, with whom Hemingway had fished in Michigan. Joining them was Lady Duff Twysden, bright and beautiful, with a boy's haircut, who was going through a divorce. Her intended, Pat Guthrie, a Scotsman fond of the vine, was part of the group, as was Harold Loeb, who had been the first Jewish student at Princeton. Loeb and Duff had just spent a romantic interlude at the coastal resort of St. Jean-de-Luz. Together all these people marveled at the bullfighting skill of Cayetano Ordóñez, who fought under the name Niño de la Palma. But even the simple things went badly this year. When Ordóñez presented Hadley with the ear of a bull, she left it behind, unceremoniously, in a drawer in her hotel room. When Ernest and Bill went north to fish the Irati, they found it fouled from logging operations. The celebrations in Pamplona degenerated into jealous quarrels, with Hemingway and Loeb nearly coming to blows over Duff. Although they shook hands and apologized, the emotions were tense and the pleasure of the week was compromised. The fiesta had been ruined, and the friendships would never be the same. Yet in these events and feelings Hemingway had found the subject for his first novel.

Hemingway remained in Spain after the festival, writing the first draft of *Fiesta,* as it was then called, in six French notebooks. The central figure was to be the matador, and the events opened in Spain. The narrator was a journalist, alternately called "Hem" and Jake, who had been left impotent as the result of a wound sustained in the World War I. Although Hemingway gave his characters fictional names, essentially he followed the broad outlines of what had actually happened just a few weeks before. Later, back in Paris, he decided to change the focus of the novel, making the central character Brett Ashley and providing two chapters of biographical background about Brett and Jake.[2] The opening action was then set in Paris, with the journey to Spain to follow. Hemingway finished that draft on September 21, 1925, and set it aside to write a satire of Sherwood Anderson's fiction entitled *The Torrents of Spring*. He resumed work on the novel in Schruns, Austria, where he and Hadley spent the winter, and when the revision was complete he sent it off to his new publisher in New York, Charles Scribner's Sons. Meanwhile, F. Scott Fitzgerald read this draft and advised Hemingway to cut the first two chapters, beginning now not with Brett but with Robert Cohn and eliminating the background information about how Brett and Jake fell in love. The novel was published on October 22, 1926, and retailed for the price of $2.00. It was quickly hailed as a fictional masterpiece, widely reviewed in the major newspapers, and Hemingway was suddenly the center of attention. Columnists rushed to describe him, his charm, his manly bulk, and he came to be regarded as a man's man, who wrote dramatic fiction about war, violence, and adventure. That view of him has been sustained in the popular imagination.

Yet *The Sun Also Rises* is much more a novel of character than of event, and the action would seem empty were it not for the rich texture of personalities that interact throughout the book. The foremost among these, inevitably, is Jake Barnes, because it is he who tells the story – in retrospect, after all the events have taken place. It is important to remember that none of the other characters appear in the present; they exist in the narrative only in the memory and telling of Jake Barnes, and he is free to relate incidents and conversations, people and places, as he chooses. At the time of the telling, shortly after the fiesta, he has been through a great deal and cannot be trusted for objectivity. His negative portrait of Robert Cohn, for example, is skewed by his bitterness at the time of the telling, for it is clear that the two men had been good friends in Paris, before Cohn got involved with Brett Ashley.[3] Jake has lost much during the summer of 1925, more than any other person in the book, and the very telling of the novel seems to be a confessional, an attempt to come to terms with what has happened, how his relationships have changed, what remains to give him the strength to get on with his life. His friendship with Robert Cohn has been destroyed; he has compromised his standing among the aficionados of Pamplona, and it would seem unlikely that he can go back for another fiesta, at least not to the hotel run by Montoya; and, most important, his love and respect for Brett have been tarnished. In short, Jake is not the same person after the festival that he was before. If it must be said that he had already lost more than he deserved in World War I, he loses still more during the celebration in Spain, for much of what had sustained him is gone. He is certainly one of the most isolated and vulnerable figures in American literature, and he narrates out of his disillusionment and pain, his grief evident throughout. As he says about himself, all he wants is to figure out how he can live in the world. It would seem that telling what happened is part of the process of learning how to live in the special circumstances of his world.

Those special circumstances derive from a war that had brought devastation to Europe on a scale never before imagined. Over eight million men had died in the trenches, countless others had been mutilated, and the consequences of the destruction were everywhere apparent. Young men, especially, bore the physical and psychological legacy of that experience, and this was a period in which they were, as a group, suspicious of the abstract ideals of courage, heroism, and grand national purpose.[4] Many of them felt uncomfortable in the idealistic and conservative society of the United States after the war, and the initiation of Prohibition with the Volstead Act in 1919 only served to underscore their disenchantment with mainstream America. For the intelligentsia, the trial of John Thomas Scopes in 1925 for teaching evolution, and the national uproar that attended the confrontation between conservative Christianity and modern science, further deepened the rift between the younger generation and established values.

Hemingway humanized this dichotomy in the character of Jake Barnes by creating a man who bears the wounds of the war in a profoundly personal way yet combines his disillusionment with traditional American values of hard work and just compensation.[5] It is surely an oversimplification to see Jake as an uncompromised representative of lost-generation radicalism, for he exhibits much of the midwestern values he sometimes satirizes. He is religious enough to pray frequently even throughout the pagan rituals of the fiesta in Pamplona, yet he mocks Puritanism and literal approaches to Scripture at every opportunity, particularly on his fishing expedition with Bill Gorton. He works hard, takes his profession seriously, and attempts to be just in his dealings with other people, yet he enjoys the mocking of the American middle class that is Bill Gorton's specialty. Above all, it is his judgment that provides the normative sensibility for assessing the people and events of the novel. But to grasp the meaning of what he relates, it is essential to understand the psychological context in which he tells it.

In the few comments he makes about events prior to the summer of 1925, it is clear that he was a pilot in Italy when he was wounded and sent to a hospital in Milan, where he met Brett, a British V.A.D., a nurse's aid. They fell in love, and their relationship apparently deepened until he learned that he was impotent, at which point they thought it best to go their separate ways. In the course of things, Jake was sent to England for convalescence, and there he saw Brett again; they discovered that they were still in love. In material that does not appear in the novel (Hemingway cut it from the manuscripts), Jake explains that he went home to the United States in 1916 to work on a newspaper and to forget about Brett. With a partner, he started the Continental Press Association and made it a success. He moved to Paris in 1920 to handle the news from Europe, and he has been working there for five years when Brett comes back into his life. Although Hemingway excised these details in the course of revision, he added nothing to contradict this basic account of the events that lead up to the beginning of the novel.

In the nine years between London and Paris, Jake has managed to learn how to live in a man's world, devoting himself to his work, to friendships, and to sports, participating in tennis, swimming, and fishing and observing boxing, bicycle racing, and, especially, bullfighting, about which he seems to have sufficient expertise to impress even the Spaniards. His wound has not changed his relationships with men, and he makes friends easily, exchanging banter with strangers and wit with his friends. He loves Paris, derives satisfaction from his profession, and knows how to enjoy even the simple things in life, the streets and buildings and historic locations near his apartment on the Boulevard St. Michel. To the extent that he lives in a man's world, his life is satisfying enough, but his deepest feelings are for Brett Ashley. His love for her, and his pain and disillusionment at the impossibility of their having a life together, underscore everything he relates.

Brett is not only a woman but an extraordinary woman for the age, a point not clear unless she is considered in historical context. From this perspective, the women in *The Sun Also Rises* might be regarded as more interesting than the men. The role of women in society had been changing with each decade for a century, always with a good deal of social conflict and ideological struggle. The fact that Anthony Comstock had been successful in 1873 in lobbying Congress to forbid the dissemination of information about birth control is an indication of where American society had been, and Comstock was still a sufficiently dynamic force in 1915 that President Woodrow Wilson appointed him to represent America at the International Purity Conference.[6] But the culture of the 1920s was something new, embracing the first generation of women to smoke, drink, and use divorce as a solution to a bad marriage.[7] Although American society was changing rapidly, as was evident in the passage of the Nineteenth Amendment on August 26, 1920, which enfranchised women in American politics for the first time, it was no match for the social liberalism of France. By the 1920s there were some eighty feminist societies in Paris enrolling more than sixty thousand women in support of their cause; to some extent their influence on sexual mores and social codes is given embodiment in the character of Brett Ashley.[8]

Brett is by no means the first representation of a sexually liberated, freethinking woman in American literature but rather an embodiment of what became known as the "New Woman" in nineteenth-century fiction. Hester

Prynne in Nathaniel Hawthorne's *The Scarlet Letter* is perhaps the best known of these iconoclastic figures, because her infidelity conflicts so directly with the rigid Puritan codes of the society in which she lives. But even more remarkable is her strength of character in confronting the very culture that has judged her, eventually winning the respect and admiration of the community.[9] Soon after the Civil War, John William De Forest's *Miss Ravenel's Conversion from Secession to Loyalty* featured a Mrs. Larue, who uses sex in a calculated strategy to gain social and financial advantage.[10] By the 1890s, one of the most important decades in American literature, the figure had become common: Celia Madden in Harold Frederic's *The Damnation of Theron Ware*,[11] Edna Pontellier in Kate Chopin's *The Awakening*,[12] Nellie in Stephen Crane's *Maggie*[13] are all strong women who design a code of conduct for themselves that is free of the prescribed gender roles and sexual restraints of traditional society. One of the most remarkable is Rose Dutcher in Hamlin Garland's *Rose of Dutcher's Coolly*. She not only experiments with sexuality but goes on to take a university degree in journalism and to enter a profession in a position equal to that of her male colleagues.[14] When she decides to marry, she does so on the basis of a marriage contract that spells out the mutual responsibilities and equal prerogatives of husband and wife. At the turn of the century, in *Sister Carrie*, a novel based closely on the life of his sister, Theodore Dreiser created Carrie Meeber, who lives with a man without benefit of marriage, leaves him for another man of greater cultivation and social standing, and then deserts him when her career as an actress in New York is well established.[15] That she does so without authorial condemnation, without overt punishment, made Dreiser's first novel deeply controversial.

In the context of American literary history, Brett Ashley is thus not a dramatically new character, nor is she the most socially radical of these New Woman figures.[16] Indeed, in some senses, she is more conservative than the norm of these characters. Unlike Celia Madden, Brett has married, intends to be married again, and would quickly marry Jake if his condition permitted them to live together. Edna Pontellier, of course, despises marriage and the role of wife and mother. Unlike Nellie and Mrs. Larue, Brett is not interested in exploiting her considerable erotic power for economic gain, refusing $10,000 to spend a weekend with Count Mippipopolous, for example. What she shares in common with these figures is an indomitable will and strength of character that allow her to explore her own prerogatives, to forge her own relationships, and to attempt to find pleasure and satisfaction in tragic circumstances not of her making.

Her portrait in the novel is conditioned by the fact that Jake describes her after all the events have taken place – after her indiscretion with Robert, after she compromised Jake with Montoya by seducing Romero, after the pain and disillusionment she has caused Jake. Perhaps that is why the first scene in which Brett appears is underscored with bitterness and disgust and ends in pain and separation.[17] Brett appears, ironically for a woman of unusually active heterosexual appetite, with a group of male homosexuals at the *bal musette* on the Rue de la Montagne Sainte Geneviève, a street named for a French nun, the patron saint of Paris. At the time he first sees her, Jake is in the company of Georgette, a prostitute he picked up for dinner. Both of these lovers are with inappropriate companions, and they gravitate to each other with unstated assurance. Jake is offended by the effeminate manner of Brett's companions, and she jibes him about the restraint of trade that his date represents. From the beginning, the world is out of sexual order, the social evening is a parody of erotic potential, and the deeper irony is that this pathology is at the very heart of Jake and Brett's relationship. Their conversation in the taxi reveals the central problem of the novel: that they love one another, that they feel there is nothing they can do about it, that it is painful and destructive for them to be together (24). Whatever else happens is driven by this fact, and it is impossible for them to change it. The central dilemma for Jake is whether he can change the situation by finding some satisfaction in life. The problem for Brett is that she needs the companionship of a man, and no one but Jake can offer her much beyond fleeting sexual pleasure.

The depth of this dilemma is evident in the second scene involving Brett, when Jake, alone in his apartment, cannot stop the torturous thoughts of her, his wound, and their life apart, and he cries uncontrollably (31). It is clear that Jake is emotionally unstable: His mind starts to work, and he cannot control it. When Brett comes to his apartment with Count Mippipopolous, revealing that the count offered her money to spend a weekend with him, Jake's anguish is only renewed. The next day, when Jake and Robert talk about Brett, it is clear that Cohn is also drawn to her, a situation Jake tries to relieve by informing him that she is engaged to Mike Campbell. Cohn also misinterprets Brett, thinking that she was born to a title, a woman of good breeding, absolutely fine.

The Paris action in book 1 ends with Brett and the count returning to Jake's apartment. When the count asks Jake and Brett why they do not get married, Jake makes an ironic comment about how they want to lead their own lives, and Brett says she wants to have a career. This scene (53–62) reiterates several key points: that they love each other deeply but find their situation impossible; that their affection for each other is evident to the people around them; that Jake's condition is not widely known; that there is little reason to be optimistic that they will find a solution to their problem in the course of the action. When the group moves to Zelli's for an evening of dancing, there is a subtle reminder of Brett's promiscuity when the black drummer in the band waves at her. Biographically, this gesture derives from a widely circulated rumor about Duff Twysden in 1925, that she had left England because of an affair with a black musician. In context, Brett's comment that he is a great friend of hers is ironic, as is the drummer's song about a two-timing woman. Significantly, Jake here provides ellipses, rather than the words, to the rest of the song, and with this reminder of their dilemma, Jake leaves the party. By the end of book 1 Jake has established himself in his narration as a man of sensitivity and deep pain, who loves Brett but finds it agonizing to be reminded of the loss he has suffered. He has introduced Brett as a beautiful woman of impressive erotic attraction, who loves him but can do nothing about it, while revealing her quick insight and wit, her standards for her own behavior, and her needs as a New Woman. The following two books each reveal a different dimension of her personality.

The interaction of the central characters of the novel in book 2 increases the stakes. In this part, the narrative irony of retrospection is dramatically increased, and it should not be forgotten that Jake is telling these events after everything has happened, so that he knows, at the time of rendition, how it will all turn out. This insight is frequently overlooked, so that the drama of the first scene is almost entirely missed. What happens here is that Brett has told Jake that she is taking a holiday in San Sebastian, just as Robert tells him that he will be spending some time in the country. At the time, Jake does not know that they have planned to go off together. Nor is there reason for him to suspect as much, because their only meeting was the brief encounter at the dance. Brett sends Jake a card from San Sebastian saying everything is healthy and quiet, and Jake is free to think about other matters. From the time of the telling, however, the scene is much richer. Jake now knows that they went off together. Robert must have made arrangements with Brett at the dance, or soon after, because very little time elapses between then and their trip. Robert clearly misrepresents the nature of his trip, compromising his friendship with Jake, and Brett lies through omission. Book 2 thus opens on the theme of betrayal, an idea that deepens with each progressive scene.

Jake does not discover the truth about the San Sebastian trip for several weeks. Even when he and Brett have drinks at the Closerie des Lilas on her return, Brett conceals the true nature of her sojourn, passing the experience off as "interesting" if not very enjoyable. Her comment that she never saw anyone there because she never went out, a seemingly innocuous remark, is painfully ironic in its sexual suggestions when Jake eventually realizes that she was with Robert (74–76). Later, at the Café Select, Brett and Mike Campbell, newly arrived in Paris, join the conversation, which quickly turns to Brett's erotic power. Jake observes Brett's legs, noticing that she wears no hosiery. Mike is more direct, commenting repeatedly that Brett is a lovely "piece" and suggesting that they turn in early.

The emphasis on Brett's sexuality and promiscuity becomes more acute in the scene at the Dingo Bar the next day, when Brett confesses to Jake that she went to San Sebastian with Robert (81–84). His anger, and her lack of contrition, reveal the difficulty they are having in working out a strategy of personal interaction. Jake is astonished at the idea that Robert has been invited to join the group in Pamplona, uniting Brett's most recent lover with her fiancé in the highly charged, pagan atmosphere of the fiesta. But Jake cannot foresee Brett's destructive affair there with Pedro Romero.

The Pamplona action is at the heart of book 2, and it places Brett in a world she does not understand. The fact that she has never seen a bullfight suggests that she has not spent much time in Spain and that she knows little of Spanish customs. If Brett as New Woman was very much at home in the progressive atmosphere of Paris, she could not be more alien in the conservative world of traditional Spain, where young ladies are chaperoned until marriage.[18] Here Brett's tight sweaters and short hair, gregarious manner, and social liberties amaze the women of Pamplona, and they constantly stare at her throughout the fiesta (137). Part of the pagan element of the fiesta, she plays the role of Circe, the enchantress who turns men into swine in Homer's *Osyssey;* the men dance around her, literally and figuratively, with strings of garlic around their necks.[19]

The action before the bullfights begin is filled with powerful emotions: the lust of Robert and Mike; Mike's open rage at Robert Cohn, both for the affair and for his obtuse intrusion in Pamplona; and Jake's more disguised pain and disgust at the situation. And at the center of it all is Brett. The only truly healthy scenes in the Spanish section of the novel are the ones when Brett is not present, particularly the fishing trip Jake and Bill take to Burguette. As long as Jake is with her, Brett rekindles his emotional pathology. Even hearing her voice outside his door is painful for him (147) and stresses his isolation and despair. Alone in the night, unable to sleep for thinking about her, he says "to hell with you" to the woman he loves (148). When Jake takes Brett to church with him, he prays devoutly; she then has her fortune told, engaging in a superstition of pre-Christian origin (150–51).

Later, when Jake goes into the chapel of San Fermín, Brett is stopped at the door for not wearing a hat. More and more, Jake and Brett live in different worlds.

When the rocket goes up announcing the beginning of the fiesta, Brett becomes even more the central figure. She has apparently never seen a corrida before, and Jake explains it all to her in great detail. He watches her closely to see how she takes it, especially the goring of the horses. Far from being repulsed, she is fascinated and wants to sit in the front row, close to the action. She is intrigued by the ritual violence in the ring, a counterpoint to the sexual violence all around her, but she is even more attracted to Pedro Romero, the nineteen-year-old bullfighter from Ronda (165). The operative emotion would seem to be lust, not love, because before she ever speaks to him she has decided to seduce him. At the second bullfight, Brett cannot take her eyes off the handsome young matador in the tight trousers. Jake seems to feel that her interest is in the art of the sport, and informs her that the next bull will be the last one. "Not really," she says, implying that *her* next bull will be the matador himself, a prediction that proves correct. That her interest in Pedro is sexual and not a case of admiration of his craft becomes evident later, when he presents her with an ear from the bull he has just killed and she forgets it in the hotel (199).

That she involves Jake in her pursuit of Pedro proves to be doubly destructive, because one of the things that has given value and direction to Jake's life has been his dedication to codes of conduct, none of them more clearly defined, or more deeply felt, than those of the bullring. The conversations between Montoya and Jake are explicit in their admiration of Pedro, in the feeling that he is something special, almost sacred, a person they are obligated to protect. That is why Jake advises Montoya not to give the invitation from the American ambassador to Romero: the fear is that the ambassador and his party are powerful people who do not understand the value of a truly great bullfighter, and their influence might injure him in some way. Jake does not care if they talk to the matador Marcial Lalanda, whose skills are not unique, but there is a clear understanding between Montoya and Jake that Pedro must not be harmed (171–72). It is significant that Montoya discusses this matter with Jake: Pamplona is filled with Spaniards who follow bullfighting, but Montoya does not consult them, it is clear that Jake's understanding of the sport forms a special bond between them.

That is the context for Jake's betrayal of this bond when he introduces Brett to Pedro. In doing so he demonstrates that his loyalty to her is stronger than his commitment to the code of the aficionado. This issue is played out twice. In the first scene, Jake simply invites Pedro to have a drink with them in the café, introducing Brett to Pedro in the normal course of things. Montoya observes this activity with grave disapproval, looking at Brett, her bare shoulders, the cognac Pedro is drinking (177). When Pedro leaves, Brett's comments are focused on sexual attraction, speculating about how he gets into such tight clothes, stressing his good looks. As Jake and Brett leave the group and stroll around town, Brett complains about Robert, how the tension of his presence bores her. Jake comments that having Robert around must be hard on Mike, but he does not articulate the obvious: that it is also hard on him.

This is the moment when, in response to Jake's heartfelt comment that he is still in love with her, Brett confesses that she is a "goner," passionately in love with Pedro (183). Because Brett has only spoken to Pedro once, and then in the most superficial of circumstances, her concept of love seems pathetically juvenile for a twice-married woman of thirty-four, a point she acknowledges when she says she has lost her self-respect and calls herself a "bitch" (183–84). Jake then agrees to facilitate her conquest of Romero, and takes her back to the café. This act is Jake's deepest betrayal of his personal values, and his telling of the details of the scene constitutes a confession, a purgation through rendition. Once Jake sees that Brett and Romero are deeply engaged in conversation, and that the bullfighter understands not only her overt flirtation but the meaning of Jake's departure, that it indicates his approval of the romance, that it will not be an insult to him for Romero to become involved with her, Jake leaves the café. He returns shortly thereafter, glancing into the room from outside, and confirms that they have left. His gaze lingers on the scene until the waiter clears the table, indicating that Jake is not insensitive to what he has done.

A great deal of violence, of all kinds, results from Brett's conquest of Pedro. Robert, who seemed able to deal with the idea of Mike as her fiancé, is violently angry about her affair with Romero. He knocks Jake out in the Café Suizo and then breaks down crying. He has also hit Mike, although not so seriously. Later, Jake learns that when Robert left the café, he went to the hotel and severely beat Romero. Jake, Mike, Robert, and Pedro have all been injured by Brett's desire for a young man half her age, not understanding his world or his stature in it. Robert and Jake, old friends in Paris, will never be friends again. Montoya does not acknowledge Jake when they pass on the stairs, a point that is mentioned three times. Pedro has lost his innocence, and he has been beaten badly in a fight; Mike has lost the woman he intended to marry; and, although she does not yet realize it, Brett has lost another portion of her dwindling self-respect. It is at this point, on the matter of the enormous cost of her sexuality, that book 2 ends.

Book 3, the brief conclusion of the novel, presents yet another side of Brett, the vulnerable woman capable of dependence and contrition, having risen above the simple fulfillment of sensual desire, needing support from Jake. This section is all aftermath; Brett and Pedro are in Madrid as Bill, Mike, and Jake drive together to the coast before separating. Jake has a brief respite in Bayonne and then goes on to San Sebastian, where he gets the telegram from Brett saying that she is in trouble and needs him. That Jake is willing to go to Madrid to assist her indicates that he still loves her, that her indiscretions have not killed that part of him, and that he is resigned to the pain that continued association with her is likely to bring. Brett has had her own painful recognition, realizing that Pedro was ashamed of her, that he wanted to change her, expecting her to grow her hair out and become a proper Spanish woman. The thought of what she has been through makes her weep, in counterpoint to Jake's crying in the early stages of the novel. Brett takes satisfaction in deciding not to be a bitch, but there is little else to give either of them solace. Brett's closing remark, that they could have had a good life together, elicits only a cynical reply from Jake, "Isn't it pretty to think so," which ends the novel.

In the three sections of *Sun*, Jake has shown somewhat different dimensions of the woman he loves – the only woman he will ever love, for he has no chance for another relationship. He can remember the brief relationship they had in the hospital, before he learned of his impotence; he well knows how destructive their relationship is for them now; and only with irony can he contemplate the fine life they might have had together. Jake has shown Brett in Paris to be charming and witty and inordinately sensual, and beneath the surface he has suggested the pain in their lives, the wounds they carry from the war. In the Spanish section he has recounted the physical and emotional violence that derived from her allure and her acquisitive sexuality; and he has ended by revealing his enduring love and her vulnerability. He has grown, as his recounting of the events demonstrates, but he has also made many mistakes, betrayed many values that were important to him. And it has become clear that Brett is the central figure in his psychic drama, the memory he cannot escape, the core of his life even though they can never be married.

But there is yet another context in which Brett must be perceived, for the full complexity of her character requires that she be considered in contrast to the other women in the novel. As a New Woman, she is remarkable not only when measured against men but in comparison to the women around her. It is from this perspective that the secondary female characters in the novel become particularly interesting. These other women function in a variety of ways, from the promotion of lost-generation values, to reminding Jake of what he has lost, to setting Brett Ashley in relief, juxtaposed against alternate models of feminine behavior.

Remembering that everything included in the narrative must mean something to Jake at the time of the telling or he would not bother to include it, characters mentioned only briefly, even in a single line, must have some significance. For example, few readers would remember the name of Katherine Kirby, who is mentioned but never actually appears in the novel, yet the fleeting reference to her plays a dramatic role. When Jake first encounters Brett at the dance, and they take their first taxi ride together, it is clear that they love each other deeply, find the impossibility of their relationship a torture, and think it best to stay away from each other. Jake, in his loneliness, has been able to construct a code of values in work, sport, and daily life that gives him some stability in spite of his loss. In the first complete manuscript, Jake was quite explicit on this point:

> The thing I would like to make my reader believe, however incredible, is that such a passion and longing could exist in me for Brett Ashley that I would sometimes feel that it would tear me to pieces and yet in the intervals when I was not seeing Brett, and they were the greater part of the time, I lived a very happy life.[20]

This insight is dramatized in the published novel, and the precipitating event comes just after his first encounter with Brett when Jake returns to his apartment and opens the wedding announcement from Mr. and Mrs. Aloysius Kirby regarding the marriage of their daughter Katherine. It is this document that sets Jake's mind working: "There was a crest on the announcement. Like Zizi the Greek duke. And that count. The count was funny. Brett had a title, too. Lady Ashley. To hell with Brett. To hell with you, Lady Ashley" (30). This is the stream-of-consciousness scene in which Jake thinks about his wound, about the Ospedale Maggiore where he met Brett after he was wounded, and about seeing her again in England during his convalescence: "I lay awake thinking and my mind jumping around. Then I couldn't keep away from it, and I started to think about Brett. . . . Then all of a sudden I started to cry" (31). The mention of the wedding of Katherine Kirby, a name Jake does not even recognize, serves to remind him of his impossible relationship with Brett. In many ways this is the most emotional incident in book 1, and it shows Hemingway's skill in using indirect suggestion through an apparently casual reference.

In similar fashion a pattern of references reinforces Jake's sense of romantic loss. For example, just after Brett returns to Paris from her escapade in San Sebastian, and before she reveals that she went there with Robert, Jake and Bill take an evening stroll through the streets of Paris, lingering on a bridge to enjoy Notre Dame at night. Jake remembers that "a man and a girl passed us. They were walking with their arms around each other" (77). Hemingway must have thought this reminder of courtship important, for the passage is not in the original manuscript,[21] and he took the trouble to add it later. On the same level is the mention of the husband and wife and young son who share a compartment with Jake and Bill on the trip to Spain (85–88). They are middle-class, conventional, and not very interesting, precisely the sort of people Jake and Bill later satirize, and yet they are an embodiment of the family Jake will be unable to have. Similarly, after the devastation of Pamplona, when Jake swims out to the raft in San Sebastian, he dwells on the young lovers (235) and the Spanish nurse (Brett had been a nurse) with the beautiful Spanish children next to the soldier with one arm (237).

Jake's retrospective observations on the women associated with Robert Cohn are particularly bitter, given the events of the summer. Jake, who can have neither romance nor family, provides the details of Robert's wife and their three children, further discrediting Robert by suggesting that he had squandered in self-indulgence what Jake has come to value so highly. That Robert's wealthy wife left him for "a miniature painter," an interestingly ambiguous phrase, further suggests that he is a failure in love – a matter of little consequence at the time of the first chapter but dramatically pertinent after Brett has run off with, and then rejected, him. That Robert's mother, alluded to but not actually present in the novel, gives him an allowance of $300 a month casts her wayward son in the role of child, in contrast to Jake's self-sufficient status and devotion to his profession.

In this respect it is significant that Hemingway deleted from the manuscript all references to Jake's own mother, the subject of a long passage in the first draft:

> I was quite young and my parents were going through a period of great religious fervour that there were ⟨many⟩ several things my mother said she would rather see me in my grave than do. They were quite unimportant things such as smoking cigarettes, gambling, and drinking and the last two were quite unthought of and far off sins [ms p. 47].

Although this passage continues at length, it casts Jake in the role of son and somewhat ameliorates his isolation in the world. If Jake were to have a mother and family in the United States, and his loneliness and depression became intolerable, he could always go home; his condition would not be so devastating as it is in his solitary despair, with no alternative to his life in Paris. Yet Jake seems a bit old to be dwelling on maternal prohibitions, a concern out of keeping with the jaded and world-weary crowd of Left Bank expatriates. In any event, Jake's reminiscences of boyhood, including the scene in which he and his mother attend the funeral of Uncle Jacob, after whom he was named, were deleted after the first typescript. One excised comment, relating to the funeral, was especially pertinent to Jake's values: "It seemed strange that anything I could do would make her wish to see me in that condition [i.e., dead, like Uncle Jacob] and it ⟨warped me⟩ prejudiced me against all her views and moral values" [ms p. 50]. What young Jake specifically rejects is his mother's cruel Puritanism, which she values even above the life of her son. Jake vows, even as a child, to have nothing to do with it, and it is this memory that originally informs the satiric dialogue between Jake and Bill on the banks of the Irati. The scene is not only a mockery of the simplistic fundamentalism of William Jennings Bryan and his role in the Scopes trial of 1925, but also represents Jake's personal rejection of his mother's Puritanical admonitions. But Hemingway was wise to delete all references to Jake's mother: It would diminish the tragic tone of the novel if Jake's iconoclastic cynicism were portrayed as a rebellion against a supercilious mother rather than as the inexorable and ubiquitous psychological consequence of the war and his wound.

The scenes involving Frances Clyne are particularly resonant considering the time of Jake's narration. On one level, Robert's treatment of Frances stands in direct contrast to Jake's relationship with Brett. Jake has just suffered through the multifaceted humiliations of Pamplona, the recognition of her ignominious fling with Robert, the devastation of her seduction of Pedro Romero, and yet, when she needs him, he goes to Madrid to rescue her. Robert, in contrast, has an affair with Frances for three years, rejects her when he becomes infatuated with Brett, and sends her off to England (69). Jake is obviously the hero in this contrast of personalities, and his telling of it gives him a revenge against Robert that he never enjoys in the action of the novel.

But it is in contrast to Brett that Frances is most interesting. Whereas Brett is loving without constraints, Frances is domineering, jealous, possessive, and determined to marry Robert (5). To demonstrate these attributes, Hemingway has Jake recall a scene in 1924 in which he and Robert and Frances had dinner in Paris. When Jake mentions his plans to take Robert to Strasbourg, where a girl he knows could show them the town, Jake feels a kick under the table and switches his proposed trip to another location. Robert is unable to confront Frances directly and has to excuse himself to explain her jealousy to Jake. "I rather liked him and evidently she led him quite a life," Jake then remarks (7).

The second major scene with Frances takes place a year later, after Robert has become intrigued with Brett. In her desperation, Frances confides in Jake: "We have dreadful scenes, and he cries and begs me to be reasonable, but he says he just can't do it" (47). When the three of them meet for a drink at the Select, Frances baits Robert publicly, talking to Jake about him in the third person and openly voicing his most deplorable traits: "She turned to me with that terribly bright smile. It was very satisfactory to her to have an audience for this" (49). The cruelty of her taunts is too much for Jake, and he escapes by going into the bar: "Cohn looked up as I went in. His face was white. Why did he sit there? Why did he keep on taking it like that?" (51). Here, early in the narrative Jake is relating, Robert is discredited in romance, portrayed as insincere in his relationships and as ineffectual in dealing with women. Frances is presented in terms that contrast directly with Brett's relationship with Jake – her pained acceptance of tragedy, her independence of spirit, her pervading and undemanding love.

The prostitute Georgette Hobin functions in the novel in a similar fashion. The section that Jake narrates about her reveals his sense of irony and suggests for the first time that he is "sick" as a result of the war. Jake's encounter with Georgette allows Hemingway to introduce Jake's sexual dysfunction prior to his meeting with Brett, where the consequences are more deeply felt. It also shows Jake's need of companionship to assuage his loneliness and his ethic of fair compensation, when he leaves money for her at the dance (23). The galley proof of the novel, interestingly, contained another prostitute, a "two-hundred-pound meteoric glad girl called Flossie, who had what is known as a 'heart of gold,' lovely skin and hair and appetite, and an invulnerability to hang-overs."22 This reference was deleted when the first two chapters were cut, leaving Georgette alone in the trade. But his evening with Georgette was not a unique experience for Jake, for he observes that he had dined with prostitutes before, although not for a long time, and had forgotten how dull it could be (16).

As a prostitute with a venereal disease, Georgette embodies the degradation of sex for money, a point underscored by her bad teeth and disastrous smile. She can be a subject of humor only as a flat character, with no real background, no explanation of how she came to Paris, no concern for what became of her. Were she presented with depth, were the situation described from her point of view, a life wasted and without promise, her characterization would be tragic, not unlike that of Jake himself. So it is important strategically that Jake not get involved with her. In the manuscript, Jake kisses her passionately during the taxi ride, bringing him more closely into her world. This passage was deleted before publication, although this scene with her closely paralleled the ride he takes with Brett a few pages later.[23] Having Jake kiss anther woman would diminish the impact of his kissing Brett and make Jake look more like an adventurer than a sincere but hopeless lover. Georgette, who does not like Paris and exchanges sexual favors for money, is persistently set in contrast to Brett, who loves Paris and refuses a great deal of money to go away with Count Mippipopolous. Still, it is suggestive that when Brett comes to Jake's apartment late at night, and has her problems with the concierge, Jake first misinterprets the situation: "Then I heard Brett's voice. Half asleep I had been sure it was Georgette. I don't know why. She could not have known my address" (32). Although this may be no more than the confusion of semiconsciousness, it seems unlikely that the dialect of a Belgian streetwalker would closely resemble that of a British nurse. Some comparison, or contrast, seems called for.

The character of Georgette accomplishes several other things. For one, it demonstrates that Jake is a quick study, sensing that Georgette knows how to play her clients. When she objects to the restaurant Jake has chosen, calling it "no great thing," he responds, "Maybe you would rather go to Foyot's. Why don't you keep the cab and go on?" (16). Later, when they join the other revelers, she becomes the butt of a good deal of humor. Jake introduces her ("I wish to present my fiancée, Mademoiselle Georgette Leblanc") with great irony, not only because of the improbability of his being engaged but because the most famous chanteuse in Paris at the time was the real Georgette LeBlanc, the former mistress of Maeterlinck and also a beautiful lesbian, involved at the time with Margaret Anderson.[24] A savvy reader of the time would recognize the multiple ironies of an impotent man pretending to be engaged to a famous lesbian singer. The context emphasizes how obtuse Mrs. Braddocks is, for she not only does not get the joke but, having had it explained to her, feels it necessary to explain it to others (18). Mrs. Braddock's lack of perception contrasts with Brett's quick assessment of the situation. One additional dimension to the Georgette scene is that the prostitute instantly objects to Frances's arch and domineering manner – a manner Robert was apparently oblivious to all along. Hence this brief scene with Georgette does a great deal for the novel, introducing the central problem with Jake, the ironic sexual humor that pervades the action, the lost-generation pathology eroding the relationships. It may well have been for this reason that when F. Scott Fitzgerald first read the manuscript, he suggested to Hemingway that it begin when Jake picks up Georgette.[25]

Another character almost totally ignored in Hemingway criticism is Edna, the extraordinarily attractive young woman Bill met at Biarritz. Mike speaks to her in terms that parallel those of the earlier scene with Brett. Mike says, "I say, she is a lovely girl. Where have I been? Where have I been looking all this while? You're a lovely thing" (180). Edna goes off with Mike and Bill, leaving Brett with Jake to confess that she is obsessed with Pedro. When Brett leaves to be with Romero, Edna functions as her surrogate in the group: Edna is there when Jake is knocked out by Robert. Later, Jake takes her to see the holding pens before the running of the bulls, as he had with Brett, and she is there in the arena when the bulls come in, screaming as the bulls enter. She wants Mike and Bill to get into the ring with them, and she enjoys the excitement of the fiesta without complications. She and Bill appear to be the only truly healthy people in the novel, although she lacks Bill's delightful humor, and she disappears into the crowd when Brett returns to the group for Pedro's final appearance. As a temporary substitute, she has no place in the group once Brett has come back. Still, Brett emerges as unique even when measured against Edna, who resembles her in many respects, for Edna has no special meaning for Jake, and he does not dwell on her personality.

Viewed in the context of the double time of the novel, and with a special concern for what would be of interest to Jake at the time of the telling, it is not surprising that his narrative should focus on Brett and the spectrum of women around her. Jake's wound, after all, primarily transforms his relationships with women. His orientation to work; his interest in boxing, trout fishing, bicycle racing, tennis, and bullfighting; his lively conversation and masculine camaradarie are not diminished by his impotence, but it compromises his relationships with women, especially his romance with Brett. The depth of his anguish is evident, nearly a decade after he was wounded, in his emotional pathology, in the despair he reveals in his Paris apartment. It makes sense that, as he reviews the events of the summer, he should dwell on the meaning of his loss, the life he and Brett might have had, and what remains for him.

The "loss" in the "lost generation" is sustained primarily by him, and it makes for powerful fiction. The novel works, ultimately, because Jake, in anomalous circumstances, nevertheless presents a normative sensibility in the story he tells. He emerges as a man of intelligence, humor, and good sense who lost more than he deserved in World War I but learned how to make a life for himself. In the summer of 1925, he ruined much of what had sustained him. To come to terms with his emotional devastation, he tells his novel, a cathartic reiteration that focuses not so much on the masculine world of violence and adventure as on Brett and the women who surround her.

NOTES

1. For an account of Hemingway's adventures in World War I, see Henry S. Villard and James Nagel, eds. *Hemingway in Love and War: The Lost Diary of Agnes von Kurowsky, Her Letters, and Correspondence of Ernest Hemingway* (Boston: Northeastern University Press, 1989). This volume contains letters and a diary by Agnes von Kurowsky, letters home by Hemingway, a reminiscence by another ambulance driver who was in the hospital with Hemingway, and other material relating to Hemingway's service in the Red Cross.

2. As Linda Wagner-Martin points out, the original opening presented a much more positive portrait of Brett than does the published novel. In the manuscript the emphasis is on her vulnerability, her fear of being alone, her grace and resiliency. See "Women in Hemingway's Early Fiction," *College Literature* 7.3 (1980): 239–47.

3. For a more detailed examination of the relationship between Jake and Robert Cohn, see James Nagel, "Narrational Values and Robert Cohn in *The Sun Also Rises,*" *Hemingway: From Michigan to the World,* ed. Joseph Waldmeir and Frederic Svoboda (East Lansing: Michigan State University Press, 1994).

4. See Wendy Martin, "Brett Ashley as New Woman in *The Sun Also Rises,*" *New Essays on The Sun Also Rises,* ed. Linda Wagner-Martin (New York: Cambridge University Press, 1987), p. 65.

5. For an excellent discussion of Jake's dedication to the idea of paying for what he receives, see Scott Donaldson, "The Morality of Compensation," *By Force of Will: The Life and Art of Ernest Hemingway* (New York: Viking, 1977), pp. 21–33.

6. See Sibbie O'Sullivan, "Love and Friendship/Man and Woman in *The Sun Also Rises,*" *Arizona Quarterly* 44 (Summer 1988): 80.

7. See Michael S. Reynolds, The Sun Also Rises: *A Novel of the Twenties* (Boston: Twayne, 1988), p. 3.

8. See Martin 68.

9. Nathaniel Hawthorne, *The Scarlet Letter* (Boston: Ticknor and Fields, 1850).

10. John William De Forest, *Miss Ravenel's Conversion from Secession to Loyalty* (New York: Harper, 1867).

11. Harold Frederic, *The Damnation of Theron Ware* (Chicago: Stone and Kimball, 1896).

12. Kate Chopin, *The Awakening* (Chicago: Stone, 1899).

13. Stephen Crane, *Maggie: A Girl of the Streets* (New York: D. Appleton, 1896).

14. Hamlin Garland, *Rose of Dutcher's Coolly* (Chicago: Stone and Kimball, 1895).

15. Theodore Dreiser, *Sister Carrie* (New York: Doubleday, Page, 1900).

16. For an alternative discussion of Brett in the context of the New Woman, see Martin 65–82. Martin does not discuss any of the works to which I refer, however, confining herself to general remarks about the role of the New Woman figure.

17. Ernest Hemingway, *The Sun Also Rises* (New York: Charles Scribner's Sons, 1926), pp. 20–29. All citations refer to this text.

18. For an excellent discussion of the role of Spanish values in the novel, see Edward F. Stanton, *Hemingway and Spain: A Pursuit* (Seattle: University of Washington Press, 1989).

19. The men dance around Brett on p. 155. For the best essay on Brett as Circe, see Mark Spilka, "The Death of Love in *The Sun Also Rises*," *Twelve Original Essays on Great American Novels*, ed. Charles Shapiro (Detroit: Wayne State University Press, 1958), pp. 238–56.

20. Hemingway's earliest manuscripts of the novel have been published as *Ernest Hemingway: The Sun Also Rises. A Facsimile Edition*, ed. Matthew J. Bruccoli, 2 vols. (Detroit: Omnigraphics, 1990). All references to the first manuscript draft of the novel refer to the page numbers in the facsimile edition by Bruccoli, the most accessible source. Because the pagination is continuous throughout these two volumes, I will cite only the page number, as in [ms p. 47]. In the transcription from handwriting, I will use ⟨⟩ to indicate deleted material, {} for Hemingway's insertions, and [] for editorial interpolations and bibliographical data.

21. See *Facsimile Edition* 222. The young lovers on the bridge are nowhere to be found.

22. Frederic Joseph Svoboda, *Hemingway and* The Sun Also Rises: *The Crafting of a Style* (Lawrence: University Press of Kansas, 1983), p. 135.

23. *Facsimile Edition* 89.

24. For more background on the historic Georgette LeBlanc, see Linda Wagner-Martin, "Racial and Sexual Coding in Hemingway's *The Sun Also Rises*," *Hemingway Review* 10.20 (1991): 39–41.

25. See Svoboda 98.

WORKS CITED

Bruccoli, Matthew J., ed. *Ernest Hemingway,* The Sun Also Rises: *A Facsimile Edition.* 2 vols. Detroit: Omnigraphics, 1990.

Chopin, Kate. *The Awakening.* Chicago: Stone, 1899.

Crane, Stephen. *Maggie: A Girl of the Streets.* New York: D. Appleton, 1896.

De Forest, John William. *Miss Ravenel's Conversion from Secession to Loyalty.* New York: Harper, 1867.

Donaldson, Scott. *By Force of Will: The Life and Art of Ernest Hemingway.* New York: Viking, 1977.

Dreiser, Theodore. *Sister Carrie.* New York: Doubleday, Page, 1900.

Frederic, Harold. *The Damnation of Theron Ware.* Chicago: Stone and Kimball, 1896.

Garland, Hamlin. *Rose of Dutcher's Coolly.* Chicago: Stone and Kimball, 1895.

Hawthorne, Nathaniel. *The Scarlet Letter.* Boston: Ticknor and Fields, 1850.

Hemingway, Ernest. *The Sun Also Rises.* New York: Charles Scribner's Sons, 1926.

Martin, Wendy. "Brett Ashley as New Woman in *The Sun Also Rises.*" *New Essays on The Sun Also Rises.* Ed. Linda Wagner-Martin. New York: Cambridge University Press, 1987, 65–82.

Nagel, James. "Catherine Barkley and Retrospective Narration in *A Farewell to Arms.*" *Ernest Hemingway: Six Decades of Criticism.* Ed. Linda W. Wagner. East Lansing: Michigan State University Press, 1987, 171–85.

———. "Narrational Values and Robert Cohn in *The Sun Also Rises.*" *Hemingway: From Michigan to the World.* Ed. Joseph Waldmeir and Frederic Svoboda. East Lansing: Michigan State University Press, 1994.

O'Sullivan, Sibbie. "Love and Friendship/Man and Woman in *The Sun Also Rises.*" *Arizona Quarterly* 44 (Summer 1988): 76–97.

Reynolds, Michael S. The Sun Also Rises: *A Novel of the Twenties.* Boston: Twayne, 1988.

Spilka, Mark. "The Death of Love in *The Sun Also Rises.*" *Twelve Original Essays on Great American Novels.* Ed. Charles Shapiro. Detroit: Wayne State University Press, 1958, 238–56.

Stanton, Edward F. *Hemingway and Spain: A Pursuit.* Seattle: University of Washington Press, 1989.

Svoboda, Frederic Joseph. *Hemingway and* The Sun Also Rises: *The Crafting of a Style.* Lawrence: University Press of Kansas, 1983.

Villard, Henry S., and James Nagel. *Hemingway in Love and War: The Lost Diary of Agnes von Kurowsky.* Boston: Northeastern University Press, 1989.

Wagner-Martin, Linda. "Racial and Sexual Coding in Hemingway's *The Sun Also Rises,*" *Hemingway Review* 10.20 (1991): 39–41.

———. "Women in Hemingway's Early Fiction." *College Literature* 7.3 (1980):239–47.

6

MICHAEL REYNOLDS

A Farewell to Arms: Doctors in the House of Love

A text, as we are now almost too much aware, is never the same text twice. Words once translucent become opaque; issues once current become historical footnotes. The concerns of one generation are rejected by the next only to be rediscovered by their grandchildren in a different context. A century and a half ago Ralph Waldo Emerson told us that each generation has to write its own books. He might have added that each generation also has to reinterpret the books it has inherited from the past. *A Farewell to Arms* was written for the generation who experienced the Great European War that we now call World War I. The next generation of readers brought to the text its experience from World War II. We are now past the third generation with its Vietnam experience and well into postmodernist readings.

The first two generations of readers grew up with the public image of Hemingway engraved on their collective consciousness, a condition that encouraged misleading and frequently irrelevant biographical readings of Hemingway's fiction. The author opened his texts to such readings when he used recognizable prototypes from the Left Bank as characters in his first novel, *The Sun Also Rises* (1926). Afterwards it became an easy generalization to say that Hemingway wrote only about his own firsthand experiences and that his central male character was a thinly veiled self-portrait. This Hemingway Hero, like his creator, grew older as he engaged in the Hemingway interests: bullfighting, hunting, fishing, boxing, and war. That Hemingway never fought in the bullring, hunted African game only twice, never caught a giant marlin on a hand line, was never a professional boxer, and never served as a soldier in any capacity could not dissuade those readers who needed his actual life to be as exciting as his fictive world. That this need was real says more about the period and its readers than it does about the author and his texts.

As late as 1963 the biographical blurb on the Hemingway paperbacks told us that in World War I, Hemingway "served as an ambulance driver and infantryman with the Italian army." Another publisher's blurb tells us that Hemingway "was invalided home, having been seriously wounded while serving with the infantry." The truth was that Hemingway served a few weeks as a Red Cross ambulance driver on the Italian front in 1918 before being injured by an Austrian mortar burst while distributing chocolate to Italian troops on the Piave River. He turned nineteen in the Milan hospital, where he fell in love with an American nurse, Agnes von Kurowsky, who was eight years his senior and who eventually sent him back to America before telling him that she was too old for him. There was just enough correlation to encourage the reading of *A Farewell to Arms* as Hemingway biography.

We should have known better. Frederic Henry's experience on the Italian front bears only superficial resemblance to that of his author. Frederic is older, more sexually experienced, more widely traveled, and better read than was Hemingway at nineteen. Frederic, fluent in Italian, is an insider; befriended by bar men and diplomats, he understands the war in a way that young Hemingway never did in Italy. When Frederic tells us, "In the late summer of that year we lived in a house in a village that looked across the river and the plain to the mountains," he speaks of a time and place that Hemingway never experienced. "The late summer of that year" is August 1915, when Hemingway was at Walloon Lake preparing for his sophomore year in high school. Hemingway had never seen Frederic's terrain before he wrote the novel. He had never been to Plava, where Frederic is wounded; he had never been on the Bainsizza plateau, where Frederic is stationed the morning of the massive Austrian breakthrough at Caporetto. During the October 1917 retreat from Caporetto, Hemingway was a cub reporter in Kansas City. By the time he reached the Italian front in June 1918, the battle lines on the Venetian plain were far removed from Gorizia and the Isonzo River. In the early 1950s when Carlos Baker was preparing his seminal study, *Hemingway: The Writer as Artist* (1952), he asked Hemingway about Frederic Henry's wounding on the "Piave River." In reply Hemingway pointed out that he, not Frederic, was wounded on the Piave. Lt. Henry's wounding, he said, was on a different river altogether.[1]

It was not until the 1970s that readers began to compare the novel's specific topography and military references with the Italian terrain and the detailed accounts of the Great European War as it was fought in northern Italy. We discovered that *A Farewell to Arms* was a map accurate down to the smallest details, that the Friulian plain, the river crossing at Plava, the streets of Milan, Frederic's retreat from the Bainsizza, and his night journey up Lake Maggiore were so accurately described that one could follow the novel's progress on large- and small-scale maps (see Reynolds, *Hemingway's*

First War). We found that every battle Frederic mentions was, in fact, an actual engagement whose results were accurately reported. The Italian debacle at Caporetto was so embarrassingly accurate that the fascist government banned the novel from Italian publication until after World War II. Italians who had taken part in the retreat assumed that Hemingway had been with them, for how else could he have been so knowledgeable about troop behavior, weather and road conditions, or the precise timetable of the retreat? At the Tagliamento River bridge, Frederic encounters the drumhead court that is executing deserters and suspected spies. Only the Second Army, to which Frederic belongs, crossed at the Codroipo bridge, and it was only at this crossing that such executions took place. Later, when Frederic leaps aboard the train at Latisana, he smashes his head against a piece of heavy artillery; Lt. Henry does not know that it belongs to the First Army, but Hemingway has positioned his character with the precision of a travel agent to meet this train.

Once we examined these details, which were more important to the writer than the reader, their source became rather obvious: Hemingway had to read a lot of books researching the background for his fiction. On the morning of the Austro-Hungarian breakthrough at Caporetto, Frederic Henry tells us that on the Bainsizza plateau, "the Croatians came over across the mountain meadows and through the patches of woods and into the front line" (186). As Austrian battle maps and postwar histories showed, the Bainsizza was the only place on the entire northern Italian front where Croatian troops were deployed. The accurate detail of Hemingway's military narrative came from his postwar reading, not from firsthand experience. For almost any other author, such reading and research would have been expected, but Hemingway's public image with its attendant anti-intellectual pose prevented such assumptions and encouraged a certain condescension on the part of critics. That first generation of critics was in awe of Joyce, Pound, and Eliot, who wore their intellectual credentials on their sleeves; those same critics saw Hemingway as a talented but primitive naif who did not understand his fiction so well as they. What else could they, with their Ivy League degrees, think about a young writer with only a high school education? It was not until the 1980s that the full picture of Hemingway's self-education emerged. Now we know that each year between 1910 and 1940 about two hundred books passed through his hands. When he died, he left six thousand to eight thousand books in his Cuban library.[2]

As the literary history of the novel emerged, its revelations undermined the public Hemingway image and set *A Farewell to Arms* free to become a classic on its own merits rather than as Hemingway biography. Intertextual references, previously unsuspected because we knew the naif Hemingway would not do such a thing, now became apparent. The author left us plenty of clues, but we were slow learners. In 1942, when Hemingway edited a collection called *Men at War,* he said in his introduction,

> The best account of actual human beings behaving during a world shaking event is Stendhal's picture of young Fabarizio at the battle of Waterloo. . . . Stendhal served with Napoleon and saw some of the greatest battles of the world. But all he ever wrote about war is the one long passage from "La Chartreuse de Parme."(xx)

It took us another thirty years to take seriously the possibility that there might be some relationship between *A Farewell to Arms* and *The Charterhouse of Parma.*[3]

When the holograph manuscript was opened to scholars (c. 1970),[4] overt intertexual references, which had disappeared in revision, suggested other avenues, some of which have yet to be explored. For example, the relationship between Hemingway and T. S. Eliot has drawn little critical interest despite the several signs pointing the way. Hemingway's library included everything Eliot ever published, including his essays. In first draft, when Frederic wakes from his operation, he tells us, "It is not like death's other kingdom" – a clear reference to Eliot's "The Hollow Men" (1925). Among the long list of possible titles for the novel, Hemingway included a revised quote from Marlowe's *The Jew of Malta:* "I have committed fornication but that was in another country and besides the wench is dead." He might have read Marlowe, but a closer source was Eliot's use of the same quote as his epigraph to "Portrait of a Lady." When the German translation of *A Farewell to Arms* appeared, it was titled *In Ein Andern Land,* and the quote from Marlowe appeared as the translation's epigraph.

In the past ten years, critical readers have come to the text less in awe of its author, less encumbered by the baggage of their fathers. The posthumous publication of Hemingway's *Garden of Eden* with its strong androgynous theme has also been therapeutic for readers, giving them good reason to reexamine earlier works. As a result we are now looking more closely at Hemingway's art and less closely at the artist's private life. Interesting work is being done of Frederic as narrator, on the narrative devices themselves, and on the characters from feminist and Lacanian perspectives. Postmodernists are beginning to realize that Hemingway texts, above or below the waterline, are frequently concerned with the problems of the writer writing. And the old historicism has recycled as new historicism, adding Marxist concerns, which someone soon will apply to the subtext of social unrest that

Hemingway has embedded in this novel. My interest here, less theoretical, is in the novel's medical concerns, which have become opaque over time.

If, as Hemingway often said, one should write about what he knew best, then it is no surprise that the fiction of a doctor's son should involve medicine. *In Our Time* opens with Dr. Adams performing a cesarean section without anesthetic on an Indian woman while her husband, unable to stand his wife's screams, cuts his own throat with a straight razor. In "Cross-Country Snow," Nick, the doctor's son, is informed about the incidence of goiter among the Swiss, and when he realizes the waitress is pregnant, he wonders that he did not immediately spot her condition. Later, in "Big Two-Hearted River," Nick threads the hook through the grasshopper's thorax and into its abdomen with a surgeon's attention to detail.

In Oak Park, young Hemingway grew up with his father's medical practice, the daily routine of which indexed his days: patients coming to the doctor's home office for examination; Clarence Hemingway making house calls, first by horse and buggy, later in his black Ford; hospital rounds in the afternoons; and always the doctor carrying his black medical bag of authority. In his youth Hemingway became acutely aware of pregnant women. Grace, his mother, had four more babies before he graduated from high school, and Clarence's practice, after his 1906 course at New York's Lying-In Hospital, was increasingly obstetric. Like most children in medical families, Hemingway grew up fascinated by the mysteries in his father's medical books, first the pictures and later the texts; in the doctor's office, there hung a full-sized articulated skeleton, "Suzy Bones." From knowledge read, overheard, observed, and guessed, Hemingway was far wiser than his boyhood contemporaries about birth, death, and what lay between them, and that knowledge both informs and silently supports the text of *A Farewell to Arms*.[5]

Clarence Hemingway, invisible and silent, is a lurking presence throughout Frederic's narrative. At Key West in 1928, when Hemingway had barely one hundred manuscript pages of *Farewell* in first draft, Clarence and Grace appeared for a day's visit on their way back from a Havana vacation. The doctor's son did not need a second opinion to know his father was ill, nervous, and worried. Eight months later, with his draft complete, he visited briefly in Oak Park: His father was no better. A month later, Clarence, unable to save himself, placed a Smith & Wesson pistol against his right temple and permanently put out the light. Hemingway hurriedly returned to Oak Park to bury his father, shore up his mother's finances, and begin revising his novel in which doctors, competent or not, cannot save Catherine or her baby.

Battered heads, broken bones, auto accident, gun shot wounds to the spine, leg, stomach, head, horn wounds, gangrene, venereal disease, dysentery, shell shock – the Hemingway canon reads like Saturday night at the emergency room. *A Farewell to Arms,* in many ways, epitomizes this violence that we have come to know as what happens "in our time." Following Frederic Henry on his journey into loneliness, we see what war can do: Passini loses both legs and his life to the trench mortar shell; Frederic, leg wounded and skull possibly fractured, lies helpless in the ambulance while a nameless casualty bleeds to death above him in the dark; the deserting sergeant is casually shot and killed; Aymo is killed by the Italian rear guard; at the river, two officers are executed by firing squad; Catherine hemorrhages to death in Lausanne. Out of sight, thousands die from cholera.

Some, like Lt. Henry, survive to carry their wounds with them. In the Milan hospital where Frederic recovers first from surgery and then from jaundice, he is not alone: "There were three other patients in the hospital now, a thin boy in the Red Cross from Georgia with malaria, a nice boy, also thin, from New York with malaria and jaundice, and a fine boy who had tried to unscrew the fuse-cap from a . . . shell for a souvenir."[6] When Frederic returns, slightly limping, to Gorizia, he finds his friend, the surgeon Rinaldi, depressed by his possible case of syphilis, for which he prescribes his own treatment. "We put our faith in mercury," Rinaldi says. Or Salvarsan, the major reminds him. "A mercurial product," Rinaldi mistakenly replies (175). In those days before penicillin, the standard treatment for syphilis was mercuric chloride salve and intramuscular injections. By World War I, mercuric compounds were used in conjunction with Salvarsan, a trivalent arsenic compound also known as 606; Salvarsan and mercury, both potentially poisonous heavy metals, were alternately injected to kill the spirochetes. Painful and potentially poisonous, the injections were repeated over an eight-day period with sometimes satisfactory results.[7] That the surgeon should be so infected is ironic; that he should give Frederic advice about women is doubly ironic.

For that first generation of readers, Salvarsan needed no explanation, for syphilis was a disease whose painful cure was uncertain and whose progress was horrific. The World War II generation, secure with its new antibiotics, could afford to forget Salvarsan and the fear of syphilis. The postmodernist reader may not understand the word "Salvarsan" but he does not joke about venereal disease as his father did, for this is the age of AIDS. Were Hemingway writing the book today, Rinaldi would have been HIV-positive. "What if I have it," Rinaldi says. "Everybody has it. The whole world's got it." (175). As, indeed, the whole world of Hemingway's fiction appears sick unto death; the vineyards and fruit trees of the Friulian plain may regenerate with spring, but the war, without end in sight, celebrates spring with a new offensive. Into this sick world come Frederic and Catherine, whose desperate love is made in the face of death, made in the world of hospitals and doctors whose cures are temporary at best and deadly at worst. Nowhere in Hemingway's fiction are we more aware of medical details, specific treatments, hospital rooms, and the demeanor of doctors than in *A Farewell to Arms*.

Although *A Farewell to Arms* is commonly referred to as a great war novel, over half the novel takes place in hospitals where numerous nurses and doctors treat the several diseases, wounds, conditions, and complications that determine the narrative's flow. Frederic meets Catherine in the Gorizia hospital, makes his first pass at her in a hospital garden, beds and bowers her in the Milan hospital, and watches her die in the Lausanne hospital. In the process, the lovers exchange roles: Catherine is nurse to Frederic's wounds in Milan; at Lausanne, Frederic, disguised in white, turns the bedside knob on the gas to dull Catherine's labor pains.[8]

Throughout the narrative there are medical signs to be read, most of which center on the condition and treatment of the laconic narrator, Frederic Henry. At Plava in the field emergency station, the doctor examines Frederic's legs, both of which are filled with Austrian shrapnel, and notes: "Profound wounds of right knee and foot. Laceration of the scalp . . . with possible fracture of the skull" (59). When Rinaldi visits Frederic at the field hospital, he says there is no fracture, that the field doctor, a captain, was a "hog butcher" (64). This new diagnosis is significant: With a fractured skull, Frederic was told at Plava not to drink too much brandy in order to avoid inflammation (60). He probably should not be getting drunk on the cognac Rinaldi brings, nor should he be drinking as much as he does in the Milan hospital, where the nurse Ferguson asks Frederic about his head wound. There is a numbness at the wounded place, but he says it does not bother him. "A bump like that could make you crazy," she tells him. Not until Frederic and Catherine are snuggled down at the Guttingens' cottage above Montreux do we hear again of the wound. "I want to feel the bump on your head," Catherine says. "It's a big bump" (298). Two days later, she reminds her lover that she was "nearly crazy" when they first met. All of these signs ask us to examine Frederic's narrative with more attention to his medical condition, for he is wounded in flesh, mind, and spirit more deeply than he ever tells us outright.

Much of Frederic's treatment and its attendant signs have become rather commonplace, and we tend to read past these medical details in the same way children read past obligatory paragraphs of setting in their impatience for the action to begin. For example, in the field station at Plava, Frederic is immediately given a shot of "antitetanus" before his wounds are cleaned. In 1914, the first year of the war, the British lost eight out of every one thousand wounded to tetanus infection. In agrarian landscapes, where most of World War I was fought, cow and horse dung carry the tetanus bacilli to the soil, where they remain active indefinitely.[9] By April 1916, when Frederic is injured, medical practice prescribed "early, near-universal use of [tetanus] antitoxin, accompanied by meticulous debridement of wounds." By 1918 the tetanus rate among wounded had fallen to 0.16 per thousand.[10] Once the doctor is finished, he assures Frederic that he has "nothing to worry about if it doesn't infect and it rarely does now" (60). By 1917 excision of damaged tissue and application of a general antiseptic like iodine or bichloride of mercury had greatly reduced the incidence of infected wounds.[11]

At the new American hospital in Milan, the thin Italian doctor, with refined distaste for what may be his first war wound, numbs areas of Frederic's legs with "snow" as he probes for shrapnel. In World War I, liquid ethyl and methyl chloride sprays were available to "freeze" the body surface for localized surgery, but excessive use carried the danger of gangrene setting in afterwards. Another method used liquid carbon dioxide: "The fluid CO_2 is passed into a metal tube or the container is filled with closely packed CO_2 snow. Anesthesia is produced by contact of the metal tube with the skin."[12] On Frederic, the doctor used "something or other 'snow,'" which was probably a methyl chloride spray. As Frederic tells us, when the doctor's probe went too deep, the "anesthetized area was clearly defined by the patient" (94).

From the field hospital, the major quickly moved Frederic on to Milan, where there were "better x-ray facilities" (75). Given the nature of the wounds, the field doctor was following what had become standard military procedure: "An x-ray examination should be made in every case of joint wound, irrespective of whether the missile is retained or not, as an unsuspected foreign body or a bone injury discovered before hand may modify the operative procedure."[13] At Ospedale Maggiore, the "excitable, efficient and cheerful" doctor arranges Frederic so that he can "see personally some of the larger foreign bodies through the machine" (94). Stretched out on the x-ray table, with the x-ray tube positioned beneath him, Frederic is sitting up, his legs flat against the surface. When the x-ray tube is turned on, he and the doctor can see bones and embedded shrapnel on the green, fluoroscopic plate positioned above the wounds.[14] With the shrapnel precisely located, the tube was turned off, the fluoroscopic screen replaced with the unexposed x-ray plates, and the permanent photographs made. Although Eastman Kodak had developed an x-ray film before the end of the war, most hospitals continued to use glass plates through 1918.[15]

When the plates are developed and delivered to the American hospital, Catherine holds them up to the light, telling Frederic, "That's your right leg. . . . This is your left" (95). Later, when the house doctor and two colleagues arrive, Frederic tells us:

> I have noticed that doctors who fail in the practice of medicine have a tendency to seek one another's company and aid in consultation. A doctor who cannot take out your appendix properly will recommend to you a doctor who will be unable to remove your tonsils with success. These were three such doctors. (95)

The house doctor, examining the x-rays, mistakes the left leg for the right leg, confirming for the reader Frederic's judgment and centralizing the issue of competent and incompetent physicians. Told that he must wait six months for the shrapnel in his knee to encyst and the synovial fluid to reform before an operation can be safely done, Frederic demands a second opinion, refusing to let a first captain operate on him. "If he was any good," Frederic says, "he would be made a major" (98). The house doctor promises to send Dr. Valentini, who arrives laughing, tanned, and extremely confident. In fact, he talks and acts a good deal like Rinaldi, sharing a cognac with his patient. Frederic notes that he is a major and that he makes no mistakes with the x-ray plates. Telling Frederic that he will operate in the morning, Dr. Valentini leaves with the promise to bring Frederic better cognac. As the chapter ends, Frederic tells us again: "There was a star in a box on his sleeve because he was a major" (100).

While Frederic may place his faith in rank, the "competent" surgeons have other shared characteristics. Rinaldi, the doctor at Plava, and Dr. Valentini are all supremely confident in their abilities, sure and quick in their judgments, and good-humored. All three provide Frederic with brandy. Rinaldi and Valentini make sexual jokes about Frederic's relationship with Catherine and give him advice beyond medical. These three doctors, cut from the same bolt of cloth, are contrasted with the other three, who are altogether too serious, make no jokes, share no brandy, and are judged incompetent. None of those Frederic regards as competent bear the least resemblance to Clarence Hemingway, who did not drink, curse, or joke, and who had volunteered to deliver his son's second baby. Ernest and Pauline declined the offer.

The three physicians admired by Frederic are not tutors nor the bearers of behavioral codes: Frederic takes on none of their stoicism, none of their protective facade of humor. The irony of their competence passes without comment: Because Valentini is skillful, Frederic is returned to the front six months earlier than he would have been by the incompetent surgeons. This irony extends up and down the battle lines of the war. The more competent the medical services, the more likely the wounded will survive to return to the trenches where they can suffer more violence. Frederic, the ambulance driver, thinks Valentini is "grand." Catherine, a nurse's aid, does not care for the doctor's masculine bluster or the way he looks at her, but imagines "he's very good" (102).

On the morning following Dr. Valentini's visit, Catherine prepares Frederic for surgery with an enema, but the details of his operation are elided. Waking from anesthesia, Frederic tells us that "They only choke you. It is not like dying it is just a chemical choking so you do not feel, and afterward . . . when you throw up nothing comes but bile" (107). From these after-effects, we can surmise that Frederic was anesthetized with liquid ether dripped over a nose cone, or a gaseous mixture of ether and oxygen administered through a mask. Both methods were in wide use during the war.[16] Frederic wakes to find his leg elevated in a heavy cast supported by sand bags.

Had Frederic been wounded sixty years earlier in the American Civil War, his medical treatment would have been quick and final: At the field hospital, his leg would have been taken off at the knee, the stump cauterized, and he would have been sent away on crutches. Turn-of-the-century discoveries at the extremes of the light spectrum as well as improved operating techniques and a better understanding of infection and its prevention enabled World War I surgeons on both sides to save limbs that would have once been amputated. Through the Milan summer and into the fall, Frederic recuperates from his surgery and undergoes rehabilitation at "Ospedale Maggiore for bending the knees, mechanical treatments, baking in a box of mirrors with violet rays, massage and baths" (117). All of Frederic's therapy, then relatively new and unproven, was the beginning of what we now take for granted in physical rehabilitation: mechanical devices to retrain the muscles, heat therapy, massage, and water therapy. The "box of mirrors" reflected ultraviolet rays on Frederic's knee; this light therapy killed germs, reacted with ergosterol in the skin to produce vitamin D, and, as was later discovered, sometimes produced skin cancer.

None of this rehab, one notes, speaks to Frederic's head wound, nor does Frederic refer to it without prompting. Most of the novel's first-generation readers would have been particularly sensitive to this wound, for the media had educated them to the latest hazard of modern warfare – "shell shock." In World War II we called it "battle fatigue," in Vietnam, "post-traumatic shock syndrome." Its causes and its effects were so various that the term – shell shock – was vague at best. In extreme cases where a soldier was in close proximity to an artillery blast, the result could be death even when there were no surface wounds. The extreme overpressure of the explosion alone could cause internal hemorrhaging and death. The lesser effects of shell shock were frequently bizarre. The victim might remain mute for weeks afterward, or partially paralyzed, or suffer from amnesia; he might begin to stutter inexplicably or develop a different personality. His "moral tone" might "be changed for the worse" or he might have "altered feelings, affection, temper, or habits in general." He might also develop "melancholia, mental confusion, delusion and hallucinatory disturbances." He might suffer from headache, insomnia, or terrifying dreams.[17] After his night wounding, Frederic prefers to sleep during the day rather than at night unless Catherine is sleeping with him. In the Milan hospital, he wakes "sweating and scared," and then goes back to sleep "trying to stay outside" his dream (88). In one of his few moments of confession, Frederic says, "I know the night is not the same as the day: that all things are different, that the things of the night cannot be explained in the day, because they do not then exist, and the night can be a dreadful time for lonely people" (249). When Count Greppi asks him if he has religious belief, Frederic tells him that his belief comes only at night (263).

Despite Frederic's reticence, his behavior should let the reader see that he has been changed by his violent wounding. Before the blast at Plava, Frederic treated his relationship with Catherine as a game. When she slaps him for attempting to kiss her, he tells us, "I felt I had a certain advantage. . . . I was angry and yet certain, seeing it all ahead like the moves in a chess game" (26). Four days later, in the garden, Catherine says, "You did say you loved me, didn't you?" Frederic tells us, " 'Yes,' I lied. 'I love you.' I had not said it before" (30). And later, "This was a game, like bridge, in which you said things instead of playing cards. Like bridge you had to pretend you were playing for money or playing for some stakes" (31). After Frederic's wounding, he is a changed man. When Catherine walks into his hospital room in Milan, we are told, "When I saw her I was in love with her. Everything turned over inside of me. . . . God knows I had not wanted to fall in love with her. I had not wanted to fall in love with any one. But God knows I had." Before the blast at Plava, Frederic was certain that he would not die in this war; afterwards he has lost this false sense of immortality. Vulnerable and crippled, he turns somewhat desperately to Catherine for support. Call it love, call it need, call it psychic dependence, but the only difference between Frederic in the nurse's garden and in the Milan hospital is his violent wounding. Like a victim of shell shock, he exhibits altered feelings, affection, temper, and habits.

However, as much could be said about Catherine Barkley, whose behavior is certainly erratic enough to compare with Frederic's. In fact, Catherine exhibits many of the traits associated with war stress on the home-bound women who each day scanned the military casualty lists for the names of their husbands, sons, and lovers. When we first meet her, in April 1917, we discover that her fiancé of eight years was killed in the battle of the Somme, which began on the Western Front in July 1916. The British forces lost sixty thousand men on the first day of the Somme; five months later six hundred thousand British men were dead. The autumn rains turned the mud so deep that men drowned in it. When the battle was declared over, the front lines remained much as had been; nothing had changed except for the deaths. Catherine tells Frederic that she began her nursing career at the end of 1915, when her fiancé enlisted. She says, "I remember having a silly idea he might come to the hospital where I was. With a saber cut, I suppose, and a bandage around his head. Or shot through the shoulder. Something picturesque. . . .He didn't have a sabre cut. They blew him all to bits" (20). Had she known what the war would be like, she would have married him before he left: "I could have given him that anyway," she says (19).

During Frederic's next two visits with Catherine, her behavior is erratic and perplexing. First she slaps him when he attempts to kiss her; then she allows the kiss, which ends with her crying on his shoulder, saying, "You will be good to me, won't you? . . . Because we're going to have a strange life" (27). Frederic is pleasantly confused. On his third visit, Catherine becomes a different woman altogether, instructing him in his role, telling him what to call her and how to say certain phrases. She is, quite obviously, acting out a reunion with her dead fiancé. Frederic tells us that "she was probably a little crazy. It was all right if she was. I did not care what I was getting into" (30). Just as suddenly Catherine "came back from wherever she had been" and tells him that they are playing a rotten game that is over for the evening. She tells her confused would-be lover, "I had a very fine little show and I'm all right now. You see I'm not mad and I'm not gone off. It's only a little sometimes" (31). He tries to continue the game to press his sexual advantage, but she cuts him off, telling him that his pronunciation of her name sounds nothing like her dead fiancé's voice. Later Catherine and

Frederic will joke about this night when she was "Scotch and crazy," but there is no laughter as they part, and Frederic makes no comment.

Except for a brief moment when she gives Frederic a Saint Anthony medal before his wounding, Catherine does not see him again until she is transferred to the Milan hospital. When she walks into his room, Frederic's legs are bandaged and he has a head wound not unlike the one Catherine once imagined for her fianceé. Here her fantasy of caring for her wounded man is carried out in reality. No sooner is she in the room than she is in his bed, nurse and lover to her supine soldier. Their sexual union makes them both more whole, relieving Catherine's guilt for not giving herself to her dead fiancé while comforting Frederic's night fears. Both are living for each other's moment, completely interdependent. As the summer waxes, Frederic becomes her religion, and he replaces the lost company of soldiers with his love for her. As they learn at the San Siro track, life is a fixed race in which there are no winners. Support must be taken and given when chance permits, for against the backdrop of the Italian front, they are but inconsequential specks whose lives will be missed by no one but each other. Both he and she are war wounded, and both use each other, in the best sense, to bind those wounds.

There, in their hospital bed, Catherine becomes pregnant while Frederic recovers from his surgery. Frederic says that he worries about "having a child" and offers to marry Catherine, but she refuses because a married nurse would be sent home. So they tell themselves they are married without benefit of ceremony, but Frederic admits, "I suppose I enjoyed not being married, really" (115). Catherine keeps her pregnancy to herself for three months, before telling Frederic. She says, "I did everything. I took everything but it didn't make any difference" (138). For those postmodernists who grew up with the birth control pill, Catherine's statement may seem disingenuous. For those who know of Margaret Sanger's long fight to bring birth control information into public domain, Catherine's problem might appear to be a lack of contraceptive means. Neither supposition is correct. In 1918 no available contraceptive was as effective as the birth control pill would prove to be in the 1960s. However, there were several methods of contraception available to both Catherine and Frederic. Sanger's fight was to promote understanding of those methods that were known and practiced by most of the educated Western world. Frederic, for example, certainly knew about the condom, a device available in limited quantities from the mid-nineteenth century and perfected during World War I using the vulcanizing technology developed in sealing and repairing air balloons. Catherine's choices were wider. She could have used a douche, a sponge, a cervical cap, or a diaphragm in conjunction with a lactic or boric acid spermatocide, methods widely available in 1917. She also might have used an intrauterine device (1909) such as a loop made of cat gut or silver.[18]

What Catherine may have *taken* is more problematic. In 1917 there were no oral contraceptives, but folk pharmacology did prescribe certain drugs that were believed to interrupt a pregnancy. Quinine, for example, taken in large doses, was thought to terminate a pregnancy, and ergot, used obstetrically to start or complete uterine contractions, might eliminate a pregnancy in the first trimester. In fact, though, none of the drugs then available were particularly effective in terminating a pregnancy. That the nurse, Catherine, would have tried to prevent, or even terminate conception is understandable; that Frederic apparently left the problem to her says a lot about male lack of responsibility at that time.

Books 3 and 4 have almost no medical detail: Frederic retreats with the Second Army only to desert at the river; Catherine abandons her nursing duties; they reunite at Stresa and escape into Switzerland, where her pregnancy proceeds toward term without apparent complication. In early spring, just as the war renews itself, Catherine goes into labor in the Lausanne hospital. Most of book 5 focuses on that last day of Catherine's life. The reader watches as she slowly crumbles under the pain of her extended and fruitless labor. Frederic, having played many false roles, finds himself in white doctor's garb in the prep room, administering the pain-numbing gas to Catherine. The gas was nitrous oxide, an analgesia in fairly common use by 1918. Masking the pain, it was found, did not interfere with the delivery process up to the point of the actual delivery. Catherine's somewhat giddy responses during the early stages of her delivery can be attributed to the nitrous oxide, sometimes called "laughing gas." By 1915 the gas was thought to be "the ideal drug for conducting labors. It is the most volatile of anesthetics, in that it acts more quickly, and its effects pass away very rapidly. It is practically free from danger even when continued . . . over many hours."[19] However, prolonged use beyond six hours was not suggested. Catherine begins labor at three in the morning. She is not taken to the operating room until roughly seven in the evening after using the gas for over twelve hours. By the time the doctor and Frederic have decided to perform a cesarean section, the gas no longer effectively blocks her pain. Frederic turns the dial on the gas regulator to three and then four. "I wished the doctor would come back," he says. "I was afraid of the numbers above two" (323).

After Catherine has been in labor the entire day, the doctor tells Frederic that she appears unable to have the baby naturally. He suggests the only two alternatives: a high forceps delivery or a cesarean section. He warns Frederic that the forceps delivery "can tear and be quite dangerous besides being possibly bad for the child." The *high* of the high forceps method means that the baby has not begun to move down the birth canal; the surgeon literally reaches into the uterus with a metal forceps and pulls the baby to light. This birthing method, no longer used today, held great risk of maiming the baby's head and causing permanent internal damage. It held some risk, as well, for the mother's life: A torn uterus could result in septic shock or serious bleeding. When Frederic asks about the danger of a cesarean section specifically to Catherine without mentioning the baby, he is told, "It should be no greater than the danger of an ordinary delivery" (321). Reassuring Frederic, the doctor says that if it were his wife, he would do the cesarean, which had less risk of infection than the high forceps method.

All of this was true under normal conditions. By 1918 the cesarean section had undergone considerable improvement from its early days of 30 percent to 45 percent mortality rate for the mother and 17 percent to 45 percent for the baby. By 1910 the operation's mortality rate for the mother had dropped to between 3 percent and 10 percent, depending on when it was performed. By 1918 the mortality rate for mothers was less than 2 percent if the operation were performed early in labor, rising to almost 10 percent if performed late in labor. The risk to Catherine's life from a high forceps delivery was at least 25 percent.[20] The doctor quite rightly advises the cesarean section and Frederic finally agrees. When Frederic sees Catherine next, she asks, "Did you tell him he could do it?" (322). Given the wife-as-property attitude of the period and Catherine's badly deteriorated physical condition, not to mention the effects of the nitrous oxide gas, it is understandable that the doctor would require Frederic's consent. And given Frederic's day-long vigil and the anxiety of the situation, perhaps it is understandable that he does not consult with Catherine, nor does he require a second opinion as he did when his own leg was at risk. But it is worth noting that this doctor, despite his confidence, has none of the identifying traits associated with earlier doctors whom Frederic judged competent: He has none of Valentini's confidence, makes no sexual jokes, and provides no cognac.

The operation, which we do not see because Frederic does not look, seems to proceed smoothly enough. The baby boy is born and Frederic watches the doctor "sewing up the great long, forcep-spread, thick-edged wound." This brief description sounds like the conclusion to the older, so-called classic cesarean, in which the abdomen was opened with a longitudinal cut and the uterus was taken completely out of the abdomen, cut open, and the baby removed. By 1918 many surgeons preferred a smaller, latitudinal cut at the base of the uterus, which was less invasive and lessened the risk of peritoneal infection. It is only after Frederic has visited Catherine that the nurse tells him that his child was born dead: "They couldn't start him breathing. The cord was caught around his neck or something" (327). Frederic recalls that he had not felt the child kicking in Catherine's womb for at least a week. Frederic, thinking that Catherine is safe, goes out of the hospital for a late supper; when he returns, Catherine has begun to hemorrhage, and the doctors cannot stop it as she quickly bleeds to death. Her hemorrhaging was probably due to two causes. When the placenta is removed, the blood vessels connecting it to the wall of the uterus continue to pump blood until the uterus contracts, sealing them off. In a normal delivery this contraction takes place without problems; however, in cases of prolonged labor in which the mother's strength is badly depleted, the uterus may not contract and the bleeding will be difficult to stop. In Catherine's case, her dead baby may have worsened her condition. If a fetus dies in the womb, a strange chemical reaction can take place in the mother's body whereby all of her blood clotting agents are absorbed, leaving her without natural means to shut down bleeding.

Frederic may have had no knowledge of such complications, but Hemingway certainly did. Not only was his father an obstetrician, but just weeks before he finished *A Farewell to Arms,* he observed a Kansas City doctor perform a successful cesarean section on his wife, Pauline Hemingway, after twenty-four hours of labor. Given his great interest in all things medical, it is reasonably certain that he discussed all the details and possibilities with his wife's surgeon.[21]

For a novel supposedly about love and war, we see little of war, and who can see love, that supreme abstraction? More clearly in focus is the human condition: the drive to propagate in the close proximity of death played out against the backdrop of ritual violence. The story that Frederic is left to narrate does not reflect well on the displaced American. He has done nothing particularly brave, nothing heroic. His medals were awarded for an "industrial accident." Unable to carry out his orders during the retreat, he lost his ambulances, most of his men, and finally his military identity during the muddy retreat. The priest once told him that to love was to serve, to sacrifice one's self for another. Never do we see him sacrifice himself for Catherine. Their escape into Switzerland is to save his life, not hers. Her pregnancy, which is half his responsibility, eventually kills her. Frederic, blown about by the deterministic forces at play, is a man to whom unpleasant things happen, not because he is the hero born to bear them, but because he happens to be standing at the wrong place at the wrong time. At the end he is as isolated from the world as American foreign policy was in 1929 when the novel was published.

In this novel that Hemingway once thought of calling "A Sentimental Education," Frederic Henry learns that he is not immortal, that he needs Catherine beyond sexuality, that life is neither fair nor foul, and that there is little he can do about it. The surgeon, skillful or not, can only postpone, not abrogate death. As Frederic tells Catherine, one always feels trapped biologically. The novel's wealth of medical detail calls our attention to our own vulnerability: We are all permanently at risk, trusting in doctors, medical and metaphorical, to preserve us in a world where we have little control. As with the ants on the burning log (327–28), one may die quick and early, or late and scarred; we are born into the world's hospital, each of us a terminal case.

NOTES

1. Originally read in the Carlos Baker files at Princeton; now at the Stanford University Library.

2. See Michael Reynolds, *Hemingway's Reading, 1910–1940* (Princeton: Princeton University Press, 1981); and James Brasch and Joseph Sigman, *Hemingway's Library: A Composite Record* (New York: Garland, 1981).

3. See Robert O. Stephens, "Hemingway and Stendhal: The Matrix of *A Farewell to Arms*," *PMLA* 88 (March 1973): 271–80.

4. The manuscript was deposited at Harvard's Houghton Library in 1959, but its presence did not become generally known until 1970.

5. Note that, like many doctors' children, Hemingway often exaggerated his own illness, for, as a child, it was one of the easiest ways to get his father's attention. *Black's Medical Dictionary* was part of Hemingway's permanent library, and late in life he carried with him his medical file, which is now at the Kennedy Library.

6. Ernest Hemingway, *A Farewell to Arms* (New York: Charles Scribner's Sons, 1929, 1957), pp. 107–8. Further references will refer parenthetically to this text.

7. Albert Neisser, *On Modern Syphilotherapy with Particular Reference to Salvarsan*, first published in 1911 in German and translated by Isabelle von Sazenhofen Wartenberg (Baltimore: Johns Hopkins University Press, 1945), pp. 13–27

8. See Reynolds, *Hemingway's First War: The Making of* A Farewell to Arms (Princeton: Princeton University Press, 1976). Although I stand by my early work, I am no longer reading the same text I did in my youth. If I contradict myself, I contradict myself.

9. Arthur F. Hurst, *Medical Diseases of the War* (London: Edward Arnold, 1918), pp. 250–79.

10. *Cambridge World History of Human Disease,* ed. Kenneth F. Kiple (Cambridge: Cambridge University Press, 1993), p. 1045.

11. *Medical Services: Surgery of the War,* vol. 1 (London: Stationer's Office, 1922), p. 243.

12. Heinrich Braun, *Local Anesthesia,* trans. Percy Shields (New York: Lea and Febeger, 1914), p. 50.

13. *Medical Services: Surgery of the War,* vol. 2, p. 301.

14. *United States Army X-Ray Manual* (New York: Paul B. Hoeber, 1919), p. 203.

15. Ruth and Edward Baker, *The Rays: A History of Radiology* (Baltimore: Williams and Wilkins, 1959), p. 204.

16. James T. Wathney, *Anesthesia,* 2nd rev. ed. (New York: Macmillan, 1925), p. 690.

17. E. W. White, "Shell Shock and Neurasthenia," *Journal of the American Medical Association* 70.21 (May 25, 1918): 1570–71; R. Eager, "War Psychoses in Cases of Shell Shock," p. 1571.

18. See *The History of Contraception* (pamphlet) prepared for the Medical Committee by Beryl Suitters, published by International Planned Parenthood Association [n.d.]. William H. Robertson, *An Illustrated History of Contraception* (Park Ridge, N.J.: Parthenon, 1989), pp. 107–20.

19. "Eutocia by Means of Nitrous Oxide Gas." *Journal of the American Medical Association* 64.14 (April 3, 1915): 1188.

20. John Harley Young, *Caesarean Section: History and Development* (London: H. K. Lewis, 1944), pp. 141–215.

21. It may be significant that Hemingway gave the holograph manuscript to Pauline's surgeon, Don Carlos Guffey.

WORKS CITED

Baker, Carlos. *Hemingway: The Writer as Artist.* Princeton: University Press, 1952.

Baker, Ruth and Edward. *The Rays: A History of Radiology.* Baltimore: Williams and Wilkins, 1959.

Brasch, James, and Joseph Sigman. *Hemingway's Library: A Composite Record.* New York: Garland, 1981.

Braun, Heinrich. *Local Anesthesia.* Trans. Percy Shields. New York: Lea and Febeger, 1914.

Cambridge World History of Human Disease. Ed. Kenneth F. Kiple. Cambridge: Cambridge University Press, 1993.

"Eutocia by Means of Nitrous Oxide Gas." *Journal of the American Medical Association* 64.14.(April 3, 1915).

Hemingway, Ernest. *A Farewell to Arms.* New York: Charles Scribner's Sons, 1929.

Hurst, Arthur F. *Medical Diseases of the War.* London: Edward Arnold, 1918.

Medical Services: Surgery of the War. Vol. 1 and 2. London: Stationer's Office, 1922.

Men at War: The Best War Stories of All Time. Ed. and Introd. Ernest Hemingway. New York: Crown, 1942.

Neisser, Albert. *On Modern Syphilotherapy with Particular Reference to Salvarsan.*

Trans. Isabelle von Sazenhofen Wartenberg. Baltimore: Johns Hopkins University Press, 1945.

Reynolds, Michael. *Hemingway's First War: The Making of* A Farewell to Arms. Princeton: Princeton University Press, 1976.

———. *Hemingway's Reading, 1910–1940.* Princeton: Princeton University Press, 1981.

Robertson, William H. *An Illustrated History of Contraception.* Park Ridge, N.J.: Parthenon, 1989.

Stephens, Robert O. "Hemingway and Stendhal: The Matrix of *A Farewell to Arms.*" *PMLA* 88 (March 1973): 271–80.

Suitters, Beryl. *The History of Contraception* (pamphlet). International Planned Parenthood Association, n.d.

United States Army X-Ray Manual. New York: Paul B. Hoeber, 1919.

Wathney, James T. *Anesthesia.* 2nd rev. ed. New York: Macmillan, 1925.

White, E. W. "Shell Shock and Neurasthenia," and Eager, R. "War Psychoses in Cases of Shell Shock." *Journal of the American Medical Association* 70.21 (May 25, 1918): 1570–71.

Young, John Harley. *Caesarean Section: History and Development.* London: H. K. Lewis, 1944.

7

ROBERT E. FLEMING

Hemingway's Late Fiction: Breaking New Ground

When he returned to Cuba after World War II, Ernest Hemingway faced the necessity of resurrecting his moribund literary career. He had closed out the 1930s with a triumphant novel about the Spanish civil war, confounding the critics who had declared his career to be over. But during World War II he had forsaken his art to serve as a *Collier's* correspondent – although he had actually published only six dispatches[1] – and had confined his literary efforts to two long free verse poems written to Mary Welsh, whom he married in 1946. It was time to return to his real vocation.

Hemingway could not mark his return to letters by writing a mere journeyman novel or a few stories reminiscent of his prewar work. As he would observe in 1954, a writer of a certain standing had to strive continuously to push beyond his previous limits:

> For a true writer each book should be a new beginning where he tries again for something that is beyond attainment. He should always try for something that has never been done or that others have tried and failed. Then sometimes, with great luck, he will succeed.
>
> How simple the writing of literature would be if it were only necessary to write in another way what has been well written. It is because we have had such great writers in the past that a writer is driven far out past where he can go, out to where no one can help him.[2]

It has become fashionable among critics to suggest that after the war he rested on his laurels or became so affected by his own public persona that he was no longer able to create the sort of major literary work he had produced in the 1920s and the 1930s. This view overlooks Hemingway's willingness to experiment, to take real chances, in attempts to better his own earlier efforts. Whatever one thinks of the value of *Across the River and into the Trees* and the two posthumously published novels, in those three works Hemingway attempted to venture into new territory. As he put it in a 1950 interview with Harvey Breit, "Should I repeat myself? I don't think so. . . .

In writing I have moved through arithmetic, through plane geometry and algebra, and now I am in calculus."[3]

Soon after returning to Cuba, Hemingway began a novel reminiscent of his own life in France in the 1920s, later published in severely edited form as *The Garden of Eden*. He shelved that project temporarily to write a big book about the sea, posthumously published as *Islands in the Stream*. In turn, he interrupted his writing on that book in 1949 to expand a work that began as a short story into a book-length study of a middle-aged military officer's death in Venice.

ACROSS THE RIVER AND INTO THE TREES

In 1950 Hemingway published his first novel in ten years. It is the story of Richard Cantwell, a fifty-year-old American colonel in love with Renata, a nineteen-year-old Italian countess. During a three-day stay in Venice, Cantwell eats, drinks, and makes love to his countess. As he is leaving Venice, he suffers the last in a series of heart attacks and dies. Reviewers disliked the book intensely and it became the target of several parodies. But is the book the unqualified failure that it first appeared to be?

Judged strictly as a realistic love story, the novel fails. Despite the fact that she is based on a real person (Adriana Ivancich), Renata lacks plausibility. She is perhaps better viewed as a symbolic character. Her name, as Arthur Waldhorn has noted, means "reborn," and Cantwell's love for her is as much a desire to recapture the "beauty and innocence [Cantwell] nostalgically yearns for"[4] as a physical or sexual desire. Furthermore, *Across the River and into the Trees* is not only a story about love: It is also a story about war and about confronting death. In fact, several comments Hemingway made about the book suggest that it was not his chief intention to produce a realistic novel. Rather, he seems to have intended a more symbolic work than any he had written in the 1920s and 1930s, and the chief subject matter of that work was the recent war. Responding to reviewers' criticism that *Across the River and into the Trees* lacked action, Hemingway told Harvey Breit "they can say anything about nothing happening in *Across the River*, but all that happens is the defense of the lower Piave, the breakthrough in Normandy, the taking of Paris and the destruction of the 22nd Inf. Reg. in Hurtgen forest plus a man who loves a girl and dies." He describes his approach to this material as consisting of "three-cushion shots" (Breit 61–62).

One such three-cushion shot is apparent in the novel's title, which is based on the last words of Confederate General Thomas J. (Stonewall) Jackson –

"Let us cross over the river and rest under the shade of the trees" (*ARIT* 307). Colonel Cantwell is an avatar of this Civil War hero. Renata's name works with this pattern of symbolism, suggesting Cantwell's rebirth or perhaps his reunion with an earlier state of existence. The union between Cantwell and Renata, often treated as the ridiculous daydream of a writer who is undergoing the male menopause, is on one level the attempt of a dying man to rediscover the youth that he once was or the attempt of a hardened, pragmatic soldier to unite with his long-estranged anima. It is appropriate that the encounter takes place in Venice, for Cantwell's love affair with that city predates his metaphor-laden love affair with Renata by nearly thirty years.

As an eighteen-year-old junior officer in the Italian infantry, Richard Cantwell fought the Austrians outside Venice. He was first wounded slightly and spent his convalescent leave in that city; then he was nearly mortally wounded near the Piave. These early associations with Venice make him feel that it is "his" town. His wide acquaintance among the boatmen, bartenders, headwaiters, and porters of the town suggest a local boy returning to his hometown, not a member of the army that has conquered fascist Italy. Renata seems designed to suggest to readers the open and innocent soul of the man that Cantwell once was, a man they see only in certain brief memories that the colonel's surroundings evoke.

In contrast to his remembered self, Cantwell looks at his driver, a boy who, in spite of his "combat infantryman badge, his Purple Heart, and the other things he wore, was in no sense a soldier but only a man placed, against his will, in uniform" (22). This young conscript, with his pragmatic view of life, is ironically given the same surname, Jackson, as the heroic Civil War general. The contrast inherent in that naming points up the difference between modern war and nineteenth-century war. As the colonel relives former times in preparation for death, he thinks constantly of how he has seen the world change, following up a theme that Hemingway had introduced in "The Snows of Kilimanjaro" almost fifteen years earlier.

Because the colonel is a military man, *Across the River and into the Trees* becomes a subtle meditation on war in modern times. Whereas once the leader of soldiers was revered for personal bravery and fighting ability, the modern military establishment distrusts officers who have fought personally as Cantwell has done. The architect of the Allied victory in Europe, Dwight D. Eisenhower, is criticized as "some politician in uniform who has never killed in his life, except with his mouth over the telephone, or on paper" (234). Cantwell sizes Eisenhower up as a presidential candidate in the postwar civilian world rather than as a true soldier of his own stamp.

Among the soldiers who appear in Cantwell's memories and the stories he tells Renata, none really recalls Stonewall Jackson except Cantwell himself. Although Hemingway does not refer to Jackson's death except for the allusion in the title and a brief passage near the end of the book, the parallel between him and Cantwell is reinforced by knowledge of the way Jackson died. While conducting a reconnaissance with his staff between Confederate and Federal lines, he was shot by his own troops. (Jackson himself remarked that all of his wounds were from his own men.) Cantwell has suffered a similar attack at the hands of his own army. Promoted to brigadier general because of his merits as a leader, he is assigned an impossible attack on an impregnable target that probably has no military significance but is "important because it got into the newspapers" (233). After inevitably losing his command, Cantwell is subjected to "friendly fire" from the military establishment, who strip him of his star to cover up the foolishness of their own orders. Jackson died a lingering death from pneumonia after his wound; Cantwell eventually succumbs to a heart condition presumably aggravated by the stress he has had to endure.

Hemingway's attempt to move from arithmetic through plane geometry and algebra and into calculus resulted in his least successful book. Perhaps in compressing his account of some of the major battles of the recent war into a few pages of Colonel Cantwell's reminiscences, he encountered the limits of the iceberg principle that had worked so brilliantly in his works of the 1920s and 1930s. Disappointment over the book's reception did not curtail his work on other experimental fiction, but it did make him hesitant to publish until he was sure of the power of his work. *The Old Man and the Sea* was published during his lifetime because it had been read and pronounced impregnable to criticism by several critical readers. His two larger novels remained unfinished when he died, victims of his uncertainty. Nevertheless, both illustrate new developments in his fiction.

ISLANDS IN THE STREAM

Hemingway began *Islands in the Stream* as the study of a writer, Roger Hancock, and his relationships with his several former wives and his three children. Early during the composition of the work, Hemingway reduced Roger's role to that of a supporting character, changed his surname from Hancock to Davis, and created a new character who is the father of the three boys originally envisioned as Roger's children. This new protagonist, Thomas Hudson, is a painter rather than a writer, but he shares the problem common to all artists of splitting his energy and attention between his role as artist and his roles as lover, husband, and father. During the course of World War II (covered in the second and third books of the novel), Hudson abandons his art as well as his family to become a reluctant warrior, fighting off depression when he thinks of his dead sons and the one great love of his life, and dreaming how he will use what he has learned during the war if his life should be spared.

Islands in the Stream was projected as three-fourths of a long novel about the sea, and was written over a period of half a dozen years. In the latter half of 1946 and early 1947, Hemingway completed close to one thousand pages of handwritten manuscript that in substance constituted book 1 of *Islands*.[5] He set aside this work-in-progress when his son Patrick became ill in the spring of 1947, and then turned his attention to *Across the River and into the Trees*. He did not go back to his novel of the sea until December 1950, when he wrote the first draft of book 2 in a furious three-week burst. Then, early in 1951, he composed the first draft of *The Old Man and the Sea* before resuming work on the concluding section of *Islands*. But the break he took to complete the enormously popular tale of Santiago and the great fish was not really an interruption to his sea novel, as Carlos Baker persuasively argues, for *The Old Man and the Sea* was itself conceived as a concluding section to that larger project.

The four-book novel Hemingway had in mind would have begun with a lengthy section leading up to World War II (this eventually became "Bimini," the opening section of *Islands*), followed by two studies of Thomas Hudson as he participated in the war: "Cuba" and "At Sea" – the first emphasizing his emotional strain when not in action and the second showing him engaged in battle. Finally, the novel would have closed, after Hudson's death at the end of book 3, with a book that showed a return to normalcy on the Gulf Stream, with an old man fishing using a centuries-old technique and living in harmony with nature (*The Old Man and the Sea*). The first and last books would have been united by twin stories of fishing battles – one between Thomas Hudson's second son and a giant fish and the other between Santiago and his marlin.

Islands in the Stream was not designed to be a continuous narrative like *A Farewell to Arms* or *For Whom the Bell Tolls*. Except for "At Sea," which begins soon after "Cuba," each new book would begin a considerable time after the previous book; old characters would disappear with or without explanation and new supporting characters would be added. In this way the reader would have been somewhat prepared for the appearance of a new protagonist, Santiago, after the death of Hudson in the final battle of "At Sea," yet the contrast between the first three books and the last would have produced a shock that might have increased the impact of the final segment as well as of the novel as a whole.

Hemingway, of course, did not follow this plan. In March 1951 he had suggested to Charles Scribner Jr. that the sea book would be ready for fall 1952 publication, but a few months later, he reversed that decision, quite probably because of the negative reception of *Across the River and into the Trees*.[6] Instead, needing a victory over reviewers and critics, he allowed Leland Hayward to persuade him to publish *The Old Man and the Sea* separately, first in an issue of *Life* and then in a Scribner's edition. Although Hemingway's reputation was restored by his small masterpiece, its separate publication left *Islands in the Stream* without its original ending and may explain why Hemingway never completed the novel. Yet there are fine things in the sea novel that make its posthumous publication in 1970 an event of considerable significance.

The first book of *Islands in the Stream*, "Bimini," tells the story of a visit to Bimini by the three sons of Thomas Hudson in 1936.[7] Hudson's closest friend, writer Roger Davis, is visiting at the same time and shares the duties and joys of fatherhood with Hudson (as well he might; the boys had been his own sons in the first manuscript version of the novel). Hudson and Roger are doubles who illustrate two versions of the modern artist: Hudson is the pure artist for whom everything else is relegated to a secondary rank; Roger is the flawed artist who is more human and more vulnerable than the perfect artist. Hudson enjoys having his sons with him, but there is a reserve in his attitude toward them – and toward all of humanity.

After an earlier life during which he loved various women, married at least two of them, begot three children, fought in a war, and traveled the world, Hudson has renounced all else in favor of his art. At times it seems that Hudson has taken refuge in art because his relationships with people have disappointed him; he seems actively to crave isolation. He tells himself that he is willing to be "selfish" and "ruthless" where his art is concerned and to maintain a harsh discipline that is nearly monastic. He isolates himself from women, once his downfall, by willing himself not to fall in love with them. He holds the commercial world at bay through his refusal to have anything to do with the marketing of his paintings: He works only through a New York dealer.

In contrast to Hudson, Roger illustrates most of the pitfalls to which an artist can fall victim. He continues to make disastrous alliances with women, favoring those who subject him to their sadism. To the detriment of his art, he continues to lead an adventurous life that has caused some critics to confuse him with his own literary heroes. He has aimed his writing at commercial markets for so long that he has lost all artistic integrity and fears that he is no longer able to do the serious work he once was capable of. When he appears in *Islands in the Stream,* he has just left Hollywood, where he did some screenwriting and nearly killed another man in a brawl.

If, as Carlos Baker has maintained, Thomas Hudson represents a narcissistic and idealized picture of Hemingway's own life at middle age,[8] Roger suggests the dark self that Hemingway might have feared he had become. Although Roger owes a few facets of his character – the screenwriting and his pandering to the mass markets – to F. Scott Fitzgerald, he has far more in common with his creator. Roger has been accused of repeatedly retelling his own autobiographical story, his heroines are all versions of the same woman, he has been involved with the communist cause in Spain, and the critics have delighted in reporting that he is "washed up" every time his career has faltered. If Hudson bears away the palm as true artist, however, Roger's fallibility lends him a saving humanity. The boys enjoy a closeness with Roger that they cannot hope to achieve with their father.

Hudson insists on working each morning before joining the boys. He tells himself that maintaining his work schedule is merely protective – that he is working even when his sons are with him so that he will not miss them so much when they are gone – but this justification has a hollow ring. In one scene, Hudson paints in the morning while Roger plays and swims with the boys. When Hudson pauses in his work, he looks down from the elevated porch where he has been working like an Olympian figure surveying lesser beings (176–77).

Hudson's attitude toward his sons is highlighted by one of the most exciting events in "Bimini." The boys are spear-fishing in dangerous waters while the adults keep watch for sharks. Hudson's first mate sees a hammerhead shark swimming toward Hudson's second son David and sounds the alarm. Hudson responds by firing at the shark repeatedly with his 6.5 mm Mannlicher, but is unable to hit the shark. After the rifle is empty, the boy is saved by the marksmanship of Eddy the mate, who shoots the shark with his own Thompson submachine gun. Eddy's ability to hit the shark with a weapon designed for close-quarters combat after Hudson misses repeatedly with an accurate long-range rifle (the same model used by Margot Macomber in making her most famous shot) raises interesting psychological questions. Is Hudson unable to hit the shark because he has "buck fever," because his very desire to hit the shark and save David makes him too nervous to shoot accurately? Or is his missing a sort of Freudian slip that betrays a subconscious desire to rid himself of one of his few remaining human ties?

The real-life event that inspired this episode has been related by Gregory Hemingway, allowing a comparison of fact and fiction that might shed some light on the question. Although he was grudging in his praise for his father's heroism, Gregory wrote that it was he who was threatened by the shark and that his father jumped into the water to save him.[9] Hudson's inability to take the same kind of aggressive action to save his son suggests that Hemingway intended to emphasize Hudson's choice of art over his human ties. All three sons eventually die in the course of the book: David and Andy are killed in an auto accident in France near the end of "Bimini," and Tom Jr. is killed flying with the RAF during the hiatus between "Bimini" and "Cuba."

The estrangement between Hudson and his sons is again emphasized during another major event in "Bimini," David's unsuccessful struggle to land a huge fish. Like David's narrow escape from the shark, this episode is also a fictional elaboration of a real-life event. Gregory Hemingway has written about how, when his brother Patrick was allowed to sit in the fighting chair of the *Pilar* while the adults ate lunch, he hooked a huge fish and lost $500 worth of rod, reel, and line (*Papa* 26). David Hudson hooks his fish and fights an epic battle to boat it, losing it just as Eddy the mate is about to gaff the fish.

As in the painting scene, Thomas Hudson is once more looking down on the action from an elevated position on the flying bridge of the boat while Roger is on deck encouraging and helping David. After David loses the fish, it is Roger who ministers to the boy. Hudson seems able to react to his son's action only through his art; he paints two pictures of the fish when they return to shore. But as a father, Hudson is unable to comfort his son. Significantly, he is shut out of an exchange between Roger and the boy when Roger tells David something that makes him feel better – a remark that Hudson never hears.

This fishing passage ties "Bimini" to *The Old Man and the Sea* not only because of similar action but because of certain specific images and even verbal similarities. Like Santiago, whose name recalls Saint James, David is called a "saint" and a "martyr" by his older brother Tom (125). David's wounded hands and feet, like Santiago's wounded hands, recall the stigmata that bind some saints to Christ (130, 133). Eddy the mate tells David near the beginning of his fight with the fish that it is nearly towing the boat (115), just as Santiago's boat is literally towed by his fish. After his ordeal, David lies face down on the bunk in much the same posture as Santiago when he falls asleep after returning home. And, like Santiago, David paradoxically wishes the fish well: He tells his brothers and Roger that as the ordeal lengthened, he began to love the fish "more than anything on earth" (142). Just as Santiago acknowledges a kinship when he tells the fish that he does not care which of them kills the other (as if the line that connects them were some metaphysical link), the boy states that he is willing to die fighting his fish (114). David goes even further in recognizing a merging of his identity and that of the fish when he says that during the hardest parts of the struggle, he "couldn't tell which was him and which was me" (142). Speaking of his encounter with the shark just before this episode, David anticipates the words of Santiago: "I just went too far out" (90).

Roger's easy acceptance of the boys contrasts sharply with Hudson's distance from them. When Hudson begins to make sketches for the first painting of David's fish, the boy watches his father's work and makes cautious suggestions, but he retracts those suggestions and apologizes when Hudson gently but firmly defends the sketch as he has made it. David returns when the sketch is finished and tactfully praises its accuracy. Hudson's deliberate separation of family from work is contrasted to the early years in Paris, when he took time for leisurely walks in the parks with his eldest son Tom. Young Tom's vivid memories of "Mr. Joyce" and "Mr. Fitzgerald" show that he was then familiar with his father's artistic circles. Now, like his brothers, he is deliberately kept at a distance from Hudson's work.

Roger, on the other hand, not only has plenty of time for the boys, but refuses to become too serious about his own work. He laughs with the boys when they jokingly bring up the various charges leveled by the critics and joins them in an elaborate spoof – played out for the benefit of a group of American tourists – of the public image of the writer. But if Roger Davis is a better father figure than Thomas Hudson, his art suffers by comparison. He is a man who devotes much of his time to art; Hudson is an artist. The gulf between Hudson and his doppelgänger Roger is apparent not only in their relationship with Hudson's sons but in two significant episodes involving Roger.

Early in the book, Roger is goaded into engaging a boorish yachtsman in a fistfight. He punishes the man unmercifully before knocking him out, then faces the man down when he seeks to avenge the beating by confronting Roger with a shotgun. When his adrenalin has worn off, Roger feels terribly guilty about the fight. Late in "Bimini," Roger meets Audrey Bruce, a young woman who, as a schoolgirl, idolized both Roger and Hudson when she knew them in France. Roger falls in love with Audrey, and near the end of this segment of the novel, the couple leaves for Hudson's ranch, where Roger will try to regain his power to write good fiction. Unlike Roger (and anticipating Santiago) Hudson is no longer engaged closely enough with life to fight or fall in love. It will take a world war to draw him back into a human conflict, and he thinks of love as a thing of the past, possible only with his first wife, from whom he is irretrievably estranged.

The artistic difference between the doubles is also explored in a scene that echoes Morley Callaghan's recollected conversation with Hemingway in the 1920s: Hemingway had said that when an artist suffered from an emotionally painful experience, he must use the pain. For example, Hemingway explained, if a writer was present at the funeral of his own father, one side of him existed in the son who mourned his father, but the artistic side would stand aloof, observing and storing away the emotional response for some future use in his art.

Early in "Bimini," Roger tells Hudson and the boys about the most painful emotional experience he had ever suffered. When he was twelve, he and his brother David had a canoeing accident in which David drowned. Because he was a year older than David, Roger has always felt that his father considered him responsible. Worse, his own conscience has bothered him because he failed to save his brother. Yet Roger has never written about this powerful experience, fearing the emotional confrontation of putting the event down in words. When Hudson tells Roger that if he will simply "bite on the nail," the experience will result in a fine novel, Roger hints that reawakening his suppressed emotions might lead to suicide.

The end of "Bimini" finds Thomas Hudson alone, and it is as he is attempting to conquer his loneliness with work that he receives a telegram about the death of his two youngest sons, along with their mother, in France. Hudson's sorrow is real but restrained as he prepares to sail on the *Ile de France*. His sorrow is not brought about by memories of the boys or regrets at not having been a better father but simply by his contemplation of a great void or abyss that marks the emptiness of life. This he regards as the true hell man faces, as opposed to that depicted in Dante's *Divine Comedy*, or as the end of the world as he himself has drawn it in his apocalyptic painting for Mr. Bobby's waterfront bar. When Eddy tries to comfort him by saying that he still has his oldest son Tom, Hudson replies that this is true for the present – foreshadowing Tom's death during the time that elapses between the first and second books of the novel.

"Cuba," the second book of *Islands in the Stream*, is the least successful of the three because it is the most static. Hudson is suspended between past and future eventful periods – the loss of his sons and his artistic career in the past and the search for the crew of a German U-boat in the future – and the story does little but reveal the former and anticipate the latter. The death of

Tom Jr. is not disclosed until midway through the book (262–63), but earlier Hudson has made a mental note that he must not think about his sons, and he is clearly depressed.

The chief event in "Cuba" is a meeting with Hudson's first wife, Tom's mother and the one true love of Hudson's life. She comes to find him in the Floridita bar in Havana and accompanies him to his *finca* outside the city, where they make love and reminisce. Something about his depression allows her to guess that Tom Jr. is dead, and she asks Hudson if it is true. He answers with one significant word: "Sure" (319). Just as Hudson has foreseen Tom's death after his brothers were killed at the end of "Bimini," he now takes it for granted that the death of Tom was inevitable. Tom's mother similarly anticipates Hudson's own death, when she elliptically talks to Boise the cat after Hudson has left to answer an emergency message calling him back to sea duty. She says, "Both of them" (327), implying that Hudson will soon die like their lost son.

Deprived of his art by the need to become a man of action, in the time remaining to him Hudson must content himself with contemplating his own first-class art collection and evaluating with his practiced painter's eye some of the scenes around him. In the end, the works of other artists mean little to him, and he knows that he will never translate his own visions to canvas.

"Cuba" ends with premonitions of Hudson's death. His first wife has good reason to assume that he will be killed at sea, for she has asked him whether it is likely and he has tersely replied, "Very" (321). In the last few pages of the section, he offers her any of the paintings in his house, as well as any of Tom's letters and any books she wants. As he leaves the *finca,* Hudson reflects that he has lost his sons, his one great love, and his honor. All that he has left to sustain him is his duty. That duty will direct him toward a fatal battle in the last segment of *Islands in the Stream,* as Hudson, once a sport fisherman, must become a "fisher of men" in an ironic perversion of the biblical injunction.

"At Sea" begins with a dramatic contrast. The opening passage, in which Hudson and his crew approach an island off the coast of Cuba, describes a scene of natural beauty that might have delighted Hudson when he was an active painter. Now the long white beach, the picturesque row of palm trees, and the blue water of a natural harbor has become a potentially hostile environment because the crew of a crippled German submarine is thought to have taken refuge on the island. The Germans are gone, but they left behind a horror that contrasts with the pastoral beauty of the white beach. In a small fishing village just out of sight of the harbor are nine decaying bodies, and Hudson assumes the duty of performing postmortems on them.

After a brief descriptive passage echoing *The Waste Land* – land crabs rattle in the dry brush, Hudson reflects on the long absence of rain, and he thinks of how long he and his men have been waiting fruitlessly for something to happen – Hudson enters the village and digs the fatal bullets out of the bodies. They are 9 mm bullets with black tips, the type used in Schmeisser submachine guns. Before putting the bullets into his pocket, Hudson dwells on their dual meaning. He is satisfied because the bullets prove the presence of the German sailors he and his men have been seeking; on the other hand, he has a premonition that the four bullets are harbingers of his own death. Much like his son David and Santiago thinking of their two fishes, Hudson realizes that "we have our enemies and they cannot escape. Neither can we" (337).

The feeling of a connection or comradeship between the hunter and the hunted is reinforced when Hudson's men find a dying German sailor. In spite of the fact that he is the enemy, their first impression of the young German is that his suffering has rendered him saintlike. Like Harry in "The Snows of Kilimanjaro," the boy is rotting away from gangrene, but unlike Harry, his closeness to death has brought him a peaceful detachment from the world. He refuses to give any information about his shipmates. Peters, the interpreter, speaks "lovingly" to the boy, and Hudson offers morphine to make his death less painful.

As Hudson and his crew continue their search for the U-boat crew, Hemingway escalates the tension. Hudson has lost radio contact with his base, placing his crew in the same predicament as their German prey, who are cut off from help from their allies. Hudson's inability to communicate with his home base underscores his earlier inability to communicate with his loved ones; his isolation at sea recalls the self-imposed isolation from his sons during their visit in "Bimini." When a message does come through, it is oracular and seems to predict death as surely as Colonel Cantwell's (and Stonewall Jackson's) last utterance about crossing the river. Hudson is told to "Continue searching carefully westward" (368) – on the literal level an order to sweep the north coast of Cuba as he moves toward Havana, but on the symbolic level an allusion to his lifelong journey toward death. Hudson feels tension because of sensations of déjà vu (414), and at one point the boat moves into a narrow channel that recalls the aspect of the river entering the swamp in "Big Two-Hearted River," while on a tactical level the narrowness of the channel deprives Hudson of maneuvering room. Like Santiago, Hudson views the sea as a woman, but this feminine sea is a treacherous woman who is likely to tip the balance capriciously toward Hudson's enemies.

The tension is relieved at times by Hudson's reflection on his former life as an artist. On one occasion, returning to his boat during the heavy rain that finally (and symbolically) breaks the drought, Hudson sees his men standing on the stern naked, soaping themselves and letting the rain rinse them clean as if they were in a shower. Hudson thinks of Cézanne's bathers and then of how Eakins might have painted it. Finally, he realizes that he too would be painting the scene if he were again a painter instead of a warrior. Like Harry in "The Snows of Kilimanjaro," mentally writing his stories when it is too late, Hudson makes mental notes for a sketch of the scene. Similarly, before the end of the novel, Hudson thinks several times of landscapes that he could paint. Two of his final thoughts concern the lessons from the war that he could use in his painting if only he survived, and a sense of regret that he will never paint the beautiful lagoon his boat is approaching just before he dies. But events recall Hudson from his contemplation of artistic questions. He and his crew are ambushed by the Germans in another narrow channel, and Hudson, steering his craft from the flying bridge, is shot. His friend and crewman Willie pronounces a fitting epitaph: He says that Hudson never understands anyone who loves him. Thomas Hudson's detachment from the human race has become permanent.

Had Hemingway lived to complete *Islands in the Stream*, it would have marked a new direction for him. Not only would he have explored two subjects about which he knew a great deal and had never written at length – fatherhood and painting – but he would have transcended the conventional nineteenth-century structure that marks his published novels. Even in its current form, unfinished by Hemingway and edited by other hands after his death, *Islands in the Stream* is a powerful work that repays careful reading.

THE GARDEN OF EDEN

The other major work Hemingway left unfinished when he died was an ambitious and complex novel – perhaps written to compete with Fitzgerald's *Tender Is the Night* – that became the basis for the heavily edited published version of *The Garden of Eden*. As Hemingway planned the novel, the plot would have revolved around two sexual triangles composed of three artistic men, the wives of two of these men, and an unattached woman. The triangles would have been linked by the sexual involvement of the two wives with one another. As in *Islands in the Stream,* one of the two principal artists would have been a writer, the other a painter. Hemingway nearly completed one of the triangle plots, composed large segments of the second, then wrote a brief chapter that he labeled a "provisional ending" for the novel. When Scribner's editor Tom Jenks edited the large incomplete manuscript, he omitted the unfinished triangle involving painter Nick Sheldon, his wife Barbara, and her lover Andrew Murray, presumably because too much of the story remained unfinished; he ignored the provisional ending by choice.

Incomplete as the resulting book is in relation to the entire manuscript, it adds two new dimensions to the Hemingway canon. It treats sexuality more frankly and examines the creative life more critically and at greater length than any other Hemingway book. The sexual theme, which treats a triangle in which two women and a man are romantically involved – the two women with each other and the man with each in turn – has received the most attention, but Hemingway's meditations on the life of the writer are perhaps even more significant.

Like *Tender is the Night*, *The Garden of Eden* tells the story of a gifted young American expatriate who is torn between pursuing his career and becoming a caretaker for his wealthy wife. Fitzgerald's Dick Diver chooses to sacrifice his career as a psychologist to devote himself to the care of his wife Nicole. In a variation on this theme Hemingway's protagonist, David Bourne, refuses to abandon his writing to care for his wife Catherine, even when her madness threatens to end in suicide. Catherine reacts by becoming increasingly hostile to David's writing, finally burning his manuscripts while he is absent. Fitzgerald created two triangles by introducing Rosemary Hoyt, who becomes Dick Diver's lover, and Tommy Barban, who becomes Nicole's. Hemingway combines and complicates the roles in his triangle in the character of Marita, who becomes first the lover of Catherine and then of David.

Just as astute readers of *Tender Is the Night* were able to identify sources for Fitzgerald's characters – the author and his wife Zelda, and Gerald and Sara Murphy – readers of *Garden* will note biographical sources for characters and events in the novel. Catherine Bourne looks a great deal like Pauline Pfeiffer Hemingway, and her burning the manuscripts echoes Hadley Richardson Hemingway's accidental loss of a small piece of luggage containing all of Hemingway's manuscripts in 1922. Like David, Hemingway was a rising but penniless author when he married Pauline in 1927. When he first began the novel just after World War II, Hemingway was first engaged and then newly married to his fourth wife Mary, a petite woman, whose name is given to the third member of the *Garden* triangle, Marita, or "little Mary." The manuscript novel multiplied the autobiographical elements. Nick and

Barbara Sheldon are near-photographic recreations of Hemingway and Hadley as they appeared during the early 1920s, and Andy Murray is closely modeled on John Dos Passos.

The sexual theme of the novel and the theme of David as successful artist but unsuccessful husband are inextricably linked. At the beginning of the novel, the Bournes are on their honeymoon, and though David is not writing he knows that he will soon return to his career. He has some misgivings, which at first seem unjustified, about how Catherine will take his immersion in his work. When he begins to write steadily, however, Catherine indulges in sexual games to try to win back his attention. When her first attempts to upstage David's writing fail, Catherine engages in increasingly bizarre behavior, and when her sexual escapades fail to win him back, she descends to insanity.

Catherine's first sexual ploy is to assume the dominant male role in their lovemaking and to encourage David to attune himself mentally to a passive female role. She has her hair cut short like a British schoolboy's and bleached; she speaks in public about undergoing a metamorphosis into a male. She next tries to objectify her sexual interchangeability with David by transforming him into an image of herself. She entices him into having his hair cut exactly like hers and bleached so that the couple, who have already been mistaken for brother and sister, become apparent twins. Catherine attempts to counter what she views as David's obsession with an artistic endeavor of her own, with their lives as the canvas upon which she paints. She will later propose collaboration in his art as another way of countering his solitary pursuit.

When David persists in his writing, Catherine makes the acquaintance of Marita, a younger woman the Bournes meet in the company of another woman of approximately her own age who displays signs of sexual jealousy when Marita speaks to the Bournes. Catherine immediately recognizes Marita's bisexuality, first teasing David by suggesting that Marita is in love with him and then speculating that Marita may be in love with her, as other women have unsuccessfully been in the past. In spite of (or because of) her perception that Marita may be in love with both David and her, Catherine soon invites Marita, her hair now cut exactly like Catherine's and David's, to stay at the same country hotel where they are living, and to make a threesome with the Bournes at meals and on excursions to the beach.

Shortly after Catherine brings Marita into the hotel, David finds the two women in bed together. Far from hiding the affair she is having with Marita, Catherine insists on telling David in detail about her sexual feelings for the younger woman. At the same time, she encourages David to become interested in Marita, referring to both of them as his wives, suggesting that they all swim naked together, and even inviting David into bed with the two of them at the same time.

The sexual plot in the published novel ends when Catherine leaves David and Marita alone in the south of France. She proposes to take the couple's Bugatti – bought with her own money – but David, recalling that Catherine's father "killed himself in a car" (61), possibly on purpose, convinces her to take the train. This is the only suggestion in the published novel that Catherine may be suicidal, although the manuscript is explicit on the point. David and Marita end the bizarre love story by reverting to a life of heterosexual monogamy as David attempts to rebuild his literary career.

Hemingway's provisional ending, like that of *The Old Man and the Sea* as ending for *Islands in the Stream,* would probably have been appended rather abruptly to the text. It pictures a couple on the beach, zooms in on them as if with a modern movie camera, and discloses that they are David and Catherine, not David and Marita as might have been expected. In spite of her recent release from an institution in Switzerland, Catherine assumes that she will again succumb to madness, and she extracts a promise from David that if things go bad for her again, he will join her in a suicide pact. David has come to resemble Dick Diver in his role of caretaker rather than lover. Had this ending been attached to the novel as Scribner's published it, the novel would have seemed of a piece with all of Hemingway's other work, illustrating the 1930s theme of "winner take nothing."

Parallel to the triangular love story in *Garden* is a story about David as artist that is perhaps even more striking. The novel takes up a theme that Hemingway had touched upon as early as "The Sea Change" (1931) and another theme that is central to "The Snows of Kilimanjaro" (1936); on the first page of the manuscript of *Garden* David is given the same name as the protagonist of "The Sea Change," Phil, and he is preoccupied with not letting the fate of Harry, of "Snows," befall him. Phil betrays his humanity by parasitically feeding off the emotional and sexual life of the woman he has been in love with, planning to use her story in his fiction. Conversely, Harry allows his wealthy wife to consume much of his vitality as a writer and dies without finishing some of his best stories, betrayed by the comfortable life that marriage to a wealthy woman has made possible. Further, there is a metafictional layer to *Garden* that appears nowhere else in Hemingway's fiction. Although he has treated writers elsewhere, he does not depict them engaged in the act of creating literature. In *Garden* he does just that.

When David and Catherine are first introduced, they are on their honeymoon and life seems idyllic to Catherine. David, on the other hand, knows that trouble lies ahead for them when he turns to his writing again. He recognizes that writers are selfish, stealing time from their loved ones to devote to their work, and he resolves to make it clear to Catherine that he regrets the isolation imposed by his art. Nevertheless, by the second chapter of the novel, David and Catherine have their first quarrel over David's writing, brought on by the arrival of a package of press clippings forwarded by his publisher. With uncanny intuition, Catherine tells David that the clippings frighten her, that they depict another man from the David Bourne she married, and that they could destroy David.

David realizes that Catherine is dangerously close to the truth. It is not so much the clippings that threaten their marriage as it is what they represent – David's obsession with the act of writing itself rather than his wish for the acclaim his work may bring him. The couple conclude the argument with an apparently innocuous agreement. They will retire to a remote area where there will be few distractions. David will write, and Catherine will amuse herself. But as the novel progresses, David's work increasingly estranges him from Catherine, who fights to retain him not only by distracting him with her sexuality but by offering to become his artistic collaborator.

If hawks do not share, as Hemingway observed in *A Moveable Feast,* neither do artists. David, who early in his marriage had cautioned himself about spending too much time on his writing, loses his sense of proportion once he is in the grip of one of his stories. He conveys a sense of his superiority over Catherine because he has devoted himself to an artistic project while she is hedonistically enjoying herself, and she bristles over his air of satisfaction after doing a good morning's work. When he is in his writing room, he literally forgets Catherine and his increasingly troubled marriage and moves from France back to Africa (the setting of his fiction) in much the same way that Hemingway, recalling his early years in Paris, wrote of leaving Paris behind and transporting himself to northern Michigan.

The difference is that the process is idyllic as recalled in *A Moveable Feast* but ruinous in *Garden.* Writing becomes a narcotic to David, who begins to use it as an escape mechanism. His reality becomes Africa to such an extent that on one occasion, when he hears the sound of a car intruding from the real world, he is startled by it. In the beginning of the book, he was concerned about how his writing would affect Catherine; now he is oblivious to her growing mental illness for large periods of his days. His obsession with privacy is emphasized by his habit of locking his work in a suitcase in a locked room, as if to underscore the compartmentalization of his life. His isolation threatens to undermine his humanity. When Marita speaks of other important things in life besides his writing, David privately reflects that "there are no other things" (140).

Catherine seeks to become part of David's hidden life by offering up her own privacy on the altar of his art. She suggests that he take up as his subject their life together. She will even help him by providing exciting incidents such as the triangle with Marita. By cooperating with the writer's tendency toward voyeurism, Catherine exacerbates one serious flaw of the artist, the tendency to use other people rather than to deal with them on human terms. Catherine also offers to underwrite the cost of the new book's publication and its illustration by emerging modern painters. David begins the account, which the two call their "narrative," but once he turns to a difficult story about his father that has been simmering in his subconscious for years, he sees the marital narrative for what it is – a sterile literary exercise. He then stops work on it, an act that Catherine interprets as desertion of her personally.

A similar view of David's writing as the core of his nature is present in the triangle plot. Although Catherine encourages David to sleep with Marita, she is seriously offended by Marita's defense of David's obsessive work on a recently completed story. She becomes enraged when she learns that David has allowed Marita to read the story before he has shown it to her. She tears the little exercise book containing the story in half, foreshadowing her later destruction of all the manuscripts.

Finally, in *Garden* as in no other work, Hemingway dwells on the act of writing, exploring the workings of a writer's mind as he probes his way into the treatment of a story. From his depiction of David as a triumphant young writer to a nearly defeated one struggling against writer's block, Hemingway deals with the working problems of the artist, employing, varying, and enlarging on concepts that he had expressed in interviews or written about in his fiction.

Near the beginning of *Garden,* David's creativity has been bottled up by his artistic inactivity during his courtship of Catherine, their marriage, and their honeymoon. When he begins to write, the work flows easily, but David admonishes himself not to let the creative process become oversimplified. He tells himself that he must recognize the complexity of the human issues he is dealing with and then write about them in deceptively simple terms. The passage might serve as a defense against the charge once made by William Faulkner that Hemingway rated lower than many modernists because of the simplicity of his writing – or, as Faulkner put it, his failure to take chances in his art.[10]

In the next chapter, as David continues his work, Hemingway varies one of the symbols – which he had used previously and would use again in interviews and nonfiction – to explain his employing of unstated factors that underlie the surface of his fiction. David thinks of his own writing not, like Hemingway, in terms of an iceberg and its huge underwater mass belied by its lesser mass above the waterline, but in terms of apparently placid water that hides a potentially dangerous reef. The uninitiated will perceive only the smooth surface, but David knows that he has concealed a reef, and he creates a "light feathering" (42) on the surface that will alert the sensitive reader to the "sinister" layer concealed below.

The manuscript of the novel emphasizes David's creative life and the problems he confronts, in composing fiction. Writing about Africa, for example, David faces the same dilemma Hemingway had expressed in nautical terms in *The Old Man and the Sea* and in his Nobel Prize acceptance speech. Driven out beyond previous literary tradition, David realizes that he must invent ways to write about his African experience because no previous novelist in English has preceded him in depicting the culture of the black Africans he had grown up with. And he must allow the tribal secrets he knows to inform his writing without betraying the confidence of the Africans who have shared their lives with him.

David also has his own personal reticences to work out. He and his father have become estranged in spite of the fact that, like Nick Adams and his father, they were once very close. David realizes that his most powerful memories – his most valuable literary assets – are tied to his father and to the sense of betrayal connected to his recollections of their relationship. Yet he can use this material only by taking a certain psychological risk. Especially in the manuscript, but to a lesser degree in the published version of the novel, the reader is able to follow David as he explores the labyrinth of his emotions concerning his father, giving a sense of the process of discovery that comes to the writer while he is working.

At the same time, the text reflects back on Hemingway as author. For while he depicts David as writer dredging up the painful details of his past and putting them down on paper, he must recall his own estrangement from his father. And as Hemingway depicts David uncomfortably setting down the "narrative" of his troubled marriage with Catherine, he must draw on another of the most painful experiences of his own life, the breakup of his marriage to Hadley and the beginnings of his romance with Pauline – the real-life triangle that inspired his literary ménage à trois.

There are many other reflections of Hemingway's self-consciousness about his art in *Garden*. Both the positive and negative features of the creative life – the joy mingled with exhaustion that comes at the end of a day's work, reminiscent of some of the passages in *A Moveable Feast* – are woven into the narrative. So are darker reflections. At times it seems that David's only life is his life as a writer: He returns to real life with regret, leaving behind his writing until he can pick it up again the next day. David's writer's block after Catherine has destroyed his manuscripts has a clear parallel in sexual impotence. Some of Marita's comforting words when he reports a fruitless day's attempts to work suggest what she might say to him after a sexual failure. Thus, much of *Garden* treats the creation of literature. As in no other Hemingway work, the reader gets the sense of watching over the shoulder of the artist as he produces a work about the creation of art. In this respect, *The Garden of Eden,* had it been finished, could have marked Hemingway's emergence from modernism into postmodernism.

The conventional critical view has been that Hemingway's career was truncated by his participation in World War II. According to that viewpoint, his postwar efforts resulted in a series of failures relieved only by the publication of one small masterpiece – *The Old Man and the Sea* – and a bittersweet posthumous sketchbook treating the happier period of his apprenticeship in Paris – *A Moveable Feast.* While it is true that the years from 1946 to his death in 1961 did not see the publication of another big novel, Hemingway never stopped attempting to grow, or in his own terms, to explore the territory far out beyond where the artist could go. If he was not successful, at least he sought his own limit, the point at which his literary reach exceeded his grasp.

NOTES

1. Hemingway's World War II reports to *Collier's,* published between July 22, 1944 and November 18, 1944, ranged from the D-Day invasion to the fighting on the Siegfried Line. For a bibliography, see Carlos Baker's "A Working Check-List of Hemingway's Prose, Poetry, and Journalism – with Notes," in his *Hemingway: The Writer as Artist,* 4th ed. (Princeton: Princeton University Press, 1973), p. 414.

2. Quoted in Baker, *Writer as Artist* 339.

3. Harvey Breit, "Talk with Mr. Hemingway," reprinted in *Conversations with Ernest Hemingway,* ed. Matthew J. Bruccoli (Jackson: University of Mississippi Press, 1986), p. 62. Hemingway would use calculus as a metaphor within the text of the novel as well. While Cantwell is talking to the gran maestro, the headwaiter at the Gritti with whom he served in World War I, the gran maestro reflects that because the colonel has been a general officer, he thinks "in terms that were as far beyond [the gran maestro] as calculus is distant from a man who has only the knowledge of arithmetic" (62–63).

4. Arthur Waldhorn, *A Reader's Guide to Ernest Hemingway* (New York: Farrar, Straus and Giroux, 1972), p. 184.

5. Baker, 379–80.

6. Ibid., 382.
7. Ibid., 379.
8. Ibid., 384–88.
9. Gregory H. Hemingway, *Papa: A Personal Memoir* (Boston: Houghton Mifflin, 1976), pp. 64–67.
10. Carlos Baker, *Ernest Hemingway: A Life Story* (New York: Charles Scribner's Sons, 1969), 461.

WORKS CITED

Baker, Carlos. *Ernest Hemingway: A Life Story.* New York: Charles Scribner's Sons, 1969.
———. *Hemingway: The Writer as Artist.* 4th ed. Princeton: Princeton University Press, 1973.
Breit, Harvey. "Talk with Mr. Hemingway." Reprinted in *Conversations with Ernest Hemingway,* ed. Matthew J. Bruccoli. Jackson: University of Mississippi Press, 1986, 60–62.
Fleming, Robert E. *The Face in the Mirror: Hemingway's Writers.* Tuscaloosa: University of Alabama Press, 1994.
Hemingway, Gregory H. *Papa: A Personal Memoir.* Boston: Houghton Mifflin, 1976.
Hemingway, Patrick. "*Islands in the Stream:* A Son Remembers." *Ernest Hemingway: The Writer in Context.* Ed. James Nagel. Madison: University of Wisconsin Press, 1984, 13–18.
Jones, Richard B. "Mimesis and Metafiction in Hemingway's *The Garden of Eden.*" *Hemingway Review* 7.1 (1987): 2–13.
Waldhorn, Arthur. *A Reader's Guide to Ernest Hemingway.* New York: Farrar, Straus and Giroux, 1972.

8

KENETH KINNAMON

Hemingway and Politics

With a few exceptions, Hemingway's biographers have discounted his interest in and understanding of politics. In his foreword to *Ernest Hemingway: A Life Story,* Carlos Baker summarizes many of the paradoxical, even contradictory, aspects of his complex subject, calling him politically a "fierce individualist . . . who believed that that government is best which governs least." In his intellectual inventory of Hemingway in *By Force of Will,* Scott Donaldson follows suit, finding the consistent pattern of his political stance to be "the ideas of conservative Republicanism," deeply distrustful of big government and jealous of the autonomy of the individual person. "Basically bored with politics" according to the biography by Jeffrey Meyers, Hemingway responded to the call of the left in the 1930s in a "half-hearted" way with *To Have and Have Not,* which represents "only a token commitment to the class struggle." Kenneth Lynn's *Hemingway* brings a neoconservative as well as psychoanalytical perspective to the life and works, arguing that his political naiveté allowed Hemingway to become a communist dupe. James Mellow's recent *Hemingway: A Life without Consequences,* discussing the writer's relationship to the communist magazine *New Masses,* characterizes his political stance as that of "an individualist first and liberal second." Under the combined influence of Martha Gellhorn and the outbreak of civil war in Spain, however, Hemingway embraced what Mellow styles "the politics of desperation." And even the most authoritative biographer, Michael Reynolds, announces in *The Young Hemingway* that postwar cynicism and journalistic experience soured politics for the fledgling author: "Never a radical, Hemingway became apolitical and remained so for the rest of his life," making him "one of the least overtly political writers of his generation."[1]

Yet Hemingway's life, journalism, and imaginative writing show a continuing awareness of politics from early childhood, when his heroes included his grandfathers, both committed Republicans, and Theodore Roosevelt, the dominant American politician of the first decade of the century, right down to the victory of the Castro revolution in Cuba and the election of John F. Kennedy, to whose inaugural Hemingway was invited. The strong personality of his mother expressed itself in many ways, one of which was commitment to the suffrage and temperance movements. One of her son's early memories was attending a political meeting with her in Nantucket (Reynolds, *Young Hemingway* 106); another was recalled in a love letter to Mary Welsh cataloging the excitement of Chicago "with my Grandfather . . . and Theodore Roosevelt with the hearty clasp and the high squeeky [sic] voice."[2]

Although Roosevelt's trust-busting, Bull Moose variety of progressive Republicanism carried Hemingway's hometown in national elections, the pervasive gentility and insularity of Oak Park, Illinois, were less attractive to the boy. Working as a cub reporter in Kansas City after graduation from high school, he encountered a rawer kind of life. His beginner's status did not entitle him to a byline, but his reportorial beat included the railroad station, where he interviewed visiting celebrities, including, one supposes, some politicians. In the city room where he typed his stories, exposure to rough urban politics was inevitable. After seven months on the *Kansas City Star* Hemingway, having failed his physical examination because of weak vision, volunteered for Red Cross ambulance duty in the Great War that was ravaging Europe. In France and then in Italy he encountered not only war but the state politics that is "the womb in which war is developed."[3] While convalescing in northern Italy after being wounded in the Veneto, Hemingway met the elderly Count Emanuele Greppi, whose political sagacity, diplomatic experience, and courtly charm deeply impressed the young man, who later used him as the prototype of Count Greffi in *A Farewell to Arms*. In 1950 Hemingway wrote to Charles Scribner that Greppi served as his mentor in the complexities of European politics (*SL* 751).

Returning to America after the war, Hemingway spent his first year convalescing and writing sketches and short stories, then went to Toronto to serve as a companion to the crippled son of a wealthy family. There he began contributing to the *Toronto Star*. Over the four years of his association with this newspaper, he wrote almost two hundred articles. Many were human interest stories, but well over half were political, mostly concerned with Europe and the Near East. Covering postwar conferences, conflicts, and tensions, the young journalist wrote knowledgeably about the World Economic Conference in Genoa, the rise of fascism in Italy, the effects of runaway inflation in Germany, Mustapha Kemal and the evacuation of Constantinople and Thrace, Franco-German tension in the Ruhr, the revolutionary unrest in the European proletariat, and occasionally about Canadian and American political issues. Such political figures as Clemenceau, Poincaré, the Soviet diplomat George Tchitcherin, Aleksandr Stambouliski of Bulgaria, Chancellor Schober of Austria, Mussolini, Kemal, Count Apponyi, and Lloyd George receive extended treatment, and D'Annunzio, Lenin, Trotsky, Eamon de Valera, King Constantine, King Victor Emmanuel, Leon Daudet, Wilson, and numerous others make at least cameo appearances. Anyone doubting Hemingway's political expertise should read him on "Russia Spoiling the French Game" (October 23, 1922), "Turks Distrust Kemal Pasha" (October 24, 1922), or "King Business in Europe" (September 15, 1923).[4] Torontonians who read his dispatches to the *Star* regularly received a good education in some of the issues and personalities of contemporary European politics.

As Hemingway's work for the *Star* ended and his literary efforts began to appear in print in his and the century's middle twenties, his direct exposure to politics decreased and his interest subsided somewhat. Nevertheless, his political awareness continued to appear in his correspondence. In a letter of March 17, 1924, Hemingway teased Ezra Pound for his admiration for Mussolini by beginning with the salutation "Dear Duce." Praising Spain in a November letter to his old friend Howell Jenkins, he contrasted the situation in the other southern European peninsula: "They treat you like shit in Italy now. All post war fascisti, bad food and hysterics" (*SL* 131). Even more relevant complaints about the Mussolini government appear in a letter of February 2, 1925, to the same recipient. Writing to John Dos Passos on April 22 he referred sarcastically to Hindenberg and the Junker monarchists. In the following year, when the first issue of *New Masses* came out, Hemingway accurately called it "some sort of a house organ" (*SL* 218) in a letter to Sherwood Anderson. To his painter friend Waldo Peirce at the end of 1927 he denounced dictatorships in both Italy and Primo de Rivera's Spain. While in Kansas City in the summer of 1928 for the birth of his son Patrick, "he looked in at the nomination of Herbert Hoover at the Republican National Convention, retiring in disgust at the machinations of the politicians" (Baker, *Life Story* 194). The Great Depression was not far away, but Hemingway noted that it had already arrived in Key West.

In his imaginative writing of this first major period of his career, political issues appear more often than has generally been noticed or acknowledged, though they seldom become a major theme. In "Out of Season," one of three stories in Hemingway's first published book (1923), the drunken gardener-fishing guide Peduzzi extends greetings as he walks through town with his clients. Silently and rather sinisterly, "the bank clerk stared at him from the door of the Fascist cafe."[5] Of the ten poems in the same book, "Roosevelt" is an ambivalent eulogy to a childhood hero, and "Captives," "Champs d'Honneur," and "Riparto D'Assalto" express the disillusion-ment with the Great War that was the most widely held political opinion among literary intellectuals at the time and that was to receive its definitive statement six years later in *A Farewell to Arms*. Similar sentiments are behind a third of the eighteen short sketches called "chapters" comprising *in our time* (1924) and appearing again in *In Our Time* (1925). In addition, the 1930 edition of that collection contains "On the Quai at Smyrna," derived from Hemingway's journalistic coverage of the Greco-Turkish con-flict, and the overtly political story "The Revolutionist," which had ap-peared as a "chapter" of *in our time*. A few months later the short satirical novel *The Torrents of Spring* was published with a sarcastic dedication to S. Stanwood Mencken, a right-winger committed to keeping alive the red scare with the preposterous claim that there were more than half a million Com-munists in the United States, and to his antagonist H. L. Mencken. In the next novel, *The Sun Also Rises,* the banter of Jake Barnes and Bill Gorton on their fishing trip north of Pamplona includes references to both foreign and domestic politics: Primo de Rivera and the rebellion in the Riff as well as Lincoln and Grant, the temperance movement, William Jennings Bryan, and President Coolidge. Coolidge is also mentioned in "Banal Story" in *Men without Women* (1927), a collection that includes two Italian stories of political significance. "In Another Country" is set in Milan at a rehabilita-tion hospital for wounded military personnel during the war. Walking through "the communist quarter" to the Café Cova, the narrator and three other young officers must pass by wineshops filled with hostile workers, some shouting, "A basso gli ufficiali!" ("Down with officers!").[6] Much more unpleasant is the political situation after the war as depicted in "Che Ti Dice la Patria?" This story first appeared as a nonfictional report on a trip Hemingway and Guy Hickok took to Italy in March 1927. The country that Hemingway had loved so much only a decade earlier had become under Mussolini a rude, threatening, dangerous, corrupt place. That is what the country's domination by fascism said to him. Finally, at the end of the decade, came *A Farewell to Arms.* Whatever else that great novel may say, its statement against the Great War is clear and convincing.

As in the previous decade, Hemingway's letters during the 1930s are sprinkled with political references, especially when he is writing to Dos Passos. Traveling to Spain in May 1931 to collect more material for *Death in the Afternoon,* he observed closely the complicated Spanish political scene, reporting on it to Dos Passos in a letter of June 26 that is virtually a disquisition on the subject. Hemingway still felt at home in Spain, but Italy was another matter. As he made plans for an African safari with Henry Strater early in 1932, he stipulated that the boat from Marseilles to Mombassa not stop at an Italian port because he did not want to be beaten up. As the Depression deepened many writers were moving left, but Hemingway, who had moved in that direction more than a decade earlier, resisted the tendency. As the presidential election approached, with the "Country . . . all busted" (*SL* 372), he wrote Guy Hickok, the unattractive choices were "The Paralytic Demagogue/The Syphilitic Baby/The Sentimental Reformer/The Yes-Man of Moscow" (*SL* 373), that is, Franklin D. Roosevelt, Herbert Hoover, Norman Thomas, and William Z. Foster. A year later he wrote from Madrid to his conservative mother-in-law, noting confusion and corruption in Spain but something worse in Germany: "I hate Hitler because he is working for one thing: war" (*SL* 398). When "one of my best pals" (*SL* 411), the communist revolutionary and painter Luis Quintanilla, was arrested in Spain in October 1934, Hemingway financed a benefit show of his work in New York and wrote an introduction to the exhibition catalogue. A new epistolary friend was the Soviet critic and translator Ivan Kashkeen, with whom he discussed literature and politics in correspondence beginning August 19, 1935.

During these years Hemingway was following closely Caribbean as well as European politics. Gerardo Machado's brutal dictatorship had been overthrown in Cuba in 1933, but political turmoil continued on that unhappy island. Ninety miles north in Key West, where the Hemingways had been living since 1928, the Federal Emergency Relief Administration was trying to respond to the collapse of the economy, but Hemingway was sharply critical of its efforts. When a disastrous hurricane hit the Keys on the night of August 31, 1935, the appalling loss of life in the Civilian Conservation Corps work camps, filled with war veterans including many of the bonus marchers, enraged Hemingway, who blamed not only the Miami Weather Bureau but New Deal bureaucrats in Washington, who delayed a rescue train until it was too late. Not satisfied with venting his anger in his correspondence, he wrote "Who Murdered the Vets?" for *New Masses* in September and in December sent a congratulatory telegram on the occasion of the twenty-fifth anniversary of the magazine that nine years earlier he had reviled.

Cuban and Key West materials form the substance of "One Trip Across" (1934) and "The Tradesman's Return" (1936), which constitute the first two parts of *To Have and Have Not* (1937), the author's most political book to date. By the time of publication the Spanish civil war had been under way for over a year, and Hemingway was itching to get involved. As early as September 26, 1936 he had written to Maxwell Perkins: "I hate to have missed this Spanish thing worse than anything in the world but have to have this book [*THAHN*] finished first" (*SL* 454–55). There was no question where his loyalties lay. In December he told Perkins. "I've paid two guys over there to fight (transportation and cash to Spanish border) already. . . . Franco is a good general but a son of a bitch of the first magnitude" (*SL* 455). By January 1937 Hemingway was in New York helping Prudencio de Pereda on a propaganda film for the Loyalists, and late the following month he was sailing to France. On March 16 he arrived in Spain as an accredited correspondent for the North American Newspaper Alliance. For over a year he covered the bloody conflict, often under fire, writing thirty-one dispatches for publication in European and Canadian as well as American newspapers. During this period he and Joris Ivens made the film *The Spanish Earth* to raise public concern about what was happening in and to his most loved country. Back in the States in the late spring and early summer of 1937, Hemingway narrated the sound track for the film, showed it to Franklin and Eleanor Roosevelt in the White House, gave antifascist speeches at the Second American Writers' Congress in New York and at a successful fundraising event in Hollywood sponsored by Frederic March, wrote an article for *Pravda*, and did whatever else he could to aid the cause that constituted the deepest political commitment of his life. When he returned to Europe again in August, he continued his reporting on the war and enlarged his circle of friends, especially among the political activists of the International Brigades.

While hosting soldiers and journalists in his hotel room rocked by artillery fire in besieged Madrid and traveling to the Aragon front to cover important battles, Hemingway somehow managed to write the highly political play *The Fifth Column,* followed by four short stories on the war and by *For Whom the Bell Tolls.* Early in 1938 he returned to Key West, but he was back in Spain on April 1 in time to witness Franco's rapid, relentless advance toward Catalonia. Though he tried to maintain optimism after this cruelest of Aprils, it became increasingly difficult to do so. Returning to Key West, in a July article for *Ken* he urged President Roosevelt to provide aid at last to Spain, but FDR continued his policy of nonintervention, leading Hemingway to predict in *Ken* on August 11 that war would break out within a year as a consequence of continuing appeasement of fascism. Six weeks later Chamberlain signed the Munich Pact, six months after that Franco received a telegram from Pope Pius XII giving thanks "for Spain's Catholic victory," and five months later, on September 1, 1939, Hitler unleashed the blitzkrieg against Poland. Hemingway, whose political pre-science has too often gone unremarked, had missed his prediction by only twenty-one days.

As the United States moved closer to involvement in 1940 and 1941, Hemingway declined to write "flagwaving stuff" (*SL* 506), but would, he said, fight. Soon after his marriage to Martha Gellhorn, however, she received an assignment from *Collier's* to report on the Chinese-Japanese war, and Hemingway wangled a similar assignment from the new left-liberal New York newspaper *PM*. They spent a month in Hong Kong, where Hemingway met the widow of Sun Yat-sen, before moving on to a war zone. In Chungking he met with Generalissimo and Madame Chiang Kai-shek as well as the American ambassador to discuss the military and political situation. In his articles for *PM* he pointed out China's need for assistance in its struggle to repel aggression, noting also that the Soviet Union was giving aid. The situation was reminiscent of Spain.

Recognizing as he did Japan's threat, Hemingway was appalled by the lack of U.S. preparation revealed at Pearl Harbor. To Charles Scribner he wrote despairingly: "Through our (American) laziness, criminal careless-ness, and blind arrogance we are fucked in this war as of the first day and we are going to have Christ's own bitter time to win it if, when, and ever" (*SL* 532). His first contribution to the war effort was the anthology *Men at War*. In the introduction he expresses his hatred of both war and "all the politicians whose mismanagement, gullibility, cupidity, selfishness and am-bition brought on this present war and made it inevitable." He also reiter-ated the political position he had consistently maintained for twenty years: "We must win [the war] never forgetting what we are fighting for, in order that while we are fighting Fascism we do not slip into the ideas and ideals of Fascism" (*Men at War* 5, xi–xii). Having contributed to the effort to stop fascism in Spain, he now organized the "Crook Factory," with the support if not at the instigation of the U.S. ambassador to Cuba, Spruille Braden, to conduct espionage on the Falangists and other Nazi sympathizers on the island. His associates in this enterprise were several friends from the Spanish civil war, including the talented radical composer and former Loyalist gener-al Gustavo Durán, as well as members of the embassy staff. From spying Hemingway progressed to patrolling for Nazi submarines on his fishing vessel the *Pilar*, equipped for the purpose by Braden and the Chief of Naval Intelligence for Central America. Although the *Pilar* did not engage in actual combat with submarines, as Hemingway was to fantasize in his posthumous novel *Islands in the Stream*, during its two years of activity, according to Ambassador Braden, the operation "obtained valuable information on the location of German subs on various occasions" (Meyers, *Hemingway: A Biography* 388).

But the real action that Hemingway longed for was in the European theater. His wife had left the Finca Vigia for London in late October 1943 as war correspondent for *Collier's*, returning in March. In May they were both in Europe, Hemingway having secured a contract of his own with *Collier's*. Though not on the same ship, they were both offshore at Omaha Beach on D-Day, June 6, 1944. Hemingway was back in London when the Germans began to launch their buzzbombs, two of which struck not far from him. He flew with the RAF over enemy territory several times before crossing over to Normandy to see ground action. There he met Colonel Charles "Buck" Lanham, with whom he was to develop a close friendship as he accompanied the 22nd Infantry Regiment in Normandy and later, after the liberation of Paris, in Belgium and on into Germany. He was often under fire, especially as the leader of a French guerrilla group on the way to Paris and in the terrible fighting in the Hürtgen Forest with Lanham and the 22nd. Only after the Allied victory was obvious to all did Hemingway leave on March 6, 1945, a month after the Yalta Conference and a month before V-E Day. The second war against fascism, unlike the first, had been won.

In the sixteen remaining years of his life, Hemingway's interest in politics continued. In the months immediately following the war his letters discuss such political issues and figures as the cancellation of the Lend-Lease program; Pétain, whom he "never liked . . . neither as a general, a man nor a politician" (*SL* 595); the Soviet Union; and such British fascists as Oswald Mosley and William Joyce ("Lord Haw-Haw"). In a letter to the Soviet writer Konstantin Simonov on June 20, 1946, Hemingway affirmed his antifascism, criticized Churchill, and endorsed Soviet-American friendship. Writing to Charles Scribner in 1947 he approved Martha Gellhorn's attack in *The New Republic* on the House Un-American Activities Committee, and in the same year he scoffed at the notion that political unrest in Colombia was sponsored by the Kremlin. As anticommunist hysteria was sweeping the United States, he found it necessary to affirm to Charles Scribner Jr. that he could "take an oath at any time that I am not nor never have been a member of the C.P. [Communist Party]" (*SL* 641). As for congressional investigating committees, in a 1949 letter he fantasized his response to any question about being subversive: "You cocksucker, when did you come to this country and where were your people in 1776–9, 1861–5, 1914–18, and 1941–45?" (*SL* 659). As for Senator McCarthy, Hemingway in 1950 issued this invitation to the Finca Vigia: "You can come down here and fight for free, without any publicity, with an old character like me who is fifty years old and weighs 209 and thinks you are a shit, Senator, and would knock you on your ass the best day you ever lived" (*SL* 693). While disillusioned with American politics, he followed the Cuban revolution with interest and approbation. He was less than favorable to the Mau-Mau uprising in Kenya. As he complained to sometimes disbelieving friends, he was hounded by the FBI. One of his last letters was to John F. Kennedy, praising him for his inaugural address and expressing his admiration and hope for the new administration.

There can be no doubt, then, that Hemingway had a serious interest in politics during his entire adult life. It was only one of many interests, of course, and certainly less intense than his interest in writing or fishing or hunting or bullfighting or travel. But it conditioned his worldview and found its way into his imaginative writing, especially in the 1930s. The question remains, however: What was his own political position? As a man of strong opinions, he was certainly not content to remain an impartial observer of the international and domestic scene. He was not, like his old Spanish refugee at the bridge, "without politics."7

Because he was not a consistent political thinker, however, he did not adhere to a systematic political theory. Unresolved contradictions recur in his political pronouncements, but certain central themes can be traced. First, though interested in politics, he disliked politicians and especially distrusted their appeals to patriotism. In Kansas City as a cub reporter he observed political corruption involving a city hospital during a smallpox epidemic. In World War I he experienced the human consequences of political rivalries in Europe. The loss of idealism shared by his generation has received no more memorable statement than Frederic Henry's thoughts in *A Farewell to Arms,* elicited by his patriotic friend Gino's comment that one should not speak of losing the war because "what has been done this summer cannot have been done in vain": "I did not say anything. I was always embarrassed by the words sacred, glorious, and sacrifice and the expression in vain. We had heard them, sometimes standing in the rain almost out of earshot, so that only the shouted words came through, and had read them, on proclamations that were slapped up by billposters over other proclamations, now for a long time, and the things that were glorious had no glory and the sacrifices were like the stockyards in Chicago if nothing was done with the meat except to bury it."8

After the war Hemingway worked in Chicago for the *Cooperative Commonwealth,* the magazine of the Cooperative Society of America, ostensibly a political-economic scheme to improve the lot of rural midwesterners. As it turned out, the society was a financial fraud designed by founder Harrison

Parker to bilk millions from the members. Another disillusionment. As a reporter for the *Toronto Star* Hemingway satirized Mayor Thomas Church as a gladhanding politician pretending to be a sports fan and wrote of political murders in Chicago. On the international scene he excoriated Poincaré and the other reactionary, shortsighted, vindictive, stupid French politicians in power in an article dated February 4, 1922, but he was more favorable to Poincaré five weeks later. His coverage of the Genoa Conference in April and May was avowedly impartial, but some of his sketches of Europe's political leaders are less than flattering. Subsequently he interviewed Mussolini twice, on the second occasion calling him "the biggest bluff in Europe" (*Dateline: Toronto* 255). On the domestic scene he made sardonic comments in his correspondence about Warren G. Harding, Calvin Coolidge, and Herbert Hoover. He was, if anything, even more caustic about the New Deal, calling his formerly beloved Key West "this F.E.R.A. Jew administered phony of a town" (*SL* 410). In *Green Hills of Africa* the New Deal is called "Some sort of Y.M.C.A. show. Starry eyed bastards spending money that somebody will have to pay. Everybody in our town quit work to go on relief. Fishermen all turned carpenters. Reverse of the Bible."[9] FDR, "The Paralytic Demagogue," Hemingway held responsible for the deaths of the veterans in the Keys during the hurricane of 1935 as well as the U.S. failure to aid the Spanish Republic. Other politicians and public figures criticized by Hemingway in the late 1940s and early 1950s include Harry Truman, Cardinal Spellman, Juan Antonio de Rivera, Mayor O'Dwyer of New York, Winston Churchill, Dwight Eisenhower, and Mussolini. From 1954 to the end, such a list would include De Gaulle, Ezra Pound, Eisenhower, Nixon, Adlai Stevenson, Estes Kefauver, John Kasper (the racist admirer of Pound); and Fulgencio Batista. Writing to Mary Welsh in 1945, he included "any liveing [sic] politicians" (*SL* 600) in a list of people he did not believe.

The second salient characteristic of Hemingway's political position was a strong individualism hostile to control by any exterior force, whether literary critic, wife, or government. His personality was powerful, not to say domineering, and he asserted it among his friends and associates, many of whom readily followed his leadership. As for government bureaucracies, *noli me tangere* might well have been his motto. To Dos Passos he wrote on May 30, 1932: "I can't be a Communist because I hate tyranny and, I suppose, government. . . . I can't stand *any* bloody government. . . . No larger unit than the village can exist without things being impossible" (*SL* 360). In another letter to Dos Passos he called himself an anarchist. To his Russian translator, the critic Ivan Kashkeen, he wrote three years later: "I cannot be a communist now because I believe in only one thing: liberty. . . . All the state has ever meant to me is unjust taxation. . . . I believe in the absolute minimum of government." As he went on to explain, the writer is a kind of an Ishmael, an antipatriot: "He owes no allegiance to any government. If he is a good writer he will never like the government he lives under. His hand should be against it and its hand will always be against him" (*SL* 419). Such autonomy was essential to maintain the integrity necessary to serve truth, the artist's deepest moral obligation.

Hemingway's dislike of politicians and his prickly individualism have long been recognized, but the third and even more important component of his politics has been underestimated, insufficiently acknowledged, or ignored altogether. From the beginning to the end of his adult life, he had deep sympathies with the left, especially the revolutionary left. An example of the neglect of his leftism is the matter of the great American Socialist Eugene V. Debs. In their full-scale biographies of Hemingway, neither Kenneth Lynn nor James Mellow mentions Debs. Michael Reynolds mentions Debs twice in *The Young Hemingway* only as historical background, not connecting him to the young war veteran from Oak Park. Only Carlos Baker makes such a connection, stating somewhat misleadingly that Hemingway did not wish to choose between Roosevelt and Hoover in 1932 "since his favorite candidate was still Eugene Debs" (Baker, *Life Story* 231). Relying on Baker, not understanding the import of the word "still," and forgetting that Debs died in 1926, Jeffrey Meyers states that "Hemingway supported the Socialist Eugene Debs for President in 1932" (Meyers, *Hemingway: A Biography* 109). The truth, as Hemingway related it to Lillian Ross in 1948, is that he cast his first and only vote in a U.S. presidential election for the founder of American socialism: "I cast the only vote for Debs in our precinct. Never voted after that. In the death of our candidate I retired from giddy political whirl" (*SL* 648). Eight years later he explained to J. Donald Adams that he voted for Debs because "he was an honest man and in jail" (*SL* 871), as if on the American political scene the only place for an honest man was in jail. One thinks of Thoreau. It is especially significant that Hemingway was still recalling (and implicitly endorsing) Debs so late in life.

When Hemingway characterized the Democratic, Republican, socialist, and communist candidates in the 1932 presidential campaign, his least unfavorable epithet, "The Sentimental Reformer," was attached to the socialist Norman Thomas. But unlike Thomas, a Presbyterian minister and graduate of Princeton and Union Theological Seminary, Debs was more than a reformer; he was a class-conscious railroad worker, union organizer and official, pioneer of the movement for industrial unions, one of the founders of the Industrial Workers of the World, and opponent of American intervention in the Mexican revolution and of American participation in World War I. He also celebrated the success of the Bolshevik revolution. As Debs was entering prison on Palm Sunday 1919, after conviction under the Espionage Act for a speech he gave in Canton, Ohio, the previous year, he declared himself "a flaming revolutionist."[10] The next year Hemingway voted for him.

A couple of months later he met Isaac Don Levine, who covered Russia for the *Chicago Daily News*. Impressed, Hemingway wrote to his mother that "Levine is an excellent fellow and gave us the cold dope on Rooshia" (*SL* 44), and proceeded to read the correspondent's book, *The Russian Revolution* (Reynolds, *Young Hemingway* 193), a favorable account. After his marriage to Hadley Richardson and the departure of the couple to Paris at the end of 1921, Hemingway learned more about the Soviets the following spring at the Genoa Conference, where he wrote more for the *Toronto Star* about the Russian delegation than about any other. Additional information was doubtless gleaned from fellow journalists Lincoln Steffens and Max Eastman, both of whom were enthusiastic supporters of the Bolsheviks. Eager to see Russia for himself, Hemingway received credentials for the trip from the *Star*, and even provided an author's note for *Poetry* magazine, stating that he was "at present in Russia as staff correspondent" (*SL* 70), but the trip never came off. From Genoa he returned to Paris in time for May Day 1922, when a large communist demonstration was broken up by police. Confined to bed with a throat infection, he did not witness the event, but he was impressed enough by newspaper accounts to mention it in a letter to his father and to describe it brilliantly in a sentence that moved his writing from journalism to literature: "I have watched the police charge the crowd with swords as they milled back into Paris through the Porte Maillot on the first of May and seen the frightened proud look on the white beaten-up face of the sixteen year old kid who looked like a prep school quarter back and had just shot two policemen" (Baker, *Life Story* 91). Italian Communists, ubiquitous in the north of the country, were less formidable: "The North Italian Red is father of a family and a good workman six days out of seven; on the seventh he talks politics" (*Dateline: Toronto* 131), often fueled by too much chianti. Congenial and convivial, these Reds are no match in street battles with the bands of young Fascists, as Hemingway ruefully admits.

As sympathetic as he was toward the Bolsheviks in Russia, the easygoing Genoese Reds, or his "new God" (*SL* 101) in 1923, the recently assassinated Mexican revolutionary Pancho Villa, Hemingway had little use for parlor radicals or new converts back home. When Max Eastman's *Masses* was revived as *New Masses* in 1926, he called it "the most peurile [sic] and shitty house organ I've ever seen" (*SL* 216), though he did send it "An Alpine Idyll." Similar cracks appeared the next few months in letters to Sherwood Anderson and Maxwell Perkins, and he also poked fun at the sentimental reformism of *New Republic* in the poem "The Earnest Liberal's Lament," enclosed in a letter to Waldo Peirce. When literary intellectuals were moving left in the early 1930s, Hemingway made a startling comment in a letter to Scott Fitzgerald: "Have you become a Communist like Bunny [Edmund] Wilson? In 1919–20–21 when we were all paid up Communists Bunny and all those guys thot it was all tripe – as indeed it proved to be – but suppose everybody has to go through some political or religious faith sooner or later. Personally would rather go through things sooner and get your disillusions behind you instead of ahead of you" (*SL* 339). Because there is no evidence elsewhere that he was in fact a "paid up Communist" and because he later denied that he had ever been a Communist, one must interpret this statement as humorous hyperbole, but it does confirm other indications of his early sympathy with the revolutionary left. After all, his writing of the 1920s included the touching story of "The Revolutionist," tortured by the Hungarian Whites but still full of illusions: "He believed altogether in the world revolution" (*IOT* 106). And another peripatetic revolutionary was the protagonist of the aborted "A New Slain Knight," the major fictional project between *The Sun Also Rises* and *A Farewell to Arms.*[11]

When Hemingway's great work on tauromachy, *Death in the Afternoon,* appeared in 1932, the concluding page seemed clearly to repudiate, at least in his own work, increasingly fashionable literary radicalism: "Let those who want to save the world if you can get to see it clear and as a whole."[12] In *Green Hills of Africa* (1935), the criticism becomes even more pointed: "Writers should work alone. . . . Otherwise they become like writers in New York. All angleworms in a bottle, trying to derive knowledge and nourishment from their own contact and from the bottle. Sometimes the bottle is shaped art, sometimes economics, sometimes economic-religion. But once inside the bottle they stay there" (*GHOA* 21–22). He was especially apprehensive about the dangers of ideological or party control of the creative process. Praising 1919 as "bloody splendid" (*SL* 354), even better than *The 42nd Parallel,* Hemingway went on to warn Dos Passos about left didacticism. When Paul Romaine expressed the hope that Hemingway would write about more socially significant subjects than bulls and the lost generation, he bristled: "That is so much horseshit. I do not follow the fashions in politics, letters, religion etc" (*SL* 363).

But even as he resisted pressure from the American left, Hemingway traveled to Madrid in May 1931, only a month after the overthrow of the dictator Primo de Rivera and the departure of King Alfonso XIII. He found the political scene exhilarating but chaotic, with Republicans constituting a large majority but split among themselves into a bewildering variety of parties and factions, not to mention regional interests. Helping him make sense of the situation was a new Spanish friend, the radical Luis Quintanilla. At the end of the year the Constitution of the Second Republic was passed, declaring Spain "a democratic republic of workers of every class, organized in a regime of liberty and justice."[13] These were the ideals and the country to which Hemingway made the most profound political commitment of his life in the civil war that was to follow in less than five years.

But first there was the deteriorating situation at home. As an old sympathizer with the revolutionary left, his sympathy recharged by his trip to Spain, he was not to be lectured by pinkish, bookish types in the States. To Paul Romaine he wrote angrily on August 9, 1932: "I will not outline my political beliefs to you since I have no need to and since I could be jailed for their publication but if they are not much further left than yours which sound like a sentimental socialism, I will move them further over" (SL 365). There was no denying, as he wrote to Guy Hickok in October, that the "Country is all busted. . . . 200,000 guys on the road like the wild kids in Russia. . . . Well well well this depression is hell" (SL 372, 373). But Stalinism was certainly not the way out. Indeed, he wrote to Dos Passos at this time, "I suppose I am an anarchist. . . . To hell with the Church when it becomes a state and the hell with the State when it becomes a church" (SL 375). At times, though, Hemingway seems to demand constancy above all. Thus in 1933 he was critical of Scott Fitzgerald for turning to communism but two months later called Max Eastman, who had angered him with his scathing review of Death in the Afternoon, "a traitor in politics" (SL 394) because he was turning away from it.

Hemingway's culminating statement in the mid-1930s on revolution, politics, and writing is surely "Old Newsman Writes: A Letter from Cuba." Using an unnamed newspaper columnist (clearly Heywood Broun) as an example, Hemingway here deplores easy talk of revolution by writers without an adequate knowledge of history or a sufficiently analytical intelligence. He explains: "The world was much closer to revolution in the years after the war than it is now. In those days we who believed in it looked for it at any time, expected it, hoped for it – for it was the logical thing. But everywhere it came it was aborted." The reason, he came to believe, was that "there can never be a Communist revolution without, first, a complete military debacle." The debacle was complete in Russia. Italy came close to revolution after Caporetto, but rallied its military effort in the spring and summer of 1918. French troops rebelled and were marching on Paris in 1917, but Clemenceau turned the tide with ruthless suppression of all who did not wish to pursue the war, even to the extent of ordering a saber charge by the Guard Republicaine on a parade of mutilated veterans – thus anticipating Hoover's use of troops to rout the bonus marchers in Washington. The implication throughout is not that Hemingway no longer wanted revolution in 1934 after wanting it in the early 1920s, but that now the conditions were not propitious, for economic crisis was not a sufficient cause. Serious writers, moreover, should have a commitment to their art that goes beyond politics or the personal rewards that politics may bring. Hemingway's statement of his aesthetic creed in "Old Newsman Writes" is similar to those he made elsewhere, but it bears quoting: "All good books are alike in that they are truer than if they had really happened and after you are finished reading one you will feel that all that happened to you and afterwards it all belongs to you; the good and the bad, the ecstasy, the remorse and sorrow, the people and the places and how the weather was." These qualities, he explains, constitute the permanent value of such a book as *War and Peace,* not "the big Political Thought passages"[14] that are topical and therefore transient. Only the dedicated writer working alone can hope to achieve literature. Writers' collectives and left didacticism cannot.

If the duty of a writer is to write, the duty of the revolutionary is to work for the revolution. Both vocations require extraordinary commitment. One of the few favorably presented minor characters in *To Have and Have Not* is the Communist Nelson Jacks, "a tall, thin man with a scar that ran from one corner of his eye down over his chin." Unlike the rowdy drunks among the other vets crowding Freddy's Bar in Key West, Jacks is calm and focused. To Richard Gordon, the fashionably radical novelist character based on Dos Passos, Jacks comments: "It takes discipline and abnegation to be a Communist; a rummy can't be a Communist." Writing a novel on the Gastonia textile strike, Gordon had earlier received praise for his fiction at the Lilac Time, a watering place for the Haves, but his admirer turns out to be literally crazy. The literary judgment of Jacks is quite different. When Gordon asks his opinion of his books, Jacks says that he did not like them

"Why?"
"I don't like to say."
"Go ahead."
"I thought they were shit," the tall man said and turned away.

Presumably Jacks will continue his lonely, dedicated life as a peripatetic communist organizer. Before working with the bonus marchers he had been in "Mexico, Cuba, South America, and around."[15]

Of Hemingway's next three works, *The Spanish Earth* is a propaganda film made in collaboration with a Dutch Communist, and both *The Fifth Column* and *For Whom the Bell Tolls* have communist protagonists. In the play Philip Rawlings is a counterespionage agent in Madrid reporting to Antonio, a character based on the city's chief of the Servicio de Investigación Militar, the Communist Pepe Quintanilla, the brother of Hemingway's good friend Luis Quintanilla. Philip's romantic interest is Dorothy Bridges, a leggy blonde reminiscent of Martha Gellhorn. When his attraction to her and his disgust with the dirty business his work involves – including assassination and torture – threaten to compromise his dedication to the cause, his comrade Max reminds him of the ends these means are designed to achieve: "You do it so *everyone* will have a good breakfast like that. You do it so *no one* will ever be hungry. You do it so men will not have to fear ill health or old age; so they can live and work in dignity and not as slaves" (*The Fifth Column* 79). Once enjoying wealth and the pleasures it brings, Philip has given up his lifestyle to serve the revolution, and at the end of the play he must give up Dorothy as well: "I've been to all those places [Saint Tropez, Paris, Nairobi, Kitzbuhel, Havana, etc.] and I've left them all behind. And where I go now I go alone, or with others who go there for the same reason I go" (*The Fifth Column* 98). So Philip achieves the requisite communist abnegation and discipline that Nelson Jacks prescribes.

If Philip Rawlings is ambivalent about the issue of means and ends, Robert Jordan of *For Whom the Bell Tolls* is even more so. In the beginning, as a volunteer in the International Brigades, he felt his political faith with a religious intensity: "Like the feeling you expected to have but did not have when you made your first communion. It was a feeling of consecration to a duty toward all the oppressed of the world which would be as difficult and embarrassing to speak about as religious experience and yet it was authentic as the feeling you had when you heard Bach, or stood in Chartres Cathedral or the Cathedral at León and saw the light coming through the great windows. . . . It gave you a part in something that you could believe in wholly and completely. . . . It was something that you had never known before but that you had experienced now and you gave such importance to it and the reasons for it that your own death seemed of complete unimportance. . . . But the best thing was that there was something you could do about this feeling. . . . You could fight."[16] And fight he did: "You learned the dry-mouthed, fear-purged, surging ecstasy of battle and you fought that summer and that fall for all the poor in the world, against all the tyranny, for all the things that you believed and for the new world that you had been educated into" (*FWBT* 236). This was the zealous faith of crusading communism, the spirit of Velasquez 63, the headquarters of the International Brigades. Who has described the communist faith better than Hemingway, who did not share it but respected it deeply? The climate was different at Gaylord's, the hotel housing some of the high Russian officers and journalists. Cynicism – or realism – was the prevailing mood here, where the food was good despite the siege of the city and where the reality behind the propaganda was known to all. But such characters as Karkov, modeled after the *Pravda* and *Izvestia* correspondent Mikhail Koltsov, and General Golz, modeled after the Polish General "Walter," were admirable in their distinctive ways and, after their fashion, perhaps equally committed. Jordan himself becomes increasingly uncomfortable with the discrepancy between appearance and reality in the conduct of the war. In the longest stream-of-consciousness passage in the novel he is deeply troubled by the necessity of using fascistic methods to stop fascism: "You were fighting against exactly what you were doing and being forced into doing to have any chance of winning" (*FWBT* 162). With these serious reservations he was still willing to "be under Communist discipline for the duration of the war" (*FWBT* 163), even if, as he tries to tell himself, he had no politics now. Not quite a Communist anymore, perhaps, Jordan is still and always, like his creator, an antifascist. On the second of his three days with Pablo's band in the Guadarramas he continues his interior political dialogue: "You're not a real Marxist and you know it. You believe in Liberty, Equality and Fraternity. You believe in Life, Liberty and the Pursuit of Happiness" (*FWBT* 305). But a fascist victory in Spain will prevent realization of the goals of the French and American revolutions as well as the dictatorship of the proletariat, a classless society, and a state economy.

The achievement of *For Whom the Bell Tolls,* Hemingway's greatest novel, transcends partisanship in its artistic integrity. If the horrors of fascism are made manifest, the massacre of the fascists in Pablo's village is perhaps even more graphically depicted. And surely no character in the work is etched more acidly than the murderous madman André Marty, commander of the International Brigades. The author's commitment to truth eschews propaganda. The result is an affirmation of human struggle, indeed of humanity itself, as well as perhaps the finest novel of Spain by a non-Spaniard. However, its matrix is its author's longstanding sympathy for the revolutionary left, his love of Spain, and his friendship with such Communists as Luis Quintanilla, Gustav Regler, Milton Wolff, Karol Swierezenski ("Walter"), Gustavo Durán, Freddy Keller, Mikhail Koltsov, Mamsurov Judji-Umar, Hans Kahle, Werner Heilbrun, José Luis Herrera Sotolongo, Joris Ivens, Maté Zelka (General "Lukacz"), Alexis Eisner, Ilya Ehrenburg, Phil Detro, Roman Karmen, Nicolas Guillén, Roman Nicolau, and others. As he once told Joseph North, "I like Communists when they're soldiers, but when they're priests, I hate them" (Baker, *Life Story* 330). Hemingway was never a dupe of the Communists, but neither did he allow his discomfort with their duplicity or brutality to override his conviction that their discipline offered the best chance to save the Republic, stop fascist aggression, and prevent another world war. As he wrote to Edmund Wilson years later about his association with Communists in the civil war: "This was not a Stalinist experience. These were episodes in the defence of the Spanish Republic" (*SL* 794).

What Hemingway later sardonically called his "premature antifascism"[17] became timely when World War II arrived. Eager for action, he first organized the "Crook Factory" and subsequently went to the European theater. Again, as he wrote to Mary Welsh on September 11, 1944, he was happy fighting fascism: "Know what you fight for and where and why and to what ends" (*SL* 566). It was good, but it was not Spain. In a letter to Charles Scribner after the war, Hemingway sorts out his loyalties: "to Scribners . . . the Spanish Republic, the 4th U.S. Infantry Division and the 22nd Infantry Regiment. I have felt much more deeply about the 12th International Brigade and my children and Mary" (*SL* 638). On the occasion of the tenth anniversary reunion of the Veterans of the Abraham Lincoln Brigade in New York in 1947, Hemingway could not attend in person but he recorded his prose eulogy "On the American Dead in Spain," first published in *New Masses* in 1939, along with some prefatory comments to be played at the dinner.

Some of these loyalties were bound to make Hemingway a suspicious character to Senator Joseph McCarthy, the House Un-American Activities, and vigilante groups during the anticommunist hysteria of the 1940s and 1950s. He was under close scrutiny by the FBI during the last two decades of his life. His response was to mock and defy the witch-hunters.

The hunt might have become more intense if Washington had been aware of the help Hemingway was providing to Cuban Communists. Dr. José Luis Herrera Sotolongo, whom he had met in Spain, escaped a death sentence imposed by Franco and was living in exile in Cuba, where he became Hemingway's personal physician and one of his closest friends. Herrera Sotolongo met Fidel Castro while the latter was still studying at the University of Havana and later participated in the rebellion against the dictator

Fulgencio Batista. Hemingway himself had supported the overthrow of the former dictator Gerardo Machado in 1933. When the outlawed Cuban Communist Party began its agitation against the Batista regime, Hemingway supported the effort with donations totaling $20,000, the largest sum contributed by a foreigner. After the Party was legalized, Hemingway continued his financial support of both Cuban and Spanish Communists through Emiliano Loza and Herrera Sotolongo. He also became involved in an unsuccessful conspiracy to overthrow another Caribbean dictator, Rafael Leonidas Trujillo of the Dominican Republic.[18]

When Castro came down from the Sierra Maestra for the final phase of the Cuban revolution, Hemingway had mixed feelings. From Ketchum he wrote to his son Patrick in late November 1958 expressing serious reservations: "I am not a big fear danger pussy but living in a country where no one is right – both sides atrocious – knowing what sort of stuff and murder will go on when the new ones come in – seeing the abuses of those in now – I am fed on it" (*SL* 888). But after Castro's total victory and Batista's flight from Havana "with his chief murderers and thieves," Hemingway was glad to see him go, writing to Gianfranco Ivancich on January 7, 1959: "Sic transit hijo de puta" ["So passes the son of a bitch"] (*SL* 890). Later the same month he wrote to L. K. Brague Jr. that "Things are OK with us in Cuba. A friend I was in Spain with is one of the new govt. . . . With all the vested U.S. interests they will be bucking to try to give the Cubans a square shake for the first time ever. . . . Castro is up against a hell of a lot of money. The Island is so rich and has always been stolen blind. If he could run a straight government it would be wonderful" (*SL* 892). After Castro had been in power a year, Hemingway was still defending the revolution. Arriving back in Havana after the dangerous summer of 1959 in Spain, he kissed the Cuban flag on arrival and declared, "I am happy to be here again, because I consider myself one more Cuban. . . . My sympathies are with the Cuban Revolution and all our difficulties. I don't want to be considered a *Yanqui*" (Fuentes, *Hemingway in Cuba* 274). He approved of some of the executions of Batista thugs, bitterly decried by the American press, adding: "I have complete faith in the Castro Revolution because it has the support of the Cuban people. I believe in his cause" (Fuentes, *Hemingway in Cuba* 275). Or, as he put it in a letter to Buck Lanham on January 12, 1960, "I believe completely in the historical necessity of the Cuban Revolution" (*SL* 899). For the forty years of his adult life, Hemingway had believed in revolution.

One wonders what Hemingway would have made of the collapse of communism in the Soviet Union and Eastern Europe in *our* time. Surely his individualism would have rebelled against the regimentation that seems inevitable when the state becomes a church. Perhaps, despite his impatience with politicians, he would be attracted to Felipe González, the democratic Socialist now leading Spain. Hemingway once expressed some grudging admiration for the socialist prime minister during the early years of the civil war, Francisco Largo Caballero. To support democratic Socialism at the end of the century would have been consistent with his support of Eugene V. Debs in 1920. Despite his individualism and his distrust of politicians, Ernest Hemingway was always on the left.

NOTES

1. Carlos Baker, *Ernest Hemingway: A Life Story* (New York: Charles Scribner's Sons, 1969), p. ix; Scott Donaldson, *By Force of Will: The Life and Art of Ernest Hemingway* (New York: Viking, 1977), p. 123; Jeffrey Meyers, *Hemingway: A Biography* (New York: Harper and Row, 1985), pp. 296, 292; James R. Mellow, *Hemingway: A Life without Consequences* (Boston: Houghton Mifflin, 1992), pp. 473, 483; Michael Reynolds, *The Young Hemingway* (Oxford: Basil Blackwell, 1986), p. 194.

2. Carlos Baker, ed., *Ernest Hemingway: Selected Letters, 1917–1961* (New York: Charles Scribner's Sons, 1981), p. 597.

3. Ernest Hemingway, ed., *Men at War: The Best War Stories of All Time* (New York: Crown, 1942), p. 2. The quotation is from von Clausewitz.

4. Ernest Hemingway, *Dateline: Toronto,* ed. William White (New York: Charles Scribner's Sons, 1985), pp. 233–36, 295–300.

5. Ernest Hemingway, *In Our Time* (New York: Charles Scribner's Sons, 1930), p. 126.

6. Ernest Hemingway, *Men without Women* (New York: Charles Scribner's Sons, 1927), p. 31.

7. Ernest Hemingway, "Old Man at the Bridge," in *The Fifth Column and the First Forty-Nine Stories* (New York: Charles Scribner's Sons, 1938), p. 177.

8. Ernest Hemingway, *A Farewell to Arms* (New York: Charles Scribner's Sons, 1929), pp. 184–85.

9. Ernest Hemingway, *Green Hills of Africa* (New York: Charles Scribner's Sons, 1935), p. 191.

10. Ray Ginger, *Eugene V. Debs: A Biography* (New York: Collier, 1962), p. 406.

11. Michael Reynolds, *Hemingway: The American Homecoming* (Oxford: Basil Blackwell, 1992), pp. 145–57.

12. Ernest Hemingway, *Death in the Afternoon* (New York: Charles Scribner's Sons, 1932), p. 278.

13. Rhea Marsh Smith, *Spain: A Modern History* (Ann Arbor, Mich.: University of Michigan Press, 1965), p. 435.

14. Ernest Hemingway, *Byline: Ernest Hemingway,* ed. William White (New York: Charles Scribner's Sons, 1967), pp. 180, 184.

15. Ernest Hemingway, *To Have and Have Not* (New York: Charles Scribner's Sons, 1937), pp. 203, 206, 210, 209.

16. Ernest Hemingway, *For Whom the Bell Tolls* (New York: Charles Scribner's Sons, 1940), p. 235.

17. Cary Nelson, ed., *Remembering Spain: Hemingway's Civil War Eulogy and the Veterans of the Abraham Lincoln Brigade* (Urbana: University of Illinois Press, 1944), p. 19.

18. Norberto Fuentes, *Hemingway in Cuba* (Secaucus, N.J.: Lyle Stuart, 1984), pp. 57, 187–89, 252–54.

WORKS CITED

Baker, Carlos. *Ernest Hemingway: A Life Story.* New York: Charles Scribner's Sons, 1969.

Donaldson, Scott. *By Force of Will: The Life and Art of Ernest Hemingway.* New York: Viking, 1977.

Fenton, Charles A. *The Apprenticeship of Ernest Hemingway: The Early Years.* New York: Farrar, Straus and Young, 1954.

Fuentes, Norberto. *Hemingway in Cuba.* Secaucus, N.J.: Lyle Stuart, 1984.

Hanneman, Audre. *Ernest Hemingway: A Comprehensive Bibliography.* Princeton: Princeton University Press, 1967; *Supplement to Ernest Hemingway: A Comprehensive Bibliography.* Princeton: Princeton University Press, 1975.

Kobler, J. F. *Ernest Hemingway: Journalist and Artist.* Ann Arbor, Mich.: UMI Research Press, 1985.

Lynn, Kenneth. *Hemingway.* New York: Simon and Schuster, 1987.

Mellow, James R. *Hemingway: A Life without Consequences.* Boston: Houghton Mifflin, 1992.

Meyers, Jeffrey. *Hemingway: A Biography.* New York: Harper and Row, 1985.

———, ed. *Hemingway: The Critical Heritage.* London: Routledge and Kegan Paul, 1982.

Michalczyk, John J., and Sergio Villani, eds. "Malraux, Hemingway, and Embattled Spain." Special issue of *North Dakota Quarterly* 60.2 (Spring 1992).

Nelson, Cary, ed. *Remembering Spain: Hemingway's Civil War Eulogy and the Veterans of the Abraham Lincoln Brigade.* Urbana: University of Illinois Press, 1994.

Reynolds, Michael. *The Young Hemingway.* Oxford: Basil Blackwell, 1986.

———. *Hemingway: The Paris Years.* Oxford: Basil Blackwell, 1989.

———. *Hemingway: The American Homecoming.* Oxford: Basil Blackwell, 1992.

Stephens, Robert O. *Hemingway's Nonfiction: The Public Voice.* Chapel Hill: University of North Carolina Press, 1968.

Watson, William Braasch. "Joris Ivens and the Communists: Bringing Hemingway into the Spanish Civil War. *Blowing the Bridge: Essays on Hemingway and* For Whom the Bell Tolls. Ed. Rena Sanderson. Westport, Conn.: Greenwood, 37–57.

———, ed. "Spanish Civil War Issue." *The Hemingway Review* 7.2 (Spring 1988).

9

RENA SANDERSON

Hemingway and Gender History

In a letter written to Charles Scribner in 1949, Ernest Hemingway listed "Mr. Turgenieff" and "Mr. Maupassant" as authors he had beaten in the ring. Among his prospective opponents were "Mr. Henry James," "Mr. Cervantes," and the redoubtable "Dr. Tolstoi." Finally, he mentioned "some guys nobody could ever beat like Mr. Shakespeare (The Champion) and Mr. Anonymous" (*SL* 673). In the notorious 1950 Lillian Ross interview published in *The New Yorker,* Hemingway, with the same self-conscious braggadocio, repeated this list of authors and declared himself literary heavyweight champion, having won the title in the 1920s and defended it ever since (Ross 49).

Hemingway's boxing metaphor and the male opponents (emphasized by the masculine forms of address) neatly convey his belief – this was before the discovery that Anonymous was a woman – that the world of writing should be a man's world, a boxing gym, no women allowed. And truly, his *New Yorker* performance and other, even less subtle, public displays have made "Papa Hemingway" synonymous with a stereotypical notion of masculinity. It is a standard rule of reading imaginative literature that one should distinguish between an author's actual life and the lives that appear in his or her fiction, but for many readers – especially women – Hemingway's fame as a man makes this rule hard to observe (Abbott 612). The accusation of male chauvinism hangs over the man and his work.

From the very beginning of Hemingway's career, critics made an issue of the "masculinity" in his writings. His early stories won wide critical praise for their stoic, understated, "masculine" style and their graphic depiction of male pursuits and attitudes. Then, by the early 1930s, Hemingway was working deliberately to develop and embellish a masculine public image of himself (Raeburn) But as he turned into a male celebrity as well as one of America's best-known authors, some serious readers began to have second thoughts. In 1940 Edmund Wilson, an early admirer of Hemingway, was one of the first to criticize his "growing antagonism" to women (237).

Critics of the novels declared that Hemingway could not depict women or that he was better at depicting men without women (Fiedler; Wilson). It became common for critics to divide his fictional women into either castrators or love-slaves, either "bitches" or helpmates – the simplicity of the dichotomy presumably mirroring Hemingway's own sexist mind-set (Whitlow 10–15).

With the rise of the women's movement in the 1960s and of feminist criticism in departments of literature, Hemingway became Enemy Number One for many critics, who accused him of perpetuating sexist stereotypes in his writing (Fetterley; Rogers). The early feminist attacks unquestionably diminished his literary reputation in some academic circles and reduced the study of his work in high school and university classrooms. These same attacks, however, led to a broader reevaluation of his work. The resulting rereadings have given new visibility to Hemingway's female characters (and their strengths) and have revealed his own sensitivity to gender issues, thus casting doubts on the old assumption that his writings were one-sidedly masculine (Martin, "Brett Ashley"; Wagner; Wexler; Whitlow). That assumption has been further undermined by the claim that Hemingway had unresolved androgynous inclinations (Lynn; Spilka), a claim possibly supported by *The Garden of Eden,* the novel whose incomplete manuscript became available for study in the mid-1970s and which was published in abridged form in 1986. It remains to be seen whether this "new" Hemingway, the writer who treated gender issues in their full diversity and complexity, will win over his feminist critics and recover his once central place in the canon (Balbert; Merrill).

My purpose here, however, is not primarily to secure justice (or mercy) for Hemingway. What I hope to show is that his depiction of women and of gender issues may be fruitfully approached by placing it in its historical and biographical contexts. His fictional females reflect his responses to the ongoing reformulations of gender in the culture at large and to such specific manifestations as the rise of women within the literary world. In reaction to these changes, Hemingway fashioned an ideal – at once modern and nostalgic – of reciprocity between the sexes, an ideal he pursued in his fiction for his entire career.

It is generally accepted today that what we call gender is both an effect of biology and a social construction (and in patriarchal societies, that construction will tend to favor men over women). Hemingway was born at a time (1899) when the position of women – at least within the white, middle-class world he inhabited – was undergoing major change. It is not an overstatement to say that this dislocation of sexual traditions and assumptions about gender roles, this reconstruction of gender, was in some sense a trauma for Hemingway and for others in his generation. When he arrived at young manhood, there was a struggle – fierce but only partly recognized – between men and women over personal and sexual freedom, economic independence, and political power. That war between the sexes had a decisive effect on his thinking and writing about women, and anyone who wants to understand the confused history of gender relations in twentieth-century America would do well to read him closely. Scholars have recently drawn attention to the important role that gender issues played in the making of modernism and in that period's definitions of artistic success (Ammons; Brown; Gilbert and Gubar; Huyssen; Kiberd; Scott; Showalter). Hemingway was a witness to, and a major participant in, the broad cultural struggles of his time, especially the rise of modernism and the gender war. Not surprisingly, he and his writings (nearly inseparable, perhaps) became a significant site of those struggles. By contextualizing the man and his work, we can better understand their importance in our time.

In nineteenth-century America men and women were assumed to be, by nature, complementary opposites. American society was, in effect, divided into male and female spheres, each sphere being associated with certain gendered values. The man's sphere required the attributes of emotional and moral toughness necessary for survival in the competitive public world. The woman's sphere, like a safe shelter from the world, was aligned with what Welter (152) calls the "cardinal virtues" of true womanhood – purity, piety, domesticity, and submissiveness.

Beginning as early as 1830, this division came to be challenged by a feminist undercurrent that grew stronger throughout the century (Millett). By the time American women gained the right to vote in 1920, a modern "New Woman" had appeared who made the popular Gibson girl of the 1890s – as well as the political feminists and social reformers who had helped to gain the vote – seem outdated. Linking the modern girl to a loosening of morals that took place between 1900 and 1920, historian James McGovern describes her boyish appearance as the antithesis to the previous century's ideals of maternal and modest femininity (431). Perhaps the best known manifestation of the New Woman was the sexually permissive flapper, an urban creature who was young and tomboyish in appearance and behavior. Unlike earlier hour-glass-shaped, fully-skirted women, the flapper had short hair, bound her chest, wore short straight-cut dresses, played golf, drove a car, smoked, danced, drank, and displayed various degrees of sexual promiscuity.

Although most women were not flappers, they were much more physical and athletic than their mothers had been. In 1927 an article entitled "Feminist – New Style" in *Harper's Magazine* declared the newly evolved modern woman to be a composite figure, a boyish girl who combined the flapper's physical freedom, sexuality, and stamina with feminist self-assertiveness and traditional domestic femininity, a woman who could happily combine pleasure, career, and marriage. To the advanced young man of the time, this New Woman must have seemed the perfect companion – fearless, bright, eager to participate in work, in play, in marital sex (Schneider and Schneider 148). We know that Hemingway welcomed and praised tomboyish qualities in his four wives – Hadley's hiking, skiing, and easygoing companionship, Pauline's riding and shooting, Martha's hunting, and Mary's expertise as deep-sea fisherwoman. Quite clearly, the New Woman contributed heavily to Hemingway's own image of the ideal woman.

Aside, of course, from Hemingway's intimate relationships with women, we can identify at least three other sources of his early exposure to changing ideas about sexuality: his upbringing, his reading, and his travels as an ambulance driver during World War I in Italy and as a newlywed expatriate in Europe. Like others of his generation, he was reared in an environment of loosening gender distinctions. His own parents divided their roles according to the ideals of "companionate marriage" or equal partnership that gained popularity during the Progressive Era. That Grace Hemingway pursued her own artistic and occupational interests in music and painting and that her husband Dr. Clarence Hemingway assumed such domestic functions as cooking may be taken as signs of the time. Yet Hemingway's comments suggest that he resented his mother's domineering and regarded his father's response to her as submissive, even cowardly (Kert 152; Lynn; Spilka).

The ongoing process of liberation from Victorian sexual teachings was promoted, throughout the 1920s, by a popularized version of Freud that viewed humans as driven by and defined by inescapable sexual instincts. Though it is uncertain if Hemingway actually read Freud, we know that in 1920 and 1921 he read and recommended to friends the voluminous *Studies in Psychology* by sexologist Havelock Ellis. He sent three volumes to Hadley and they exchanged "essays" on the topic (Reynolds, *Young Hemingway* 185). Ellis, a British physician, was a Darwinist who sought to place men and women within the order of the animal kingdom. Though he recognized women's sexuality and encouraged its liberation, he also believed there were natural differences between men and women that should guide their behavior (Harris 133).

When Hemingway wrote his first publishable fiction in Paris in the 1920s, he was himself in his mid-twenties, an eager observer of the modern scene.

Gertrude Stein describes him, at twenty-three, as "extraordinarily good-looking . . . with passionately interested, rather than interesting eyes. He sat in front of Gertrude Stein and listened and looked" (Stein 212). Stein, of course, was the legendary lesbian hostess of the most stimulating salon for writers and artist in Paris. To Hemingway and to many others, she was a kind of literary mother. In fact, she has been compared to Hemingway's actual mother Grace not only in age and appearance but also in self-confidence, artistic ambitions, homosexual preferences (Grace was suspected of having an affair with another woman), and the complicated response both women provoked in the writer from Oak Park. During Hemingway's youth, his most serious relationships involved older, more mature women. His first passions – the nurse Agnes von Kurowsky, his first wife Hadley, Duff Twysden (the model for Brett Ashley), and his second wife Pauline – were all several years older than he was.

In Paris of the early 1920s postwar feminism was most prominent, with over eighty feminist societies representing more than sixty thousand members (Martin, "Brett Ashley" 68). Although not all of these feminists would have agreed that the recognition of women's sexuality amounted to liberation, many of the women Hemingway encountered in Paris embraced the modern sexual freedom. Period photographs of Montparnasse capture the sexual ambience of the place: Studio models, dancers, artists, and women writers are shown swimming and partying in mixed groups, or crossdressed in male attire, or posing in the nude. In memoirs, these women write of uninhibited sex with multiple partners. And among this extensive community of sexually experimental and lesbian women writers and artists were many who occupied central positions in the artistic and publishing circles Hemingway frequented in Paris (Benstock; Meyers). This community included Sylvia Beach, Natalie Barney, Janet Flanner, Hilda Doolittle, Bryher (Winifred Ellerman), Margaret Anderson, Djuna Barnes, and, of course, Gertrude Stein and Alice B. Toklas. Hemingway's stance as a fledgling writer surrounded by such women probably helps explain the important challenge often posed by experienced, powerful, and sexually ambiguous women in his life and works.

Hemingway's response to the Bohemian and sexually permissive environment of Paris was ambivalent. Although he derided the hypocritical narrow-mindedness of the American middle class and told wild tales of his own sexual prowess (SL 243), he also condemned promiscuity (Donaldson 175–81). In turning away from the sexual anarchy of the times, Hemingway adopted a kind of philosophical primitivism. In this he resembled many others of his generation who developed, in reaction to modern complexities, a moral and aesthetic interest in the primitive (Torgovnick). Stimulated by such critiques as Oswald Spengler's *The Decline of the West* (1918) and T. S. Eliot's *The Waste Land* (1922), they undertook a quest for essential values that modern civilization, in their view, had abandoned. This quest took highly diverse forms, such as the interest in ancient myths and rituals (e.g., James Frazer's *The Golden Bough* [1922]); the popularization of African motifs in music (jazz), dance, fashions, decor, and art; and the rise of political reaction, leading eventually to fascism.

In Hemingway's case, the quest for personal wholeness and enduring values was carried out largely within his writing and lasted for his entire career. The repeated motif of a lost paradise appears in his earliest stories and again, more markedly, in his later books. From one work to another, his characters seek to recapture what he called "the happiness of the Garden that a man must lose" (Baker 460). In Hemingway's literary imagination, these attempts to recover paradise take two basic forms. The first occurs away from civilization, in the outdoors, where men might discover that "all mean egotism vanishes" and experience a transcendental oneness with the universe (Emerson, "Nature"). The second way of attaining prelapsarian bliss is by establishing (ideally, in a natural setting) a complementary union with a member of the opposite sex. The search for such a relationship runs throughout Hemingway's fiction. In a sense, he wrote variations, more or less developed, on a single fantasy: A man finds his ideal woman, and together they flee from civilization into some pastoral retreat where they are united through their love against the rest of the world. Most often, this fantasy remains largely implied or unspoken in his stories. One might say it is present by its absence. Just as the depiction of a desolate landscape may evoke in the reader's mind its opposite – the beautiful scene that might have been, if only such and such were true – so Hemingway's often bleak stories imply the solution (reciprocal heterosexual love) to the unhappiness they depict. But except for *A Farewell to Arms,* where Edenic life becomes for a time the center of the story, paradise in Hemingway's fiction can, at best, only be glimpsed.

Hemingway frequently makes this theme central in his work (Smith). But this is not to say that he creates only one type of woman: His search for complementary relations between the sexes expresses itself in a wide range of fictional females. The modern, complex woman (e.g., Lady Brett Ashley [*SAR*]), although appealing in many ways, does not normally achieve true reciprocity with a man. Hemingway shows that between the New Woman and the New Man there are, in the language of today's divorce court, "irreconcilable differences." The modern woman who complements the modern man is the rare exception (Catherine Barkley [*FTA*], Marie Morgan [*THAHN*]). In Hemingway's later fiction the contradictory features of the modern woman are split into separate characters: Her negative traits are clearly identified and rejected, and her desirable characteristics are enlarged into positive female figures (e.g., Maria [*FWBT*], and Renata [*ARIT*]) who in their relationships with men return the longing for union. In her most developed form, Hemingway's ideal woman is a wishful restoration of the boyish New Woman of the 1910s and 1920s purged of the features that caused intimidation, conflict, and the threat of emasculation. Just as Hemingway's "philosophical primitivism" may be understood as an antidote to modern civilization, Hemingway's fictive women may be seen as his wishful makeover of modern women.

Hemingway's writings of the 1920s – the short story collections *In Our Time* (1925) and *Men without Women* (1927), and the novels *The Sun Also Rises* (1926) and *A Farewell to Arms* (1929) – were praised for their contemporary quality. Indeed, they offer studies of the lives and relationships of New Men and New Women complicated by distinctly modern problems. In the short stories, love relationships fail consistently, but it is precisely Hemingway's depiction of the corruption, the loss, or the absence of love that magnifies its value (Harding 114). The first collection, *In Our Time* (1925), interweaves tales of modern life with twelve vignettes (interchapters) focusing on modern and ancient violence. While the vignettes show an exclusively masculine world of war, crime, and bullfighting, most of the stories show men and women engaged in the modern war of the sexes. The sequence of the stories highlights the flight from a world of romantic and marital discord into the refuge of an exclusively male territory. Contrary to the charge that Hemingway prefers to depict men without women, these stories stress the interdependence, however unhappy, between the sexes.

Another common but mistaken assumption about Hemingway's fiction is that he automatically sides with his fictional males. In fact, the stories in his first collection are consistently sympathetic to women, who are often revealed to be more mature than their mates. Although in their own world Hemingway's men have an implied code of stoic manliness by which to define themselves, in their relationships to women that code does not assure success. In these early stories the men seem very passive in response to women; they are either indifferent or insensitive, unwilling or unable to take action or to accept responsibility for the way things turn out. Several of Hemingway's finest and best known early stories pivot on this very point: "Indian Camp," "The Doctor and the Doctor's Wife," "The End of Something," "Mr. and Mrs. Elliot," "Cat in the Rain," and "Out of Season."

These so-called marital tales from *In Our Time,* like several stories in *Men without Women,* stress the discord in marriage caused by distinctly modern sexual problems: homoeroticism, divorce, abortion, venereal disease, infidelity. At best, marriage seems merely insurance against loneliness.

In his first novel, *The Sun Also Rises* (1926), Hemingway distinguishes between the impermanent beliefs and practices of his generation (including its gender constructions and sexual mores) and the natural, biological cycles that assure the perpetuation of the race and the survival of the earth. Hemingway stressed that the two epigraphs introducing the book – one from Gertrude Stein and one from Ecclesiastes – were to be played off against each other: "The point of the book to me was that the earth abideth forever – having a great deal of fondness and admiration for the earth and not a hell of a lot for my generation" (*SL* 229). Hemingway's explanation illuminates the book's structural contrast between the modern lost generation and the enduring "earth" of the Spanish landscape and of the ancient rituals that will outlast the passing generations. In terms of gender definitions, it amounts to a contrast between the sterility of contemporary sexual relations and the regenerative force of primordial impulses.

Hemingway's choice of subject for this novel may have been partly influenced by the literary marketplace. Prior to its publication by Boni and Liveright, *In Our Time* had been turned down by Doran Company. In a letter written in early January 1925, Hemingway reported the rejection and then went on to mention that a German literary scout had asked him to help find stories "told by real American flappers with all the utterest insolence of this kind of animals." Hemingway bristled: "That's the latest dope on the selling market" (*SL* 143). Yet, in the summer of that year he wrote *The Sun Also Rises,* centered on Lady Brett Ashley, who despite her British title is the most flapper-like character Hemingway ever created.

A number of scholars recognize *The Sun Also Rises* as documenting the shift in gender constructions that followed World War I and the societal effects of that shift (Martin, "Brett Ashley"; O'Sullivan; Reynolds, *Sun Also Rises;* Spilka). Though Brett and Jake are understood to embody new gender relations, there is no clear critical consensus about how we should interpret this couple or the clusters of bar-hopping men and women, adulterers, homosexuals, and prostitutes that surround them

At least in her appearance, Brett is the epitome of the modern woman. She is not merely fashionable, but sets the trend toward the boyish look. Her hair is "brushed back like a boy's. She started all that." At the same time, she looks like a "fast" woman: "She was built with curves like the hull of a racing yacht, and you missed none of it with that wool jersey" (22). She is the antithesis of her corseted, ruffled, and straitlaced Victorian foremother. Her appearance seems to combine popular contemporary images from Hollywood (e.g., movie star Clara Bow) and from the world of advertising (e.g., magazine ads showing women smoking cigarettes): She is a *sexy* modern woman.

Though it has been suggested that Hemingway respects the New Woman represented by Brett (O'Sullivan 76), others think that he was ambivalent about the first Freudian generation of women (Reynolds, *Sun Also Rises* 65). Pretty clearly, Brett evokes an ambivalent response from the men around her: They find her very attractive, but she is also more than they can handle (Spilka 2). She is a modern Circe who causes men to degrade themselves. Hemingway himself passed indirect judgment on her when he declared the book's central idea to be "Promiscuity no solution" (*SL* 545).

The original opening, which was left out of the published book (on the advice of F. Scott Fitzgerald), introduced Brett sympathetically as the central character of the book and as a victim of psychological damage (Wagner 67). In the printed version of the book, sympathy for Brett is played down somewhat. It takes a while for us to discover that, at thirty-four, she has lost the person she loved to the war, that she has been married twice, that she was emotionally abused in the past, and that she drinks too much.

Brett's character is filtered through the mind of Jake Barnes, who narrates the book and is responsible for our picture of her. Jake has received a war wound that has left him impotent but still subject to sexual desires. Brett and Jake understand each other, communicate well in few words, and feel mutual sexual attraction. They might make a good couple, were it not for Jake's impotence.

But it is more than Jake's inability to perform that prevents them from building a life together: It is Brett's sexual liberation, the supposed selfishness of her modern refusal to suppress or overlook her own sexual needs, which makes Jake's impotence a fatal obstacle. The consequence of a physical wound incurred in battle, his impotence is paradoxically a badge of manly courage. By standards of an earlier time, when respectable women were not suppose to enjoy sex anyway, Jake's handicap might have made no difference to a woman who did not want to bear children. But Brett will not accept sexual deprivation, will not suffer just because Jake suffers. His impotence, then, needs to be seen as more than just a physical wound or a personal dilemma: It reflects the sexual attitudes and gender conflicts of the time.

It should be noted that Brett is not a truly liberated woman. Like the New Woman of the 1920s, she is a transitional figure between the protected, idealized wife and the modern, self-reliant woman. While she embraces the ethic of sexual freedom, she has not established her financial independence and seems to have no scruples about letting men pay her tab. A hybrid between two traditional images – the wife and the prostitute – she accepts money and protection from men, and in exchange offers them her body and her flattering presence (Martin, "Brett Ashley" 72). Ironically, Jake, the man who most often picks up her tab, will never be able to collect her debt to him. The only cautious, responsible person in the group, he is left to pay the price, literally and figuratively, for everyone else's lack of responsibility. Like other men in Hemingway's early fiction, he is an embodiment of male passivity.

In other words, Brett resembles a traditional man in her sexual expectations, and Jake resembles a traditional woman in his sexual unavailability and his uncomplaining tolerance of others' inconsiderations. The reversal, both overt and implied, in their gender roles signals that something has gone awry between the sexes.

Their personal gender dislocation mirrors sexual confusion in the society at large. Parisian nightlife illustrates the disappearance of traditional moral standards and the replacement of love by an array of sexual arrangements void of reproduction. Impotent and lonely Jake treats a sick prostitute to dinner; sexy Brett keeps the company of homosexuals. The homosexuals, in turn, like to dance with the prostitute Georgette, for whom Jake invents the last name of Leblanc. This was Hemingway's little in-joke, a jab at the Parisian lesbian writer Georgette LeBlanc (Wagner-Martin).

The novel offers, as a contrast to decadent Paris, two sites of primitive purity. The first is Burguete in the Spanish mountains. Jake and Bill make an idyllic fishing expedition there, which Brett, notably, fails to join. The second is the world of bullfighting, which Brett corrupts. Through association with primitive pagan fertility rites, the bullfights in Spain celebrate the fertility of the earth and of humanity. The corrida stages and celebrates male virility, symbolized by the phallus of the bull and by male competition (between the bulls). Just as the neutered steer in the ring keeps the bulls calm, impotent Jake maintains order between the competitors for Brett's favors. More important, Jake negotiates between Brett and the bullfighter Pedro Romero. A hapless observer of Brett's entanglements throughout much of the book, Jake breaks through his passiveness only to instruct Brett on Pedro's exceptional qualities as performer: "Romero was the whole show. . . . I sat beside Brett and explained to Brett what it was all about" (167). As Jake's surrogate, Romero performs heroically for Brett both in the ring and in bed (Reynolds, *Sun Also Rises* 37). And Jake comes to think of himself as a pimp who has allowed Brett's modern amorality to corrupt Romero's personal honor and the noble traditions of bullfighting itself.

The several reasons Brett offers for her decision not to marry Romero are inconsistent and suggest her own confusion. She objects that he would demand that she grow her hair long: "Me, with long hair. I'd look so like hell" (242). A sexually potent, old-fashioned man, Romero wants a traditional woman as his wife, but Brett refuses to give up her modern, unfeminine ways. Yet she also gives a more noble, altruistic explanation: She broke off the relationship because it "was bad for him" (243) and because she decided "not to be one of these bitches that ruins children" (245).

In his next major female character – Catherine Barkley, the heroine of *A Farewell to Arms* – Hemingway presents a woman who is both modern and principled. Some critics have attacked Catherine as an especially disturbing example of Hemingway's one-dimensional, submissive, simpering, and self-effacing female (Fetterley; Fiedler; Martin, "Seduced and Abandoned"); others regard her as an independent, self-contained individual who chooses to love Frederic Henry and is loved by him in return (Lewis; Miller; Wexler; Whitlow). Some readers stress that the story is told by Frederic (who should not be confused with Hemingway), and that our picture of Catherine is created by Frederic's selective memory (Lewis; Nagel). Others point out that the lovers are acting in the extraordinary and extenuating circumstances of war (Spanier). Still others remind us that Catherine, like the other characters, changes and develops throughout the book (Phelan; Whitlow). Increasingly in recent criticism, Catherine has been vindicated as one of Hemingway's strong, heroic individuals.

Measured by the gender standards current during World War I and extending into the late 1920s when Hemingway composed the book, Catherine emerges as a modern, independent young woman – quite possibly Hemingway's definition, at the time, of the ideal woman. Essentially, she is an improved – actually more modern – version of Brett. Catherine is just as sexually liberated but, as a self-supporting nurse, is more emancipated than the financially dependent and irresponsible Brett. Moreover, Catherine is perfectly monogamous and faithful. Her ethical and moral standards are much more orthodox. True to ideals of the New Woman that emerged during Hemingway's youth (McGovern), Catherine is a good sport and pal, possessing traditional maternal and domestic qualities (without, however, their institutional rigidity). She is self-reliant and competent but without that cruelty or mannishness displayed by some strong women in Hemingway's later fiction. She is ready and qualified to run away with the man she loves and to help him domesticate the world of his wishful dreams.

Contrary to Leslie Fiedler's assertion that Hemingway's men prefer each other's company and the dangers of the manly world to the responsibilities associated with women and civilization (355), the protagonist of this novel flees from the corrupt and untrustworthy male world into a woman's arms. As the book opens, a naive Frederic is surrounded by father surrogates, is called "baby" and "good boy," and behaves thoughtlessly. Introduced to Catherine, he is perfectly willing to lie to make his conquest. But when Catherine sees through his game and insists on honesty (31), she is establishing the ethical terms for a relationship that will become their private retreat from a deceptive, lawless world.

It is not so much that Catherine is more noble than Frederic; she is simply more experienced. Like Brett, Catherine has lost her true love to the war, but unlike Brett she seems strengthened rather than demoralized by the experience. In retrospect, she realizes that she "didn't know about anything" before the death of her fiancé (19). After that death, she behaves like someone who has been psychologically wounded by the war and by the loss of her first love, but she endures and gradually comes to realize the finality of death and what that implies for the living. Typical of Hemingway's heroic figures, Catherine not only accepts her pain but shares her insights and growth with Frederic. What the priest and Catherine know (before Frederic himself discovers it) is that the only certainty in life is the imminence of death. In contrast to Frederic, who explains "winefully" the uselessness of his good intentions, the priest and Catherine realize that dissipation equals defeat and that the only choice is to snatch "a fine life" out of the jaws of death, to carve meaning out of meaninglessness, spirituality out of worldliness.

Following his desertion from the front, Frederic adopts Catherine's perspective that "there's only us two and in the world there's all the rest of them" (139). Together, he says, they are "never lonely and never afraid" (249). Catherine and Frederic are married by nature, through their compatibility, if not by law, and their moments of togetherness add up to a flight from civilization into a prelapsarian state. When Frederic lets Catherine's long hair down and they are inside of it, it feels as if they were "inside a tent or behind a falls" (114). The scene anticipates the getaway scene in the rowboat when Frederic uses the umbrella as a makeshift sail to propel the couple toward freedom. Like Huck Finn and Jim (the runaways in one of the books Hemingway admired most), Frederic and Catherine manage to improvise and to make a home for themselves wherever they are, however outlawed the territory. Often – as in the hotel and in the rowboat – everything becomes much more homey once they share a meal (153, 275). Finally as Joyce Wexler has pointed out, there is a symbolic parallel between the description of the lovers' home in winter in Switzerland and the landscape of the priest's beloved home in the Abruzzi. The parallel hints that their "oneness" signals a loss of self-consciousness comparable to that of a mystical, spiritual experience. With the right woman, so the novel seems to say, paradise may be regained.

A Farewell to Arms is the only book by Hemingway that centers on a fully developed and happy modern love affair. It may be his happiest book because in it he gave fullest expression to his fantasy of paradise on earth. And even here the fantasy is qualified – not only, of course, by Catherine's death, but by our knowledge that she is the creation of Frederic's bereaved memory. Hemingway said that he rewrote the last chapter of A Farewell to Arms over forty times. That it ends with the death of Catherine and the (stillborn) son does not prove, as Judith Fetterley charges, that the book's "message to women readers" is that "the only good woman is a dead one" (71). Rather, the ending sounds the final note of fatalism and Frederic's realization that he cannot avoid losing "the happiness of the Garden that a man must lose" (Baker 460).

After the publication of A Farewell to Arms, a new and more authoritative Hemingway emerged, a he-man of exaggerated virility and masculine expertise. This Hemingway can best be understood as the author's defensive response to what he saw as a general takeover by women. He found evidence of this takeover both in his personal life and in the culture at large.

His father's suicide in December 1928 bitterly reminded him of the failure of his parents' marriage, a failure Hemingway blamed on his mother's bullying and on his father's inability to stand up to her. Linda Wagner suggests that it was at this point that Hemingway stopped believing in the "mystic ideal of a genuine love" between a man and a woman (69). By this time, too, his own marriage to Hadley was over, and he was remarried to Pauline. Years later, when he reflected back on these events, Hemingway stated flatly that his mother "forced [his] father to suicide" (SL 670). And in his autobiographical A Moveable Feast, published posthumously in 1964, he blamed Pauline for the destruction of his first marriage but also presented himself, unflatteringly, as a passive victim of circumstances. It may be that he found his father's passivity within himself, and he reacted by constructing a more active, courageous, masculine persona.

Starting in the early 1930s, as John Raeburn shows, Hemingway used his writing to cultivate a public image of masculinity. By choosing manly topics, he appropriated territory that, although not off-limits to women, gave him an advantage and permitted him to establish himself as a male authority figure. With the exception of his short story collection *Winner Take Nothing* (1933), Hemingway wrote nonfiction that concentrated on the world of men. In 1932, for example, appeared his book on bullfighting, *Death in the Afternoon,* which led Clifton Fadiman to identify Hemingway as a Byronic culture hero (Stephens 124–28), while Max Eastman called him a swaggering fraud compensating for his insecurity through a show of "red-blooded masculinity" (Stephens 131).

This shift in Hemingway's self-definition fitted into a broader contemporary movement, a defensive cultural "re-masculinization" of American society intended to shore up its patriarchal basis (Faludi; Millett xiii). The backlash of the 1930s was a reaction to the growing influence of two groups of women. The first group, which coalesced in the late nineteenth century, consisted of the traditional female culture-bearers who applied domestic values to the public sphere. The second group was comprised of a diverse range of New Women, including political feminists, flappers, and career women. Within the literary world, Hemingway was only one of several leading male authors whose writings express an anxiety over the power of women in that world (Ammons; Showalter). In his correspondence, Hemingway frequently shows defensiveness or hostility toward women who compete with men (e.g., *SL* 264–65, 388, 399). Competition from female writers and the female influence in the publishing industry on critical standards and on popular tastes threatened to stigmatize the writing profession as effeminate and to devalue the style and marketability of men's writings. In particular, years of cultural work by women reformers threatened to "feminize" standards of propriety and censorship. Hemingway showed his awareness of these forces in a letter to Maxwell Perkins of June 7, 1929, in which he objected to "emasculating" editorial requests for the removal of passages that might prove offensive. Distinguishing first-rate writing from "genteel writing" (associated with women), he declared, "you should not go backwards" toward more restrictive standards (*SL* 297). The comparison of censorship to "emasculation," a comparison Hemingway used with growing frequency (Gould), demonstrates once again that he thought of writing in gendered terms.

In 1933 Hemingway found himself attacked in two separate autobiographies by well-known and powerful American women writers, Gertrude Stein and Margaret Anderson, the latter a co-editor of the *Little Review* (1922–29) and a prominent figure in the Parisian literary lesbian scene. In a letter to the writer Janet Flanner, Hemingway calls Anderson "nice" and "pretty" and "flutter brained," and he refutes her contention that his interests in bullfighting, deep-sea fishing, and boxing are "simulated" (*SL* 388).

In the same letter, he declares that he had been "very fond" of Stein until "she pushed [his] face in a dozen times" (*SL* 387). But Stein, in her *The Autobiography of Alice B. Toklas,* spoke of Hemingway as "yellow" (216), physically "fragile" (218), and "ninety percent Rotarian" (220), and said that he had learned the craft of writing from Sherwood Anderson and from Stein "without understanding it" (216). Stein's published remarks stung Hemingway, and he counterattacked repeatedly, both in private and in print (*GHOA, FWBT, AMF*).

From 1933 to 1936, Hemingway wrote, for *Esquire,* twenty-five letter-essays on masculine themes (fishing, bullfighting, boxing, hunting, politics, and writing). Although these contributions to the new magazine for men helped establish him as a celebrity figure, they also hurt his critical reputation. Some suspect that he bragged about his sportsmanship in the *Esquire* pieces in response to Stein's belittling of his courage (Raeburn). The manuscript of his next book, *Green Hills of Africa,* contained direct attacks on Stein. When Scribner's objected, Hemingway fumed in a letter to Max Perkins: "What would you like me to put in place of bitch? Fat bitch? Lousy bitch? Old Bitch? Lesbian Bitch?" And then he immediately switched topics, asserting, "I will survive this unpopularity [with critics]" – revealing that this was the real issue (*SL* 423). Stein, through the success of her autobiography, enjoyed the momentary advantage in their ongoing competition.

When *Green Hills of Africa* – about big-game hunting – appeared in 1935, the critics "killed" it and Hemingway went into a serious depression (*SL* 426). By January 1936 he confessed: "Thought I was facing impotence, inability to write, insomnia and was going to blow my lousy head off" (cited in Meyers 252). At this low point in his career – a comparatively brief period, when he gave vent to his most misogynist feelings – he was increasingly inclined to blame his problems as a writer on his corruption by wealthy women in his life: both through the financial support he received from his wife Pauline, and through his adulterous affair, intermittently between 1931 an 1936, with Jane Mason, a wealthy married woman fourteen years his junior.

These feelings were vented in a series of safari writings, which put on trial both castrating "bitches" and their cowardly men. *Green Hills of Africa* already introduced as a minor, veiled theme the conflicts between powerful women and their impotent, bitter men, conflicts that Hemingway depicted more fully in two short stories, "The Short Happy Life of Francis Macomber" and "The Snows of Kilimanjaro." In both stories the husband perceives the woman to be in charge and resents her for it. In "The Short Happy Life of Francis Macomber," Margot Macomber openly cuckolds her wealthy but ineffectual husband Francis. During the hunt, however, he rids himself of his fears and becomes a brave man. But before he can act out his newly gained courage and leave his wife, she shoots him dead, either by accident or by intention. Although Margot Macomber is one of the best known examples of a Hemingway bitch, the story implies that the woman's behavior is inseparable from the failure of her husband. In "The Snows of Kilimanjaro," this implied connection is made explicit. The dying writer Harry finally admits to himself that he has no right to call his wife Helen a bitch and to blame her for his own failure: "She shot very well this good, this rich bitch, this kindly caretaker and destroyer of his talent. Nonsense. He had destroyed his talent himself. Why should he blame this woman because she kept him well?" (*SS* 45). Ultimately, both stories find fault with the man rather than with the woman.

Although Hemingway has been condemned for depicting women as "bitches," very few such women actually appear in his writings, and almost exclusively during the 1930s. The few times that Hemingway embodies his fears of powerful women in a fictive "bitch," he is attacking not only or primarily the woman but rather male passivity and dependence on women – traits he found in himself. Writing retrospectively in 1943, he admitted: "Take as good a woman as Pauline – a hell of a wonderful woman – and once she turns mean. Although, of course, it is your own actions that turn her mean. Mine I mean" (*SL* 554).

In the safari stories "The Short Happy Life of Francis Macomber" and "The Snows of Kilimanjaro," primitive nature and the proximity of death cut through the pretenses and lies of civilized life, forcing men to confront the truth about themselves – especially the truth about their unmanly response to women. In Hemingway's next novel, *To Have and Have Not* (1937), the author's celebration of the primitive merges with gender prescriptions. In this book, the first since *A Farewell to Arms* to include women in more than just a passing manner, Hemingway recommends, as an alternative to modern gender conflicts, manly and womanly behavior of natural primitive form that borders on the beastly.

To Have and Have Not consists of two loosely interwoven plots that align the contrast between socioeconomic classes with a contrast between marital situations. The first plot depicts the hard boiled, violent world of Harry Morgan and his wife Marie; the second shows the unhappy lives and marital infidelities of the writer Richard Gordon, his wife Helen, and their wealthy friends. Harry Morgan enjoys a satisfactory if carnal relationship with his wife. Harry, who has only his "*cojones* to peddle," sinks hopelessly into a life of crime, but he knows that he is doing it to support a wife who without question adores him. At forty-five, Marie is an aging, "heavy-set, big, blue-eyed woman, with bleached-blonde hair" (176), but Harry tells her that she is "better" than anyone else. Indeed Marie is an exceptional woman, loving and yet strong enough to grieve deeply for the death of Harry without being crushed by it. Marie is very much a person of her own who can give without losing herself.

Although we may be offended by the brutish features of this working-class couple, we see that their relationship is presented as their refuge in a hostile, fallen world. In the environment of romanticized poverty, Harry and Marie have little else but each other. They are social outsiders who, in an admittedly more vulgar and fierce way than Frederic and Catherine (*FTA*), have created for themselves on the margins of society a "fine life" which, of course, cannot last.

By contrast, the rich fail in their relationships, and Hemingway exposes the sordidness of their marital and extramarital affairs. Nevertheless, a wide range of narrative techniques – including interior monologues (242–46, 257–62) and a fiery feminist speech (185–86) – provides insights into the different perspectives of all the characters, but especially those of the women (Nolan).

More than any other Hemingway novel, *To Have and Have Not* shows the author's awareness that perspective is everything. Whatever the blind spots in Hemingway's perception of women, he was not utterly unaware of them. In an ironically amusing passage, the writer Richard Gordon, after a glimpse of Marie Morgan, assumes that he has "seen, in a flash of perception, the whole inner life of that type of woman" (177). We know, however, that Gordon's speculations about her life are absolutely wrong. Though Gordon is sometimes seen as a caricature of the writer John Dos Passos, this passage may also be read as Hemingway's own acknowledgment of the difficulties writers encounter when they create characters of the opposite sex.

As early as December 1936, Hemingway met and began an affair with Martha Gellhorn. During 1939 and 1940, while he was working on *For Whom the Bell Tolls*, he made the final break with Pauline and openly displayed his commitment to Martha, his third wife. But the very qualities he admired in Martha – courage, independence, and political engagement – caused her to leave him on lengthy assignments as a roving war correspondent for *Collier's*, absences that made Hemingway aware of his emotional dependence on her (Lynn 481). And her competition with him as a journalist and writer was largely responsible for the marriage's failure (*SL* 576).

Hemingway wrote *For Whom the Bell Tolls* (1940) at the end of a decade of attacks on his work and his person. In a sense, the novel confronts the fear of emasculation, the fear of powerlessness and of loss; loss of identity, of courage, of sexuality, of (pro)creativity, of life itself. Throughout the novel, the characters speak literally and metaphorically of *cojones* – Spanish for "balls" – and of what befalls the man who loses them. As conceived in this book (and throughout the 1930s in Hemingway's life and fiction), the danger of emasculation comes from the mannish woman who challenges the man's sexual and artistic authority. The stories of Kashkin, Finito, and Pablo all present foreboding examples of emasculation. In the most extreme case, the man emasculated by a bullying woman, like Jordan's father (and Hemingway's), is driven to shoot himself (339). But Jordan, unlike his predecessors (Kashkin and Hemingway's own father), retains his manly identity through his courageous behavior.

What makes Jordan's success possible is that in this novel the threatening woman and the romantic heroine are not the same. That is, Hemingway resolved his own long-standing fear of emasculation by splitting the intimidating woman of his earlier fiction into two separate characters. In Pilar and Maria, he created separate embodiments of those female qualities he feared and those he loved.

Pilar is an incarnation of the archetypal woman in her most fearsome guise. She has the ability to detect "the odor of death" on a doomed man (253). When asked to describe this odor, she says that one part of it is the smell that arises on a ship in the midst of a storm at sea, when one feels "faint and hollow in the stomach" (254). The second part is an olfactory witches' brew: the kiss of an old woman who has drunk "the blood of beasts that are slaughtered" (255), the smell of a refuse pail with dead chrysanthemums (255–56) and of slop jars from brothels containing the "odor of love's labor lost mixed sweetly with soapy water and cigarette butts," the odor of a gunny sack containing wet earth, rotten flowers, and the "doings" of old prostitutes who perform sex acts at night in the park – in short, "the smell that is both the death and birth of a man" (256). Thus identified with the cycles of births and death (and the sea), Pilar may be read as the archetypal Great Mother, both nurturing and terrifying (Gladstein 66–72).

Jordan respects Pilar for her solidity and endurance – he compares her to a mountain (136) – but he also fears her as a rival. Her experience makes her a superb teacher, mentor, and leader to the guerrilla band. She epitomizes the mannish woman whose superiority threatens the man's performance. In age and maturity, confidence, nurturance, leadership ability, and maternal appearance she resembles both Hemingway's mother and Gertrude Stein. She resembles them as well in her possible lesbian inclinations, making her a potential sexual rival to Jordan for Maria's favors (154–55; Gould 73–75).

More significant for Jordan, a would-be writer, is Pilar's storytelling ability – her most convincing teaching tool – which fills him with admiration and envy. After her long, harrowing account of the massacre at the *Ayuntamiento,* he thinks, "If that woman could only write. He would try to write it and if he had luck and could remember it perhaps he could get it down as she told it. God, how she could tell a story" (134). One imagines Hemingway winking at the reader: "Look how *I* can *write* a story," he seems to say. Pilar's artistic, oracular dimension links her to the author himself, as well as to female models like Grace Hemingway and Gertrude Stein. That Hemingway had Stein in mind while composing *For Whom the Bell Tolls* is clear from the gratuitous literary in-joke that appears later in the book during a rustic breakfast scene. When Augustín banters with Jordan about the offensive odor of onions, Jordan says that, except for its odor, an onion is like a rose. "Mighty like the rose. A rose is a rose is an onion," he says. "An onion is an onion is an onion." Not content with reducing Stein's famous remark about the (mighty) rose to a remark about smelly onions, he has Jordan think to himself, "a stone is a stein is a rock is a boulder is a pebble" (289) – the woman rival diminished from an imposing boulder to a tiny pebble.

In contrast to Pilar, Maria is a woman Jordan can love without fear of emasculation. Like Brett (*SAR*) and Catherine (*FTA*), Maria is a war victim, but she is younger and more childlike. Having been gang-raped by the Fascists, she is more fragile than any of Hemingways' other women. Lacking the callousness of Brett or the worldliness of Catherine, she is in need of protection and guidance. Her vulnerability is stressed by the comparisons between her and a variety of soft, helpless animals; his term of endearment for her – *guapa* ("little rabbit") – combines that vulnerability with the sexual innuendo of the Spanish term. At the same time, Maria is associated throughout with sunlight and earthly beauty, testifying to her essential health.

What we have identified as Hemingway's solution to the confusions of modern life – reciprocity between the sexes, achieved in a natural setting remote from society – is well illustrated by the love between Jordan and Maria. Maria is the female principle that complements Jordan's male nature; her qualities unite with his, and the idyllic love affair blossoms. Maria imagines that she and Jordan will be "as one animal of the forest and be so close that neither one can tell that one of us is one and not the other" (262). In describing (or rather, not describing) their lovemaking, Hemingway mysteriously invokes the cosmos. His incantatory verbal rendering of the sex act (which goes beyond mere sex) suggests a transcendental fusion of the couple with each other and with the universe: "for now always one now; one only one, there is no other one but one now, one . . . one and one is one . . ." (379). The book's best-known (and sometimes ridiculed) line – "And then the earth moved" (160) – is Hemingway's attempt to convey the significance and the rarity of true organic union between the sexes.

For all the intensity of the love scenes, however, *For Whom the Bell Tolls* ultimately conveys the failure of romantic love. It is not simply that love will not stop the fascist advance. Blowing up the bridge will not stop the Fascists, either. Jordan knows this, and yet he goes through with his mission. He came to Spain to defend the Republic, not to fulfill his own longing for a perfect mate (a longing he may not have had before he met Maria). He has his orders and he will carry them out. When he breaks his leg in the ensuing battle, he knows he must stay behind, in a suicidal rear guard action, while the others flee. He tells the weeping Maria, "What I do now I do alone. I could not do it well with thee" (463). Jordan then returns Maria to Pilar, from whom he had first received her.

It is noteworthy that complementarity here (to the extent that it is possible at all) requires the woman to be a "girl-woman" – a requirement that is repeated in Hemingway's later fiction. The book raises the possibility that Maria is infertile (354), suggesting that she will long retain her childlike qualities, the main source of her appeal to Jordan. Her infertility would bypass the kind of conflict that often arises between Hemingway's men and women when they are confronted with pregnancy and parenthood. Jordan declares that Maria is not only his wife but also the sister and the daughter he never had – but whether in one role or in all three, Maria herself is silence. Though she tries to tell Jordan the story of her rape, he does not want to hear it (350); Pilar, too, has instructed her to remain silent about her suffering. In her role as "daughter-listener," Maria anticipates the transformation in Hemingway's subsequent novels (*ARIT, IIS, OMATS*) of the complementary female into a filial figure (girl or boy) who provides an attentive audience for an older speaker.

Perhaps one reason Hemingway wrote and published so little in the 1940s was that he needed to redefine his stance and methods. As it was for millions of others, the decade for Hemingway was filled with turmoil. His World War II experiences, his marriage to Martha Gellhorn (1940–45), his divorce from Martha and marriage to Mary Welsh (1945), and many scares and losses due to accidents, illness, and death, especially in the second half of the 1940s (Baker 456–63). Fitzgerald died in 1940, Joyce in 1941, Stein in 1946; and between 1947 and 1952 came the deaths of Katie Dos Passos, his lawyer Morris Speiser, Pauline, Charles Scribner, and his mother Grace Hemingway.

Though he had not been publishing, he still wanted to be heard. As the 1940s ended, a battered Hemingway was granting lengthy interviews and providing extensive biographical information to Malcolm Cowley, Lillian Ross, and other reporters and literary scholars. This eagerness to be heard, the author's need for an audience, appears fictionally in his later writings (some published posthumously). In various forms, an instructional male–female relationship grows in importance and accordingly modifies Hemingway's concept of the ideal woman. The early fiction generally depicted a young man's initiation (or failed initiation) into carnal or spiritual knowledge by a more mature woman. *Death in the Afternoon* dramatically changed that pattern by presenting a male narrator who instructs an Old Lady on bullfighting, his own masculine territory of expertise. Starting with *For Whom the Bell Tolls,* and repeated in *Across the River and into the Trees, The Old Man and the Sea,* and *Islands in the Stream,* a young, innocent, and adoring pupil appears as the ideal mate and audience for an increasingly older and more jaded protagonist (a pattern that may reflect, among other things, Hemingway's own aging). In the progression from the mystical lovemaking shared by Robert and Maria (*FWBT*) to Colonel Cantwell's petting of Renata in the gondola (*ARIT*) to the platonic, filial instructions given to young boys (*OMATS* and IIS), sexual intercourse is replaced by an ideal narrative situation.

One of the features that runs throughout Hemingway's writing is the recurrence of failed communication between men and women. Linguistic studies of gender-linked differences in language that result in miscommunication confirm what we have long known – Hemingway had a great ear for dialogue (Smiley). In his renderings of common speech, he captures those moments when men and women stop truly hearing each other.

In *Across the River and into the Trees* the male protagonist must tell his story to soothe his psychological wounds, and the success of this undertaking requires a sympathetic female audience. Colonel Cantwell, like Hemingway, is over fifty years old, has lost three women, and calls Renata (allegedly based on the real-life Adriana Ivancich) his last love. Repeatedly, he asks her if she finds his stories boring (236, 240), and she replies emphatically, "You never bore me" (236). A little later she explains: "Don't you see you need to tell me things to purge your bitterness?" (240). The colonel hopes to gain immortality through Renata (whose name means "reborn"), not by reproduction but by passing on his knowledge. Through a process that brings together teacher and student, experience and innocence, they attain complementarity.

Ironically, Adriana, for whom Hemingway wrote *Across the River and into the Trees,* did not like the book and told Hemingway that she found it, of all things, boring. Almost all the critics agreed.

In *The Old Man and the Sea,* as in *Islands in the Stream* (1970) – the posthumously published novel to which the published novella originally belonged – Hemingway offers a world nearly devoid of real women, and their absence is a cause for sadness. Though the fisherman Santiago finds an audience in the boy Manolin, it is only partial compensation for the loss, through death, of his wife. Santiago has removed her photograph from the wall because the sight of it makes him feel "too lonely" (16).

The one woman in the book who has a speaking part is the tourist who notices, among the floating garbage in the harbor, the marlin's "great long spine with a huge tail at the end" (126). She asks the waiter for an explanation, but will not wait for it. Instead she leaps hastily to the conclusion that the skeleton belongs to a shark. She also refuses to listen to an accurate account of the old man's struggle and fails to appreciate the accomplishment behind his failure (Swan 155–56).

Though many reviewers called the book a parable, most had in mind a parable about Man and Fate. Mark Schorer was among the few who understood it as a parable about Hemingway's lonely struggle to master his art (Stephens 359). At the time, of course, no one knew that it would be the last book Hemingway would publish. With the advantage of hindsight, we can see Schorer was right. Written after the failure of *Across the River and into the Trees,* the novella opens with a line that speaks of a long period without a success ("eighty-four days now without taking a fish"). At the time of its writing, Hemingway felt his contemporaries had failed to appreciate his work: He had been savaged by critical sharks. Even though most of his attackers were men, the final incomprehension of Santiago's achievement is put in the mouth of a woman. That Hemingway should embody the critics' hostility toward his work in a female figure amounts to an admission that his rival was woman (Spilka 262). He feminized the things that hurt his career.

Taken as a metatextual clue, the woman's lack of appreciation may partly explain Hemingway's flight, in this late novella, from historically bound reality into the archetypal. For the true woman in the book is the sea itself (Swan), which, according to countless myths and legends, is a woman, the origin of life and a destroyer of life as well (Lederer 233–37; Neumann 47–

48, 217–22). Santiago thinks mythically. He tells us that those who love the seas call her *la mar.* "Sometimes those who love her [the sea] say bad things of her but they are always said as though she were a woman" (29). Santiago knows and accepts the ambivalent double nature of the mother-sea: He "always thought of her as feminine and as something that gave or withheld great favours" (30). In the end, *la mar* withholds Santiago's catch, but the old man (unlike some of Hemingway's other protagonists) blames no one else – not even the cruel mother-sea – but only himself for having gone out "too far" (120). Within his failure he knows there is achievement. Like Santiago, Hemingway perhaps "went out too far"; like Santiago, he "may be destroyed but not defeated" (103). The fisherman returns home. In the book's final line, he dreams of lions. The world's failure to understand what he has done is a matter of indifference. He still has his dreams, his private landscape.

Hemingway's move to an archetypal representation of woman had been attempted before. Pilar (*FWBT*) was plainly conceived in such terms, the indestructible, timeless Spanish Earth, the double-sided Great Mother who knows the secrets of life and death. And even earlier, Hemingway employed the passage from Ecclesiastes as an epigraph (*SAR*) to stress the eternal natural cycle: "All the rivers run into the sea; yet the sea is not full; unto the place from whence the rivers come, thither they return again." Regardless of the success or failure of any individual or any generation, "the earth abideth forever" (Ecclesiastes 1: 7, 4; *SL* 229).

"Mr. Shakespeare (The Champion)," after long holding the mirror up to nature, turned in the end away from his own brand of verisimilitude and toward pure romance, stories of forgiveness and magical restoration. And somewhat like the champ, Hemingway, too, withdrew from the concrete and historical and moved into the timeless world of the creative unconscious (dreams, the sea, childhood memory, the archetypal). The Young Man had the New Woman, both carefully described and located in a specific time and place. The Old Man has the Sea, *la mar,* the Great Mother, timeless and outside of history.

The Old Man and the Sea, then, may be read as Hemingway's acceptance of ultimate failure, a reconciliation with the idea that victory – never to be despised – is temporary, for all, as the Preacher reminds us, is vanity. It is therefore no small irony that when the novella was published in *Life* magazine (September 1, 1952), it was widely hailed as proof that the old master still had his powers. The book won the Pulitzer Prize in 1953 and paved the way for Hemingway's Nobel Prize in 1954. And its popular reception in the conservative Eisenhower 1950s suggests that its essentialist, archetypal presentation of woman was well suited to that decade's prevailing ideology of gender.

Analyzing Hemingway's posthumous publications is a tricky business, because we cannot know with certainty why he left them unpublished in his lifetime, nor, without consulting the original manuscripts, the full extent of the editorial emendations and omissions. It is sufficient to note that the posthumous works – such as *A Moveable Feast* (1964), "The Last Good Country" (*NAS* [1972]), and *The Garden of Eden* (1986) – show his continuing preoccupation with the motifs we have already discussed. While critics have mined these works (especially *The Garden of Eden*) for further evidence of Hemingway's fascination with the writing/gender nexus (Lynn; Spilka), their psychological readings should be supplemented by an awareness of historical contexts. Although Hemingway's fictional treatment of gender necessarily proceeded from his personal psychology, that very personality was shaped by, and was reacting to, biographical and historical circumstances that included the increasing influence of women within the literary world and over American culture generally.

One important way to understand Hemingway's depiction of women is as a reassertion of patriarchal power in American literature and culture. Reading his work provides an opportunity to reflect upon the gendered nature of the literary canon and of the American cultural history that canon is supposed to reflect. Although he was far from alone in the attempt to reestablish male domination in the cultural sphere, he stands out as a major figure in that effort, a culture hero (or villain) whose life and work had a marked effect on the history of gender in the twentieth century.

WORKS CITED

Abbott, Porter, H. "Autobiography, Autography, Fiction: Groundwork for a Taxonomy of Textual Categories." *New Literary History* 19.3 (Spring 1988): 597–615.

Ammons, Elizabeth. *Conflicting Stories: American Women Writers at the Turn into the Twentieth Century.* New York: Oxford University Press, 1992.

Baker, Carlos. *Ernest Hemingway: A Life Story.* New York: Charles Scribner's Sons, 1969.

Balbert, Peter. "From Hemingway to Lawrence to Mailer: Survival and Sexual Identity in *A Farewell to Arms*." *The Hemingway Review* 3.1 (Fall 1983): 30–43.

Benstock, Shari. *Women of the Left Bank.* Austin: University of Texas Press, 1986.

Brown, Dorothy M. *Setting a Course: American Women in the 1920s.* Boston: Twayne, 1987.

Donaldson, Scott. *By Force of Will: The Life and Art of Ernest Hemingway.* New York: Viking, 1977.

Faludi, Susan. *Backlash: The Undeclared War against American Women.* New York: Doubleday, 1991.

Fetterley, Judith. *The Resisting Reader: A Feminist Approach to American Fiction.* Bloomington: Indiana University Press, 1978.

Fiedler, Leslie A. *Love and Death in the American Novel.* Rev. ed. New York: Dell, 1960.

Gilbert, Sandra, and Susan Gubar. *No Man's Land: The Place of the Woman Writer in the Twentieth Century.* 2 vols. New Haven: Yale University Press, 1988–89.

Gladstein, Mimi Reisel. *The Indestructible Woman in Faulkner, Hemingway, and Steinbeck.* Ann Arbor, Mich.: UMI Research Press, 1986.

Gould, Thomas E. " 'A Tiny Operation with Great Effect': Authorial Revision and Editorial Emasculation in the Manuscript of Hemingway's *For Whom the Bell Tolls.*" *Blowing the Bridge: Essays on Hemingway and* For Whom the Bell Tolls. Ed. Rena Sanderson. New York: Greenwood Press, 1992, 67–81.

Harding, Brian. "Ernest Hemingway: Men with, or without Women." *American Declarations of Love.* Ed. Ann Massa. New York: St. Martin's, 1990, 104–21.

Harris, Barbara. *Beyond Her Sphere: Women and the Professions in American History.* Westport, Conn.: Greenwood, 1978.

Hemingway, Ernest. *Across the River and into the Trees.* New York: Charles Scribner's Sons, 1950.

———. *The Complete Short Stories of Ernest Hemingway: The Finca Vigía Edition.* New York: Charles Scribner's Sons, 1987.

———. *Death in the Afternoon.* New York: Charles Scribner's Sons, 1932.

———. *Ernest Hemingway: Selected Letters, 1917–1961.* Ed. Carlos Baker. New York: Charles Scribner's Sons, 1981.

———. *A Farewell to Arms.* New York: Charles Scribner's Sons, 1929.

———. *For Whom the Bell Tolls.* New York: Charles Scribner's Sons, 1940.

———. *The Garden of Eden.* New York: Charles Scribner's Sons, 1986.

———. *Green Hills of Africa.* New York: Charles Scribner's Sons, 1935.

———. *In Our Time.* New York: Charles Scribner's Sons, 1925.

———. *Men without Women.* New York: Charles Scribner's Sons, 1927.

———. *A Moveable Feast.* New York: Charles Scribner's Sons, 1964.

———. *The Nick Adams Stories.* New York: Charles Scribner's Sons, 1972.

———. *The Old Man and the Sea.* New York: Charles Scribner's Sons, 1952.

———. *The Sun Also Rises.* New York: Charles Scribner's Sons, 1926.

———. *To Have and Have Not.* New York: Charles Scribner's Sons, 1937.

———. *Winner Take Nothing.* New York: Charles Scribner's Sons, 1933.

Huyssen, Andreas. "Mass Culture as Woman: Modernism's Other." *Studies in Entertainment: Critical Approaches to Mass Culture.* Ed. Tania Modleski. Bloomington: Indiana University Press, 1986, 188–207.

Kert, Bernice. *The Hemingway Women.* New York: Norton, 1983.

Kiberd, Declan. *Men and Feminism in Modern Literature.* New York: St. Martin's, 1985.

Lederer, Wolfgang. *The Fear of Women.* New York: Harcourt, 1968.

Lewis, Robert W. *A Farewell to Arms: The War of the Words.* Boston: Twayne, 1992.

Lynn, Kenneth S. *Hemingway.* New York: Simon and Schuster, 1987.

Martin, Wendy. "Brett Ashley as New Woman in *The Sun Also Rises.*" *New Essays on* The Sun Also Rises. Ed. Linda Wagner-Martin. Cambridge: Cambridge University Press, 1987, 65–82.

———. "Seduced and Abandoned in the New World: The Image of Woman in American Fiction." *Woman in Sexist Society.* New York: Basic Books, 1971, 226–39.

McGovern, James R. "The American Woman's Pre-World War I Freedom in Manners and Morals." *Out American Sisters.* 4th ed. Ed. Jean E. Friedman et al. Lexington, Mass.: Heath, 1987, 426–46.

Merrill, Robert. "Demoting Hemingway: Feminist Criticism and the Canon." *American Literature* 60.2 (May 1988): 255–68.

Meyers, Jeffrey. *Hemingway: A Biography.* New York: Harper and Row, 1985.

Miller, Linda Patterson. "Hemingway's Women: A Reassessment." *Hemingway in Italy and Other Essays.* Ed. Robert W. Lewis. New York: Praeger, 1990, 3–9.

Millett, Kate. *Sexual Politics.* New York: Simon and Schuster, [1969] 1990.

Nagel, James. "Catherine Barkley and Retrospective Narration in *A Farewell to Arms.*" *Ernest Hemingway: Six Decades of Criticism.* Ed. Linda W. Wagner. East Lansing: Michigan State University Press, 1987, 171–85.

Neumann, Erich. *The Great Mother: An Analysis of an Archetype.* 2nd ed. Princeton: Princeton University Press, 1963.

Nolan, Charles J., Jr. "Hemingway's Women's Movement." *Ernest Hemingway: Six Decades of Criticism.* Ed. Linda W. Wagner. East Lansing: Michigan State University Press, 1987, 209–19.

O'Sullivan, Sibbie. "Love and Friendship/Man and Woman in *The Sun Also Rises.*" *Arizona Quarterly* 44.2 (Summer 1988): 76–97.

Phelan, James. "Narrative Discourse, Literary Character, and Ideology." *Reading Narrative: Form, Ethics, Ideology.* Ed. James Phelan. Columbus: Ohio State University Press, 1989, 132–46.

Raeburn, John. *Fame Became of Him: Hemingway as Public Writer.* Bloomington: Indiana University Press, 1984.

Reynolds, Michael. The Sun Also Rises: *A Novel of the Twenties.* Boston: Twayne, 1988.

———. *The Young Hemingway.* Oxford: Basil Blackwell, 1986.

Rogers, Katherine M. *The Troublesome Helpmate: A History of Misogyny in Literature.* Seattle: University of Washington Press, 1966.

Ross, Lillian. "How Do You Like It Now, Gentlemen?" *The New Yorker,* May 13, 1950, 36–62.

Schneider, Dorothy, and Carl J. Schneider. *American Women in the Progressive Era, 1900–1920.* New York: Facts on File, 1993.

Scott, Bonnie Kime, ed. *The Gender of Modernism: A Critical Anthology.* Bloomington: Indiana University Press, 1990.

Showalter, Elaine. "The Other Lost Generation." *Sister's Choice: Tradition and Change in American Women's Writing.* Oxford: Clarendon, 1991, 104–26.

Smiley, Pamela. "Gender-Linked Miscommunication in 'Hills Like White Elephants.' " *The Hemingway Review* 8.1 (Fall 1988): 2–12.

Smith, Carol H. "Women and the Loss of Eden in Hemingway's Mythology." *Ernest Hemingway: The Writer in Context.* Ed. James Nagel. Madison: University of Wisconsin Press, 1984, 129–44.

Spanier, Sandra Whipple. "Hemingway's Unknown Soldier: Catherine Barkley, the Critics, and the Great War." *New Essays on* A Farewell to Arms. Ed. Scott Donaldson. Cambridge: Cambridge University Press, 1990, 75–108.

Spilka, Mark. *Hemingway's Quarrel with Androgyny.* Lincoln: University of Nebraska Press, 1990.

Stein, Gertrude. *The Autobiography of Alice B. Toklas.* New York: Random House, 1933.

Stephens, Robert O. *Ernest Hemingway: The Critical Reception.* New York: Burt Franklin, 1977.

Swan, Martin. "*The Old Man and the Sea:* Women Taken for Granted." *Visages de la féminité.* Ed. A.-J. Bullier and J.-M. Racault. St. Denis: Université de la Réunion, 1984. 147–163.

Torgovnick, Marianna. *Gone Primitive: Savage Intellects, Modern Lives.* Chicago: University of Chicago Press, 1990.

Wagner, Linda W. " 'Proud and Friendly and Gently': Women in Hemingway's Early Fiction." *Ernest Hemingway: The Papers of a Writer.* Ed. Bernard Oldsey. New York: Garland, 1981, 63–71.

Wagner-Martin, Linda. "Racial and Sexual Coding in Hemingway's *The Sun Also Rises.*" *Hemingway Review* 10.2 (Spring 1991): 39–41.

Welter, Barbara. "The Cult of True Womanhood: 1820–1860." *American Quarterly* 18 (1966): 151–74.

Wexler, Joyce. "E.R.A. for Hemingway: A Feminist Defense of *A Farewell to Arms.*" *The Georgia Review* 35.1 (Spring 1981): 111–23.

Whitlow, Roger. *Cassandra's Daughters: The Women in Hemingway.* Westport, Conn.: Greenwood, 1984.

Wilson, Edmund. *The Wound and the Bow.* New York: Oxford University Press, 1947.

IO

J. GERALD KENNEDY

Hemingway, Hadley, and Paris: The Persistence of Desire

In 1933, five years after moving to Key West with his second wife, Pauline Pfeiffer, Ernest Hemingway revisited Paris and there composed a travel letter for *Esquire* magazine about the "gloomy" mood of the city where he had spent six momentous years in the 1920s. His return seemed "a big mistake": Some old friends had killed themselves, others clung to the past by scribbling memoirs, and everyone seemed "very discouraged." The painters complained that nobody was buying their work, and the big cafés in Montparnasse teemed with "refugees from Nazi terror" – as well as with German spies. Everyone assumed the stark inevitability of another world war. But Hemingway's somber report seemed finally to mask a private grief, betrayed near the end of the letter when he evoked the plangent image of the city as a forsaken mistress:

> Paris is very beautiful this fall. It was a fine place to be quite young in and it is a necessary part of a man's education. We all loved it once and we lie if we say we didn't. But she is like a mistress who does not grow old and she has other lovers now. She was old to start with but we did not know it then. We thought she was just older than we were, and that was attractive then. So when we did not love her any more we held it against her. But that was wrong because she is always the same age and she always has new lovers.[1]

Like an experienced lover, Paris had indeed played a "necessary part" in Hemingway's "education"; but having exhausted his passion for the city in the late 1920s, he now reproached himself for spurning her ("that was wrong") and metaphorized her as a timeless, inexhaustible mistress. He nevertheless conceded the irrevocability of the break, admitting in the final paragraph that he now loved "something else." He thus seemed to bid a last farewell to the city that had propelled him from obscurity to fame.

Hemingway had ample reason to acknowledge his love for Paris and his appreciation of her influence. In a mere six years there he had – in the words of poet Archibald MacLeish – crafted "a style for his time." The city had brought him in touch with Gertrude Stein and Ezra Pound, the two great literary innovators who read his early work, offered useful critiques, and instructed him in the life of writing; it fostered his friendship with Sylvia Beach, whose Shakespeare and Company bookstore and lending library made possible the voracious reading that taught him the language of modern fiction. Paris put him in contact with the Irish exile James Joyce, then revolutionizing the novel with the dazzling, stream-of-consciousness method of *Ulysses*. On the Left Bank, Hemingway met Ford Madox Ford, Ernest Walsh, and other editors of the little magazines to which he subsequently contributed. His assignments as Paris-based correspondent for the *Toronto Star* took him to Greece, Turkey, Italy, Germany, and Spain, giving him a perspective on the violent postwar era that enriched his early fiction. Hemingway's years in France also freed him from the conventions and constraints of American puritanism (as epitomized by his parents, Clarence and Grace Hemingway) and placed him in a milieu conducive to writing and alive with artistic activity.

During the 1920s, the decade that the French call *les années folles* ("the crazy years"), Paris was arguably the capital of high modernism, the place, as Stein aptly put it, "where the twentieth century was." Many of the most profoundly experimental currents in modern art, music, and literature flowed from the City of Light – from Picasso and Duchamp, from Stravinsky, Poulenc, and Satie, from Breton, Proust, Stein, and Joyce. To live there during those reckless, exuberant years, surrounded by books and art, was a piece of incalculable luck. As Hemingway later acknowledged in *A Moveable Feast:* "To have come on all this new world of writing, with time to read in a city like Paris where there was a way of living well and working, no matter how poor you were, was like having a great treasure given to you" (*AMF* 134). It would be hard to conceive of more fortunate circumstances for becoming a serious author, and as the already-famous Hemingway composed his "Paris Letter" in 1933, he conceded that he owed a great deal to his ancient "mistress."

By the very metaphor that links his literary apprenticeship with his love life, however, Hemingway also manifests a private remorse for betraying his first wife, Hadley Richardson, and thus breaking up the marriage that defined the early years in Paris. Eight years younger than his bride, Hemingway had married Hadley in September 1921, and just three months later they sailed to France on the advice of Hemingway's Chicago mentor, Sherwood Anderson. Hemingway had gotten a brief glimpse of Paris in 1918 en route to Italy as a volunteer for the Red Cross ambulance corps, and Anderson convinced him that the Left Bank was the place to launch his career, providing crucial letters of introduction to Stein, Pound, and Beach. Thanks mainly to an inheritance from Hadley's uncle, the couple rented a fourth-floor flat on the rue du Cardinal Lemoine in the Latin Quarter. In that working-class neighborhood, Hemingway accomplished the hard work of learning how to write "true sentences" without "scrollwork or ornament" (*AMF* 4–5).

The author's posthumously published memoir supplies ample evidence of the "lovely magic time" Ernest and Hadley spent together, mostly in Europe, from the end of 1921 until the "nightmare winter" of 1925–26 and the "murderous summer" that followed, when Ernest fell in love with Pauline, Hadley's "temporary best friend," shattering the happiness associated with "the first part of Paris" (*AMF* 207, 209, 211). Those early years saw the appearance of two Paris chapbooks (*Three Stories and Ten Poems* and *in our time*); the publication of a brilliant story sequence, *In Our Time*; and the composition of his first novel, *The Sun Also Rises*. They also produced two epochal events: Hadley's loss in a Paris train station of the suitcase containing all of Ernest's working manuscripts (with carbons); and the birth in Toronto about ten months later of the couple's son, John Hadley Nicanor Hemingway. Biographers generally agree that the loss of the manuscripts – which Ernest never forgot nor entirely forgave – helped doom a relationship soon thereafter complicated by Hadley's pregnancy.

Enduring four difficult months in Canada, the couple returned to Paris with their son "Bumby" in early 1924 and took an apartment on the rue Notre-Dame-des-Champs. There Ernest recovered his creative momentum; at Gertrude Stein's atelier he stopped playing the dutiful student, and, relying on self-discipline and his own ear for dialogue, he achieved a concentrated new style. During that year he completed three of his finest short stories: "Indian Camp," "Soldier's Home," and "Big Two-Hearted River." Imperceptibly, though, life in Paris changed the young man from Oak Park; he plunged into the ego-driven, crass competitiveness of an international literary scene and found himself simultaneously tantalized by the prospect of a love affair. As in bullfighting – a sport he had discovered in 1923 – the thrill of a possible liaison derived from risk, from the sheer proximity of danger. Always audacious and ambitious, Hemingway by the mid-1920s had become a self-absorbed careerist, a young man in a hurry, yoked in marriage to an older woman who, in his eyes, was growing somewhat matronly. He loved Hadley but also relished the attention of chic, sexually adventurous women. When Hemingway wrote in *Esquire* about the "mistress" whose age he came to resent, he was implicitly commenting on his inconstancy to his first wife.

He was also alluding, more broadly, to the connections among his love of

Paris, his commitment to writing, and his troubled marital relations (which by late 1933 included his second marriage). Those three preoccupations seemed intertwined by geographical and historical destiny. In one of the truest sentences he ever composed, Hemingway observed of his fateful break with Hadley in 1926: "Paris was never to be the same again although it was always Paris and you changed as it changed" (*AMF* 211). Over the four decades of his active career, his relationship to the city varied with the course of his personal life; he sojourned there with each of his four wives, witnessed the liberation of Paris during World War II, and returned nostalgically in the 1950s as an aging, ailing writer. From his sardonic evocation of the nightworld of Montparnasse in *The Sun Also Rises* to the romanticized Eden recalled in *A Moveable Feast,* Hemingway returned to Paris obsessively as a locus of longing. If his fictional treatment of the city reflects the complications of his private life, it also reveals the unmistakable persistence of his desire for Paris, a desire linked in his writing with a succession of influential female characters.

The Sun Also Rises, Hemingway's first major effort to represent the seductive effect of Paris – interestingly, on an expatriate American writer-journalist – included a revealing preliminary move: He literally cut Hadley out of the story. In the earliest existing draft of *The Sun Also Rises,* Hemingway had used the names of those real-life friends who had traveled from Montparnasse to Pamplona to attend the fiesta of San Fermín in 1925, including "Hem" and Hadley, who figure as central characters. But reworking his opening pages a few weeks later, he changed the names: the seductive barfly from Great Britain, Duff Twysden – with whom Ernest had flirted brazenly in Pamplona – became Brett Ashley; her bisexual companion, Pat Guthrie, became Mike Campbell; Hemingway's fishing pals Don Stewart and Bill Smith merged to form Bill Gorton; and pugnacious Harold Loeb became first Gerald and then Robert Cohn. "Hem" became (curiously) the impotent Jake Barnes, and perhaps most revealingly, Hadley vanished from the narrative altogether.[2] This shift eventually allowed Hemingway to foreground the poignant, never-to-be-consummated love affair between Jake and Brett and eliminated the inconvenience of an extraneous wife. It also detached the novel from its autobiographical origins and enabled the author to invent more freely. While it would be a vast oversimplification to regard the relationship between Jake and Brett as a sublimated version of Hemingway's attraction to Duff Twysden in 1925, the deletion of Hadley unmistakably prefigures Hemingway's separation from his first wife a year later, after another dangerous summer in Spain. The editorial excision seems in retrospect something like a coded divorce notice.

According to his memoirs, Hemingway the writer had already been experimenting with a method of conscious omission, possibly suggested by Stein, whereby "you could omit anything if you knew that you omitted and the omitted part would strengthen the story and make people feel something more than they understood" (*AMF* 75). Naturally, not all of his cuts produced residual implications. But if Hemingway's elimination of Hadley from the novel suggests a concerted effort to efface the personal, autobiographical element, it also obliges us to consider whether, by the author's own logic, that omission also contributes a subtle dimension or depth to the story that remains. For years we have recognized how vestiges of the suppressed narrative persist in the novel's particulars: how Brett and Robert Cohn, like Duff and Harold Loeb, spend a few sexy days together; how Jake and Bill go fishing on the Irati River, just as Hemingway did with Bill Smith, Don Stewart, and Hadley; how Jake's fistfight with Cohn reenacts Hemingway's jealous brawl with Loeb; and how the bull's ear that Pedro Romero gives to Brett recalls the one that matador Niño de la Palma presented to Hadley. But only the last detail introduces the fictional suggestion of a hidden female presence; Brett otherwise so dominates the action in Pamplona that she has no visible rival.

Unquestionably *The Sun Also Rises* tells a story quite different from the one that actually unfolded that summer in 1925 (insofar as the "actual" events can even be reconstructed).[3] Hemingway believed that "the only writing that was any good was what you made up, what you imagined," and his novel tested the strength of that assumption, building an essentially fictional plot around his impressions of the fiesta and of the drunken sexual rivalry provoked by Duff Twysden.[4] Exploring the triangular desire of Jake, Brett, and Romero, Hemingway pushed his story decisively beyond the steamy personal material that formed his point of departure. Causing Jake to sacrifice his status as aficionado to gratify Brett's lust for the bullfighter, the author staged a complicated, ironic crisis of values that seemed to many readers to epitomize the moral confusion of the period. Hemingway did not simply embellish or fictionalize an episode from his immediate experience; he invented characters motivated by needs and compulsions that seemed both rigorously personal and broadly representative of the postwar lost generation. But he could never completely divest the narrative of its autobiographical origins, nor could he entirely eliminate Hadley from the story.

As the writing progressed, Hemingway saw that in order to make the craziness in Pamplona intelligible, he had to begin his narrative in Paris. Although comprising only one-third of the novel, this section reveals by indirection – literally, by the reflected image that Jake contemplates in the mirror – the sexual wound that circumscribes his relation to Brett and haunts his tortured psyche. Through the symbolic geography of Jake's Paris, Hemingway further suggests the conflicting impulses that turn his love for her into a living hell. And lying behind, or beneath, this elaboration of Jake's suffering, readers conversant with *A Moveable Feast* may glimpse, like an erased yet partly legible script, a concealed story figured in topographical references associated with Hadley. Insofar as her omission from the novel left any discernible traces, they persist mainly in Hemingway's figuration of Paris.

Early in book 1, for example, when Jake tries to alleviate his loneliness by picking up Georgette, the Belgian *poule,* he takes her to Lavigne's restaurant on the boulevard Montparnasse – the same restaurant where Ernest and Hadley dined so frequently in 1924–25 that they had their own personal napkin rings in the rack on the wall. In his memoir Hemingway speaks of eating *cassoulet* and drinking "good Cahors wine" at the "Nègre de Toulouse," an eatery located close to the apartment "over the sawmill" (*AMF* 99–101). After expressing initial disappointment Georgette concedes: "It isn't bad here. . . . It isn't chic, but the food is all right" (*SAR* 16). Hemingway perhaps used the familiar setting for authenticity, or as a commercial favor to the owner; but his inevitable association of the place with conjugal meals makes his decision to have Jake and Georgette dine there a more intriguing tactic, either a deliberate (and scandalous) recasting of dinner with Hadley or an ironic imposition of domestic routine.

The conversation at the restaurant establishes yet another autobiographical connection, for when Henry Braddocks (a thinly disguised Ford Madox Ford) invites Jake to come to the dancing-club in the Pantheon Quarter, he evokes a scene familiar to Ernest and Hadley, whose apartment on the rue du Cardinal Lemoine was located directly above a working-class *bal musette*. To distance himself from Jake and to accentuate the novel's theme of gender trouble, Hemingway shifted the setting to the rue de la Montagne Sainte Geneviève, thereby evoking a more controversial dance hall in the same *quartier,* frequented by homosexuals and lesbians.[5] But the underlying personal connection was with the bal musette on rue du Cardinal Lemoine, for (as we see in *A Moveable Feast*) the restaurant episode in *The Sun Also Rises* apparently replicates an actual incident in which Ford insisted on explaining how to locate the night spot three floors below Hemingway's old apartment (*AMF* 84). As evidenced in "The Snows of Kilimanjaro," Hemingway continued to associate the bal musette with the flat he shared with Hadley at the beginning of their marriage (*CSS* 51).

Shuttling his characters to the dance hall in the Pantheon Quarter, Hemingway produced the unexpected encounter between Jake and Brett. Iron-ically, the impotent Jake escorts a prostitute, while the oversexed Brett (who has been "so miserable" since she last saw Jake) arrives with a group of homosexuals. When the two decide to leave together, taking a taxi to the Parc Montsouris, they follow a route that Hemingway knew intimately, for the itinerary takes them "onto a dark street behind St. Etienne du Mont," the rue Descartes, where the author had rented a writing studio for a short time in early 1922. The taxi then passes the Place Contrescarpe, the hub of the neighborhood in which the Hemingways first lived and a place described in the opening paragraph of *A Moveable Feast*. Jake and Brett continue onto "the cobbles of the rue Mouffetard," depicted in the memoir as "that won-derful narrow crowded market street which led into the Place Con-trescarpe" (*AMF* 3). Ever afterward Hemingway connected the quartier with Hadley; by a process of metonymic substitution, it became – after the divorce – a topographical sign of his remorseful devotion to her. Sending Jake and Brett through those familiar streets in the back of a darkened taxi, he must have sensed the complex irony of this transit by his thwarted lovers across terrain linked with the happy beginning of his then-unraveling mar-riage.

In a broader sense, the pattern of Jake's movements in the Paris section betrays a fundamental conflict between his need to protect himself emo-tionally through denial and avoidance and his perverse compulsion to gaze upon the erotic play from which he has been cruelly excluded. Although he lives in a Left Bank apartment on the boulevard St. Michel, he divides his time mostly between his office on the Right Bank, where he works as a newspaper correspondent, and Montparnasse, the "Quarter," where he hangs out mainly at a "new dive," the Café Select (which opened in 1925). These two areas signify opposing spheres of activity, the one associated with labor, responsibility, and male camaraderie, the other, leisure, excess, and sexual intrigue.[6] For eight chapters, Jake moves back and forth between the Right Bank and the Left, clinging by day to the routine of his job, then succumbing nightly to compulsion. "It felt pleasant going to work," he notes reassuringly (*SAR* 36); yet he follows a seemingly irresistible pattern of returning to the Quarter to witness scenes of seduction and betrayal. There he participates voyeuristically in the circulation of desire, confiding at the end of the second chapter: "I have a rotten habit of picturing the bed-room scenes of my friends" (*SAR* 13). On the Right Bank, he associates mostly with fellow journalists – like Woolsey and Krum – and in this professional milieu represses his libidinal urges (which persist despite his wound). Even when Robert Cohn, eager to talk about Brett, joins him on the Right Bank for lunch at Wetzel's and then for coffee at the Café de la Paix, Jake deflects discussion of the woman he loves: "I could feel Cohn wanted to bring up Brett again, but I held him off it. We talked about one thing and another, and I left him to come to the office" (*SAR* 40). In the daytime on the Right Bank, Jake can control his feelings for Brett; at night, on the Left Bank, it is a different matter.

Repeatedly, Jake returns to the bars and cafés of Montparnasse; when Woolsey and Krum ask him what he does at night, he explains: "Oh, I'm over in the Quarter." In the context of Hemingway's own dilemma in 1925 – when, as a young father, his urge to stray waxed as his loyalty to Hadley waned – Krum's comment about the café scene seems revealing: "I've meant to get over. . . . You know how it is, though, with a wife and kids" (*SAR* 36). Unencumbered by marriage or family, Jake becomes a regular customer at the Select, a Quarterite familiar with the nightworld and its manifold enticements. In the cafés, he witnesses the glances, gestures, and innuendo of sexual negotiation; yet barred by his injury from bedroom sports, he affects detachment and irony. In the original opening of the Paris section – deleted by Hemingway on the advice of Scott Fitzgerald – the author speaks of the Quarter as a "state of mind" characterized by contempt.[7] But Jake's persistent return to Montparnasse betokens something more akin to self-contempt, a recurrent exercise in flagellation.

During the Paris section, significantly, Jake visits the Café Select three times. His first visit occurs after the taxi ride with Brett has reconfirmed their intractable dilemma: They love each other but can never be lovers. Finding themselves sitting in the taxi "like two strangers," they go to the Select. There, Brett plays the seductress and quickly charms Count Mippipopolous, prompting Jake to "shove off," complaining of a "rotten headache." When Brett asks to see him the next day, Jake pointedly remarks: "Make it the other side of town then" (*SAR* 29). He insists on a Right Bank rendezvous, hoping to protect himself from hurt and knowing that he cannot stand to see Brett flaunting her sensuality in the eroticized Quarter. In the subsequent scene at Jake's apartment, we see for the first time the depth of his private despair: He curses Brett, ridicules his injury, and then starts to cry before falling asleep. In the middle of the night Brett wakes him up to invite him to join her and the count for champagne in the Bois de Boulogne, but Jake has endured enough for one evening. "It is awfully easy to be hard-boiled about everything in the daytime," he confesses, "but at night it is another thing" (*SAR* 34).

Predictably, Brett fails to meet Jake the next day on the Right Bank; he waits for an hour at the elegant, eminently respectable Hôtel Crillon and then takes a taxi to the Quarter, resuming his spectatorial role at the Select. This time he observes a lovers' quarrel between Cohn and his mistress, Frances Clyne. Like Jake, Frances has just been stranded at an expensive hotel: Her friend Paula (possibly a veiled reference to Pauline Pfeiffer) has failed to keep a lunch engagement at the Ritz. Privately Frances informs Jake that Cohn is preparing to cast her aside; she accuses him of leaving her so that he can "get material for a new book" through another affair – a claim not unlike the one later leveled against Hemingway, that he needed a new wife for each major novel. The tirade reveals the "dreadful scenes" excited by jealousy and savagely exposes the sexual game of chess (as Hemingway then understood it) in which female beauty and desirability declined with age as male wealth and attractiveness increased. Scornful of Cohn and indifferent to Frances's betrayal, Jake does not yet suspect that her predicament has direct implications for him: The woman with whom Cohn has already arranged a tryst is, of course, Brett Ashley.

Apparently breaking the pattern of Right Bank–Left Bank opposition, Hemingway portrays a brief scene at the end of chapter 8 in which Jake accompanies Brett and the count to Zelli's in Montmartre, a nightclub featuring black jazz. Earlier in the evening, Brett has shown self-awareness by refusing Jake's suggestion that they live together: "I don't think so. I'd just *tromper* you with everybody. You couldn't stand it" (*SAR* 55). Indeed, she has already planned to deceive Jake. At Zelli's, when the drummer shouts "You can't two time – " she suffers an ostensible *crise de conscience* about her impending trip to San Sebastian with Cohn and tells Jake: "I just feel terribly" (*SAR* 64). So does Jake; dancing close to Brett he has "the feeling as in a nightmare of it all being something repeated, something that [he] had been through and that now [he] must go through again" (*SAR* 64). In a moment of insight, Jake seems to glimpse the mechanism that compels him to repeat, over and over, the scene of male inadequacy that is itself a reenactment of the primal scene of sexual wounding during the war. Such an experience seems literally out of place on the Right Bank, but as deleted portions of the manuscript suggest, Hemingway imagined Montmartre as something like a northern extension of the Quarter. In a cancelled passage, he wrote: "There is a sort of neutral corridor leading from this Paris [Montparnasse] to Montmartre, which consists of Zelli's, Kelly's, now Shamley's and several [Negro] joints."[8] As in the Quarter, the evening at Montmartre forces on Jake the humiliation of impotence; at her hotel, Brett does not invite Jake to her room but instead pushes him away: "Good night, darling. I won't see you again" (*SAR* 65).

During Brett's brief absence from Paris, Jake enjoys a respite from pain in the company of his bibulous fishing buddy, Bill Gorton. But just after her return, he makes his third visit to the Select, near the end of an evening marked – significantly – by male bonding. As if seeking a neutral territory between the workaday world of the Right Bank and the seductive ambience of the Quarter, Jake takes Bill to dine at Madame Lecomte's restaurant on the Ile St. Louis, that refuge of tranquility on the Seine behind the noisier Ile de la Cité. After their meal the two friends admire Notre Dame, "squatting against the night sky," and then cross over to the Left Bank, having promised to meet Brett at the Select around ten o'clock. Interestingly, the pedestrian tour takes Jake once more through the working-class neighborhood associated with Hemingway's first apartment:

> We crossed the bridge and walked up the Rue du Cardinal Lemoine. It was steep walking, and we went all the way up to the Place Contrescarpe. The arc-light shone on the leaves of the trees in the square, and underneath the trees was an S bus ready to start. Music came out of the door of the Nègre Joyeux. Through the window of the Café aux Amateurs I saw the long zinc bar. Outside on the terrace working people were drinking. (SAR 77)

Their passage through the Quarter around the Place Contrescarpe effects a retracing of the earlier, fugitive journey of Jake and Brett; now, freed from the pressures of sexuality, Jake reclaims the landscape, enjoying each local detail. During the composition of "Big Two-Hearted River" Hemingway (through the persona of Nick Adams) had fantasized openly about leaving Paris, his wife ("Helen"), and the expatriate literary life to return to the rivers and lakes of Michigan where he had fished with "Bill Smith . . . and all the old gang."[9] Jake's hike with the wise-cracking Bill Gorton through that section of Paris reminiscent of the honeymoon year with Hadley – before she lost the manuscripts – seems another version of the fantasy of escape to a patently asexual world of male companionship and outdoor sport.

However delightful the promenade, though, Jake's steps lead ineluctably toward the Quarter, the Select, and another self-punishing encounter with Brett. When they arrive at the café, he instantly notes her provocative appearance: "Brett . . . was sitting on a high stool, her legs crossed. She had no stockings on" (SAR 78). She invites attention; the bare legs unmistakably signify her sexual freedom. But now Jake confronts a sorry new rival in the person of Brett's fiancé, Mike Campbell, who five times during the excruciating scene blurts out his crude compliment: "I say, Brett, you are a lovely piece" (SAR 79). His lecherous refrain only reminds Jake – once again the powerless bystander – of what he can never have. While Brett and Mike stumble off to bed, Bill and Jake settle for a boxing match: sport as displaced sexuality.

The final Parisian humiliation for Jake occurs outside the Dingo Bar on the rue Delambre. There Brett quizzes him about the proposed fishing trip to Spain and casually admits to the weekend that she has spent with Robert Cohn in San Sebastian. Beneath the laconic irony of his congratulations to Brett for sleeping with Cohn ("You might take up social service"), we perceive the mortification that Jake seems obliged to relive endlessly by virtue of his devotion to Brett. The subsequent episode in Pamplona represents the culmination of this inner conflict – through Jake's equivocal, part-sacrificial, part-vengeful gesture of arranging an assignation between the woman he loves and the bullfighter he admired. This complex act of symbolic substitution gratifies Brett and renders homage to Romero as it spites Cohn and destroys Jake's own status as an aficionado. The novel's ambiguous closing pages frame the implicit question of whether, by this strategy, Jake has freed himself from self-wounding illusion or whether he still believes – vainly – that he and Brett can "just live together" without sex (*SAR* 55). His last mordant remark ("Isn't it pretty to think so?") gives weight to the former assumption.

We cannot know to what extent Hemingway consciously explored his own emotional dilemma while writing *The Sun Also Rises*. The biographical record indicates plainly, however, that he had become enamored of Duff Twysden during the spring of 1925; Michael Reynolds writes that her effect on the author was "instant and total," sparking rumors in Left Bank cafés.[10] That summer, in Pamplona, his blatant attentions to Duff infuriated Hadley and created a rift in their relationship. But Hemingway seems to have been restrained by his own residual Oak Park morality (or by Duff's consideration for Hadley) from ever becoming her lover. That summer, as he composed the novel in hotel rooms in Madrid, Valencia, and Hendaye, Hemingway transformed the Pamplona crowd into wholly fictional characters but drew creative energy from the unresolved passions that had built up during the fiesta. His ambivalence about Hadley and his infatuation with Duff no doubt helped him experience – as a good writer must – the inner life of his protagonist, to understand intuitively the strange compulsions that might lead Jake to feel hopelessly in love with Brett yet unable to be her lover. Hemingway's sense of being torn suddenly between two women, two ways of living his life, perhaps enabled him to project Jake's alternate efforts to immerse himself in work, duty, and self-denial on the Right Bank or to risk the agony of unsatisfiable desire with Brett in Montparnasse. Hadley's moody reaction to Hemingway's flirting with Duff may have helped him understand and portray the indignity that Jake experiences on the rue De-lambre. And his deeply rooted, guilty awareness of having already begun to break away from Hadley emotionally may have induced him to incorporate into the novel so many topographical signs of his continuing attachment to her.

Months before *The Sun Also Rises* hit the bookstores in 1926, the Hemingway marriage was in shambles. In *A Moveable Feast* the author alludes to Pauline Pfeiffer's intrusion into their lives, first as Hadley's new acquaintance, then as an inseparable friend of the family, subsequently as Ernest's secret mistress, later as Hadley's open rival, and finally (after divorce and remarriage) as the second Mrs. Hemingway. Curiously, she moved into the orbit of Hemingway's life about the time that he became enamored with Duff Twysden, and at first the slender, wealthy, and fashionable Pauline took little interest in him. But by the end of 1925, when she joined the Hemingways (and Bumby) in Schruns, Austria, for skiing, the situation had altered; Pauline had (as Hemingway later wrote) "unknowingly, innocently, and unrelentingly" (*AMF* 209) begun to displace Hadley. Remembering that tumultuous season of change, Hemingway wrote: "First it is stimulating and fun and it goes on that way for a while. All things truly wicked start from an innocence. So you live day by day and enjoy what you have and do not worry. You lie and hate it and it destroys you and every day is more dangerous, but you live day to day as in a war" (*AMF* 210). Caught between two women, Hemingway attended the Pamplona fiesta again in 1926, with Pauline now installed as his not-so-secret love and Hadley resigned to the dissolution of her marriage. As later transmogrified in "A Canary for One," the final rupture occurred at the end of a long railroad journey back to the city where the Hemingways had been happy; in the closing line the narrator tersely observed: "We were returning to Paris to set up separate residences" (*CSS* 261). During a three-way separation demanded by Hadley, Pauline returned to the United States, Ernest moved into Gerald Murphy's studio on the rue Froidévaux, while Hadley relocated on the rue de Fleurus near Gertrude Stein. During this difficult waiting period, Hemingway wrote to Scott Fitzgerald: "Our life is all gone to hell which seems to be the one thing you can count on a good life to do."[11] The first part of Paris was definitively over.

After his marriage to Pauline in May 1927, Hemingway moved into a fashionable apartment on the rue Férou, near the place St. Sulpice. He avoided the cafés of Montparnasse and instead frequented Deux Magots and the Brasserie Lipp in St. Germain; a new phase of his Parisian life seemed to be opening up. But in reality he had already tired of the expatriate scene: He wrote to Jane Heap in 1925 that the city was "getting all shot to hell" and seemed no longer "like the old days"; in early 1926 he wrote from Schruns, promising to visit friends in Paris in April or May, "before the [summer] inrush of visiting Elks."[12] Perhaps symptomatically, Hemingway made little use of Paris as a fictional setting during the late 1920s. The brief scene at the Gare de Lyon that closes "A Canary for One" marks both the end of a marriage and, for several years, the virtual disappearance of the city from his writing. As Carlos Baker has noted, "Ernest's affection for Paris had entered a temporary decline," and in March 1928 he conducted his own "exile's return," resettling in Key West with Pauline.

There Hemingway toiled to complete the manuscript that became *A Farewell to Arms,* and he discovered the pleasures of deep-water fishing in the Gulf. But by September he wrote to Guy Hickok: "I am cockeyed nostalgique for Paris."[13] As if to recapture the charmed life of an earlier epoch, he returned to the rue Férou in April 1929 after a grueling year that had witnessed the birth of a son (in Kansas City), the suicide of his father in Oak Park, and the completion of the new novel. The eight-month sojourn mostly confirmed his sense, though, that he had depleted his enthusiasm for Paris; he returned to Key West in early 1930, prepared to make it his permanent home.

Hemingway was convinced that he could write about a place better – imagine it more clearly – if he were somewhere else; on the Left Bank he had written brilliantly about Michigan, and he assumed that "away from Paris [he] could write about Paris" (*AMF* 7). But his repatriation did not immediately generate much writing that was "about" Paris. "The Sea Change," apparently composed in 1930–31, contains only one passing mention of the city. But the story's subject – a young man's discovery that his "girl" has been having an affair with another woman – breaks new ground for Hemingway and indirectly associates Paris with bisexuality (or "perversion") as well as sexual betrayal (*CSS* 304). The title implies the potentially transformative effect of exile in Gay Paree, but the interior scene and implicitly interiorized action afford not so much as a glimpse of the city. In "A Way You'll Never Be," composed in 1932, the insomniac, war-haunted Nick Adams has a recurring dream on the Italian front about a church in Paris, "Sacré Coeur, blown white, like a soap bubble," in which "sometimes his girl was there and sometimes she was with someone else and he could not understand that" (*CSS* 310). Here the city shrinks to a single image, associated – in what might be understood as a displacement of male guilt – with female treachery. Scattered references in *Death in the Afternoon* (1932) and *Green Hills of Africa* (1935) indicate fleeting afterthoughts of Paris but no apparent urge to return to the Left Bank or to reconstruct in prose detail its memorable topography. Published in early 1934, his *Esquire* "Paris Letter" evokes a sympathetic image of Paris as a spurned lover but ends with a declaration ("I now love something else") that seems literally to close the book on that once-beloved place, either as a site of writing or as its subject.

By 1936, however, Hemingway had gained the emotional and temporal distance necessary to begin the consuming imaginative project of his later career: the fictional reconstruction or reclamation of his early years in Paris. Using his 1933–34 safari in Africa to construct the immediate setting of "The Snows of Kilimanjaro," he portrayed (in another suggestive move) the situation of a dying writer named Harry who has "destroyed his talent" and who toward the end of his life experiences flashbacks to all of the places and events he has saved to write about and now never will. Reminiscent of the method of Joyce or Faulkner in its use of an italicized flow of images – representing the stream of consciousness – the story offers a virtual resumé of Hemingway's travels from 1922 onward. Within this framework, which foregrounds the African scene and the writer's bitter exchanges with his wife Helen, Hemingway accords special importance to Harry's memories of Paris.

Remembrance evokes two distinct phases in the writer's life, associated with different wives and different parts of the city. With Helen, the "rich bitch" (*CSS* 45) whom Harry has married cynically in his middle years, he is obliged to ask: "Where did we stay in Paris?" (*CSS* 43). Significantly, he cannot recall the Parisian places he has known with her, the plush quarters at the Hôtel Crillon and at the Pavillion Henri-Quatre (in the suburb of St. Germain-en-Laye), which connote precisely the luxury and excess that Harry intermittently blames for the destruction of his talent. When Helen reminds him that he once "loved it there" at those elegant hotels, the writer replies sardonically, "Love is a dunghill, . . . and I'm the cock that gets on it to crow" (*CSS* 43). His self-contempt, which exceeds even his scorn for Helen, arises from his sense of failure and dissolution. The parts of Paris he has shared with Helen seem in retrospect as meaningless as the marriage that festers on the African plain.

He entertains much richer and more sustaining memories of the Paris that he knew earlier with his first wife, the one he quarreled with but also loved. In an extended flashback the writer admits betraying his first wife while on a journalistic assignment in Constantinople (which Hemingway visited in 1922), and he likewise admits his obsessive longing for another woman, "the one who left him" (*CSS* 48), a shadowy figure who recalls Agnes von Kurowsky, the Red Cross nurse whom Hemingway loved in Italy in 1918.[14]

But his feelings for that unnamed first wife nevertheless seem durable and genuine; after returning to Paris from the spectacle of the Greek-Turkish war, Harry feels "glad to be home" safely "back at the apartment with his wife that now he loved again" (CSS 49). In a subsequent flashback, he recollects more explicitly the working-class quarter where he has lived with her, remembering "the smell of dirty sweat and poverty and drunkenness at the Café des Amateurs and the whores at the Bal Musette they lived above" (CSS 51). "There was never another part of Paris that he loved like that," Hemingway writes, asserting the devotion of the dying writer (and perhaps that of the living author) to the old neighborhood and – implicitly – to the earlier marriage associated with it.

This evocation of the Quarter around the Place Contrescarpe marks an interesting move, for the ostensible focus of Harry's affection – the neighbors, the shopowners, the "sprawling trees," the ancient "white plastered houses," the narrow streets of the quartier, the "two rooms in the apartments where they lived" – conspicuously avoids direct mention of the first wife, who hovers like a ghost about the place where Harry has "written the start of all he was to do" (CSS 51). Without naming names, that is, Hemingway invests the scene of prior happiness, the tiny apartment over the bal musette, with nostalgic desire, allowing place to function as a metonym of irreplaceable human presence. Mindful of the pitfalls inherent in the autobiographical fallacy (reading the text naively as a record of the author's life), we must note the obvious about this passage: It portrays in its concrete particulars the very quartier where Hemingway launched his own career in 1922–23, and (ten years after the breakup of his first marriage) it also evokes, albeit indirectly, the memory of the woman inextricably associated with those early years. Hemingway composed the story, perhaps not coincidentally, as his marriage to Pauline foundered upon bitterness, boredom, and mistrust. Suggestively, the memory of the old neighborhood fills the dying writer with a desire for all that has been lost, all that cannot be recovered in his broken life. He observes with remorse that he has "never written about Paris. Not the Paris that he cared about" (CSS 52). Yet in "The Snows of Kilimanjaro" Hemingway had indeed begun to write about the Paris that *he* loved, initiating – in however tentative a fashion – the project of restoring Hadley to her place in the narrative.

As events transpired, though, conflict – both matrimonial and military – postponed Hemingway's work on the Paris book. During the Spanish civil war, his visits to the city with his new love, Martha Gellhorn, gave him further occasion to reflect on the persistence of desire and its ineluctable association, in his life, with Paris. During the early 1940s, however, the great problem of liberating France from Nazi occupation overshadowed the private, literary task of reconstructing the Paris years that mattered to Hemingway. A sign of his continuing longing for that lost world emerges in a 1942 letter to Hadley, where he remarks that in life "the good luck is to have had all the wonderful things and times we had. Imagine if we had been born at a time [like the present] when we could never have had Paris when we were young."[15] In 1944, Hemingway participated as a journalist-guerrilla fighter in the liberation of "the city [he] love[d] best in all the world," and shortly after the end of the war he embarked on two longer narratives that betrayed his continuing need to excavate the long-repressed story of Paris in the early years.[16]

Several months before Hemingway's fourth marriage to Mary Welsh, he conceived the idea of a three-part sea story that drew on his experiences of the early 1940s, fishing and hunting German submarines in the Gulf of Mexico. In the "Bimini" section that opens the posthumously published *Islands in the Stream* (1970), Hemingway projects details from his own past into the story of painter Thomas Hudson, who cruises the Gulf with his three sons and who remembers Paris in the 1920s, when he was married to the mother of his eldest son, Tom. When his boys ask him to talk about Paris as it was back then, Hudson obliges by reminiscing about acquaintances like Harry Crosby, James Joyce, Ezra Pound, and Ford Madox Ford. As a painter he has also known Picasso, Braque, Miro, Masson, and Pascin. He recalls the flat "over the sawmill," where he lived with baby Tom and his mother, and the nearby Closerie des Lilas and the Jardin de Luxembourg. When he is not fishing, though, Hudson mostly broods on his own loneliness and on the consciousness that through "one disastrous error of judgment" after another, he had broken up his marriage to Tom's mother. "I only really loved one woman and then lost her," he admits to himself.[17] News of young Tom's death in the war colors the action in the "Cuba" section, where Hemingway, in an act of transparent wish-fulfillment, portrays Hudson's brief, intense reunion with the woman whom he has loved and lost. In the third section, "At Sea," the painter reflects on the ephemerality of happiness, on "the time of innocence" when Hudson and his first wife would go to the Closerie together: "They would put Tom to bed and sit there together in the evenings at the old café, completely happy to be with each other" (*IIS* 449). This crucial remembrance of things past occurs just before Hudson receives a presumably fatal wound from a sniper hidden in a mangrove thicket. The painter's preoccupation with the Paris of his youth suggests Hemingway's implicit urge to memorialize his *own* past, but the fictionalizing of the *Islands* manuscript also suggests a countervailing need to disguise the autobiographical element.

The Garden of Eden, another narrative begun in 1946 and destined never to be completed, evokes the early years in Paris mainly through a subplot dropped from the abbreviated edition of the novel that appeared in 1986. While focusing mainly on the androgynous experiments of David Bourne, a young American novelist, and his sexually ambivalent wife, Catherine, this surprising novel about expatriate liaisons and gender reversals originally contained a parallel account of the sexual "changings" undertaken by painter Nick Sheldon and his wife Barbara, who live on a cobblestone street in a small, unheated studio in the fifth *arrondissement* near the Place Contrescarpe. Though they sometimes dine at the Brasserie Lipp, the Sheldons have little money and content themselves with giving each other small gifts, like the brioche Nick brings his wife for breakfast. Not coincidentally Barbara bears a striking physical resemblance to Hadley: "Her face was fresh scrubbed and very delicately freckled and her red-gold hair was shining brushed and came down to the square collar of her sweater."[18] In this subplot Hemingway seems poised to convert deeply personal material from his life with Hadley into sensational fiction. But he refrained: Except for a few wholly imagined episodes set in the south of France – one portraying Barbara's infidelity and Nick's almost simultaneous death in a bicycle accident – Hemingway dropped the Sheldons and focused most of the bulky manuscript on the Bournes and their bisexual friend Marita. *The Garden of Eden* draws its main imaginative force not from the author's nostalgia for the early days in Paris but – insofar as autobiographical sources may be discerned – from the more complicated triangular relations that developed in Schruns and on the Riviera after Pauline entered the lives of Ernest and Hadley in 1925–26.

By late 1956 Hemingway had still not written fully and directly about the Paris he cared about. Yet a stop at the Hôtel Ritz – between sojourns in Spain and Africa – apparently turned up some long-lost materials that he had been working on in 1924–25, that last good year with Hadley before everything went to ruin. Among the papers were several notebooks containing his draft of *The Sun Also Rises,* with the opening two chapters later cut from the novel at the suggestion of Scott Fitzgerald. The second of these chapters, which describes the atmosphere of mutual contempt pervading the Quarter, leads to a derisive scene between Jake and the pompous British author, Braddocks, at the Closerie des Lilas. The deleted episode would soon be transformed into a scathing reminiscence called "Ford Madox Ford and the Devil's Disciple." Mired in two long novels he was unable to complete and depressed by the obvious ebbing of his health and creativity, Hemingway discovered in this early work a sudden impetus, as if rereading the novel in his own handwriting brought back the circumstances under which he had first composed it in Madrid, Valencia, and Hendaye, and also brought back memories of Montparnasse in 1925, of Ford and Fitzgerald (both now dead), of Duff Twysden (also dead), after whom he had lusted in Pamplona, and of Hadley, who had been dropped from the novel as she was later to be displaced in his bed. Always, thoughts of Paris led back to Hadley.

In the very effort of remembrance, it seemed, Hemingway recovered something like the stylistic control that emerged from his early struggle to write "true sentences" on the rue Descartes. During the first half of 1957, possessed by a sense of urgency, he recorded the story of the Paris that he cared about, as if unwilling to repeat the fate of the dying writer in "Snows." The memoir became a conflicted project of self-representation; habitually protective of his privacy and laconic about his feelings, Hemingway nevertheless felt impelled by his own intimations of mortality to write the story of his literary beginnings and early happiness. He loaded the story, however, with insistent images of death. In "People of the Seine," for instance, he wrote, "When the cold rains kept on and killed the spring, it was as though a young person had died for no reason" (*AMF* 45). In another sketch he implied that he himself was (even in the 1920s) "The Man Who Was Marked for Death." When the tubercular Ernest Walsh tells the young Hemingway, "You're marked for Life," the author sardonically replies, "Give me time" (*AMF* 127). In 1957–58 his immediate awareness of age and debility gave his portrait of youth a fatalistic edge.

Recovering the nuanced simplicity of his early writing, Hemingway yet pursued multiple and complicated purposes in the memoir. He saw the book as an opportunity to acknowledge debts and (as he judged matters) to settle scores. Constructing a portrait gallery of literary Paris in the 1920s, he depicted the warm generosity of Sylvia Beach and Ezra Pound; he drew an admiring profile of James Joyce; he portrayed Gertrude Stein and Scott Fitzgerald in highly equivocal terms, mixing affection with disdain; he subjected Ford Madox Ford and Wyndham Lewis to scathing caricature. Hemingway also wrote lovingly about the city, especially about those favorite places he liked to go – the Auteuil race track, the book stalls along the quai, or the little park at the tip of the Ile de la Cité. No doubt recalling Joyce's *A Portrait of the Artist as a Young Man*, he crafted the sketches to tell the story of his apprenticeship "in the town best organized for a writer to write in that there is" (*AMF* 182). Recollecting the reading he did under Pound's tutelage with books borrowed from Sylvia Beach, he described the formation of his creative sensibility. He also dramatized the hard work of composing "the start of all he was to do," and he reconstructed his developing ideas about writing – as he remembered them – and the lessons he learned from Stein and Pound, as well as the ones he taught himself.

But if the education of a writer forms the principal theme of the memoir, its secondary motif emphasizes the love story of Ernest and Hadley and offers a subtle rationale for the breakup of the marriage. In a sense, *A Moveable Feast* amounts to an act of literary atonement, a tribute to the woman whose love and companionship had made the first part of Paris the best years of his life. The memoir forms a belated lyrical apology to Hadley for Hemingway's foolishness in losing her. With time running out, he finally told the personal story that he had suppressed in *The Sun Also Rises* – the story that seemed, in the flush of his enthusiasm for Duff Twysden in 1925, to have nothing to do with the longing and frustration that a wounded journalist-hero could feel. It was the story to which he had alluded in the *Esquire* "Paris Letter" that expressed his regret for having spurned an older woman, his first mistress; it was the tale he told only obliquely in "The Snows of Kilimanjaro" and in the sprawling, unfinishable novels of the 1940s and 1950s.

Significantly, the rereading of the notebook draft of *The Sun Also Rises* propelled Hemingway's penitential narrative. If Duff Twysden did not provoke the separation of 1926 and subsequent divorce, she functioned as a transitional figure, the temporary focus of that desire for secret new pleasures that would within a few months lead Hemingway into the liaison with Pauline Pfeiffer. Curiously, Duff appears in *A Moveable Feast* only as an anonymous acquaintance; by a kind of reciprocity, Hemingway now foregrounds his devotion to Hadley while concealing the flirtation with Duff that had Montparnasse buzzing in 1925. Recollecting the day that he first met Scott Fitzgerald, Hemingway remembers sitting in the Dingo Bar with "some completely worthless characters" (*AMF* 149). When Fitzgerald later asks about "those absolutely bloody British" in Ernest's company, Hemingway first denies having been with them and then reverses himself with peculiar emphasis:

> No, I remembered, there had been two British there. It was true. I remembered who they were. They had been there all right.

"Yes," I said. "Of course."

"That girl with the phony title who was so rude and that silly drunk with her. They said they were friends of yours."

"They are. And she *is* very rude sometimes." (*AMF* 153)

Hemingway's initial inability to remember Duff (and Pat Guthrie), like his refusal to insert proper names, reflects his determination to avoid the topic of his advances to her. The passing allusion mainly allows him to display a retrospective indifference toward the "rude" woman he once wanted to bed.

Clearly, though, Hemingway well remembered how he had behaved with Duff in Pamplona and how that trip had rocked his marriage. Later in the "Scott Fitzgerald" sketch, he depicts a conversation with his wife just before the 1925 trip to Spain. Hemingway has just returned from a misadventure in Lyon with Fitzgerald, and this dialogue with Hadley foreshadows marital changes to come:

"I learned one thing."

"What?"

"Never go on trips with anyone you do not love."

"Isn't that fine?"

"Yes. And we're going to Spain."

"Yes. Now it's less than six weeks before we go. And this year we won't let anyone spoil it, will we?" (*AMF* 175)

In view of the emotional damage sustained that summer, Hadley's last question reflects the kind of doomed innocence she shares with Ernest. Recurrently in *A Moveable Feast* Hemingway illustrates the precariousness of luck and happiness, and here he turns a seemingly light conversation about the trip to Spain into an exemplary moment of self-delusion, as the two congratulate themselves on being "awfully lucky." But Hemingway then imposes the ironic perspective of experience when his narrator remarks: "We both touched wood on the café table and the waiter came to see what it was we wanted. But what we wanted not he, nor anyone else, nor knocking on wood or on marble, as this café table-top was, could ever bring us. But we did not know it that night and we were very happy" (*AMF* 176).

Hemingway's gesture of atonement to Hadley involves two separate but related strategies. On the one hand, he idealizes the marriage, casting a nostalgic glow around commonplace scenes and settings. As he had in "Snows," Hemingway fondly portrays the old neighborhood around the Place Contrescarpe and recalls his first winter in Paris with Hadley in 1921–22. He remembers the writing room he rented on the rue Descartes – though forgets to say that he used it only a few weeks. And he recalls their cramped, unheated apartment, which had neither toilet nor bathroom, as a wonderful place: "With a fine view and a good mattress and springs for a comfortable bed on the floor, and pictures we liked on the wall, it was a cheerful, gay flat" (AMF 37). He omits any mention of the "quarrels" alluded to in "Snows" and depicts a seemingly ideal relationship in which the couple "ate well and cheaply and drank well and cheaply and slept well and warm together and loved each other" (AMF 51). He describes lovely walks across Paris, including the one that finds him standing on a bridge with Hadley, looking up the Seine toward the Ile de la Cité, basking in the beauty of the view: "We looked and there it all was: our river and our city and the island of our city" (AMF 55). Through the possessive pronouns he implies that they own it all; by loving each other they have gained title to Paris.

Hemingway tries to portray himself as a faithful and monogamous husband. In "A Good Café of the Place St. Michel," he observes an attractive woman but contents himself with aesthetic appreciation. She "belongs" to him in the same sense that Paris belongs to him – because he belongs to "this notebook and this pencil" – to the implements that signify his commitment to writing. Later, Hemingway displays his fidelity to Hadley in his encounter with Pascin at the Dôme. Here we glimpse the highly charged erogenous zone that was Montparnasse in the 1920s, the Quarter as frequented by Jake and Brett. Hemingway notices several acquaintances in the big cafés but remarks that "there were always much nicer-looking people that I did not know that, with the lights coming on, were hurrying to some place to drink together, to eat together and then to make love" (AMF 100). When the painter arrives with two young models in tow, he good-naturedly offers to let Hemingway "bang" one of them. After some chaffing about sex, however, the faithful husband declines to stay for dinner: "No. I go to eat with my *légitime*" (AMF 104). Hemingway's quaint use of French slang to refer to his legal wife emphasizes the gallantry of his refusing Pascin's offer.

Yet the retrospective idealizing of the relationship to Hadley could not erase the obstinate fact that the marriage began to come apart before their fourth anniversary. So Hemingway's other tactic of apology (in "There Is Never Any End to Paris") involves an elaborate rationalization of the break up that shifts responsibility partly to Pauline, the "best friend" who contrived to steal Hadley's husband; partly to the "rich" (Gerald and Sara Murphy) who encouraged Ernest to drop his less fashionable first wife; and partly to the "pilot fish" (John Dos Passos) who led the Murphys to Hemingway and thus contributed to his undoing. Very briefly, when he describes

Hadley's loss of his early manuscripts in Gare de Lyon, Hemingway also lays the groundwork for a claim he never quite makes – but nevertheless insinuates – that his wife bears some blame for the alienation of his affections. "I remember what I did in the night when I let myself into the flat and found it was true," he remarks cryptically about his return to Paris to confirm the loss of all his work (*AMF* 74).

A more conspicuous rationalizing figures in his treatment of "luck," which enables him to attribute the breakup itself to bad luck. Hemingway portrays himself carrying a rabbit's foot and knocking on wood to preserve his charmed life a little longer, but he cannot insure it indefinitely against mischance and catastrophe. In a more philosophical vein, he explains the divorce from Hadley and the end of "the first part of Paris" as a result of "hunger" – that yearning for completion, that craving for something else so indicative of human imperfection. Perhaps the most eloquent and moving passage in the memoir describes the persistence of desire:

> It was a wonderful meal at Michaud's after we got in; but when we had finished and there was no question of hunger any more the feeling that had been like hunger when we were on the bridge was still there when we caught the bus home. It was there when we came in the room and after we had gone to bed and made love in the dark, it was there. When I woke with the windows open and the moonlight on the roofs of the tall houses, it was there. I put my face away from the moonlight into the shadow but I could not sleep and lay awake thinking about it. We had both wakened twice in the night and my wife slept sweetly now with the moonlight on her face. I had tried to think it out and I was too stupid. Life had seemed so simple that morning. . . . But Paris was a very old city and we were young and nothing was simple there, not even poverty, nor sudden money, nor the moonlight, nor right and wrong nor the breathing of someone who lay beside you in the moonlight.   (*AMF* 57–58)

Although Hemingway portrays a quintessentially romantic scene, lying beside his wife in the moonlight after a good meal and lovemaking, still the hunger betrays the creaturely discontent that will lead to the rupture a few years later. Paris figures in this moral calculus as a place where nothing is simple, where "right and wrong" get mixed up, and where young people from the American Midwest may undergo rapid, profound changes that leave them strangers to each other – and perhaps even to themselves.

Hemingway knew that as well as anyone. "I wished I had died before I ever loved anyone but her," he finally writes about Hadley. Even though Paris was "always Paris and you changed as it changed," he could not shrug off the fact that he had lost Hadley through his own errors of judgment just as he had lost the Paris that he cared about. That Paris – associated first with the rue du Cardinal Lemoine and later with the rue Notre-Dame-des-Champs – had been shaped and defined by the poverty he shared with her. Although the memoir exaggerated their actual impoverishment, still the couple lived simply and frugally; they knew the common life of working people. "This is how Paris was in the early days," Hemingway concluded, "when we were very poor and very happy" (*AMF* 211). What he had realized by the early 1930s was that happiness was not simply a corollary of the poverty but virtually a consequence of it. He had no wish to romanticize penury; but what he learned, the hard way, was that wealth and fame lured him away from the simple, good life that he had known, depriving him in the process both of the Paris that he cared about and of the woman who had for a time made that world sufficient.

NOTES

1. Ernest Hemingway, "A Paris Letter," *Byline: Ernest Hemingway,* ed. William White (New York: Charles Scribner's Sons, 1967), p. 158.

2. See Frederic Joseph Svoboda, *Hemingway's* The Sun Also Rises: *The Crafting of a Style* (Lawrence: University Press of Kansas, 1983), pp. 5–10.

3. See Michael Reynolds, *Hemingway: The Paris Years* (Oxford: Basil Blackwell, 1989), pp. 298–306, for an analysis of the confusing evidence.

4. The comment about what is made up appears in "On Writing," *The Nick Adams Stories* (New York: Charles Scribner's Sons, 1972), p. 246.

5. See my discussion of this allusion in *Imagining Paris* (New Haven: Yale University Press, 1993), pp. 104–6.

6. See ibid., p. 110.

7. Svoboda 135.

8. Notebook manuscript of *The Sun Also Rises,* The Ernest Hemingway Collection, John Fitzgerald Kennedy Library, Boston, Mass., #194, 1, p. 10.

9. See "On Writing," *The Nick Adams Stories* 241–49, and note especially Nick's comment that "he always worked best when Helen was unwell. Just that much discontent and friction" (247).

10. Reynolds, *Paris Years* 289.

11. Letter to F. Scott Fitzgerald, ca. September 7, 1926, *Ernest Hemingway: Selected Letters, 1917–1961,* ed. Carlos Baker (New York: Charles Scribner's Sons, 1981), p. 217.

12. Letter to Jane Heap, ca. August 23 or 30, 1925, Jane Heap Collection, University of Wisconsin–Milwaukee; letter to Louis and Mary Bromfield, ca. March 8, 1926, *Ernest Hemingway: Selected Letters* 196.

13. Letter to Guy Hickok, September 27, 1928, Carlos Baker Papers, Princeton University.

14. See especially Henry S. Villard and James Nagel, *Hemingway in Love and War: The Lost Diary of Agnes von Kurowsky, Her Letters, and Correspondence of Ernest Hemingway* (Boston: Northeastern University Press, 1989), pp. 233–51.

15. Ernest Hemingway, letter to Hadley Mowrer, July 23, 1942, *Ernest Hemingway: Selected Letters 1917–1961* 537.

16. Ernest Hemingway, "How We Came to Paris," *ByLine: Ernest Hemingway,* 383.

17. Ernest Hemingway, *Islands in the Stream* (New York: Charles Scribner's Sons, 1970), p. 98.

18. File 422a-3, pp. 6–7, Ernest Hemingway Collection, John F. Kennedy Library, Boston, Mass.

WORKS CITED

Hemingway, Ernest. *Byline: Ernest Hemingway.* Ed. William White. New York: Charles Scribner's Sons, 1967.

The Complete Short Stories of Ernest Hemingway. New York: Charles Scribner's Sons, 1987.

Ernest Hemingway: Selected Letters, 1917–1961. Ed. Carlos Baker. New York: Charles Scribner's Sons, 1981.

The Garden of Eden. New York: Charles Scribner's Sons, 1986.

Islands in the Stream. New York: Charles Scribner's Sons, 1970.

A Moveable Feast. New York: Charles Scribner's Sons, 1964.

The Nick Adams Stories. Ed. Philip Young. New York: Charles Scribner's Sons, 1972.

The Sun Also Rises. New York: Charles Scribner's Sons, 1926.

Kennedy, J. Gerald. *Imagining Paris.* New Haven: Yale University Press, 1993.

Reynolds, Michael. *Hemingway: The Paris Years.* Oxford: Basil Blackwell, 1989.

Svoboda, Frederic Joseph. *Hemingway's* The Sun Also Rises: *The Crafting of a Style.* Lawrence: University Press of Kansas, 1983.

Villard, Henry S., and James Nagel. *Hemingway in Love and War: The Lost Diary of Agnes von Kurowsky, Her Letters, and Correspondence of Ernest Hemingway.* Boston: Northeastern University Press, 1989.

II

ALLEN JOSEPHS

Hemingway's Spanish Sensibility

[America] had been a good country and we had made a bloody mess of it.
– GHOA 285

He was in Spain, inside Spain, living her life. And his two great works, *For Whom the Bell Tolls* and *The Sun Also Rises,* blossomed out of this implantation of the roots of that powerful American tree into Iberian soil.
– Salvador de Madariaga

Ernest Hemingway wrote about many places – northern Michigan; France and Italy; Key West, Havana, and Bimini; East Africa – but no place had the effect on him, as a person or as a writer, that Spain did. In the second sentence of his last book, *The Dangerous Summer,* Hemingway claimed to like Spain better than any country except his own, and privately he said he loved Spain more than any place. To understand how and why Spain affected him so deeply is to explore the most profound mysteries of Hemingway's craft, both as stylist and as creator of narrative fiction.

The effect of place on writers is well known, especially the home place: William Faulkner's northern Mississippi or Thomas Wolfe's North Carolina highlands come readily to mind as examples. With Hemingway the case is quite different. He wrote very little about his hometown of Oak Park or nearby Chicago. Nick Adams, one of his most autobiographical characters, thinks in the story "The Killers" that he ought to get out of town. Hemingway himself did virtually the same and seldom returned.

Instead of writing about his literal home, Hemingway adopted a series of places as spiritual homes and wrote about those. In a section cut from the galleys of *Death in the Afternoon,* he explained that he had loved three peninsulas: northern Michigan, where he had spent his childhood summers hunting and fishing; Italy, where he had served as an ambulance driver in World War I; and Spain. But Michigan had been ruined by the cutting of the forests and Italy had been fouled by the Fascists; Spain was the only good country left.

What was it about Spain that so attracted him? Why was it the only good country left? All his life Hemingway, much like his contemporary Faulkner, distrusted modernity or progress, believing instead in nature and agreeing with the rabbi of Ecclesiastes that "the earth abideth for ever" (1:4 – the next verse provided the title for *The Sun Also Rises*). In all his work, from the early stories to *The Dangerous Summer,* there arises a kind of opposition between those who live in harmony with nature and those who do not. The Spanish people, especially prior to the Spanish civil war, belonged to the first group, *homo naturalis* as opposed to *homo progressus.*

Almost everyone who goes to Spain has a definite reaction to it, loving it or loathing it. The first time I went to Spain, I had the odd sensation that I had come home to a place I had never been. Now after more than thirty years of working there, I know Spain is my spiritual home, what I've come to call my psychic stamping ground. I think Spain and Cuba, long the favored and most Spanish of Spain's colonial empire, were much the same for Hemingway.

Why should this be so?

Let me answer with a question: Is there such a thing as genetic memory? We may doubt anyone can give us a very scientific answer but it is certainly true that people have visceral reactions to places they have never been, reactions that could be explained by a phenomenon such as genetic memory. What is it about East Africa, for example, that so stirs some people, Hemingway included?

In the deep recesses of our genes, do some of us somehow "remember" that humankind began there? Is it possible that atavisms – the reappearance of characteristics of some remote ancestor absent in intervening generations – occur in humans? We may never know the answer to these questions, but we can use them to give context to the idea that Hemingway was our most atavistic or primordial writer. And Spain, especially in Hemingway's early years there, was still very much a primordial place.

Before we examine Hemingway's use of Spain in his fiction, it is helpful to trace briefly his biographical involvement with Spain. Then we can consider his fiction in the light his biography sheds on it.

Hemingway stopped briefly in the south of Spain on the way home from Italy and the war in January 1919. In December 1921, on the way to Paris with his new bride Hadley, he spent a few hours at the northwestern port of Vigo. He told his friend Bill Smith that a person could stay at the best hotel for a dollar. The bay swarmed with large tuna and there were trout in the mountains as well as wonderful swimming. And the "Vino" was only two pesetas a litre (*SL* 58; in direct quotes I will keep E.H.'s eccentricities).

In 1923, Hemingway visited Spain twice, the first time in May and June, expressly to watch corridas (what we erroneously call the bullfights), and the second time in July to attend the great fiesta of San Fermín in Pamplona. Hemingway instantly appreciated *toreo* (what we call bullfighting) and seemed to have an instinctual understanding of it. In March 1925 he wrote Bill Smith that he got a bigger kick from his first corrida than anything he'd ever seen (Maurice Neville's collection). How much did Hemingway like the corridas he saw? Enough to risk taking Hadley to Pamplona in her fifth month of pregnancy and enough to name his son, born in October, John Hadley Nicanor Hemingway, the Nicanor after the great *torero* (bullfighter), Nicanor Villalta.

At year's end he wrote his friend James Gamble about corridas, commenting that Spain was the greatest country of all. He loved it because it was "unspoiled" and incredibly "tough and wonderful" (*SL* 107). He confided to William D. Horne, who served in Italy with Hemingway, that in Pamplona he'd had the best times since the war. He described the running of the bulls through the streets early in the morning and maintained that Horne would love the spectacle of the corrida. It was not brutality as they had always been taught. Instead it was "a great tragedy," and "the most beautiful thing" he had ever seen, something that took plenty of skill and guts. Hadley was "wild about it" (*SL* 87–88).

In 1924, Hemingway spent June and July in Spain, seeing corridas, especially in Madrid and Pamplona. After the fiesta he and Hadley and friends went to the mountain town of Burguete near the French border where they had fine trout fishing in the Irati River.

In November, Hemingway wrote to his wartime friend and fishing buddy Howell Jenkins that fishing in the Irati was like trout fishing on the Black in Michigan; the forests of beech and pine had never been cut; Pamplona was the "godamdest wild time" you could have; the country was the greatest anywhere; the fishing was unspoiled because there were no roads; the people had "any people in the world skinned"; and bullfighting was the "best damn stuff in the world." Hemingway's enthusiasm was boundless, as was his admiration for Spain and its people. Spain was "the only country" that had not been "shot to pieces." Italy was now just Fascists, poor food, and "hysterics," but Spain was the "real old stuff" (*SL* 130–31).

From Burguete Hemingway wrote Ezra Pound that the *plaza de toros* (bullring) was the only place left where "valor and art" could combine for success (*SL* 119). In May, Hemingway had written the influential publisher

Edward J. O'Brien about his need to find people whose "actual physical conduct" could give you a sense of admiration: Well, he had gotten "ahold of it in bull fighting. Jesus Christ yes" (*SL* 117). Hemingway was clearly beginning to associate toreo and writing and to see that both arts shared important elements. This fundamental association is one I want to emphasize strongly, here and throughout Hemingway's development.

By April 1925, Hemingway – who had not yet written a novel, although he had already done some of his finest stories – decided to write a book on the bulls. He told Max Perkins, the Scribner's editor about to sign him on, that it would be a large book with lots of good photographs (*SL* 156). As it turned out, he would write *The Sun Also Rises* first, but the taurine book, which would eventually become *Death in the Afternoon,* prefigured the novel and very likely determined the novel's centering on toreo and the fiesta of San Fermín.

In July, Hemingway would be in Pamplona the third time, now with a new group of friends, and he would turn experiences there in 1925 into the fictional basis for *The Sun Also Rises.* Before the fiesta started he returned to Burguete to fish, only to find that lumbermen had run logs down the river, destroying the fishing.

In good spirits despite the ruined stream, he wrote a funny letter to his new friend F. Scott Fitzgerald, whom he had met two months before. His idea of heaven, he told Fitzgerald, was a "big bullring" with his having two front row seats and a private trout stream outside in which no one else could fish (*SL* 166).

After Pamplona, where Hemingway watched Cayetano Ordóñez (the model for Pedro Romero in *SAR*) perform, he began to write the rough draft of *The Sun Also Rises,* originally titled *Fiesta.* It took him about two months.

Hemingway's first years visiting Spain and discovering corridas – just as his style was emerging and he was making the revolutionary breakthroughs in language in his early stories and first novel that would change the English language – were experiences not readily separable from the style itself. The twin discoveries – of Spain and toreo on one hand and of his own style on the other – are part and parcel of the same powerful aesthetic vision. Rather than coincidental, these discoveries were intentional.

Hemingway said as much on the second page of *Death in the Afternoon.* He was trying to learn to write when he first went to Spain to see corridas. He was trying to get the "real thing," what he called "the sequence of motion and fact" that produced the emotion, and the ring, where you could see life and death, violent death, was just the thing he was seeking. And instead of not liking toreo, the reaction he expected to have, he loved it.

Clearly a bonding took place for Hemingway – one that combined "art and valor," included his idea of "grace under pressure," first mentioned to Fitzgerald in April 1926 (*SL* 200), and wove together form and content, style and substance, writing and toreo. To the extent this is true, the art of toreo left an indelible impression on American literature and, by extension, on world literature.

In 1926, after extensively rewriting *The Sun Also Rises* that winter in Austria, Hemingway spent four months in Spain, seeing corridas (*SAR* was published in October). In 1927, now married to Pauline Pfeiffer, he visited Spain in July, August, and September. After a hiatus in the United States in 1928, Hemingway returned for July, August, and September of the 1929 season, befriending American matador Sidney Franklin. In 1931, hard at work on *Death in the Afternoon,* he followed the bulls all over Spain from May through September. The book came out in September 1932, marking the end of Hemingway's early, very creative period in Spain.

Hemingway dedicated 1933–35 to Africa, but on July 18, 1936, the Spanish civil war broke out, and he again focused on Spain. Also in December 1936, he met Martha Gellhorn at Sloppy Joe's in Key West. During the same period, Hemingway contributed money for ambulances for the Spanish Republic and signed with the North American Newspaper Alliance (NANA) to cover the Spanish conflict.

Early in 1937, Hemingway helped write the narration for the pro-Republican film, *Spain in Flames.* He spent mid-March to mid-May in Spain, helping Dutch director Joris Ivens film *The Spanish Earth,* observing battle sites at the Jarama River, the Arganda Bridge, and Guadalajara, where the Republicans defeated troops sent by Mussolini to help Franco.

Martha Gellhorn joined Hemingway in Madrid, and they closely observed the running battle of Madrid, including the occasional shelling of their hotel. Hemingway and Gellhorn also spent ten days in the Guadarrama mountains, just north of Madrid, touring on horseback and inspecting battle sites. Although he may not yet have known it, Hemingway was already gathering material for *For Whom the Bell Tolls,* which would take place precisely in those mountains and in that month of May 1937.

In June, Hemingway addressed the Writer's Congress in New York, speaking on behalf of the Republic and against fascism. He also wrote the narration for *The Spanish Earth* and showed the film at the White House and at Frederic March's house in Hollywood, raising ambulance money. In the fall he returned to Spain to write newspaper pieces and his only play (*The Fifth Column*). The year 1937 was Hemingway's most political year and one of the happiest times of his life. Finally, there is strong evidence that Hemingway took part in a clandestine guerrilla operation – blowing up a bridge – north of Teruel.

In 1938, Hemingway wrote pieces on Spain for *Ken* magazine, urging the United States to abandon its hypocritically neutral position and to aid the Republic. In April and May he reported on the Ebro front for NANA. After the summer in Key West working on stories about the Spanish civil war and pieces for *Ken,* he returned to Spain in the fall for the fourth and last time during the war. By this time Hemingway was deeply disappointed by the Republic's imminent loss to Generalísimo Franco.

In March 1939, in Cuba, as the Spanish civil war ended, Hemingway began to write *For Whom the Bell Tolls,* and working on it steadily for well over a year, finished it in late July 1940. It was published on October 21 to splendid reviews and became a phenomenal best-seller. This year ended Hemingway's middle period in Spain and began his residence in Cuba. In December he bought the Finca Vigía outside Havana, where he would spend almost the rest of his life.

With half of Spain dead, jailed, or exiled, Franco ran the country with a dictator's viselike grip. Foreigners were only allowed in by visa and supporters of the Republic were excluded. It was not until 1953 and rapprochement with the United States that borders were opened.

Hemingway returned immediately, heading straight for Pamplona, spending a month with old friends and going to the bulls. There was an important novelty, the young matador Antonio Ordóñez, son of Cayetano Ordóñez, whom Hemingway immediately judged better than his father "on his father's best day" (*SL* 822).

In 1954, after two airplane crashes in two days in Africa, Hemingway returned to Spain for the corridas in Madrid in May. In October he won the Nobel Prize, due largely to the success of *The Old Man and the Sea,* published in 1952. In 1956, he visited Spain in the fall, catching performances of now leading matador, Antonio Ordóñez.

Then, in 1959, Hemingway contracted with *Life* magazine to do a series of articles on the 1959 season, centering on the rivalry between Antonio Ordóñez and his brother-in-law Luis Miguel Dominguín. From May until mid-October, he assiduously followed the matadors up and down the taut bull's hide of Spain.

In 1960 he worked on the articles, now called *The Dangerous Summer,* in Cuba, writing 120,000 words instead of the 10,000 *Life* had requested of him. In August he returned to Spain ostensibly to take care of details, and while there suffered severe depression. In September, *Life* published excerpts from the manuscript Hemingway had been unable to cut. That publication ended the late period of Hemingway's involvement with Spain. On July 2, 1961, at his second home in Ketchum, Idaho, instead of preparing to go to Pamplona, Hemingway committed suicide with a shotgun.

From 1923 to 1960, Hemingway's involvement with Spain was intensely significant. That involvement follows a downward curve, as his life does, with more intensity and significance in the early and middle periods, and less in the later period. Yet in spite of the downward curve, the influence of Spain on Hemingway's adult life and works is unequaled by any other place. As a result, Hemingway's work is simply not conceivable without Spain and without Spanish values, values that often suggest a rejection of modern Western values.

Hemingway is generally credited, perhaps overly so, with writing about what he actually experienced. That was not the case with his first fictional piece about the bulls. Chapter 9 of *In Our Time*, his first collection of stories, came not from his own experience but secondhand from the painter Mike Strater, and Hemingway wrote the sketch before he saw a corrida, remembering what Strater had told him, probably almost verbatim.

Chapters 10 to 14 were written after Hemingway had actually seen corridas, and they are among the most arresting of those vignettes that concentrate in detailed and close-up fashion on brutalities – scenes of war, a hanging, police brutality, political executions, and refugees on the march – of "our time." These scenes of toreo clearly belonged in Hemingway's mind to that sense of life and death he would describe in *Death in the Afternoon*. To put it another way, these brief taurine pieces are vivid examples of what Hemingway would refer to as going "to Spain to see bullfights . . . to try to write about them for myself" (*DIA* 3). When we read these striking sketches inserted between the longer stories, we are simultaneously watching the development of Hemingway's style.

At this early stage of his *afición* (passion for the bulls), toreo was raw subject matter rather than the aesthetic experience it was to become. Yet the spectacle's fascination for Hemingway and his richly inclusive use of it indicate that he was deeply aware of how pervasive an influence it already had on him.

What stands out in these pieces is their objective examination of sensory experience and their presentation of rhetorically unencumbered descriptions of action. These important elements of Hemingway's stylistic revolution are remarkably evident in these early descriptions of toreo, and even though he did not yet fully understand the complexities of the spectacle he was so vividly portraying, his sense of it was substantially greater than anything yet written on the subject in any language other than Spanish.

Two of the vignettes include the narrator inside the action. In chapter 11, after the crowd cuts the pigtail from the disgraced matador (up to here in third person), the narrator remarks: "Afterwards I saw him at the café" (CSS 133).

Chapter 13 is told entirely in the first person and the narrator is himself a matador: Maera asks who will kill the bulls after the drunken Mexican gets gored and the narrator responds, "We, I suppose" (CSS 149). Hemingway has made extraordinary progress in the very short space from the secondhand narration of chapter 9 to the narrator as matador in chapter 13. He also introduces here the ambience of the fiesta of San Fermín, which anticipates *The Sun Also Rises:* "I heard the drums coming down the street and then the fifes and the pipes and then they came around the corner, all dancing" (CSS 149).

One of Hemingway's most distinctive stylistic traits is his use of the second person to personalize third-person narration. He employs this device in chapter 12: "If it happened right down close in front of you, you could see Villalta snarl at the bull and curse him" (CSS 141). The rest is told in third person, but the second-person bridge to the reader contributes strongly to one of Hemingway's major goals and achievements: to make the reader a part of the experience he was describing.

Finally, in chapter 14, Hemingway describes the fictional death of Maera – fictional death because Maera, a real matador, did not die in this manner and did not die until several years later, as Hemingway would record in *Death in the Afternoon.* Here the death of the matador seems a natural ending to this series of taurine sketches, all of which display violence one way or another.

The most interesting technique in this scene is the narration of the experience of Maera's dying, when everything gets larger and then smaller and then larger and then smaller and then begins "to run faster and faster as when they speed up a cinematograph film" (CSS 161). This experience was very probably related to Hemingway's own near-death experience when he was wounded at Fossalta, Italy, on the night of July 8, 1918. I am strongly inclined to believe that Hemingway's nearly overwhelming sense of life and death, stemming from that seminal incident during the war – as he wrote to his family, "Dying is a very simple thing. I've looked at death and really I know" (SL 19) – is directly related to his fascination with the primal scenes of tauromachy he was witnessing and recording in Spain.

Jake Barnes, the first-person narrator of *The Sun Also Rises*, not only witnesses corridas; he is a knowledgeable insider, a somewhat rare being for that time. Jake is a foreign aficionado, a non-Spaniard who understands and appreciates what toreo means. One of his important functions is that of guide who will assure that we also understand the importance of toreo and ultimately through toreo, the meaning of the novel.

In *The Sun Also Rises* toreo has gone beyond the immediate sensory realm of the vignettes to a highly developed, structurally integrated, aesthetic component of the novel. Toreo, in Hemingway's mind and in his fiction, had evolved from sensation into art, from being merely the subject of art to an art in its own right. And that art is at the very center of the novel.

Many think of toreo as a sport. It is not. It may be described as a spectacle, a ritual, a ceremony, a sacrifice, or an art, but never as a sport. And as Hemingway well knew by the time he wrote the novel, toreo was often described within Spain as the tragedy of the death of the bull.

Toreo is very early theater, structurally earlier than classical Greek tragedy, in which there is only the *representation* of death. In toreo, still fixed in the stage of sacrifice, the bull must actually die. By the time Hemingway wrote *The Sun Also Rises,* he understood deeply and intuitively the Spanish sense of toreo. And he used that sense, that hieratic or priestlike quality, to turn his undistinguished autobiographical draft of a few days at the fiesta of San Fermín in 1925 into one of the finest and most influential of modern novels, one that in the intervening years has only increased in fascination.

In the winter of 1925–26, Hemingway completely revised that original account in what he would call years later in his memoir *A Moveable Feast,* "the most difficult job of rewriting" he ever did. He had to take his first draft and, as he put it in a masterpiece of understatement, "make it into a novel" (202). It was in the painstaking rewriting – especially of the scenes involving the matador Pedro Romero – that Hemingway subtly brought the art of toreo to the foreground in the novel's climactic moment.

Notice that I am saying the art of toreo and not the artist himself. Romero, the artist, the torero, the matador (literally the killer), creates that art to be sure, but a close look at the language Hemingway uses in the climactic moments shows us that Romero's work, the art, the "it," is what counts: "Romero's *bullfighting* gave real emotion, because he kept the absolute *purity* of line. . . . Romero had the *old thing*" (168, emphasis added throughout). "The crowd felt *it,* even the people from Biarritz, even the American ambassador saw *it* finally:" (215). "Pedro Romero had the *greatness.* He loved *bull-fighting.* . . . Never once did he look up. He made *it* stronger that way, and did *it* for himself, too, as well as for her. . . . he did *it* for himself inside, and *it* strengthened him. . . . He gained by *it* all through the afternoon" (216). Then during Romero's second bull, "Each thing he did with this bull wiped [the fight with Cohn] out a little cleaner" (219). The artist's performance here, at the center of the arena, is not merely the center of attention; it is also the source of moral amelioration and physical antidote. Romero's triumph – over the bull and over Cohn – is firmly rooted in his art.

As Romero continues his *faena* (work with the *muleta,* the small red cloth, preparatory to killing), he achieves the kind of performance Hemingway would equate in *Death in the Afternoon* with religious ecstasy: "The crowd made him go on. They did not want the bull killed yet, they did not want it to be over. . . . And each pass as it reached the summit gave you a sudden ache inside. The crowd did not want it ever to be finished" (219–20). This is clearly the kind of faena "that takes a man out of himself and makes him feel immortal while it is proceeding," that is capable of moving the spectators "in a growing ecstasy of ordered, formal, passionate, increasing disregard for death," as Hemingway would phrase it in *Death in the Afternoon* (206–7).

The moral, spiritual, even ecstatic dimension of toreo ought not surprise us. Juan Belmonte, the great revolutionary of the modern art of toreo (whom Hemingway does not treat quite fairly in the novel), once commented that toreo is "a spiritual exercise" (Caballero 102). There is no doubt that Hemingway, too, saw it exactly in that light. In a long section cut from the end of Hemingway's seminal story, "Big Two-Hearted River," published posthumously as "On Writing," Nick Adams thinks: "His whole inner life had been bullfights all one year. . . . Maera was the greatest man he'd ever known" (*NAS* 236–37).

This, of course, is the same Maera Hemingway had fictionalized in the vignettes and the same man about whom he commented to Ezra Pound, "There is no comparison in art between Joyce and Maera – Maera by a mile" (*SL* 119). James Joyce was the contemporary writer Hemingway most admired but his comment here is only partly tongue in cheek.

The art of toreo is at the heart of the novel precisely because it is spiritual. Young, promising matadors are often called messiahs, and Hemingway used the terms "Messiah" and "Resurrexit" in his draft.

We cannot understand *The Sun Also Rises* – a novel of manners of the so-called lost generation – without taking into account the fact that the religious fiesta of San Fermín forms the center of the novel and without understanding that the nucleus of that center is the great faena Pedro Romero performs with his second bull. All the characters in the novel are measured according to their reactions to the corrida.

In the sacred time of the fiesta – what religious historians call mythic time or the eternal present or time out of time – we watch the mystery of the sacrifice of the bull in the center of the ring. In the still, sunlit center of the ring is the art of toreo and around that axis in concentric circles, each one at a greater remove from the Promethean fire at the center, revolve first Romero himself, the matador as sacrificial high priest; then Montoya, whom Hemingway once called "a highly moral hotel keeper" (SL 240), and the true aficionados, initiates in the mystery; then at varying distances Jake and Brett and the foreign aficionados, the not altogether faithful converts who have made the pilgrimage to Pamplona (which is on the great thousand-year-old medieval pilgrimage route called the Camino de Santiago, the Way of Saint James) seeking momentary solace in the fiesta; then in near darkness the uninitiated American ambassador and his entourage; and finally, altogether blind to the rising sun at the heart of the novel, alone and uncomprehending, Robert Cohn.

It was, as Hemingway wrote to Max Perkins, "a damn tragedy with the earth abiding forever as the hero" (SL 229), the tragedy of his own generation inescapably imprisoned in history, irredeemably lost in the profane time of the aftermath of the war.

Why, if not to point up the sacred nature of this mythical novel of manners, did Hemingway change his original title Fiesta to The Sun Also Rises, along the way rejecting The Lost Generation? Why if not to contrast the sacred nature of the Spanish fiesta and the profane nature of the modern world did he use as opposing epigraphs Gertrude Stein's otherwise banal dictum "You are all a lost generation," which in context becomes a virtual maxim of historical or profane time, and the poignant and poetic quote from Ecclesiastes, the cyclical and repetitive nature of which denies the importance of the individual or the individual generation and affirms the timeless essence of sacred time?

At the beginning of this essay, I posited the opposition between homo naturalis and homo progressus, which we can now also understand as the opposition between sacred time and profane time. The Sun Also Rises – in many ways his most profound novel – is Hemingway's tragedy of homo progressus's fall from primordial grace. Most critics and many readers have failed to heed his admonition to our secular age, but to do so is to incur the graceless risk of accompanying Cohn in outer darkness (Josephs, "Toreo" and "In Another Country").

It is ironic, perhaps, that Hemingway saw some semblance of salvation in the Spanish ritual of toreo, because that ritual, misunderstood and much maligned, is often anathematized in Western culture. For that reason *The Sun Also Rises* is often completely misread as a negative novel. Hemingway was evidently concerned about this situation and wrote to Max Perkins that he did not intend the book to be "a hollow or bitter satire" (*SL* 229). Perhaps in some measure to rectify misreadings of *The Sun Also Rises,* Hemingway resumed his project for the "bullfight book" (*SL* 156), in which toreo would not be the moral or spiritual axis around which a story subtly revolved, but instead the *axis mundi,* the world axis around which Hemingway's artistic vision turned.

On the last page of *Death in the Afternoon,* Hemingway claimed, almost facetiously, that he wrote the book as an "introduction to the modern Spanish bullfight," as an explanation of the spectacle "both emotionally and practically," and "because there was no book which did this in Spanish or in English" (517). However, as we have already seen, in the early pages of the book Hemingway made clear that his writing and toreo were closely connected, that, in fact, he specifically went to Spain "to see bullfights and to try to write about them for myself" (3). This book was the product of what he had learned in that process.

But it was more. In the last chapter, which begins, "If I could have made this enough of a book it would have had everything in it" (270) and goes on to catalog nostalgically some of the things left out, Hemingway made it quite apparent that his real subject was not just toreo itself but his discovery of Spain and the Spanish way of life that were best exemplified in toreo. He told Arnold Gingrich, editor of the new magazine *Esquire,* that he was glad Gingrich liked the last chapter because that was "what the book is about" even though no one (i.e., the reviewers) had seemed to notice. "They think it is just a catalog of things that were omitted" (*SL* 378).

The last chapter, chapter 20, is a long, elegiac passage on the way Spain had been in the ten years Hemingway had known it. But even that was changing as he made clear in the last paragraph: "Rafael says things are very changed and he won't go to Pamplona anymore. . . . It's all been changed for me. Let it all change" (277). The important thing was to last and to get his work done. Let those who wanted to save the world do so. What he wanted was "to see it clear and as a whole." That way "any part you make" would "represent the whole if it's made truly" (278). It was not enough of a book, he concluded, "but still there were a few things to be said. There were a few practical things to be said" (278).

Here Hemingway is echoing what is perhaps his most famous passage on writing, the analogy in *Death in the Afternoon* in which he remarks that the dignity of movement of an iceberg is due to the fact that only one-eighth of it is above water and that seven-eighths is therefore unseen (*DIA* 192). Hemingway's iceberg theory or theory of omission – that what the writer intentionally leaves out actually strengthens the writing – is precisely the principle he is operating under at the end of *Death in the Afternoon.*

Those few practical things about toreo were the visible tip of Hemingway's Spanish iceberg. By making a true part to stand for the whole, he could suggest a whole way of life that was disappearing. In the first draft of *Death in the Afternoon,* he spelled this out, saying that if "bullfighting [were] not going to survive, posterity ought to have a true contemporary account of it" (Lewis 46). By writing about the bulls he could preserve something of this last good country before the old ways succumbed, especially the atavistic spectacle of the corrida and all it signified in the ample context of Spanish life.

The only Spanish reviewer, writing for the Barcelona taurine paper *La fiesta brava* in April 1933, understood Hemingway's intentions exactly, calling it "a complete tauromachy" that fell somewhere between a "novelized biography" and a lively and knowledgeable travel book that nonetheless never lost sight of its role as "apostle" and preacher of " 'the good news' of tauromachy" to the English-speaking world (*Uno al sesgo,* my translation).

In writing an entire volume on the bulls, Hemingway injected Spanish values – the good news of tauromachy – into American literature, whether his fellow writers and the critics liked it or not.

What was involved was the profound discovery of a land, a people, and a spectacle that moved Hemingway as none ever had. The core of that experience, as he expressed it in that unparalleled description in *Death in the Afternoon,* already examined briefly, was the rare, complete faena the matador makes in preparing for the kill, the series of linked passes that leads up to the moment of truth:

> The faena that takes a man out of himself and makes him feel immortal while it is proceeding, that gives him an ecstasy, that is, while momentary, as profound as any religious ecstasy; moving all the people in the ring together and increasing in emotional intensity as it proceeds, carrying the bullfighter with it, he playing on the crowd through the bull and being moved as it responds in a growing ecstasy of ordered, formal, passionate, increasing disregard for death that leaves you, when it is over, and the death administered to the animal that has made it possible, as empty, as changed and as sad as any major emotion will leave you. (206–7)

For our purposes that is the seminal passage by Hemingway on Spain. Not only is it a perfect description of a nearly indescribable phenomenon, but that description fits perfectly the Spanish context of the corrida. Hemingway, infinitely more than any previous writer of English, understood toreo and its context from the Spanish point of view, from inside.

When Hemingway died, the distinguished Spanish writer Salvador de Madariaga made precisely that point: "He was no longer the gaping tourist, the go-getter businessman, the Protestant ever ready to frown at Catholic superstition, the progressive commiserating on backward Spain." Madariaga believed that Hemingway's understanding of toreo was "an essential factor" in his understanding of Spain: "Hemingway [understood] it from the outset and may well have been the non-Spaniard who of all time has come closest to the core of this strange form of Spanish life" (18).

What does it mean to understand the corrida from the Spanish point of view? Twentieth-century Spanish artists have frequently been antimodern, going against the materialism and rationalism we think of as normal. Unamuno is famous for disdainfully remarking, "*Que inventen ellos*" [Let the others invent]. Picasso's gift to modernism was the restoration of an ancient sense of the sacred to contemporary art, and he sometimes painted scenes of the corrida in a religious context. Hemingway once cited a phrase of Picasso on the subject: "You know it's absolutely the only thing left in the world. Bul [sic] fighting that is" ("Pamplona Letter").

Philosopher José Ortega y Gasset, not an aficionado, nevertheless maintained that an understanding of the corrida was absolutely essential to understanding Spanish history and culture from 1650 onward (9:123). And the great poet Federico García Lorca, not unlike Picasso, once remarked, "The only serious thing left in the world is toreo," affirming that "Toreo is the liturgy of the bulls, an authentic religious drama where, just as in the mass, there is the adoration and sacrifice of a God" (Forman and Josephs 95).

That is the Spanish context of the corrida. And that is Hemingway's context, the primordial and mythic context that stands in opposition to so much of our world. Only by keeping this context in mind can we understand Hemingway's use of toreo as the center of his writing on Spain in general and as the center of *Death in the Afternoon* in particular.

The corrida provides us, we should remember, with a pattern of experience or an archetype that recreates many of the most persistent myths of antiquity. The hero Gilgamesh kills the celestial bull. Mithra kills the sacred bull – with a sword. Hercules kills the maddened bull of Crete. Theseus kills the minotaur in the Cretan labyrinth and the great bull on the Plains of

Marathon. And these myths are only the tip of the iceberg of myths that become reincarnated in the romantic theater of the plaza de toros.

Hemingway was our most atavistic artist, which is why he is also the most Spanish. Sometimes he saw with the primordial vision of Lorca or of Picasso, and he sought, as they did, a hieratic restoration of values we had lost in contemporary life. In this light *Death in the Afternoon* is Hemingway's artistic creed. The work of a pioneer, a rebel, and a seer, it was a call – like the horns that announce the corrida – to recover something of what we have lost in the modern age.

His explanation and exaltation of the pristine savagery of the corrida were equivalent to resurrecting an ancient mystery religion and to rejecting much of what passed for Western values. In this sense Hemingway is one of the great romantic writers and *Death in the Afternoon* is his most romantic and his most Spanish book. It is also an essential book for understanding the rest of his work (Josephs, "A Reconsideration" and "In Another Country").

While Hemingway was gathering material for *Death in the Afternoon*, he was also observing the turmoil in the newly created second Spanish Republic. With his usual political perspicacity, Hemingway could sense trouble was brewing. As he wrote to John Dos Passos in June 1931, things were "pretty well steamed up" politically. He gave Dos Passos a rundown region by region and told him, "Been following politics closely" (*SL* 341).

When the war actually broke out, it was no surprise to Hemingway, and he commented early on that the conflict in Spain was "the dress rehearsal for the inevitable European war" (*SL* 458).

Given his previous involvement with Spain and his love for the country and the people, it is not surprising he took a personal stand in favor of the legally elected Republic and against the fascist-supported military insurgents. Had it not been for his deep affection for Spain, however, Hemingway would not have become involved. Had the dress rehearsal taken place in Poland, we would not have had a Polish version of *For Whom the Bell Tolls*. As Hemingway put it to his wife's family, "For a long time both me and my conscience have known I had to go to Spain" (*SL* 457).

He went to Spain because he loved it, and his involvement there turned out to be productive indeed. Including journalism, Hemingway wrote more about the Spanish civil war than about any other single topic: thirty syndicated news dispatches for NANA; miscellaneous pieces for *New Masses*; one for the Russian newspaper *Pravda*; twelve pieces for *Ken* magazine; the narration for the film *The Spanish Earth*; the play *The Fifth Column*; half a dozen short stories; and, of course, his longest novel, *For Whom the Bell Tolls*. The Spanish civil war literally dominates the middle period of Hemingway's writing.

For our purposes here – fiction only – we will look briefly at *The Fifth Column* and the stories and then concentrate on *For Whom the Bell Tolls*. Hemingway's fiction on the Spanish civil war can be divided into two categories. The first, the play and the stories, depict the war as Hemingway experienced events. The second, *For Whom the Bell Tolls*, is largely invented.

In the play and the stories, Hemingway was writing from firsthand knowledge. Although there is some invention involved, especially in the play, these works were largely crafted from events that Hemingway saw or took part in. He made his room in the Hotel Florida the scenario for the play and part of the story "Night before Battle." And he used his favorite Madrid bar, Chicote, as the locale for "The Denunciation," "The Butterfly and the Tank," and for the beginning of "Night before Battle."

The Spanish civil war stories have two characteristics in common. The first-person narrator in all of them is obviously Hemingway himself, correspondent, film-maker, raconteur, and famous personage. The second characteristic is that the real subject of all these stories, as well as the play, is the political nature of the conflict. Philip Rawlings, the main character in *The Fifth Column,* is also substantially autobiographical and the "girl," Dorothy Bridges, is clearly based on Martha Gellhorn, as is the girl in the story "Landscape with Figures."

Spanish critics have objected that *For Whom the Bell Tolls* does not give an accurate historical picture of the Spanish civil war. But the stories and the play, in fact, do give us an accurate rendition of that part of the war that Hemingway actually experienced, in and around Madrid.

These stories are not among Hemingway's best – with the exception of one fine story, "Under the Ridge" – but they do have a function. For better or for worse, they present Hemingway's personal version of events, events that included being on the losing side.

There is no doubt about Hemingway's disgust with the outcome of the Spanish civil war and with European politics in general, especially the democracies' capitulation to Hitler in Munich. As he told Arnold Gingrich from Paris in 1938, "Things here are so foul, now, that if you think about it you go nuts" (*SL* 473). A week later he described the European situation in a letter to Max Perkins as a "carnival of treachery and rotten-ness" (*SL* 474).

These stories about the real war, and to a lesser extent the play, precisely because they were both political and personal, served as a purging of Hemingway's feelings about the turn of events. By writing them, he got rid of the dreadful reality of the war as he had experienced it. The play and the stories, then, became a thinly veiled fictional memoir of the problems of the Spanish Republic.

That catharsis is important because it led directly into the writing of *For Whom the Bell Tolls*. Had Hemingway not written the play and especially the stories, it might have taken him much longer to write about the Spanish civil war (it took him ten years to write about World War I in *A Farewell to Arms*). As it turned out, he explained to Max Perkins that he had started on a story that he "had no intention of writing for a long time," that it was "very exciting," and that "it was a novel" (*SL* 482).

Above all, the play and the stories seem to have readied him to write the great romantic war novel he so much wanted to do. As he wrote to Tommy Shevlin in April 1939, begging out of a fishing tournament, the novel he had just started was "the most important thing" he'd ever done and this was the time in his career as a writer he had "to write a real one" (*SL* 484).

Hemingway definitely had a "real one," and he knew it. He told Max Perkins it was "20 times better" than "Night before Battle" which had been "flat where this is rounded and recalled where this is invented" (*SL* 482). This remark about material that is "invented" is the key to the difference between the "flat" stories and the "exciting" novel, and it echoes something Hemingway had told Perkins only days before: "should *always* make up stories – *not* try to remember what happened" (*SL* 479). Now, inventing rather than remembering, Hemingway would create what for many readers and critics is his greatest achievement, *For Whom the Bell Tolls* (Josephs, "Civil War Stories").

Hemingway seems to have had two goals in mind as he sat down to write *For Whom the Bell Tolls*. On the one hand he wanted to write about the specifics of the war, including the "carnival of treachery and rotten-ness" that pervaded Spain and Europe. Now that the Republic had lost, he was free to write whatever he wanted, and he became an acerbic critic of the left as well as the avowed enemy of fascism. He wanted to convey to the reader the larger truth of the Spanish conflict without engaging in partisan politics. And above all he wanted the reader to understand that the fight against fascism was essential.

Early in the novel Robert Jordan thinks that the bridge he is to blow up "can be the turning point on which the future of the human race can turn" (43). At the end of the novel, as he is about to blow up the bridge, Jordan thinks: "Today is only one day in all the days that will ever be. But what will happen in all the others that ever come can depend on what you do today" (432).

Hemingway's other goal was to write a great romantic war novel, his own version of *War and Peace,* a love story between the American volunteer Robert Jordan and the Spanish girl Maria with the real war as background. Hemingway once told the poet Archibald MacLeish that *War and Peace* was "the best book I know" (*SL* 179). Spain's civil conflict now provided Hemingway the chance to create his own twentieth-century equivalent of Tolstoy's masterpiece, to *create* – not simply to report – out of all the raw material of his own experiences in Spain since 1923. He would tell Malcolm Cowley some years later that "it wasn't just the civil war I put into it. . . . It was everything I had learned about Spain for eighteen years" (Cowley, "Portrait").

Robert Jordan has himself written a book about Spain, putting into the book "what he had discovered about Spain in ten years of traveling in it" (248). Jordan's ten years are analogous to Hemingway's eighteen, and we can strongly suspect that Jordan's book was something like *Death in the Afternoon.*

Carlos Baker has written that if you read *For Whom the Bell Tolls* fresh from *Death in the Afternoon,* you will see "how much of the old Spain has been transferred out of the manual and into the novel, always with a gain in dramatic intensity." Baker believed that *Death in the Afternoon* served "as a kind of sourcebook" for the novel (Baker 148–49). Perhaps it would be more accurate to say that both books drew from the same sources or that much of what was "left out" of *Death in the Afternoon* – scenes such as Pilar's days with the torero Finito, her description of the smell of death, or Andrés' description of the village bull baiting – found its way into *For Whom the Bell Tolls.*

Hemingway went to Spain as a writer against fascism and Jordan goes to Spain as a fighter against fascism. Had they not both discovered Spain prior to that, had Spain not already existed as a place to fight or even to die for, *For Whom the Bell Tolls* would not have come into being. Hemingway's and Jordan's love for the country and for the cause of the Spanish Republic are virtually identical. For both of them Spain – a country they love and the source of their writing – was sacred ground. Jordan even says, "I would rather have been born here" (15). As Carlos Baker knew, "The driving emotion behind *For Whom the Bell Tolls* is Hemingway's sense of the betrayal of the Spanish people" (Baker 239).

In order to combine the love and the betrayal, Hemingway imagined a guerrilla campaign within the real historical Republican offensive against La

Granja and Segovia at the end of May 1937. In the process he invented a great deal – the bridge, the cave, the guerrillas themselves had no historical counterparts in that sector – but he placed his invented elements in very real country and within a very real failed offensive, one of the turning points of the war.

In the background was the real war, but in the foreground were the invented characters Hemingway based on his experiences in the primordial Spain of *The Sun Also Rises* and *Death in the Afternoon,* characters such as Pilar the gypsy seer, Pablo the anarchistic horse trader, and El Sordo the guerrilla leader. These are characters – Baker's "Spanish people" – who are betrayed from within by their own ignorance and ineptitude, and betrayed from without by the meddling of communist political officers on the left, by the military intervention of Mussolini and Hitler on the right, and by the indifference of the democracies to the fate of the Republic.

Within this "carnival of treachery and rotten-ness" blooms the exquisite love affair between the American hero Jordan and the Spanish girl Maria. Maria, raped by the fascists, is a personification of the Spain Hemingway loved. She is innocent and pure (hence her name Maria), and a part of the fragile natural world being destroyed by the "mechanized doom" (87) of the war (hence her nickname "rabbit").

Hemingway's guerrillas are still part of the primordial world of Ecclesiastes, living within the harmony of nature, and Maria, the incarnation of Jordan's female side, whom he calls "true love" and "wife," "sister" and "daughter" (381), belongs at the heart of that vanishing world that was so vital to Hemingway. To see her as anything less is to miss one of the essential mysteries of love that binds the novel together. The mystical union of the lovers Jordan and Maria – "one and one is one" (379) – in Hemingway's imagination is the core image of Hemingway's Spain, and our remembrance of Hemingway's creation bears a distinct resemblance to the memory of Jordan that Maria takes with her, forever.

Robert Jordan is Hemingway's most complex character and only genuine hero, a man who sacrifices himself for a cause and for the love of a woman. At the novel's opening Jordan lies on the bosom of the Spanish earth and at the novel's close, seventy hours later, he is there again. As he lies there wounded, Hemingway makes an unusual psychological observation about his character: "He was completely integrated now" (471) – integrated with nature, with the earth, with the pine needles, and with the bark of the pine tree he touches. But by virtue of his sacrifice he is also integrated with the rest of humanity, bridged to the *Mankinde* of John Donne's meditation Hemingway selected for the novel's epigraph. And he is integrated with himself – having learned of his own dark side from Pilar and having felt the earth move and having known "la gloria" with Maria – integrated, in harmony with nature, sacrificing, saving.

In the novel's last sentence, Jordan can "feel his heart beating against the pine needle floor of the forest" (471), and it is the hero's heart and the lover's heart that remain with us as the closing image, the lover's heart brought into being by the love for Maria and the hero's heart brought into being by the love for Spain, brought into being and in the final image still beating (Josephs, *Undiscovered Country*).

There is a discernible progression in Hemingway's treatment of Spain, one that we can now review and bring into sharper focus. In the vignettes from *In Our Time* taurine Spain provided the raw and violent material that Hemingway was seeking. In the process of exploring *that* world for artistic purposes, he became fascinated by the spectacle – bitten by the *gusano*, the worm of *afición* or passion for the corrida.

That fascination and passion led Hemingway to use toreo and the taurine world as the spiritual center of *The Sun Also Rises;* by doing so, he made the violence of the vignettes positive, spiritual, sacred, and opposed to the terrible clock time of *this* world, of the war and its aftermath.

Death in the Afternoon no longer directly opposes the taurine world to the profane, modern, historical, Western world. Implicitly the opposition is still there, but textually Hemingway fairly ignores this world to explore the values of that world, a world he believes very much in danger of disappearing.

In *For Whom the Bell Tolls,* that world is not merely in danger of disappearing; it is threatened with extinction. Yet even as it must fight for its survival, it is that world that makes possible transcendence, integration, heroism, and love.

Hemingway was always involved with that world, with the sacred world of hunting and fishing, eating and drinking, the ritual sacrifice of toreo, love and ecstasy. And Spain, more than any other place for Hemingway, still retained the grace and harmony of that world. In essence Hemingway's Spanish sensibility was a matter of his own deep resonance with ancient Mediterranean archetypes – still present in Spain – in their most primal and unevolved state. In Spain, Hemingway found the most profound resonance of his own soul.

With *The Dangerous Summer* Hemingway attempted to effect a return to that world. Originally planned as an epilogue to *Death in the Afternoon,* the articles and the posthumously published book unfortunately seem an unintentional parody, what Hemingway himself had described as "overwritten journalism made literature by the injection of a false epic quality" (*DIA* 54).

The nostalgic descriptions of the country have some fine moments, but there is no sustained return to *that* country, to that last good country of Spain as it had existed before the civil war. By contrast, however, *The Dangerous Summer* makes us understand how good Hemingway's earlier work on Spain and its inimitable spectacle of death in the afternoon still are.

The real epilogue to Hemingway's writing about Spain and, as he wrote Wallace Meyer at Scribner's, "the epilogue to all my writing" (*SL* 757), is *The Old Man and the Sea*. Santiago is from the Canary Islands, which belong to Spain. The Canaries lie off the northwest coast of Africa and many Canary Islanders emigrated to Cuba. By making Santiago a Canary Islander, Hemingway brought together Spain, the place he loved most, and Cuba and Africa, his other favorite places. We should not forget that Santiago, Saint James, James the son of Zebedee, was a fisherman. That same Santiago is the patron saint of Spain, and the pilgrimage route to his burial shrine runs through Pamplona on the way to Santiago de Compostela.

By intentionally making Santiago Spanish, Hemingway associates him closely with Montoya and Pedro Romero, with Maria and Pilar and El Sordo and old Anselmo, with the old waiter of "A Clean Well-Lighted Place," with the torero Manuel García of "The Undefeated," with the Maera of the vignettes, and with all the toreros of *Death in the Afternoon*. Hemingway's finest characters are primitives in the best sense of that word, and Hemingway's bell tolls for them all throughout his work. It tolls for his Indians, his gypsies, his guerrillas, his toreros, and beyond them for all the fishing Santiagos plying the deep waters of the world in small boats.

We have returned to Ecclesiastes, Hemingway's most profound source: "For that which befalleth the sons of men befalleth beasts" (3:19). Like Homer's subjects, Hemingway's Spanish characters are epic people living in harmony with nature. And Santiago was his most essential creation, the one who lived most completely within nature, brother to the fish. In this Santiago is Cuban and he is Spanish, the incarnation of all that Hemingway had learned – especially from Spain. Without Hemingway's Spanish sensibility there would have been no Santiago, and twentieth-century literature would have had a different shape. Tracing the progression of Hemingway's Spanish sensibility from the violent vignettes through the night vision of Pilar and the love of Maria to Santiago's serene wisdom also helps us understand that in deep and abiding ways Hemingway was a pioneering multiculturalist, a protofeminist, and a dedicated ecologist long before our time.

WORKS CITED

Baker, Carlos. *Ernest Hemingway: The Writer as Artist.* Rev. ed. Princeton: Princeton University Press, 1972.

Caballero, Antonio. *Toros, toreros y públicos.* Bogotá: El Ancora, 1992.

Cowley, Malcolm. "A Portrait of Mr. Papa." *Life,* January 10, 1949.

Forman, Sandra, and Allen Josephs. *Only Mystery: Federico García Lorca's Poetry in Word and Image.* Gainesville: University Press of Florida, 1992.

Hemingway, Ernest. *Collected Short Stories.* New York: Charles Scribner's Sons, 1987.

    The Dangerous Summer. New York: Charles Scribner's Sons, 1985.

    Death in the Afternoon. New York: Charles Scribner's Sons, 1932.

    Ernest Hemingway: Selected Letters, 1917–1961. Ed. Carlos Baker. New York: Charles Scribner's Sons, 1981.

    For Whom the Bell Tolls. New York: Charles Scribner's Sons, 1940.

    A Moveable Feast. New York: Charles Scribner's Sons, 1964.

    The Nick Adams Stories. New York: Charles Scribner's Sons, 1972.

    "Pamplona Letter." *transatlantic review* 2.3 (October 1924): 301.

    The Sun Also Rises. New York: Charles Scribner's Sons, 1926.

Josephs, Allen. "Hemingway's Spanish Civil War Stories, or The Spanish Civil War as Reality." *Hemingway's Neglected Short Fiction: New Perspectives.* Ed. Susan F. Beegel. Ann Arbor, Mich.: UMI Research Press, 1989.

    "*Death in the Afternoon:* A Reconsideration." *The Hemingway Review* 2.1 (Fall 1982): 2–16.

    "In Another Country: Hemingway and Spain." *North Dakota Quarterly* 60.2 (Spring 1992): 50–57.

    "Toreo: The Moral Axis of *The Sun Also Rises.*" *The Hemingway Review* 6.1 (Fall 1986): 88–99.

    For Whom the Bell Tolls: *Ernest Hemingway's Undiscovered Country.* New York: Twayne, 1994.

Lewis, Robert W. "The Making of *Death in the Afternoon.*" *Ernest Hemingway: The Writer in Context.* Ed. James Nagel. Madison: University of Wisconsin Press, 1984, 31–52.

Madariaga, Salvador de. "The World Weighs a Writer's Influence." *Saturday Review* 44 (July 29, 1961): 18.

Ortega y Gasset, José. *Obras completas.* Madrid: Revista de Occidente, 1961.

"Uno al sesgo," pseud., "Libros de toros: un rato a bibliografía." *La fiesta brava* 8.314 (April 7, 1933): 4.

12

BICKFORD SYLVESTER

The Cuban Context
of *The Old Man and the Sea*

In preparing a line-by-line, word-by-word scholarly commentary on *The Old Man and the Sea,* I discovered many aspects of the narrative thus far overlooked.[1] One pattern of neglected detail refers to workaday practicalities peculiar to the locale, and very often to local customs and habits of mind – to a general Cuban cultural consciousness. Here, as in many of his other works, Hemingway unobtrusively relies on such detail to account for his characters' motivation and to reveal what is actually being referred to in much of the dialogue. In other words, he requires his readers around the world to notice the specific cultural context of his narrative and to familiarize themselves with that context in order to follow what is literally happening in the plot.

This is an approach we accept as a matter of course in reading the works of other modernists – Joyce, Pound, or Eliot, for example. Yet it is a challenge posed so subtly by Hemingway's method that it has eluded us from the very beginning, in "Out of Season" (composed April 1923), his first narrative written in the style that was to make him famous. As I have pointed out ("Hemingway's Italian *Waste Land*" esp. 79–89), readers can understand that troublesome story only by learning something about the attitudes of provincial Italian villagers living on the Austrian border after World War I. And our failure to recognize Hemingway's challenge to "think in the head" of his various other foreign characters has accounted for many a canonized misreading or marginal understanding of his works. We have tended to forget that Hemingway is at bottom a travel writer, performing the traditional novelist's function of helping us measure ourselves by and against precisely described exotics.

Accordingly, readers have largely overlooked their need to seek a Cuban explanation whenever details puzzle them – or *should* puzzle them – in *The Old Man and the Sea.* In fact, the novel requires non-Cuban readers to do considerable homework if they are to register not only many literal details of the plot, but many layers of meaning-through-indirection. I will discuss several illuminating examples of narrative details that appear extraneous, implausible, or erroneous, tempting us to dismiss them as incidental or to assume some loose symbolic significance. We will find, on the contrary, very literal, specific topical references, references we are invited to supplement by knowledge or research beyond the text. And in undertaking these assignments we will discover in each case information not only solving a puzzle, but exposing an unsuspected dimension of the narrative as a whole. Our findings throughout will suggest, I believe, the value of screening each narrative detail in Hemingway initially for its literal, topical implications before leaping to conclusions as to its symbolic import. Indeed, we will find that concrete, local applicability determines which of the potential literary, religious, mythic, or archetypal allusions potentially plausible in a given instance may in fact be central, and which secondary, peripheral, or irrelevant.

Near the beginning of *The Old Man and the Sea,* Manolin tells Santiago about the bad eyesight of the new fisherman the boy's father has apprenticed him to – a man who never went turtle spearing in the brilliant sunlight, the occupation that most commonly "kills the eyes" of local fishermen. "But," Manolin says to Santiago, who is much older than this new employer, "you went turtle-ing for years . . . and your eyes are still good." Santiago then makes the oft-quoted, obviously laden remark: "I am a strange old man"; and when the boy asks, "But are you strong enough now for the truly big fish?" Santiago replies, "I think so. And there are many tricks."

We have thought here of the tricks of the trade that the old fisherman will soon use to compensate for his waning physical strength in his struggle against the marlin, tricks that years of experience have taught him: the products of disciplined attention to a craft that for him is also a passion. We have known, too, that in Hemingway the word "strange" almost always refers to something defying conventional understanding, a mystery of nature. The word consistently refers as well to those rare people and creatures who understand the "strange" (i.e., paradoxical) logic that Hemingway most admires: the dedication to timeless principles of behavior at the expense of all concern for material success or survival. We know that Santiago is about to demonstrate this "strange" vision – this "trick," or psychological device for survival – during his ordeal with the great fish; and we assume we have grasped all the implications of his remark that he is a "strange" old man.

But when the boy asks him if he is strong enough for a big fish, Santiago's mind is still partly on how he had managed to preserve his eyesight during his years of turtle-ing. And he has a particular trick in mind, known to very few readers. In the most common method of turtle-ing in the Caribbean, the hunter drifts in a small boat, peering beneath the surface for turtles to harpoon; as a result, the damaging tropical sunlight reflected by the water shines constantly into his eyes. Yet English ships exploring the Caribbean in the seventeenth and eighteenth centuries often employed native Indians who avoided this hazard. These natives used remoras (sucker-fish) to locate turtles. The remora is a parasite, which attaches itself to a larger creature like a shark or turtle and eats the scraps drifting back when its host feeds. The native hunter simply captured a remora and put it in the water with a fishing line tied around its tail. When the fish attached its suction-cup dorsal fin to a passing turtle, the hunter could feel the extra pull on his line and had only to follow the line to the remora, quickly spear and boat the turtle, detach the hungry remora, and put it back in the water to find another host. The hunter never needed to scan the water for his prey. Apparently, Santiago's use of this technique accounts for his continuing good vision, in spite of his years spearing turtles. In this case, then, Santiago's appearance as "strange" – a natural rarity – really is a deception, the result of an insider's device, or trick, although later in the narrative, during his ordeal, he will use such triumphs of expertise over physical limitation to supplement his truly extraordinary, or "strange," emotional resources.

Only Cuban readers, of course, and only some of them, are likely to know at first reading about that remora on a leash. Yet the rest of us have been invited to find out exactly how turtle hunting in Cuba hurts the eyes (and in the process discover the traditional method for avoiding that damage). For readers can reasonably be expected to wonder how the "real old man" Hemingway later called this character can still have good eyesight (not symbolic, but physical eyesight) into his seventies, if long engaged in an occupation that "kills the eyes." Readers cannot reasonably be expected to make the automatic, initial assumption that Ernest Hemingway – of all writers – is taking poetic license. But of course that is what we have silently inferred, as we conveniently glossed over this incident, together with so many others like it in Hemingway's texts. And this oversight matters, because it has allowed us to form a false impression of Santiago. Santiago is truly "strange," truly inspiring, not because he is physically a freak of nature, or because he is emotionally "a saint rather than a man," as Norman Mailer insouciantly presumed (19). Santiago is strange because he is in every material sense "the real old man" Hemingway later called him. He is real like us, yet he behaves and thinks – with remarkable regularity – as we are able to behave and think only in our very best moments. And that is exalting to us, *because* he is human; he is possible.[2] A man his age who puts himself through the physical and emotional ordeal we see this old man endure will in reality be likely to break "something in his chest" and be dying – as Santiago is, the text subtly specifies (Sylvester, " 'They Went Through This Fiction' " 75–78). And such a man, being human, will also experience despair when his resolution occasionally falters, as Santiago's does back on shore, until at the end Manolin/Parçifal revives the old Fisher King's "strange" disregard for material failure.

Allusions like the one to the remora trick are early indications of Santiago's human fallibility, put there ... guide us away from seeing him as an icon rather than the convincing, imitable exemplar that he is. And that is an important function of his other endearing fallibilities. But these are traits readers can recognize only by minutely examining every apparently unaccountable detail of Santiago's portrayal, especially in the opening exchanges with Manolin, and by consulting reference books or other sources when still in doubt. Like Hemingway's travel narratives generally, *The Old Man and the Sea* is directed at readers who have either been to its locale, will ask someone who is from there, or will go to the history and geography books about that place and its people – readers who will do research, as we now know Hemingway did himself (Lewis 227–36; Reynolds throughout; Sylvester, "Persona" 26–30).

Another case in point is an indirect revelation of actual historical events that we must know about if we are to appreciate fully the symbolic parallels between Santiago and Joe DiMaggio, and the role of the champion in nature and society that these important parallels help define. The information is conveyed indirectly during the early dialogues between Santiago and Manolin, when they discuss an American League pennant race between DiMaggio's team, the New York Yankees, and the Detroit Tigers. This contest is taking place as they speak, in September of a year some scholars have assumed is based on a composite of DiMaggio's 1949 and 1950 seasons and is therefore a fictionalized representation of early fall in that time period. But C. Harold Hurley has recently discovered that the narrative specifies not only the year 1950, but the exact dates in September as well. And Hurley has discovered this narrative revelation by research into the topical, rather than the symbolic significance of the dialogue's details. His attention to such details as references to the numbers 84 and 85 has at last deciphered the specific relevance of this portion of the narrative.

We have wondered why the narrative presents eighty-four as the particular number of days Santiago has gone without a fish, so that the voyage he is about to undertake is his eighty-fifth attempt. And we have wondered why his always-extraordinary confidence seems to be so especially buoyed by this number that he wants to play an eighty-five in the lottery. There has been wide speculation as to possible numerological implications, archetypal and/or Christian, and other symbolic or biographical explanations for Hemingway's choice (Hurley 103–15).

But these numbers have a much more literal and topical frame of reference. They refer to the pennant race the two discuss both before and after Manolin interrupts their conversation to go for bait and food for Santiago. And it will be instructive, for all of us who study his narratives, to observe Hemingway's oblique disclosure of the connection. We are to notice that before Manolin leaves, Santiago's confidence in DiMaggio's leadership and a Yankees pennant victory is stated as an assertion of faith. But when Manolin returns, Santiago tells him: "In the American League it is the Yankees *as I said*" (emphasis added), a reference (obvious, once we notice it) to some new, firm information confirming his earlier faith. Yet all Santiago has done while Manolin has been away is sleep and read "yesterday's" newspaper. ("You study it [the baseball news] and tell me when I come back," Manolin had told him.) We are prompted, therefore, to sift through international press coverage of the Yankees in September of the two years shortly before the novel's composition (1951), and in doing so we find Santiago's good news. His newspaper is that of Monday, September 11, 1950, reporting on the Yankees' game the day before that, Sunday, September 10. On that Sunday, Joe DiMaggio, after a long period of indifferent performance at bat, hit three home runs (a record in Washington's Griffith Stadium), leading the Yankees to their *eighty-fourth* win of the season. And although the Yankees' eighty-fourth victory coincides numerically with his own eighty-fourth fallow day, Santiago is encouraged by this numerical concordance. For he knows that the Yankees' eighty-fourth win brought them within half a game of tying with powerful Detroit Tigers in the very tight pennant race that year. Further, this tells him as a Yankees follower that the Yankees then had to win only one game of a doubleheader with the mediocre Washington Senators, scheduled for the next day, Monday the 11th, to secure a tie with the idle Tigers. And because DiMaggio's return to form put the Yankees in a position to pull even with their eighty-fifth win, Santiago has renewed confidence in the potential for success of his next voyage, which happens to be his eighty-fifth (Hurley 83–84). For he is preoccupied with permutations of numbers and statistics, not only like baseball enthusiasts everywhere, but as a Cuban characteristically habituated to the lottery. And readers familiarizing themselves with the characteristic mentalities of baseball devotees and gamblers (both intimately known to Hemingway) will know that Santiago's manipulation of numbers here is typical and predictable.

Yet the numerical concordances are ancillary to a more objectively verifiable "tip of the iceberg" identifying DiMaggio's performance in Washington as the single event that confirms Santiago's faith in both DiMaggio and himself. Before we explore in detail Santiago's reaction to this game, then, we should observe how the event is obliquely specified by references to two other Yankee games on days immediately following. When Manolin returns from the Terrace with food for supper, he tells Santiago that the Yankees "lost today." We remember that "today" (present time at the beginning of the novel) is two days later than the event reported in "yesterday's paper." And readers realizing an invitation to read more baseball reports will find that the Yankees did lose a game on Tuesday, September 12, 1950. Next, readers enterprising enough to search for baseball references throughout the balance of the text will notice that during his "second day" at sea Santiago thinks about a Yankees/Tigers game being played at that moment. That is two days after the loss Manolin reported, and four days after the event so inspiring to Santiago. And a Yankees/Tigers game did take place on Thursday, September 14, 1950, four days after DiMaggio's Sunday game. Everything squares.[3] Conclusively, yet entirely by indirection, the narrative places itself in historical time. Almost by "calculus" and certainly by "three-cushion shots" (as Hemingway variously described his method of disclosure), DiMaggio's Sunday game is confirmed as the event Santiago has read of in his "yesterday's paper."[4]

To consider further the event Santiago "happily" cites to confirm his faith that "the Yankees cannot lose," DiMaggio's Sunday game was spectacular: a single event suitably matching in magnitude Santiago's outsize accomplishment, soon to follow. DiMaggio's stadium-record three home runs all traveled over four hundred feet in the spacious park; and they were, as well, part of a statistically "perfect" game (four at-bats, four hits, four runs, and four runs-batted-in). "The great DiMaggio was himself again," indeed. And in the week starting with this game, the Yankees did win their eighty-fifth victory in the doubleheader Monday, as Santiago expected – and their eighty-sixth as well, with DiMaggio contributing three of the eleven runs his team scored in those two games. DiMaggio went on, for the week as a whole, to hit six home runs in eight games, with a batting average of .467. In that single week, out of thirty at-bats he had fourteen hits, scored fourteen runs, and batted in thirteen runs: Statistically, one player accounted for twenty-seven runs, nearly half of his team's total output of fifty-eight. This was an extraordinary feat, particularly for an "old man" in baseball terms at that time (at thirty-five DiMaggio was one of the older players in the league), hampered by multiple injuries, and with sportswriters calling for his retirement as they had before his comeback in 1949.

But what matters most for the novel is that when DiMaggio came alive his personal contributions led his team to win six of its eight games that week, and emerge in first place a half-game ahead of the Tigers, prepared to grind its way to an eventual pennant. Not until the end of the novel, when Santiago wakes up Saturday morning after his own extraordinary performance and reads "the newspapers of the [days] that [he] was gone" (September 13–15), will he himself learn more details of his aging fellow champion's resurgence at bat, a sustained performance matching his own at sea. But during this dialogue on Tuesday, the day before he sets out on his eighty-fifth attempt to catch a fish, Santiago has particular reasons for being personally reassured by his knowledge that "the great DiMaggio" has returned to form, and done so despite a fallow period associated with a number almost matching that of his current, eighty-four fishless days. For Santiago has earlier gone eighty *seven* days without a fish. And if Santiago's power (his "luck") has earlier returned after eighty-seven days, it will certainly survive the present hiatus of eighty-four. That DiMaggio has made dramatic comebacks before (in 1949 especially), and has now followed with another even more dramatic, is doubly reassuring. To Santiago, DiMaggio's becoming "himself *again*" (emphasis added) includes the meaning "*once* again." It means that in champions (like DiMaggio and "*El Campeón*" Santiago) the mastery that makes them them*selves* will survive the onslaughts of time, not once but repeatedly – until at last that special quality brings them "alive" even "with their death in [them]" (as it does the marlin, the Mako shark, and Santiago himself at the narrative's end). And for this fundamental reason, the new resurgence by DiMaggio gives Santiago confidence in his next day at sea, or in an inevitable day of success soon after that – even without the numerical concordances he conceives.

All these specific topical considerations explain why it "means nothing" that the Yankees have lost a game on the day he speaks. What matters is that a champion's ability to perform, once operative, is not affected (as another, merely talented performer's might be) by a lapse of confidence over one day's reverses (or eighty-seven such reverses), any more than over the realities of physical decline. For at bottom "what makes the difference" in a champion (and sustains those on his "team") is an ability, recognized by Colonel Cantwell in *Across the River and into the Trees* (232), to make "every day a new and fine illusion" – despite the disillusionment of many a yesterday. And Santiago himself demonstrates this capacity as he speaks of faith, numbers, consonances, and luck – all of which has sounded to hasty readers like superstitious self-deception on his part (Rosenfield 50) and may appear to others as fond condescension on Hemingway's part.

On the contrary, the numerical consonances with DiMaggio's record make up one of several "informed" illusions (Baker, *Hemingway: The Writer as Artist* 273) or ritualized fictions Santiago relies upon, not because he believes in the literal content of the fictions, but because he does believe in a cause that requires him to act without hope of material success. And because he is both proud and humble enough to believe that human beings cannot act without hope of material reward, he finds ways of behaving *as if* he will succeed where he most knows he cannot (Sylvester, " 'They Went Through This Fiction' "). Despite his accurately portrayed Cuban fascination with numbers and chance, there is no evidence that Santiago believes, literally, in the cosmic significance of such easily (and obviously) manipulated "signs" as numerological consonances.[5] But there is ample evidence that he does believe in a vital connection among the species, depending on the fully extended behavior of rare individual members – creatures oriented to total commitment, without concern for practical success or personal survival.[6] That is the principle of action Santiago exemplifies as he kills the first shark to attack his fish, hitting it "with *all* his strength . . . *without hope but with resolution*" (emphasis added) – performing *as if* he could, by totally committing his resources, keep all the other sharks now coming from destroying his fish, yet fully aware that he cannot. That informed, sophisticated pretense is a "trick" far more rare and difficult than using the remora; it is a trick of the heart and mind, the "strange" way of seeing that Hemingway respected above all other human accomplishments.[7] It is the hard-won, complex vision required of the thinking "champions" in nature's scheme: the human beings in all walks of life who are able to go "far out beyond all people." Maintaining their efforts by every means necessary against their near-debilitating knowledge of the material cost, they inspire and sustain the human race at their personal expense.

As DiMaggio's team "cannot lose" in its struggle, then, neither will Santiago's team. Santiago's eighty-fifth day at sea, ending *his* slump with *his* record result, will in reality gain something precious, if not a materially tangible trophy, for the team he champions – the human species. For we will find that in his struggle with the great marlin Santiago reaffirms once again, as he has so often before, humanity's necessary connection with nature's order. In portraying the roles of Santiago and DiMaggio in the survival of their groups, therefore, Hemingway stresses in both cases the reliance of the many upon the one. This is a theme not only reinforcing the novel's occasional comparison of Santiago to Christ, but commenting on the relation of all human champions to society.

In addition to the roles of the two champions, there is a larger similarity between the Yankees' overall struggle against the resolute Tigers team of 1950 and the old man's entire struggle against the great marlin and the sharks. It is a similarity making the "September stretch" (the closing weeks) of that year's pennant race a particularly apt demonstration of this novel's most central theme: that in the order of nature intensity equals vitality. The champions of each species featured in the novel act according to a natural principle of perpetual tension, thereby maintaining for the others in their species an attunement with nature. The taut fishing line, kept for two complete rounds of the sun stretched just beneath its breaking point, is an objective correlative of that principle, which is being enacted by the man and marlin at opposite ends of that line (Sylvester, "Extended Vision" 135). And the contest between the evenly matched Yankees and Tigers of 1950 exemplified that principle. During the week timed with the novel's action the Yankees did not surge ahead with DiMaggio's resurgence, to end the tension and anxiety they had experienced all along. Throughout the week of Santiago's ordeal and well into the next week, the lead edged back and forth repeatedly by grudging half-game increments (Hurley 91–92), the two teams locked in a sustained balance of forces like that of Santiago's twenty-four-hour "hand-game" with the "great negro from Cienfuegos." This arm-wrestling scene from dawn to dawn is the novel's second objective correlative of natural order.[8] It demonstrates as well the human community's vicarious participation in that order, as these two regional champions of two villages enact nature's principle of vital tension before their enthralled spectators in the tavern at Casablanca. Hemingway could hardly have synchronized his narrative with a sustained event in contemporary baseball more felicitously objectifying this principle and the intermediary role of human championship. For in this novel, as in the world's stadiums and arenas, it is not the material quarry but the intensity of the quest that is of ultimate value to the many of us who only watch and wait.[9]

Final evidence of the need to read the baseball allusions more carefully is our neglect of a broad and ironic cultural implication. For Cubans like Manolin and Santiago, baseball is perhaps as central to the consciousness — actually mythic — as it is for Americans in the cornfields of Iowa. It is typically Cuban for Santiago's imagination to embody its special vision of championship not only in lions from his Spanish memories of African voyages, but in a baseball player from the American *Gran Ligas*. When Santiago senses that Manolin is tired of listening to an old man's memories, he says, "Go and play baseball," acknowledging the national pastime. But although the American "big show" is a dream of glory for young Cubans like Manolin and his friends, it is essentially an inaccessible dream. Santiago mentions two successful players in the majors, Mike Gonzales and the dazzlingly talented Adolpho Luque, both of whom he, with justification, considers the greatest managers in baseball. Yet they manage in the Cuban winter leagues because, as Barbour and Sattelmeyer observe (43–44), "an unwritten law" prevented them from managing in the majors. That this is the point of Hemingway's reference to these two players becomes even clearer when we discover that the unwritten law was racial, barring Cubans whether of mixed race or not, that Gonzales and Luque were accepted because both, apparently, looked white, and that only two other Cubans – Rafael Almeida and Armando Marsans, also "light-skinned" (Burns and Ward 112) – ever played in the majors until well after the novel was composed in 1951. There is cultural commentary, then, as well as archetypal symbolism and artistic symmetry conveyed when Santiago, humbly yet proudly aware of his natural aristocracy, takes DiMaggio's resurgence as a personal omen. For although a young man as talented as today's Hispanic superstars may be playing among Manolin's friends in Cojimar, it is to a fisherman's son from San Francisco that Santiago must look for El Campeón of baseball.

Predictably, Spanish and Cuban historical and cultural contexts also interact in this novel, more pervasively; and these further demonstrate the primary role of topicality in specifying relevant symbolism. There is, for example, a profound thematic pattern that we have yet to glory in, because it can only be recognized by readers willing to become familiar either with Spanish history from a Cuban perspective, or Cuban history from a Spanish perspective. Much of the novel is directly or indirectly associated with the Virgin of Cobre. Near Cobre, a small town in southeastern Cuba, is the sanctuary of Our Lady of Charity, a small statue of the Virgin Mary. An image of the Virgin hangs on Santiago's wall, as it does in most Cuban houses; the text implies that his wife may, like many other Cubans, have made a pilgrimage to the shrine and brought back this picture. In 1916, Pope Benedict XV declared the Virgin the principal patroness of Cuba. She is, then, a figure associated with Cuba's national identity. Now according to legend, this statue of the Virgin Mary was floating on a wooden board off the coast of eastern Cuba in 1628, when it was found by two Indians and a Creole in a rowboat. And it is an ancient Spanish legend that the body of Saint James (Santiago) also appeared floating on the sea, in its case already inside a boat, and was found off the coast of Spain, near Compostela, where it was said to have come from the Holy Land, even though the boat had no rudder or sail. Thus the legend of the patroness of Cuba parallels, in the Spanish New World, the far older legend of Santiago in old Spain.[10] And Hemingway has again found in history, this time cultural history, a parallel entirely relevant to his plot. For the New World legend of a mysterious boon, or blessing, discovered at sea, by humble Cubans in a rowboat, looks back to the seaborne gift of Saint James' remains off the coast of Spain, and looks forward to the modern Santiago's discovery – while at sea in a rowboat that loses its tiller – of a "great strangeness," or mystery, at the moment of the marlin's death (Sylvester, "Extended Vision" 133).

Moreover, the relic, or boon from the sea reposited at Santiago del Prado, Cuba, at the shrine of the Virgin is regarded as a spiritual endowment to the Cuban people, as the seaborne relics at Santiago de Compostela are regarded as a spiritual gift to Spain. And Santiago, the modern fisherman, brings ashore the skeletal relics of *his* "strange" encounter, skeletal remains that spiritually enrich those among the people of modern Cuba who are still capable of appreciating his values and accomplishment. As we will later consider in some detail, Santiago lives in a divided community, a village turning from the craft passion of the old Cuba to a new materialism. But those supporting national pride and old values are sustained by Santiago's circular sea journey in his wooden boat. Their traditional values will last now, in their hearts, until their next champion, Manolin, reenacts the age-old fertility rite, risking everything to maintain the vital contact between the human community and the mysteries of nature – the contact that preserves the community's sense of wonder, despite the encroaching materialism.

The historical quests contribute, as well, to another formal nicety of the work – a pattern of circles or cycles in the structure of the narrative as a whole. There are the cyclical sea journeys of Santiago's youth, from his native Canary Island to the African beaches, where he experienced an epiphany – a mystical sense of identification with young lions, nature's champions – that recurs in his consciousness throughout the narrative. Later there are the circular sea journey and epiphany of Santiago's old age, now as a Cuban. The repetition brackets his life, making it a circle, and at the same time envelops and makes the plot, about a circular voyage and life, become itself a circle. All of these cycles and circles are there for the reader to associate with the annual, cyclical pilgrimages of the Spanish and the Cuban people – to and from the shrine of Santiago in Spain, to and from the shrine of the Virgin of Cobre in Cuba.

Such historical and cultural parallels as these, together with the consciousness of North America represented by the baseball allusions, make *The Old Man and the Sea* a Cuban book, then, in far more than setting. In particular, the Spanish-Cuban concordances unify the novel by celebrating those native and European ethnic forces unifying Cuban culture: ethnic bonds that for centuries held together the Hispano-Caribbean tradition disintegrating in modern Cuba. I have no doubt that Hemingway had these cultural parallels (and more) in mind when he donated his Nobel prize medal to the sanctuary of *La Virgen de la Caridad del Cobre,* a Cuban national symbol (Stoneback, "From the rue Saint-Jacques" 13). It was a medal awarded largely because of this novel. And Hemingway called his offering "a tribute of love to the people of Cuba" – as is Santiago's sacrifice within Hemingway's novel, as is, of course, the book itself. Thus Hemingway's gift of his medal is a crowning artistic touch, a final reticulation, outside his text, of that integration of fiction and history that *is* his text.

We turn now to the most arresting narrative fact disclosed through topical details beyond common knowledge. The novel requires readers (even Cuban readers)[11] to do considerable homework if they are to register the surprising narrative fact that "the boy" Manolin is actually a young man of twenty-two, rather than a child somewhere between twelve and fourteen, as we have supposed. His age is unmistakably, if obliquely, specified by Manolin himself when he compares his family life to that of the American baseball player Dick Sisler. "The great Sisler's father was never poor," he says. "And he, the father, was playing in the Big Leagues when he was my age." When *who* was Manolin's age, Dick Sisler or his hall-of-fame father, George? The answer is that it is the father who was Manolin's age, just as our English, word order–oriented ears prompt us to choose, as we respond to the noun nearest the pronoun. Yet Hurley, the only other commentator to do the research this line requires, has assumed it must be the son, *Dick* Sisler, who was Manolin's age when his father was playing professionally. For the great George Sisler was twenty-two when he began his professional career, and retired when his son Dick was ten. Thus, as Hurley correctly deduces (97), Manolin must be either at least twenty-two or no more than ten, depending upon how we parse Hemingway's sentence. And because like most of us Hurley cannot immediately think of Manolin as considerably *older* than has been assumed, he understandably asserts that the young fisherman must be ten, somewhat younger than has been assumed.

However, if we continue our investigation even further, alerted by certain apparent implausibilities, we discover that it is a physical impossibility for Manolin to be only ten years old. At the same time, we find that the clues formerly leading readers to think of Manolin as a child are – in the context of the boy's native culture – entirely consistent with young manhood. And finally, we realize that as we think of Manolin as a young adult, other details of the narrative fall into place to form an unsuspected level of socio-economic comment in the novel.

To take the physical evidence first, surely very few adult readers of either sex can imagine themselves carrying from Santiago's boat to his shack a box the size of a large garbage can, filled with coiled fishing line weighing probably over 150 pounds and at the very least 100 pounds. Yet readers careful enough to work out the weight and size of Santiago's lines are required to think of a boy twelve to fourteen doing just that – while somehow managing to juggle the old man's gaff and harpoon. Accordingly, when such readers *also* become aware that they must choose between ten and twenty-two for Manolin's age, their decision is foregone.[12]

Of course, only readers familiar with the local equipment described can be expected to approximate these formidable dimensions immediately. But the rest of us really should become suspicious enough at some point to check on the extent of the boy's burden, even without having researched the historical evidence restricting his age. For the narrative's description of the line's thickness, composition, and enormous length is so meticulous that it eventually calls attention to itself, tempting us to compile the various specifications challengingly scattered throughout the text. Also, specifications for the lines' total length are given in two sets of figures to mark their importance, as is the evidence of the baseball dates. And when we compile them, we find that the old man carries in his boat 660 fathoms of line.[13] That is just short of 4,000 feet (three-quarters of a mile or thirteen football fields end-to-end) of "coiled, hard-braided brown" line, or "cord" "as thick around as a big pencil" (to all of my consultants a description exactly fitting lines five-sixteenths of an inch in diameter). Called "Catalan *cordel*" in the text, this Spanish line of the period was made of natural, rather than synthetic fiber. For general readers its composition is carefully, if indirectly, designated as such: After fishing, the old man takes "the heavy lines home as the dew was bad for them," because natural fibers rot, while synthetics do not. And readers consulting specialists will find that natural-fiber line is heavier than modern synthetics, even synthetics with sufficient specific gravity to sink in salt water, as Santiago's lines do. Specifically, *cordel* was made of a bast fiber, a material still used, although rarely, to make fully comparable lines in the United States. We can therefore learn that 660 fathoms of any such line – braided and five-sixteenths of an inch in diameter – weighs one-hundred-and-sixty pounds after a portion has been in the water.[14] As the text stresses, these are "heavy lines." And the bulk I mentioned is verified by commercial fishermen who daily use hand-coiled line of this length and diameter.

Philip Young, who did compute the lines' length, suspected out of general common sense that a "young boy" could not carry three-quarters of a mile of heavy line – "unless, as we are not told, the lad was actually a giant" (274–75). What we are told, of course, is that the lad was actually a powerful young man of twenty-two. And had that disclosure registered on Young, he would not have had to conclude, as he did, that Hemingway must simply have been fudging probability (274–75).

Yet to my knowledge only Young, after all, has responded to the careful description of Santiago's lines, worked out their length, and been given sufficient pause at least to comment, however precipitously, on the ostensible implausibility.[15] And the reason, I suspect, is that all of us have been distracted from conceiving of Manolin as full-grown, principally because his subservience to his father's demand that he leave Santiago for another fisherman is convincingly childlike to us, and because the references to him as "the boy" become almost a repetend.

Manolin's unquestioning subservience strikes us differently, however, when considered in the light of Cuban custom, especially at that time. In 1970, Lowry Nelson's socioeconomic study, *Rural Cuba,* described a family patriarchy still modeled on that of feudal Spain and strict to a degree that would not occur to American or European readers (174–200). Authority was slowly shifting, in some respects, from the family to the individual and the community. But a son's life, regardless of his age, remained dictated by his father until he married and actually set up housekeeping under a separate roof. This subservience was so complete, for example, that a single man did not, in his father's presence, practice the male ritual of smoking.

And during the period described in the novel there was in Cuba an abundance of such chronologically adult, yet patriarchally controlled men. According to UN demographic statistics (Schroeder 57), in 1953 (only three years later than the novel's action) 88.1 percent of Cuban males between the ages of fifteen and twenty-four were unmarried, and presumably remained dominated by their fathers. Thus in 1950, Manolin's resigned comment about his father, "I am only a boy and I must obey him," and Santiago's agreement that this is "quite normal" both faithfully represent the Cuban attitude toward a vast majority of young men. As for the term "boy," an illuminating indication of what the word means to Manolin himself is a reminiscence by Marcos Puig the Younger, chief among the young Cubans Hemingway had in mind while portraying Manolin. One day, in 1932,

Hemingway had come upon Puig and his father (whom Hemingway named as a model for Santiago) as they were bringing a large marlin alongside their small skiff. And when interviewed later about this encounter with Hemingway, Puig remarked: "I was still a young boy then" (Machlin 137). He was in fact at least twenty-two.[16] Thus Hemingway's first impression was not of a child, but of a young man exactly the earliest credible age for Manolin of the two possibilities absolutely established by the Sisler allusion. And Puig's reference to himself as "a young boy," despite his chronological age, says much about the attitudes of the fishing villages Hemingway was drawing upon in this novel. I am indebted to Allen Josephs for pointing out, moreover, that another acknowledged local model for Manolin – Manolito, a friend of Hemingway's son Gregory and presumably Gregory's age – was twenty-two when the novel appeared. Santiago, of course, refers to himself as "a boy" when he was a seaman "before the mast" at Manolin's age, hardly plausible for a ten-year-old, we note, but just right for a young man of twenty-two. And this is not surprising, when we remember perhaps the most important point of all: that in Latin America the Spanish word *muchacho*, one of the words for "boy" used in Spanish translations of the novel, applies to young males up to their early twenties, as does – in Spain – the word *chico*, also used in translations of the work.

But even apart from these primary cultural reasons for the appellation in this novel, it is characteristic of Hemingway to use "boy" in its international colloquial sense when referring to young adults in many of his works. In Hemingway's canon generally, in fact, "the boy" refers frequently to a male undergoing the very last stage of initiation into the complexities of adulthood.[17] And that, finally, is at once the social and the mythic significance of Manolin's physical and mental maturity in *The Old Man and the Sea*.

At the social level, Manolin's devotion to Santiago, and his parents' demand that he be apprenticed to a more consistently productive fisherman, reflect a major division in the local economic community. It is a conflict between progress and tradition, between craft passion and exploitation – in short, between the old Cuba and a new Cuba that Hemingway saw emerging in the 1940s. Manolin's father has opted for progress. The fisherman he chooses for his son is a middle-aged man, but his minimally competent, cautious methods yield a steady profit. Thus he is associated with the "younger fishermen" who are motivated only by the money they have been making by supplying shark livers for the booming "cod liver oil" industry in the United States in the 1930s and 1940s. These mechanized fishermen represent the decline of the old Cuban fishing culture and the beginning of an exploitative fishery. Actually, in their use of buoys and floats, they are the precursors of the disastrous "long-line" fishery that spread across the Atlantic immediately after this novel was published, and which threatens, some claim, to render all billfish extinct in all oceans by the year 2000. That is the dire prediction recently urged upon suppliers of fuel for these ships by a forthcoming documentary funded by the American Billfish Foundation. The warning demonstrates Hemingway's prescience in sensing the severe consequences of the practice he singled out for attack.

It is this far-reaching struggle between old and new, between true vocation and market-mindedness, that Manolin's adult status functions most importantly to reveal in the novel. Manolin has obviously been a satisfying character when "read" as an endearingly precocious child, attuned to Santiago's values by innate endowment alone. But when we respond to all of the evidence in the narrative, we recognize a realistically portrayed young acolyte, consciously struggling to maintain an adult compromise between his inborn idealism and a cultural paternalism he accepts (as a man) and yet (as a man) resents. With this in mind we can appreciate what Manolin really means when he says of his father's and his employer's attitudes toward him: "It is as though I were inferior." We have assumed that this is simply a child's chafing at being treated condescendingly. But we make sense of more of the novel when we realize that Manolin's father and employer dismiss his opinions because they think he is a misguided young idealist, foolishly drawn to an impractical, outdated way of life. We have a Cuban version of the American or European Babbitt, convinced that his son has foolishly fallen among priests or artists. And it is for this specific, topical reason that Manolin's father has forced him to work for a man "almost blind," metaphysically as well as physically, by Manolin's and Santiago's vocational standards.

Those standards are high, indeed, because for Santiago and Manolin craft passion reflects a sense of participation in natural order, a participation portrayed in both mythical and religious terms in the novel. The practical men against the idealists become the materialists against the mystics. The myth of the Fisher King is dominant in the novel. And as a young adult, Manolin fits into his role in that myth much more effectively than we have been able to recognize, hampered as we have been by our image of him as a child. For only an adult can be a fully credible Parçifal-figure to Santiago's Fisher King/grail keeper: a pure and potent young knight whose belief rejuvenates the aged master's failing resolution toward the end. Specialists tracing that pattern elsewhere in Hemingway's canon will find that the rejuvenating tyro is always a young adult.

In this novel social interaction shades into myth, then, and thence into religion (and vice versa). Manolin is only one of a circle of young men in the community who are devoted to sustaining Santiago, the pure craftsman, scorned though he may be by the dominant new materialists. The names of this cadre of what might be called political supporters in the community's *ethical* conflict associate them with Christ's *spiritual* disciples: "Perico" and "Pedrico" (both forms of "Peter"); Martin (as in Saint Martin), and so on. The name "Manolin," of course, is a diminutive of "Manuel," the Spanish form of "Emmanuel," the redeemer. And from the cadre of young adults, the one with this name will assume the secular and spiritual roles of the town's aged Christ-figure, Santiago, who lies dying at the end.

All of these young fishermen are thus identified with the fishers of men. And here Manolin's maturity intensifies the power of yet another set of allusions. There are several parallels to the Gospels of Saint Matthew and Saint Luke that can now be more fully glossed and appreciated as we recognize Manolin as a young man passing into full adulthood. Particularly revealing is the parallel between the novel and Matthew 4:21–22. James is in a boat with his father Zebedee and he and John "leave their father" to follow Christ. These are not children, but men, choosing – exactly as does Manolin at the end – to defy a biological parent and follow a surrogate father, in order to reject a utilitarian mode of fishing – and living – for one with spiritual dimensions.

We should not see a contradiction between Gospel and novel simply because in leaving their father for Christ the disciples seem to be exchanging "old" ways for "new," whereas in the novel the special young men abandon the new for the old. For both Christ and Santiago represent the *truly* "old thing" that informs Pedro Romero's craftsmanship in *The Sun Also Rises:* the heightened awareness of participation in nature's mysteries that in *The Old Man and the Sea* is called the "great strangeness." In this regard, Santiago is to Manolin as Montoya (guardian and tutor of that "strangeness" in *The Sun Also Rises*) is to Pedro Romero (who is nineteen and called a "boy").

Had we space here, we could reexamine Manolin's total characterization, and observe that it is uniformly consistent with his maturity. We have, however, seen enough to appreciate some of the dimensions foregrounded by his adult status. And we should ask ourselves why – if those dimensions are important – Hemingway has portrayed Manolin's immediate person and personality so ambiguously that millions of us have been allowed to see him as an early adolescent and be profoundly moved by this restricted response to the novel. Singularly, none of his physical characteristics is described, as Santiago's are; and except for carrying the line, he does or says no one thing that in his culture defines – directly and by itself – either late childhood or early manhood. That is how Hemingway makes our response depend entirely on the way we read the larger contexts we have been observing in the narrative. And here Hemingway has offered different kinds of rewards for different levels of reading. On the one hand – hinting on the cultural ambiguities of "boy" and of Manolin's deference – there is the immediate warmth of some of the most appealing romantic archetypes: Santiago as ancient youth; Manolin as wise child – Wordsworth's "father of the man," another young lion sporting "upon the shore," yet (unlike Wordsworth's child) strange in his sober acceptance of "earthly freight" ("Ode: Intimations of Immortality," epigraph and ll. 166, 126). And against these seductive attractions, profound in themselves, Hemingway offers the darker complexities we have been noticing, appropriately accessible only through an arduous process of explication requiring something of the human qualities affirmed by the novel itself: resolution, tenacity, and an initiate's understanding of the varied communities of interest abounding in the practical world. Indeed, when we respond to the full implications of the narrative, we *become* initiates as we read – in the very process of deriving realities disclosed fragmentally, as they are in life – the process required of us by the works of James and Conrad, two of Hemingway's masters in this particular creation of form as content. Of course, this level of response is the "right" reading aesthetically, because it takes into account much data otherwise inconsistent within the novel. Hemingway's achievement does not support an interpretive indeterminacy valorizing whatever associations the work may prompt in us, nor could the notion be less applicable than it is to the works of this author. In seeing Manolin as an early adolescent we have been deeply satisfied – but by what amounts to a paranovel, a closely related yet different aesthetic construct we have created out of the mythic content latent in the plot. And our response has screened out the refinement and complexity of the material's darker, more universal implications.

Yet such a restricted response is in no way unique to *The Old Man and the Sea*. In Hemingway's major works we are increasingly revising canonized interpretations that are qualified or radically corrected by newly recognized narrative facts glossed over for decades by readers distracted by his calculated ambiguity.[18] In fact, this "trick," this tour de force of narrative ambiguity, allowing a work to speak with some validity to two or more readerships and to different levels of experience within individual readers, may well be Hemingway's artistic triumph – the best-kept secret of his celebrated iceberg theory. That would certainly explain his refusal to go beyond veiled hints to correct limited readings. And in this novel that ambiguity functions with precision. For social complexity, the very dimension most readily and widely agreed to be neglected in the work as we have usually read it, is exactly what comes to our attention as we recognize Manolin's adult conflict and the underlying opposition between the Virgin and the marketplace in his shore world.

For example, I had assumed, with Friedman (284–85), that when compared to *The Bear*, Faulkner's remarkably similar treatment of nature mysticism, *The Old Man and the Sea* failed to cope adequately with the social dimension of human life. In part 4 of *The Bear* social realities convincingly mitigate the glories of Ike's transcendent iconoclasm. Against this, Santiago's supposedly unmixed sublimity has seemed to beg questions about the real conflicts between individualism and human community. However, when we realize the central role of community division in the structure of *The Old Man and the Sea*, we see that the universe of this novel is far from the socially evasive, "cozy" cosmos some have labeled it (Weeks 191). "I live in a good town," Santiago says, thinking of his supporters. But the struggle going on there between an old and new Cuba belies all charges of "sentimentality" (Toynbee 87) in the novel's worldview or in Santiago's. The conflict between craft passion and materialism ashore matches the division between noble predators and opportunistic scavengers in the sea, integrating the human community into the immemorial natural scheme.

Just as Santiago's opposition by the cowardly scavenger sharks is the additional ordeal he must bear at sea for going "far out" where the greatest marlin are found, so his human opposition – those whose passivity and greed are threatened by his stringent code – is the added burden he has borne on shore for his inflexible honor. Actually, the course of Santiago's recent life and of his impending death are even shown to be determined in part by the intense reaction of other *people* to the values he represents. Thinking Manolin a child, we have not noticed that without his aid the old man would have been unable to continue fishing and find his great marlin. Manolin's parents have not kept him from carrying the lines and arranging many of the charitable donations of food, bait, and services by the old man's other admirers. But it is because his parents' hostility has taken Manolin out of Santiago's boat that the old man undergoes, without the relief that might have saved him, the physical ordeal that ruptures his lungs "If the boy were here. . . . Yes. If the boy were here. If the boy were here." The invocation has many implications. But one of them is a comment on the human community's discomfort with those rare individuals upon whom the survival of the many depends. In his boat, the taut line from the marlin snubbed over his shoulder, Santiago is "the towing bitt" between the human and the natural worlds. Yet he must bear with that weight the antipathy of the passive majority. Blinded by practical expediency, it fears those who go "beyond all people" to preserve civilization's identification with a world larger than society – the perspective crucial to the sense of wonder that gives human life its color.

Manolin is crying each time he withdraws from Santiago's bedside in the novel's closing scenes, until we leave him quietly watching the old man sleep once more. This time Santiago will dream again of the lions, as he could not upon his return – until reminded by his dialogue with Manolin that they must both act *as if* Santiago would be going out again. For the old man's approaching death, and a champion's commitment to "pull until he dies" as does the great fish, are the true subjects of this dialogue (Sylvester, " 'They Went Through This Fiction' " 474–76). Thus Manolin's tears are not a child's tears of grief and loss, but of those emotions compounded by adult remorse, as he sees the result of the suffering he has contributed to by accepting social and parental pressures and letting Santiago go out alone. They are also tears of wonder at the final price Santiago has paid for his choice to go out "too far." For it is the price Manolin will someday pay for the choice he now makes – the choice every "boy" makes when he becomes fully a man – to honor the values central to him, whatever the cost. And there is the immediate price. "What will your family say?" Santiago asks. "I do not care," Manolin answers, and with that forgoes his touching attempt to find a considerate compromise between his parents' conventional limitations and his commitment to his high vocation. Santiago's suffering has made him see, bitterly, that the time had already come to go with the old man again. Now it is too late, too late merely to serve; on this day Manolin himself becomes *El Campeón* of the values his parents most scorn. We need not overspecify his thoughts to know that his tears reflect all these considerations during the brief rite of passage into complete manhood we observe in the concluding dialogue with his dying mentor. His grief is part of the champion's burden the old man must at last leave entirely to the young man – as he had the weight of the fishing lines. Having carried those "heavy" lines now becomes symbolic as well as tangible evidence of "the boy's" readiness,[19] as he waits reverently that afternoon to take up the full burden of championship. He perpetuates a sacrifice older than the torero's, than Christ's, than the Inuit hunter's vow: "I who was born to die shall live that the world of men may touch the world of animals." And it is reenacted in Santiago's very real Cuban village in 1950 – as always everywhere – by the few for the many, even the many who scorn their efforts.

Recognizing this human portion of nature's paradoxical scheme in *The*

Old Man and the Sea is a good place to begin in combating our persistent tendency to reduce and distort Hemingway's complex portrayals of the human condition. His reliance throughout this novel on a subtly evoked Cuban consciousness so long overlooked should also caution those who proclaim that interpretive criticism of Hemingway's work has run its course. Contemplating the wealth of implication we are directed to construe from the quotidian topicalities of this short novel, we think of Keats's summation of the romantic aesthetic: "Pack every rift with ore." It is unlikely that we have sufficiently explicated any of Hemingway's narratives. He was "a strange old man." "And" – as Santiago reminds us in this work – "there are *many* tricks" (emphasis added).

We can expect new dimensions of Hemingway's artistry to keep surfacing, on and on, as we increasingly acknowledge his modernist method and turn more readily to the library and other sources of information clarifying the narrative facts that govern his metaphors and symbols. We have only to read his works with the attention to topical and historical specificity that he exercised as he wrote.

NOTES

1. The illustrations cited in this discussion are from the book *Reading Hemingway: The Old Man and the Sea*, forthcoming from the Southern Illinois University Press in a series of scholarly commentaries on Hemingway's major works.

2. For an alternate view of Santiago's human qualities, see Brenner throughout.

3. The evidence is conclusive even without the added hint that Dick Sisler would personally affect the outcome of the National League race that year – as readers know he did in 1950, with a home run to win the pennant for Philadelphia (Monteiro 273; Barbour and Sattelmeyer 285; Hurley 78).

My summary of Hurley's derivations points up a notable feature of Hemingway's strategy here: Hemingway presents two sets of evidence, each partially establishing the historical dates of the action, which together are conclusive. We can begin with the early dialogues or with the later reference to the Tigers game (as does Hurley) – whichever catches our attention first. Either way, the sets of evidence verify each other, ruling out coincidence, error, and inadvertence. Also, the repetition gives readers a second chance, nudging them to notice the baseball dates and realize their importance. We will observe Hemingway using this strategy again to stress the importance of the fishing lines' size and weight (see n. 13).

4. The doubleheader when Santiago expects the Yankees to have recorded their eighty-fifth victory is Monday the 11th; we meet Santiago and Manolin on the evening of Tuesday the 12th, the day the Yankees lose a game; Santiago's voyage begins in the predawn hours the next morning, Wednesday the 13th; during the second day of his voyage, he thinks of a Yankees/Tigers game taking place on

Thursday the 14th; he arrives back in his village in the early hours of Saturday the 16th; Manolin wakes him later in the morning of the 16th, and that afternoon watches him sleep again as the narrative ends. See Hurley's chronology (80–82). That Santiago's week is thus set in historical time gives the novel the artistic advantages of a roman à clef, a device Hemingway exploited in his canon as a whole (see my "Persona" 21).

5. Hemingway makes Santiago's manipulation of numbers so patently forced that we are required to see the old man as either superstitious (Rosenfield 50) or profound (see n. 7). Hemingway could more easily have had Santiago go without a fish for eighty-three days (tying Zane Grey's record: for this record, see Hurley 104, 114 n. 2). Santiago's and DiMaggio's resurgences would then both be associated with the number 84; there would be no need to look ahead ingeniously to a potential tie and a potential fish in order to match eighty-fives. But Santiago's coupling of DiMaggio's eighty-fourth win with his own *first* win in eighty-four outings would have remained an illogical "apples-and-oranges" comparison. And in requiring not only Santiago, but every fully oriented reader to juggle numbers all the more, the narrative stresses the irrelevance of logic in what is, after all, an elaborate pretense.

6. See my "Extended Vision" (131–32 et passim) for opposition as necessary to life in the natural world of the novel.

7. In Hemingway's earlier works this intellectual device (familiar to him in Conrad) functions as does Wallace Stevens' concept of a "supreme fiction" (to take one of many modernist examples). It provides a rationale for what Stevens refers to in "Harmonium" as "belief without belief / Beyond belief" in a skeptical century.

8. The seemingly implausible duration of this match is not "poetic license" (see n. 15). I am indebted to my colleague B. L. Grenberg, veteran of such a marathon match and witness to another in the wilds of British Columbia, for explaining that if we assume times-out to urinate, the duration is fully credible for the very reason that the marlin can endure forty-eight hours against the boat: The young Santiago was much stronger than his opponent (who, we note, needed constant rum and cigarettes, while Santiago got no service because he needed none). Comfortably in control, Santiago chose to prolong the match out of human respect for his opponent's dignity, as the fish (for biological reasons) chooses to tow the negligible weight of the skiff slowly and steadily, rather than easily break the line: "He could ruin me by jumping or by a wild rush. But . . . he is following his plan and I am following mine." It is as a coefficient of Santiago's great power and his fellow champion's great pride and resolution that the struggle lasted and became timed with the elements to symbolize natural order. (His opponent's resolution was genuine and proud, because until Santiago instantly pinned him when the referee was about to call a tie, he had not known that Santiago was holding back. Until that moment, Santiago had used only the shifting force needed to maintain balance, slacking off when his opponent had to in order to endure, stiffening as his opponent surged.)

9. I am much indebted to Professor Hurley for looking up statistics beyond those in his study, and for graciously discussing them with me as I applied them in this parallel between the Yankees/Tigers struggle and Santiago's and in other extensions of his findings.

10. In important studies of Catholicism in Hemingway's works, Stoneback

glances perceptively at these allusions to the Virgin and Saint James, seeing them in their proper relation to Hemingway's career-long use of the pilgrimage: "From the rue Saint-Jacques" (13, 15); "'On the Road" (489); "'Review" (98).

11. Fuentes, for example, sees Manolin as a "child" (241), perhaps because Fuentes is unaware of the importance of location: "The novel could . . . have taken place in Java or the Mediterranean" (238).

12. Nor is there any doubt that Hemingway's sentence referring to the ages of Dick and George Sisler was written specifically to set verifiable, if indirect parameters for Manolin's age. For when the scriptwriters for the movie of the novel changed Manolin's line to read, "The great Sisler's father . . . played in the big leagues when he was sixteen," Hemingway wrote in "The boy was not accurate here" (Fuentes 247). His laconic comment makes clear his wish to have these interpreters of his sentence focus on the issue of George Sisler's age at the beginning and end of his well-known career, together with Dick Sisler's date of birth, get those figures right on their own (*he* would not explicate his art), and deal with the implications.

13. Because I have summarized Hemingway's two-part revelation of the baseball dates, other readers deserve the pleasure of explicating for themselves this example of the strategy.

14. For specifications I am indebted to Andrew K. Barker of the Rocky Mount Cord Co.; for the composition of *cordel* to Anthony Farraz, president of Brownell and Co.; for diameter, bulk, and practical details to Ron Schatman (who handlined for marlin) and Jack Casey, both of the American Billfish Foundation.

I see no chance that the lines' formidable weight is either unintentional or extraneous. Even a smaller line – one-quarter inch in diameter, the size of a *standard* pencil – would weigh over a hundred pounds after fishing, enough to make readers think hard about how heavy it would be for an early adolescent, let alone a ten-year-old, to carry. We can see, then, why Manolin "always" helps the elderly Santiago, who could not otherwise continue fishing, and why Manolin helps him carry "*either* the . . . lines *or* the gaff and harpoon and the sail" (emphasis added), a point Hemingway stressed in correcting the film script (Fuentes 246). The pair has regularly made separate trips, sharing the great weight of the lines on one trip and that of the remaining gear on the other. It is an all-the-more crucial narrative fact, then, that on the night and morning before Santiago's final trip Manolin is able to carry the wet lines, gaff, and harpoon to the shack and back to the boat, leaving Santiago only the mast and sail. The shifting balance of the burden shared by this twentieth-century squire and his knight prefigures the approaching end of Santiago's championship and the beginning of Manolin's at the novel's end.

15. It is unwise to assume, as does Young, that in a Hemingway narrative "allegory overwhelms reality." As instances of actual inadvertence (Donaldson, "The Case of the Vanishing American") are very rare, so are instances of facile poetic license. Thus even when an error of fact can be established, we should suspect a functional reason, rather than the indifference to reality Weeks and Young assume. In *The Old Man and the Sea* there are several genuine errors of fact, thought by some to reflect the aging Hemingway's flagging discipline (Weeks throughout). However, most errors Weeks cites are based upon incomplete scientific knowledge at the time. (So are Hemingway's erroneous assumptions that a male striped marlin might approach the

size of Santiago's fish – over 1,500 pounds – when only females do, and that a marlin that large might be found in the Atlantic, when we now know they are not.) And the other genuine errors Weeks mentions are examples of what Stoneback calls, in Hemingway's early works, "anachorism [that which is out of place] and anachronism" used calculatedly to signal the "unstated patterns . . . of a work" ("From the rue Saint-Jacques" 7). They nudge initiated readers toward truth beyond fact (Sylvester, "Extended Vision" 138) – truth that would be missed by uninitiated readers, unaware of anything wrong. But truth *through* fact is overwhelmingly the rule in Hemingway's narratives.

16. We can reasonably establish from information about Hemingway's activities at the time (Baker, *Hemingway: The Writer as Artist* 228; Fuentes 241, 419) that the incident occurred no earlier than 1932; and Puig is described as "in his late forties" in 1957 (Machlin 137).

17. In *A Farewell to Arms* Frederic Henry, in his twenties, is referred to as a boy by a variety of men and women. Donaldson (*Force of Will* 152–53) cites ten instances. (In Henry's case, of course, the label does serve to remind readers of his inappropriate innocence and irresponsibility. But the irony is effective precisely because the speakers often intend the label as it applies to young men generally.) In *Across the River and into the Trees,* Colonel Cantwell speaks of the nineteen-year-old Renata as "Boy, daughter, or whatever it is." He also remembers himself as "a boy" when he was wounded in the wear at nineteen – as does the man Ernest Hemingway in his letters: "When I was a *young boy* I was always getting shot at" (emphasis added).

18. In bibliographies of Hemingway studies for the past decade interested readers can find, for example, references to such necessary new readings of *The Sun Also Rises, A Farewell to Arms,* "The Short Happy Life of Francis Macomber," *Across the River and into the Trees,* and several of the major short stories. There are now in press or in preparation discussions of indirectly presented narrative facts hitherto overlooked or misapplied in *For Whom the Bell Tolls, Islands in the Stream,* and more short stories. The personal and artistic reasons for Hemingway's subtlety and indirection are increasingly scrutinized. For an analysis of current findings, see my "Persona" (esp. 25–34).

19. See the conclusion of note 14 above.

WORKS CITED

Baker, Carlos. *Ernest Hemingway: A Life Story.* New York: Charles Scribner's Sons, 1969.
  Hemingway: The Writer as Artist. New York: Charles Scribner's Sons, 1956.
Barbour, James, and Robert Sattelmeyer. "Baseball and Baseball Talk in *The Old Man and the Sea.*" *Fitzgerald/Hemingway Annual 1975*: 281–87.
Brenner, Gerry. The Old Man and the Sea: *Story of a Common Man.* Boston: Twayne, 1991.
Burns, Ken, and Geoffrey Ward. *Baseball: An Illustrated History.* New York: Knopf, 1994.

Donaldson, Scott. *By Force of Will: The Life and Art of Ernest Hemingway.* New York: Viking, 1977.

"The Case of the Vanishing American and Other Puzzlements in Hemingway's Fiction." *Hemingway Notes* 6 (Spring 1981): 16–19.

Friedman, Norman. *Form and Meaning in Fiction.* Athens: University of Georgia Press, 1975.

Fuentes, Norberto. *Hemingway in Cuba.* New York: Carol, 1984.

Hemingway, Ernest. *Across the River and into the Trees.* New York: Charles Scribner's Sons, 1950.

A Farewell to Arms. New York: Charles Scribner's Sons, 1929.

The Garden of Eden. New York: Charles Scribner's Sons, 1986.

The Old Man and the Sea. New York: Charles Scribner's Sons, 1952.

Ernest Hemingway: Selected Letters, 1917–1961. Ed. Carlos Baker. New York: Charles Scribner's Sons, 1981.

The Short Stories of Ernest Hemingway. New York: Charles Scribner's Sons, 1938.

Hurley, C. Harold. *Hemingway's Debt to Baseball in* The Old Man and the Sea: *A Collection of Critical Readings.* Lewiston, N.Y.: Mellen, 1992.

Lewis, Robert W. "Hemingway in Italy: Making It Up." *Journal of Modern Literature* 9 (1982): 209–36.

Machlin, Milt. "Hemingway Talking." *Conversations with Ernest Hemingway.* Ed. Matthew J. Bruccoli. Jackson: University of Mississippi Press, 1986, 130–42.

Mailer, Norman. *Advertisements for Myself.* New York: Berkley, 1959.

Monteiro, George. "Santiago, DiMaggio, and Hemingway: The Ageing Professionals of *The Old Man and the Sea.*" *Fitzgerald/Hemingway Annual 1974:* 273–80.

Nelson, Lowry. *Rural Cuba.* New York: Octagon, 1970.

Reynolds, Michael. *Hemingway: The Paris Years.* Oxford: Basil Blackwell, 1989.

Rosenfield, Claire. "New World, Old Myths." *Twentieth Century Interpretations of* The Old Man and the Sea: *A Collection of Critical Essays.* Ed. Katherine T. Jobes. Englewood Cliffs, N.J.: Prentice-Hall, 1968, 41–55.

Stoneback, H. R. "From the rue Saint-Jacques to the Pass of Roland to the 'Unfinished Church on the Edge of the Cliff.' " *The Hemingway Review* 6 (1986): 2–29.

———. "Hemingway on the Road to Roncevaux: The Pilgrimage Theme in *The Sun Also Rises.*" *VIII Congreso de la Société Rencesvals.* Pamplona: Institucion Principe de Viana, 1981, 481–89.

———. "Review of *Santiago: Saint of Two Worlds.*" *The Hemingway Review* 12 (1992): 93–98.

Sylvester, Bickford. "Hemingway's Italian *Waste Land:* The Complex Unity of 'Out of Season.' " *Hemingway's Neglected Short Fiction: New Perspectives.* Ed. Susan Beegel. Ann Arbor, Mich.: UMI Research Press, 1989, 75–98.

———. "Hemingway's Extended Vision: *The Old Man and the Sea.*" *PMLA* 81 (1966): 130–38.

_____. "The Writer as l'homme engagé: Persona as Literary Device in Malraux and Hemingway." *North Dakota Quarterly* 60 (1992): 19–38.

_____. " 'They Went through This Fiction Every Day': Informed Illusion in *The Old Man and the Sea.*" *Modern Fiction Studies* 12 (1966–67): 473–76.

Toynbee, Philip. "Hemingway." *Encounter* 17 (October 1961): 86–88.

Weeks, Robert P. "Fakery in *The Old Man and the Sea.*" *College English* 24 (1962): 188–92.

Young, Philip. *Ernest Hemingway: A Reconsideration.* New York: Harcourt, Brace and World, 1952.

13

SUSAN F. BEEGEL

Conclusion:
The Critical Reputation
of Ernest Hemingway

And you only have to do it once to get remembered by some people. But if you can do it year after year after year quite a lot of people remember and they tell their children and their children and their grandchildren remember, and if it's books they can read them. And if it's good enough it lasts forever.

- *Ernest Hemingway*[1]

Critical reputation is the reputation an author enjoys among critics, that cadre of literary professionals who decide which books will be treated as serious and important when they are published, and which will be taught in our high schools, colleges, and universities as examples of American literature. An author of great critical reputation is an author whose work is widely believed to be of permanent value in changing times, an author likely to be read by future generations yet unborn. We call the process of attaining such a critical reputation "canonization," after the process the Roman Catholic Church uses to decide whether an individual deserves public veneration and may be included in the calendar of saints.

It is important to distinguish critical reputation from best-sellerdom. For instance, when Herman Melville died in 1891, impoverished and unknown, he had not managed to sell even a single printing of his masterful *Moby-Dick,* today regarded as one of the great American novels. And some of the best-selling American novels of all time – E. P. Roe's *Barriers Burned Away,* John Fox's *Little Shepherd of Kingdom Come,* and Harold Bell Wright's *The Winning of Barbara Worth* – are today forgotten by all but a few students of popular culture.[2] Hemingway had better luck than Melville. His novels made him both well-known and well-to-do. His first, *The Sun Also Rises,* sold more than one million copies during his lifetime.[3] *The Old Man and the Sea,* published near the end of his life, reached five and a half million people when published in *Life* magazine.[4] Successful, yes, but none of Hemingway's books ever came close to matching the best-sellerdom of Margaret Mitchell's *Gone with the Wind* (more than twenty million copies in twenty-seven languages).[5]

Critical reputation also has little to do with celebrity. Hemingway's lifestyle – four marriages, bullfighting, deep-sea fishing, big-game hunting, and participation in World War I, the Spanish civil war, and World War II – made him the darling of reporters. Throughout his life, he was followed by headlines: "Worst Shot-Up Man in U.S. on Way Home," "Bull Gores Toronto Writer in Annual Pamplona Festival," "Paris Won't Let Hemingway Live a Private Life," "Hemingway Plans to Hunt Big Game in Tanganyika," "Hemingway 'Captures' Six," "Ernest Hemingway Weds Writer in Cuba."[6] His bearded face appeared in *Life* magazine so many times that he was instantly recognized by most Americans. And Hemingway suffered all of the indignities of fame in America: *Vanity Fair* published Hemingway paper dolls with little safari suits and bullfighter outfits; *Woman's Day* sought his wife's hamburger recipes.[7]

Hemingway's critical reputation was forged of something very different. Early in his career, before he had published a single word of fiction, he won the respect of established writers. In 1921, Sherwood Anderson, acclaimed author of the short story cycle *Winesburg, Ohio,* recommended that Hemingway go to Paris, and gave him letters of introduction to members of the literary avant-garde at work in that city. Gertrude Stein, Ezra Pound, and Ford Madox Ford critiqued his work and helped him publish in the experimental "little magazines" of Paris. F. Scott Fitzgerald, with the popular success of *This Side of Paradise* and the critical success of *The Great Gatsby* under his belt, placed Hemingway with his American publisher, Charles Scribner's Sons, home of the phenomenally prescient editor, Maxwell Perkins.

A partial list of the distinguished men and women of letters who chose to read and review Hemingway's work during his lifetime reads like a veritable Who's Who of twentieth-century literature: Edmund Wilson, D. H. Lawrence, Conrad Aiken, André Maurois, Virginia Woolf, Dorothy Parker, H. L. Mencken, Mario Praz, John Dos Passos, Lewis Galantière, Klaus Mann, Max Eastman, Wyndham Lewis, Bernard De Voto, Sinclair Lewis, Alfred Kazin, Malcolm Cowley, Lionel Trilling, Mark Schorer, Graham Greene, V. S. Pritchett, Arturo Barea, Evelyn Waugh, and William Faulkner.[8] Their regard for Hemingway as a writer to be taken seriously helped place him on the road to canonization.

During the 1950s, the last decade of Hemingway's life, his work began to receive serious attention from academic critics and biographers, despite considerable resistance from Hemingway himself, who was "opposed to writing about the private lives of liveing [sic] authors and psychoanalyzing them while they are alive."[9] Landmark works of scholarship published at this time included Carlos Baker's thematic study of the fiction and nonfiction, *Hemingway: The Writer as Artist;* Philip Young's controversial psychoanalytic treatment of the life and work, *Ernest Hemingway;* and Charles Fenton's examination of Hemingway's early years as a journalist, *The Apprenticeship of Ernest Hemingway.*[10] These young scholars were betting their careers that in years to come Hemingway would be considered an important figure in American literature, and they were right. By the end of the decade, Hemingway was included in such influential surveys of American literature as Charles Feidelson and Paul Brodtkorb's *Interpretations of American Literature* (1959) and Leslie Fiedler's *Love and Death in the American Novel* (1960).[11]

Publication of *The Old Man and the Sea* in 1952 played a crucial role in the development of Hemingway's critical reputation. Prior to the appearance of this crisp and lyrical novella about an old Cuban fisherman's struggle with a titanic fish, Hemingway had published nothing of distinction during the twelve years since *For Whom the Bell Tolls* (1940). The early promise of the brilliant short story collection, *In Our Time* (1925), and his finest novels, *The Sun Also Rises* (1926) and *A Farewell to Arms* (1929), seemed distant and unfulfilled. Hemingway's nonfiction of the 1930s, *Death in the Afternoon* (1932) and *Green Hills of Africa* (1935), had been disappointing by comparison, and a "novel" like *To Have and Have Not* (1937), two previously published short stories hastily cobbled together, seemed a shocking performance from a craftsman once so exacting. *Across the River and into the Trees* (1950) had been savaged by the critics, and Hemingway was widely considered to be a has-been.

The Old Man and the Sea, however, was hailed as Hemingway's triumphant return. According to Carlos Baker,

> *Life* sold 5,318,650 copies within forty-eight hours. Advance sales on the regular American edition ran to 50,000 and settled thereafter into a brisk weekly sale of 3,000. . . . [Readers] kept telephoning congratulations. Those who saw [Hemingway] personally often thanked him and burst into tears. . . . American reviewers were mostly ecstatic. Harvey Breit called the book "momentous and heartening." Joseph Henry Jackson had nothing but praise for this "miracle-play of Man against Fate." . . . Rabbis and ministers began preaching sermons on Ernest's text. For three weeks, Ernest himself averaged eighty to ninety letters a day from well-wishers.[12]

It seemed the world agreed with Hemingway's often abused wife Mary, who, after reading the manuscript, said she "forgave [him] for everything [he'd] ever done," and showed him the gooseflesh on her arms.[13]

The international success of *The Old Man and the Sea* brought Hemingway the world's most prestigious literary award, the Nobel Prize, in 1954. His citation praised him for overcoming the "brutal, callous, and cynical" tendencies of his early career to produce a work of "heroic pathos," distinguished by its "natural admiration for every individual who fights the good fight in a world of reality overshadowed by violence and death."[14] Receipt of the Nobel Prize is in many cases a guarantee of eventual canonization. With one or two exceptions, the other American writers who have won the award – Sinclair Lewis, Eugene O'Neill, Pearl S. Buck, William Faulkner, John Steinbeck, Saul Bellow, Isaac Bashevis Singer, Joseph Brodsky, and Toni Morrison – are considered pivotal figures in our literature and their works are widely taught in our institutions of higher learning.

Death, however, is the truest test of a writer's critical reputation. The "loathsome literary world," as Norman Mailer put it, is "necrophilic to the core – [critics] murder their writers, and then decorate their graves."[15] Although Mailer's bitterness is understandable, the necrophilia of critics does have a certain harsh logic. Not until authors have departed this earth can we begin to determine whether their work is, to paraphrase Hemingway, "good enough to last forever." It is far easier to capture the imaginations and speak to the concerns of one's own generation than to write meaningfully for the children, grandchildren, and great-grandchildren of the future. Again, like the saints of the Roman Catholic Church, no writer can be genuinely "canonized" until he or she is dead.

Hemingway, who never did anything once, managed to die twice. In January 1954, while on safari in Africa, he and his wife Mary were involved in two serious plane crashes in two days. The first plane, a chartered Cessna piloted by Roy Marsh, swerved to avoid a flight of ibis, collided with an abandoned telegraph wire, and plummeted into the Ugandan bush near Murchison Falls on the Nile. Badly bruised and shaken, the Hemingways and their pilot spent an uncomfortable night among curious hippos and elephants while rescuers began searching for the missing plane. But the search went wide. Marsh and the Hemingways rescued themselves the next day by flagging down a boatload of sightseers on the Nile. It took the boat until late in the afternoon to return to its berth at Butiaba; in the meantime, word flashed around the globe that Hemingway was missing and presumed dead. The second crash occurred when the Hemingways chartered another flight to take them from Butiaba to Entebbe. This time the plane crashed on takeoff and burst into flames; Hemingway, the last one out of the burning aircraft, sustained serious injuries (a concussion, cracked vertebrae, first-degree burns, and internal bruising).

Word of Hemingway's survival did not reach the outside world until the second day after the first crash, when the battered author, after yet another flight, collapsed in a Nairobi hotel room. There he had the uniquely delicious experience of reading his own obituaries. Mary Hemingway recalled it this way:

> Then the obituaries began arriving, first from London and Europe, then from the western hemisphere and India and Hong Kong, two- and three-column stories many of them, reviewing Ernest's life and appraising his work. He read and reread them enthralled and gave no attention when I suggested that the everlasting reading suggested unseemly egotism. After our day's and evening's guests departed, he read in bed. Then, heeding my objections to the light, he read in the bathroom.[16]

The African plane crashes may have been as important as the success of *The Old Man and the Sea* in precipitating Hemingway's Nobel Prize. His miraculous survival after being reported dead constituted a second "triumphant return" of the old man, and made him a sentimental favorite for the prize while it gave the Nobel committee advance assurance that their decision would be popular.

Sadly, the plane crashes also precipitated the final downturn in Hemingway's physical and mental health. A thinly controlled alcoholic throughout much of his life, he drank more heavily than usual to combat the pain of his injuries. He began to suffer from diabetes, high blood pressure, and cirrhosis of the liver. Hemingway's mental state began to deteriorate as well, and he experienced bouts of extreme paranoia (believing that the FBI and IRS were pursuing him), as well as episodes of severe depression, leading to a number of suicide attempts and eventually to his hospitalization for electroshock treatments that destroyed much of his short-term memory. Throughout this difficult period, he struggled to write, publishing "The Dangerous Summer" in *Life* magazine (1960) and bringing *A Moveable Feast* to near-completion. Finally, however, the struggle grew to be too much. On the morning of July 2, 1961, just days after his release from a psychiatric ward at the Mayo Clinic, Ernest Hemingway selected a shotgun from a basement storage room in his Ketchum, Idaho home and blew his brains out.

It is here that the continuing story of Hemingway's critical reputation, his life after death, really begins. The world mourned his passing, beginning an evaluation of his life and work truly international in scope. His receipt of the Nobel Prize, his expatriate lifestyle, and his easily translatable literary style had made him a global favorite. The *New York Times* of July 4, 1961 recorded worldwide headlines upon his death: " 'France Shocked over Hemingway,' 'Praised by Vatican Paper,' '[Manchester] *Guardian* Cites Influence,' 'Mourned in Madrid,' 'Tributes from Lisbon,' 'Work Lauded in Norway,' 'Stockholm Is Stunned,' 'Top Influence in Poland,' ' "One of Us" to Cubans,' and 'Brazilian Hails Greatness.' "[17] A special issue of the *Saturday Review* carried an article titled "The World Weighs a Writer's Influence," and included estimates of Hemingway's work by Salvador de Madariaga of Spain, Frank Moraes in India, Carlo Levi of Italy, Ilya Ehrenburg of the Soviet Union, Alan Pryce-Jones of England, and Edward Seinsticker in Japan.[18] Soviet writer Ilya Ehrenburg summarized the international response this way: "The loss of this major writer hurts. It hurts, too, that a man should have died who, through the love felt for him, has brought together people and nations otherwise remote from each other."[19]

American critics, too, were asking themselves a question best formulated by Irving Howe:

> Now that he is dead and nothing remains but a few books and the problem of his dying, perhaps we should ask the simplest, most radical of questions, what was there in Hemingway's writing that enabled him to command the loyalty of a generation? Even those of us who disliked some of his work and most of his posture, why did we too feel compelled to acknowledge the strength and resonance of his voice?[20]

The period immediately following Hemingway's death saw many retrospectives of his career as critics explored whether he was worthy of canonization. Articles such as Stanley Edgar Hyman's "The Best of Hemingway," John C. Kelly's "Ernest Hemingway (1899–1961): Formulating the Data of Experience," and C. Hugh Holman's "Ernest Hemingway: A Tribute" were commonplace.[21]

"Was 'Papa' Truly a Great Writer?" asked Maxwell Geismar in the *New York Times Book Review*.[22] Critics at work in America's colleges and universities voted a resounding "yes" with their pens. The decade of the 1960s saw the publication of nearly four hundred scholarly articles and books with Ernest Hemingway as their subject.[23] Just how rapidly Hemingway became a mainstay of high school and college classrooms is indicated by the decade's booming industry in study guides to the major novels. Cliff's Notes, Monarch Notes, Methuen Notes, Ivy Notes, Coles Notes, Merrill Guides, and Studymaster all vied for a share of the profitable Hemingway market.

The vast majority of critics at work in the academy during this period were white Anglo-Saxon Protestant males, who shared World War II as their most important historic memory. Indeed, many were combat veterans. Their favorite novel was *A Farewell to Arms,* Hemingway's romantic tragedy of love and duty in a theater of war. *The Old Man and the Sea,* with its existentialist emphasis on courage and perseverance in the face of inevitable defeat and death, came second. Among short stories they preferred those set in Africa, "The Short Happy Life of Francis Macomber" and "The Snows of Kilimanjaro," reading them as "moral tragedies tipped with irony," of dissolute men finding courage and dying "at the very moment [they commence] to live."[24] Their criticism was profoundly value-centered, focusing on heroism and existentialism, and on attitudes toward love and religion. Representative works of Hemingway criticism composed during the 1960s included John Killinger's *Hemingway and the Dead Gods: A Study in Existentialism,* Cleanth Brooks's *The Hidden God: Studies in Hemingway, Faulkner, Yeats, Eliot, and Warren,* Earl Rovit's *Ernest Hemingway,* Robert W. Lewis's *Hemingway on Love,* and Jackson Benson's *Hemingway: The Writer's Art of Self-Defense.*[25]

Philip Young, however, was the single most influential Hemingway critic during these years. His *Ernest Hemingway: A Reconsideration,* published in 1966, created a psychoanalytic paradigm, known as the "wound theory," for reading Hemingway's work. An extensive revision of Young's 1954 study, less inhibited following Hemingway's suicide, the book proposed that the author's life and art had been motivated by the trauma of his wounding in World War I (at eighteen Hemingway had been badly injured by Austrian shell and machine-gun fire while acting as a Red Cross volunteer). Young equated Hemingway with the shell-shocked Nick Adams of "A Way You'll Never Be," and viewed the author's many fictive treatments of courage and violence as repeated attempts to master the terrifying, primal scene of his 1918 wounding. From the "wound theory," Young, himself a combat veteran, evolved the notion of a Hemingway "code": "A 'grace under pressure' . . . made of the controls of honor and courage which in a life of tension and pain make a man a man and distinguish him from the people who follow random impulses, let down their hair, and are generally messy, perhaps cowardly, and without inviolable rules for how to live holding tight."[26] In Young's view, this theme is always "introduc[ed] and exemplifi[ed]" in Hemingway's fiction by a "code hero," a "consistent character" embodying the values of the code.

Like all brilliant critical theories, Young's provided a persuasive and enlightening way to read Hemingway's entire output. Many works of the

1960s, including Joseph DeFalco's *The Hero in Hemingway's Short Stories,* Leo Gurko's *Hemingway and the Pursuit of Heroism,* and Delbert Wylder's *Hemingway's Heroes* attest to Young's influence.[27] At the same time, the idea of the code hero would smother the originality of lesser critics and stifle alternative views for a long time.

Minority voices were virtually absent from the academy of the 1960s. Of the vast sea of work on Hemingway during this period, only three articles stand out as of special relevance to Americans marginalized by a dominant WASP culture: Gerald Griffin's "Hemingway's Fictive Use of the Negro: 'The Curious Quality of Incompleteness,' " Josephine Z. Knopf's "Meyer Wolfsheim and Robert Cohn: A Study of Jewish Type and Stereotype," and Michael Hoffman's "From Cohn to Herzog."[28] None was sufficient to press consideration of Hemingway's relevance to an essentially multicultural society.

Contributions by women were scarce, with only seventeen women writing about Hemingway during the first decade after his death. The seventeen speak volumes about gender and the academy in the 1960s. Nearly 25 percent were nuns, suggesting that a vow of celibacy was necessary, or at least that marriage and family were considered inappropriate for women with careers at this time. A number of women appeared as "second authors," a respectful two paces behind husbands or male colleagues. Only one woman, a 1969 graduate student, dared to challenge male-oriented subject matter and discuss female characters in Hemingway's fiction.[29] Others wrote women's magazine-style descriptions of Hemingway's homes in Key West and Cuba. Nevertheless, the decade's most important woman scholar, Audre Hanneman, produced a monumental work of permanent value: *Ernest Hemingway: A Comprehensive Bibliography.*[30] Yet perhaps it is significant that Hanneman, like Katharine Jobes (who edited a useful anthology of essays on *The Old Man and the Sea* in 1968),[31] felt more comfortable acting as a compiler than as an opinion maker.

Although the academy was silent on issues of importance to minority readers and women, the almost exclusively male critical hierarchy sometimes carried on like guys in a locker room. With their pronouncements unleavened by feminist thought and unchallenged by female colleagues, some early male critics of Hemingway man-handled his striking women characters and ignored those stories where he wrote with sensitivity from a woman's point of view. For such critics, Brett Ashley of *The Sun Also Rises* was a "Circe" who turned men into swine, Catherine Barkley of *A Farewell to Arms* a "divine lollipop," and the female protagonists of the African stories "American bitches of the most soul-destroying sort."[32] A great deal of seminal Hemingway criticism was unfortunately written in an era under the influence of Leslie Fiedler's *Love and Death in the American Novel* (1960), a tremendously popular critical work suggesting that American literature in its entirety could be interpreted as an elaboration of two ideas: that minority people make terrific sidekicks and that the only good woman is a dead one.

The dearth of minorities and women in the academy during the 1960s is probably the most significant negative influence on Hemingway's critical reputation today. When potential readers reject Hemingway as indifferent to minorities and hostile to women, they are often responding not to Hemingway's fiction, but to the indifference and hostility of some of his early critics, and a negative image of the author those influential first admirers unintentionally projected. Just as Young's notion of the code hero made it hard for subsequent critics to approach Hemingway in any other fashion, so the unconscious and deliberate biases of some early readers would make it hard for some subsequent readers to approach Hemingway at all.

In addition to a burgeoning of critical interest, the 1960s were marked by an explosion of Hemingway biographies. The marriages, the globetrotting, the wars, the adventures, and the tragic mystery of the suicide were (and are) irresistible. Hemingway's death ironically meant that public fascination with his inimitable life could now be indulged to the fullest. A crop of tawdry, exploitative biographies followed almost immediately on the heels of his suicide: Alfred G. Aronowitz and Peter Hammil's *Ernest Hemingway: The Life and Death of a Man,* Kurt D. Singer's *Hemingway: Life and Death of a Giant,* and Milt Machlin's *The Private Hell of Ernest Hemingway* hit the newsstands in paperback form almost before the body was cold.[33]

Of greater value to scholars, and held back for publication after Hemingway's death, were two sibling biographies: Leicester Hemingway's *My Brother, Ernest Hemingway* (1962) and Marcelline Hemingway Sanford's *At the Hemingways: A Family Portrait* (1962).[34] Also of value, although its brutally honest account of the suicide greatly distressed Hemingway's widow Mary, was *Papa Hemingway,* a biography by the author's friend A. E. Hotchner.[35] Lloyd Arnold, an Idaho intimate of the Hemingways, produced *High on the Wild.*[36] Another biographer with a regional emphasis, Constance Cappel Montgomery, produced *Hemingway in Michigan,* a detailed look at the childhood summers that play so vital a role in the early short stories.[37]

Many of Hemingway's literary acquaintances, including Sylvia Beach, Morley Callaghan, Kathleen Cannell, Janet Flanner, Lillian Hellman, Robert McAlmon, and Harold Loeb, responded with reminiscences to the hun-

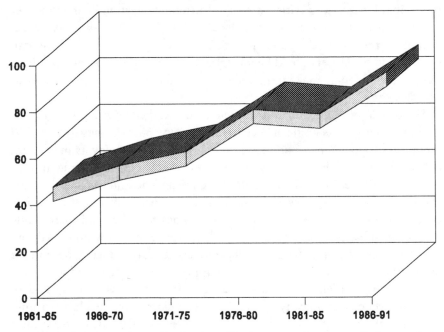

100 —

80 —

60 —

40 —

20 —

0 —

| 1961-65 | 1966-70 | 1971-75 | 1976-80 | 1981-85 | 1986-91 |

Number of scholarly articles and books about Hemingway produced annually from 1961 until 1991. (*Source:* based on the annual *MLA International Bibliography*)

ger for information. Biographies by Hemingway's most negligible acquaintances also blossomed: Jed Kiley's *Hemingway: An Old Friend Remembers* and William Seward's *My Friend Ernest Hemingway: An Affectionate Reminiscence* struck poses of imaginary intimacy.[38]

The close of the decade saw publication of a scholarly book that still endures as the finest single-volume biography, Carlos Baker's *Ernest Hemingway: A Life Story.*[39] Baker's Hemingway biography has no thesis, and is driven not by "Freudian fiddle-faddle," but by facts.[40] Baker's encyclopedic knowledge, faithful representation, and meticulous documentation of the Hemingway letters and manuscripts he was among the first to handle give *Ernest Hemingway: A Life Story* an authority as yet unsurpassed. More recent biographers may have addressed controversial issues that Baker avoided out of respect to Hemingway's widow, and they may have had access to information unavailable to Baker in the 1960s, but none has yet matched him in objectivity and scholarship.

A writer's critical reputation may languish naturally after death simply because the writer is no longer publishing, no longer stimulating critics with new work to consider. This has not been a problem for Hemingway, who continues to publish prolifically from beyond the grave. At his death he left a great deal of uncollected work, as well as three thousand pages of un-published manuscripts.[41] The 1960s saw publication of four posthumous volumes, and their carefully metered appearances no doubt account in part for his growing reputation during this period. Of these, the least significant was *Hemingway: The Wild Years,* a group of early *Toronto Star* articles hastily compiled by Gene Z. Hanrahan and published as a Dell paperback in 1962 to exploit the publicity attendant on Hemingway's suicide. His 1940 play, *The Fifth Column,* was added to four previously uncollected short stories of the Spanish civil war, to make a second, more engaging "new" Hemingway offering for 1960s readers. In *Byline: Ernest Hemingway,* bibli-ographer William White anthologized "selected articles and dispatches of four decades," sparking a critical enthusiasm for the nonfiction that culmi-nated in Robert O. Stephens' scholarly study, *Hemingway's Nonfiction: The Public Voice.*[42] By far the most momentous of the decade's posthumous publications, however, was Hemingway's previously unpublished and lyri-cal memoir of his Paris years, *A Moveable Feast.* Although questionably edited by Mary Hemingway, *A Moveable Feast* is widely and deservedly accepted as one of American literature's "books that matter."

As the 1960s drew to a close, the United States was torn apart over its growing involvement in the Vietnam War. A majority of predominantly conservative, middle-class Americans viewed the war as a necessary attempt to halt the spread of communism in Asia. Many of their college-age chil-dren, who possessed no right to vote but could be forcibly drafted to fight in this conflict,[43] viewed the Vietnam War as fundamentally racist (one poster referred to the war as "white men sending black men to kill yellow men to defend a nation stolen from red men") and an obscene effort to obliterate an agrarian people who scarcely threatened the United States superpower and its military-industrial complex. In the watershed year of 1968, the nation changed forever as the Viet Cong poured into South Vietnam during the Tet Offensive, civil rights leader Martin Luther King Jr. and liberal presidential candidate Senator Robert Kennedy were assassinated, massive antiwar dem-onstrations at the Democratic National Convention turned into violent riot-ing, and Republican Richard M. Nixon was elected president.

As the 1970s began conservatives sought an end to mounting unrest on campus. "If it takes a bloodbath, then let's get it over with," pronounced California Governor Ronald Reagan.[44] The bloodbath took place on May 18, 1970, when National Guardsmen opened fire on students protesting the war at Kent State University, killing four. The shots were heard around the world, and commemorated in forums as diverse as a poem by dissident

Soviet writer Yevgeny Yevtushenko, and a rock 'n' roll ballad by Neil Young:[45]

> Tin soldiers and Nixon coming.
> We're finally on our own.
> This summer I hear the drumming,
> Four dead in Ohio.
> Four dead in Ohio.

But the incident at Kent State did not "get it over with." By year's end 448 colleges and universities were either closed or on strike, and the nation's tension over the war did not ease until 1973, when the United States signed a ceasefire with North Vietnam.

What does all of this have to do with Hemingway's critical reputation? The truest test of an author's critical reputation is the ability to remain relevant to successive generations, and perhaps no generation gap in American history was as profound as that between the children of the 1960s and their World War II–forged parents. For those who had, like Hemingway himself, participated in the global struggle to end fascism and had stoically confronted horrors like the walking barrages of Hürtgen Forest, the issue of "grace under pressure" was all-consuming. Yet to survive the 1970s, Hemingway's work would have to appeal to a generation he had never known nor imagined, a generation that did not believe that communism was a global threat and had refused military service en masse.

Statistics show that Hemingway's critical reputation met the challenges of the 1970s with ease. The decade saw production of some 729 scholarly books and articles about his work and life, up 42 percent from the 1960s. In part, Hemingway's fictional treatment of World War I and its aftermath assisted him posthumously in bridging the gap between the World War II and Vietnam generations. He believed that World War I was "the most colossal, murderous, mismanaged butchery that has ever taken place on earth," and hated both war itself and "all the politicians whose mismanagement, gullibility, cupidity, selfishness, and ambition" create wars.[46] Yet he also believed, writing before Vietnam, that "once we have a war there is only one thing to do. It must be won. For defeat brings worse things than war."[47] Both subsequent generations could draw nourishment from his writing – he gave courage to one ("no thing that can ever happen to you from the air can ever be worse than the shelling men lived through on the Western front in 1916 and 1917"[48]) and cynicism to the other ("Abstract words such as honor, glory, courage, or hallow were obscene beside the concrete names of villages, the names of rivers, the numbers of regiments and the dates" [*FTA* 185]).

Change happens slowly in American colleges and universities, despite events like the Kent State tragedy and widespread strikes. The torch is not passed to a new generation overnight; it takes from four to ten years to earn a Ph.D., and another seven years to win tenure. Not until the late 1980s did the Vietnam generation begin to assume dominance in the academy. As the 1970s began, the World War II generation was still in command, but as the decade progressed, new critical trends slowly began to infiltrate Hemingway studies.

Not surprisingly, *The Sun Also Rises* was the favorite Hemingway novel of the 1970s. Its lost-generation characters, alienated by World War I and self-anesthetized with alcohol, were familiar and appealing to an equally lost generation alienated by Vietnam and experimenting with drugs. *A Farewell to Arms* remained immensely popular, its tragic juxtaposition of love and war still supremely relevant. *For Whom the Bell Tolls,* with its complex treatment of the political corruption, atrocities, and futile loss of life on both sides of the Spanish civil war, also increased its audience, while *The Old Man and the Sea,* with its simplistic approach to courage and endurance in the face of adversity, began to decline in popularity.

Philip Young's notion of a code hero continued to be influential in the 1970s, dominating doctoral dissertations such as Gary D. Elliott's "The Hemingway Hero's Quest for Faith" and Bhim Singh Dahiya's "The Hero in Hemingway: A Study in Development."[49] Predictably, however, the post–Vietnam generation was less interested in heroism for heroism's sake, and there were also glimmerings of discontent with this paradigm for reading Hemingway. "Throw away Your Hemingway Codebook," urged Philip K. Jason in an article for *Indirections,* while Charles Stetler and Gerald Locklin advocated "Decoding the Hemingway Hero" in an essay for *Hemingway Notes.*[50]

There were other factors at large in the academy of the 1970s as well. In 1972 a constitutional amendment (known as the ERA, or Equal Rights Amendment) prohibiting gender discrimination against women was sent to the states for ratification. That same year, a number of colleges and universities previously closed to women (Dartmouth College, Rutgers, and Yale University are three examples) opened their doors for the first time. Across the United States, women organized to work for passage of the amendment. ERA would eventually fail, but it left behind a highly organized and extremely angry feminist movement with improved access to higher education.

If Hemingway's writing was, as Philip Young suggested, almost entirely concerned with "what makes a man a man," how would his reputation survive both the advent of 1970s-style feminism and a fresh influx of women into American colleges and universities?

Feminism's impact on Hemingway studies, like that of the Vietnam War, was almost immediate and surprisingly positive. The number of women scholars at work on Hemingway rose from 7 percent of the whole in the 1960s to 13 percent in the 1970s. Women remained a distinct minority, to be sure, but their numbers almost doubled in a single decade. Some, such as Mary Jim Josephs in "The Hunting Metaphor in Hemingway and Faulkner" and Charlotte Kretzoi in "Hemingway on Bullfights and Aesthetics,"[51] tackled Hemingway's masculine subject matter. Others, such as Carole Vopat in "The End of *The Sun Also Rises*: A New Beginning" and Trisha Ingman in "Symbolic Motifs in 'A Canary for One,' " chose gender-neutral territory.[52] Still others began for the first time to explore matters of interest to women readers: Pamella Farley's "Form and Function: The Image of Woman in Selected Works of Hemingway and Fitzgerald," Deborah Fisher's "Genuine Heroines: Hemingway Style," and Janet Lynne Pearson's "Hemingway's Women."[53] Some, like Anne Greco in "Margot Macomber: Bitch Goddess Exonerated" and Sunita Jain in "Of Women and Bitches: Two Hemingway Heroines Exonerated," would challenge the assumptions of their male colleagues.[54] Nor were woman scholars always complimentary to Hemingway. Judith Fetterley's "*A Farewell to Arms*: Hemingway's 'Resentful Cryptogram,' " remains one of the best-known feminist assaults on the author's hostility to women.[55] By 1978 there were even hints of a developing backlash, as William Spofford published "Beyond the Feminist Perspective: Love in *A Farewell to Arms*."[56]

If women became increasingly involved in Hemingway studies during the 1970s, scholars interested in issues of race and ethnicity did not. Only Paul Marx, in "Hemingway and Ethics," briefly pondered the subject, concluding, with a well-developed sense of the obvious, that Hemingway's use of racial and ethnic epithets in his 1920s stories was the result of "cultural influences."[57] And only J. F. Kobler's "Hemingway's 'The Sea Change': A Sympathetic View of Homosexuality" dared introduce a subject seldom discussed in the pre-AIDS era of the 1970s.[58]

Influence studies were far and away the dominant critical trend of the decade. Now that Hemingway's canonization seemed assured, critics rushed to rank him among accepted literary figures. In article after article, Hemingway is compared to acknowledged "greats" of American literature (Poe, Thoreau, Emerson, Melville, Twain, Adams, Dreiser) and to leading lights of his own generation (Anderson, Bellow, Wolfe, Faulkner, Fitzgerald, Stein-beck, Wister, Eliot, Thurber). He is ranked as well with European and British writers (Dante, Flaubert, Mérimée, Proust, Malraux, Stendhal, Camus, Gide, Tolstoy, Mann, Nietzsche, Baroja, Gironella, Joyce, Shaw, Huxley – even Lewis Carroll and H. Rider Haggard). And Hemingway's achievements are used as a yardstick against which younger writers (Ralph Ellison, Joseph Heller, John Updike) are measured.

The 1970s also marked the real beginning of a phenomenon known as the "Hemingway industry." So many critics were now at work on Hemingway that the available spectrum of generalist journals could not accommodate their productivity. In 1970, Matthew J. Bruccoli founded *The Fitzgerald-Hemingway Annual* to provide an additional forum for publication. When this journal folded in 1979, Kenneth Rosen picked up the torch and created *Hemingway Notes,* a publication devoted exclusively to Hemingway studies and still going strong today as *The Hemingway Review.*

The burgeoning of Hemingway studies during this period may be the reason why many of the decade's most important books were devoted to helping scholars get a grip on the now considerable literature about Hem-ingway: Arthur Waldhorn's *A Reader's Guide to Ernest Hemingway* and *Ernest Hemingway: A Collection of Criticism,* Audre Hanneman's *Supple-ment to* Ernest Hemingway: *A Comprehensive Bibliography,* Linda Wag-ner's *Ernest Hemingway: Five Decades of Criticism* and *Ernest Hemingway: A Reference Guide,* Richard Astro and Jackson Benson's anthology, *Hem-ingway in Our Time,* and Benson's own collection, *The Short Stories of Ernest Hemingway: Critical Essays.*[59]

The year 1975 marked an event of lasting importance to Hemingway's critical reputation, as a large collection of manuscripts (some 19,500 pages)[60] and letters left at his death opened to the public at a branch of the National Archives in Waltham, Massachusetts. Prior to this date, textual studies of Hemingway's work had taken the form of niggling over misprints, a type of criticism Hemingway himself once labeled the "missing laundry list school."[61] Now, however, textual studies took on depth, richness, and importance, as scholars could examine multiple drafts of the famous novels and short stories, and study Hemingway's process of composition in detail. Michael S. Reynolds' *Hemingway's First War: The Making of A Farewell to Arms* and Bernard Oldsey's *Hemingway's Hidden Craft: The Writing of A Farewell to Arms* followed almost immediately.[62]

The production of Hemingway biographies continued unabated during the 1970s. Once again, a number were slight and exploitative, out to take advantage of the always salable Hemingway name. S. Kip Farrington's *Fish-*

ing with Hemingway and Glassell, Vernon (Jake) Klimo and Will Oursler's *Hemingway and Jake: An Extraordinary Friendship,* and Richard E. Hardy and John G. Cull's *Hemingway: A Psychological Portrait* are examples.[63]

More valuable acquaintance biographies also flourished. Reminiscences of Hemingway appear in Malcolm Cowley's *A Second Flowering: Works and Days of the Lost Generation,* Arnold Gingrich's *Nothing but People: The Early Days at Esquire, A Personal History, 1928–1958,* and Ina Mae Schleden and Marion Rawls Herzog's *Ernest Hemingway as Recalled by His High School Contemporaries.*[64] In this genre, Bertram D. Sarason's *Hemingway and the Sun Set* was particularly significant, gathering the recollections of the actual 1920s expatriates fictionalized in *The Sun Also Rises.*[65]

Hemingway family members continued to participate in the biographical rush. Widow Mary Hemingway published *How It Was,* weighing in at five hundred plus pages.[66] Madelaine Hemingway Miller produced *Ernie: Hemingway's Sister "Sunny" Remembers,* and youngest son Gregory Hemingway the embittered *Papa: A Personal Memoir.*[67] Each is valuable in reconstructing aspects of Hemingway's performance as husband, brother, and father.

In the shadow of Carlos Baker, and unable, as yet, to take full advantage of the newly opened Hemingway papers, scholarly biography in the 1970s was relatively quiet – a sort of calm before the biographical storm of the 1980s. Scott Donaldson's 1977 study, *By Force of Will: The Life and Art of Ernest Hemingway,* was the most important biography of the decade, a critical work focusing in detail on the life's shaping of the work.[68] James McLendon added *Papa: Hemingway in Key West* to the regional biographies of the previous decade, and Alice Hunt Sokoloff added significantly to growing interest in Hemingway's relationships with women in *Hadley: The First Mrs. Hemingway.*[69]

In the 1970s, as in the 1960s, Hemingway's critical reputation continued to be augmented by posthumous publication. Matthew Bruccoli edited two collections important to an appreciation of Hemingway's young years: *Ernest Hemingway's Apprenticeship: Oak Park, 1916–1917* (an anthology of Hemingway's contributions to his high school newspaper and literary magazine) and *Ernest Hemingway, Cub Reporter: Kansas City Star Stories* (containing his earliest professional journalism).[70] Nicholas Gerogiannis contributed an anthology of Hemingway's *Complete Poems,* never the author's strong suit, but previously unavailable except in a pirated edition.[71]

These offerings were trivial, however, beside the posthumous publication of a new novel, *Islands in the Stream* (1970). Incomplete, rambling, and like

A Moveable Feast extensively edited without explanation, *Islands* seemed to critics "a very strange book full of pleasing and disastrous things," and "a gallant wreck of a novel."[72] The tortured and sometimes tortuous tale of painter Thomas Hudson, his betrayal of the women who loved him and final loss of his sons, his loneliness and violent death, all set against a Caribbean background that Edmund Wilson felt included "the best of Hemingway's descriptions of nature," gave the novel, in Paul Theroux's words, "the tone of a suicide note."[73] *Islands in the Stream* has yet to be adequately explored by critics, but its appearance in 1970 helped keep Hemingway's reputation fresh, giving the public the impression that "a great writer's ghost [was] handing down books intact from Heaven."[74]

Despite the success of *Islands in the Stream*, a 1972 short story collection, *The Nick Adams Stories,* was the most influential posthumous publication of the decade. Editor Philip Young, with his characteristic audacity, sought to "improve" on Hemingway by retrieving all of his stories about the character Nick Adams, and some stories that *might* be about Nick Adams, from collections published during Hemingway's lifetime – *In Our Time, Men without Women,* and *Winner Take Nothing.* Young then rearranged the stories "in chronological sequence," so that "the events of Nick's life [would] make up a meaningful narrative in which a memorable character grows from child to adolescent to soldier, veteran, writer, and parent – a sequence closely paralleling the events of Hemingway's own life" (*NAS* 6). Young also drew on the Hemingway manuscripts, which he had helped inventory, for previously unpublished materials about Nick that would "fill substantial gaps" in Young's narrative (*NAS* 7). This "fascinating and valuable bit of creative editing," as Louis Rubin called it, greatly enhanced critical interest in the Nick Adams stories, and deepened critical confusion about where Hemingway's life ended and his fiction began.[75]

The year 1980 began the Reagan–Bush era, as Ronald Reagan was elected president of the United States. A two-term president, followed in office by his vice president, George Bush, Reagan left an indelible mark on the nation and its colleges and universities. The Reagan and Bush administrations were perhaps best known for their belief in "voodoo economics," a notion that if the rich are taxed less, they will invest their savings and new wealth will "trickle down" to all sectors of the economy. Instead of encouraging investment, however, these theories led to feverish speculation, the engrossment of more and more wealth by fewer and fewer people, and finally, in 1986, a major stock market crash followed by the collapse of the nation's savings and loan industry and double-digit unemployment in many states. State colleges and universities were devastated by the loss of tax support (programs were terminated, employees laid off, hiring frozen, tuitions increased, salaries reduced, and equipment and infrastructure left to age and crumble), while private institutions, dependent on carefully invested endowments, were injured, to a lesser extent, by market volatility.

At the same time, the Vietnam-era students who remembered Reagan well from another ("if it takes a bloodbath") context were earning tenure and assuming positions of leadership in the beleaguered American academy. They felt profoundly threatened by the new conservatism, whose attacks on 1970s legislation menaced much that they had worked for – including freedom of choice for women and equal opportunities for minorities. From 1986 on, as the Reagan–Bush era showed little sign of winding down and American colleges and universities were everywhere being "'downsized," the Vietnam generation reacted with a concerted effort to return liberal values to the academy. They began to view America as a "multicultural" society, including the voices of women and minorities in the canon of American literature and literary criticism. At times too, they overreacted to Reaganism with an intolerance labeled "political correctness," an effort to silence alternative views and dictate values.

In the first five years of this decade, Hemingway studies reached a plateau and even declined slightly, as scholars produced an average of seventy articles and books a year. Because the early 1980s were marked by several events that ought to have stimulated work on Hemingway, it is difficult to explain why the tide of Hemingway scholarship, having risen steadily throughout the 1960s and 1970s, should have peaked, albeit temporarily, at this juncture. In 1980, the Hemingway manuscripts were moved from the National Archives to a specially designed room in Boston's brand-new John F. Kennedy Library. The collection was opened with great fanfare and a conference that drew scholars from around the nation and led to formation of The Hemingway Society, an organization that would grow from thirty to six hundred members as the decade progressed. In 1981, *Hemingway Notes* became a full-fledged journal, *The Hemingway Review,* which would win one thousand subscribers by decade's end. And Carlos Baker, the grand old man of Hemingway studies, blessed fellow scholars with a thick volume, *Ernest Hemingway: Selected Letters, 1917–1961,* helping place innumerable aspects of Hemingway's life and work in context.[76]

Certainly Hemingway specialists rejoiced in and were stimulated by the events of 1980 and 1981: the new availability of manuscripts and letters, their own society and journal. Many scholars whose names are household words in Hemingway studies today – Michael Reynolds, Paul Smith, Bernard Oldsey, Joseph Flora, Linda Wagner, Jeffrey Meyers, Mark Spilka,

Gerry Brenner, Bernice Kert – were intensely active during the early 1980s. The falloff in Hemingway studies during this period must rather be attributed to the indifference of scholars with wider-ranging or more general concerns. In the early 1980s literary critics as a whole seemed uninterested in Hemingway.

Their apathy can be ascribed in part to a literary theory called deconstruction, imported from France, much in vogue as the Reagan–Bush era began, and appropriate to the period's valueless obsession with getting and spending and general ennui with "meaningful discourse" (people were, perhaps, exhausted by the passionate and divisive insistence on values and meanings that characterized the nation's struggle over Vietnam). One theorist describes deconstruction this way:

> We inhabit . . . an indeterminate universe. Everything is mediated entirely through language – the only way we can know anything is by using words. And the words of any discourse constantly shift their meaning. Everything depends on interpretation, and no interpretation is more correct than another. The proper attitude is to regard all interpretations as equally "not true and not false." To insist that a given piece of discourse means something specific and decided is to elevate one meaning at the expense of the others. It is to uphold a hierarchy of values, and that renders one guilty of a dictatorial urge. Fascism, in short.[77]

Hemingway's prose, based on his belief in the ability of concrete language to construct an objective reality, his craftsmanlike insistence that language is a tool of the writer, and not vice versa, would prove extremely resistant to the critical method of deconstruction. A typical Hemingway sentence – "There was a low, dark room with saddles and harness, and hay-forks made of white wood, and clusters of canvas rope-soled shoes and hams and slabs of bacon and white garlics and long sausages hanging from the roof" (*SAR* 106) – was difficult to deconstruct, to interpret as equally not true and not false, or as elevating one meaning over another. It was simpler for deconstructionists to ignore Hemingway, and for Hemingway scholars to ignore deconstruction.

During the reign of deconstruction, Hemingwayans labored instead at a variety of projects. After the previous decade's rash of influence studies, Hemingway's status as a widely read and highly literary writer became taken for granted. Michael S. Reynolds' 1981 compendium, *Hemingway's Reading, 1910–1940*, and James D. Brasch and Joseph Sigman's *Hemingway's Library: A Composite Record* of the same year, created in two complementary volumes a complete record of Hemingway's reading from childhood through old age.[78] Jeffrey Meyers produced an important compendium of a different sort, *Hemingway: The Critical Heritage,* collecting the most influential reviews of Hemingway's work.[79]

The early 1980s also saw a burst of interest in Hemingway's relationship with Hollywood. Gene D. Phillips' *Hemingway and Film* and Frank M. Laurence's *Hemingway and the Movies* explored the many screen adaptations of Hemingway's novels and short stories, and the Hemingway Collection at the John F. Kennedy Library hosted a conference on Hemingway and film.[80] However, perhaps because the movies made from Hemingway's fiction are as negligible as they are numerous (only Howard Hawks' *To Have and Have Not,* starring Humphrey Bogart and Lauren Bacall, with screenplay by Jules Furthman and William Faulkner, stands out as an exception – and Hemingway's novel is virtually unrecognizable in the film), this critical fad was as short-lived as it was intense.

Despite the academy's growing interest in multiculturalism, such readings gained no ground in Hemingway studies during the 1980s. Rather, critics interested in multiculturalism tended to ignore the author as "politically incorrect." There were just two apologetic articles on Hemingway's handling of race: Gregory Green's " 'A Matter of Color: Hemingway's Criticism of Race Prejudice" and Joyce Dyer's "Hemingway's Use of the Pejorative Term 'Nigger' in 'The Battler.' "[81] Charles Stetler and Gerald Locklin, in "Beneath the Tip of the Iceberg in Hemingway's 'The Mother of a Queen,' " were more critical, reading the story as both homophobic and misogynistic, while Ernest Fontana, in "Hemingway's 'A Pursuit Race,' " saw a "horror of homosexuality" as driving the short story.[82] Barry Gross, writing about Hemingway's anti-Semitism in "Yours Sincerely, Sinclair Levy," was quite straightforward: "Hemingway never lets the reader forget that Cohn is a Jew, not an unattractive character who happens to be a Jew but a character who is unattractive because he is a Jew."[83]

During the 1980s the involvement of women in Hemingway studies continued to grow, albeit more slowly than in the 1970s. Many focused on rehabilitating Hemingway for feminist readers, on making him "correct." We had Linda W. Wagner's " 'Proud and friendly and gently': Women in Hemingway's Early Fiction," Joyce Wexler's "E.R.A. for Hemingway: A Feminist Defense of *A Farewell to Arms,*" Alice Hall Petry's "Coming of Age in Hortons Bay: Hemingway's 'Up in Michigan,' " Sandra Spanier's "Catherine Barkley and the Hemingway Code: Ritual and Survival in *A Farewell to Arms,*" Mimi Reisel Gladstein's *The Indestructible Woman in Faulkner, Hemingway, and Steinbeck,* and Pamela Smiley's "Gender-Linked Miscommunication in 'Hills Like White Elephants.' "[84] Some male readers embraced their arguments (Charles J. Nolan in "Hemingway's Women's

Movement," and J. Andrew Wainwright in "The Far Shore: Gender Complexities in Hemingway's 'Indian Camp' ").[85] Some did not (Bert Bender in "Margot Macomber's Gimlet").[86]

Philip Young, too, continued to be influential at least through 1982, when Joseph Flora published his *Hemingway's Nick Adams*,[87] a detailed critical study and evaluation of Young's Hemingway narrative. But there was trouble brewing. In 1981, and again in 1983, an aggressive scholar named Kenneth Lynn attacked Young's "wound theory" at the roots, discounting the testimony of Hemingway's contemporaries Edmund Wilson and Malcolm Cowley that the short story "Big Two-Hearted River" was about Nick Adams' recovery from the trauma of war.[88] Lynn's assertions prompted a bitter and public argument among himself, Cowley, and finally Young, and it became clear that the "wound" and the "code" were about to be muscled off the stage of Hemingway studies.[89]

It was not so clear, early in the 1980s, what would replace Young's powerful paradigms for reading Hemingway. There were, however, inklings, in Mark Spilka's 1982 essay, "Hemingway and Fauntleroy: An Androgynous Pursuit," and Gerry Brenner's 1983 psychoanalytic study, *Concealments in Hemingway's Works*.[90] Although neither Spilka nor Brenner can be called a deconstructionist, both absorbed the irreverence of that theoretical school. And because both these critics have been deeply influenced by feminist thought, it is natural that their irreverence should be directed toward Hemingway's façade of hypermasculinity, which they set about dismantling with psychoanalytic tools. For Spilka, Hemingway's "strenuous defense of maleness becomes part of a larger struggle with his own androgynous impulses," while Brenner asserts that "Beneath his masculine swagger lay puerile diffidence. An advocate of courage, he was fear-ridden."[91] Their ideas were not new – in 1933, a critic named Max Eastman, in a notorious review called "Bull in the Afternoon," had tried to expose Hemingway's masculine posturing as "a wearing of false hair on the chest"[92] – but they had never before taken center stage in Hemingway studies. Indeed, little attention was paid to Spilka's and Brenner's ideas during the early 1980s.

In 1985, a remarkable series of events began that ended the plateau in Hemingway studies. From 1985 through 1991, the last year of this survey, the productivity of Hemingway scholars surged upward more sharply than ever before, doubling, and in some years almost tripling the output seen in the energetic period of canonization immediately following Hemingway's death. Sadly, the first, and perhaps most important factor in this surge, was the final illness and death of Hemingway's widow, Mary.

When Mary Hemingway became unable to manage the literary affairs of her late husband's estate, her trustees embarked upon a flurry of publication. Whereas Mary had been relatively cautious about placing Hemingway's remaining uncollected and unpublished work before the public, her trustees brought out more "new" Hemingway books in two years than Mary had permitted in the previous decade. The year 1985 saw the publication of *Dateline: Toronto, The Complete* Toronto Star *Dispatches, 1920–1924*, edited by William White, and a book-length version of Hemingway's *Life* magazine article, "The Dangerous Summer," padded with previously unpublished materials and an introduction by James Michener. The year 1986 saw publication of a Hemingway novel, *The Garden of Eden*, as well as Mary's death in November. The year 1987 brought *The Complete Short Stories of Ernest Hemingway*, a volume in progress during Mary's final illness. With the possible exception of *Dateline: Toronto*, all of these books were hastily and disastrously edited; they are rife with glaring omissions and misrepresentations of manuscript materials. Reviews of these posthumous publications, as well as scholarly indignation about the poor quality of their editing,[93] represented one factor in the scholarly surge.

Despite such difficulties, the appearance of *The Garden of Eden* was one of the most important benchmarks in Hemingway studies. Although textual scholars concur that the novel Scribner's published is only one-third of the novel Hemingway wrote, its treatment of feminine madness, male androgyny, bisexuality, and lesbianism was sufficient to prompt a radical reassessment of Hemingway's canonical output. These themes, of course, are omnipresent in the work published during Hemingway's lifetime, but nowhere treated with the candor of *Eden*, which brings them to the fore. Prior to publication of *The Garden of Eden*, most readers of Hemingway could only focus in a simplistic way on Young's question about "what makes a man a man." Now that question was enlarged to include what makes a man a woman? what makes a woman a woman? what makes a woman a man? what makes men and women heterosexual? homosexual? bisexual? where are the boundaries of gender? and what importance does gender have in our makeups? With so many new questions to answer, Hemingway scholarship exploded, and today the flawed text of *The Garden of Eden* is almost as often read and criticized as *The Sun Also Rises* and *A Farewell to Arms*. The novel's complex gender issues did more than any number of feminist apologies to make Hemingway politically correct, dispel the notion of his intolerance, and undo the damage of Hemingway criticism's early misogyny. Following publication of *The Garden of Eden*, the number of women in Hemingway studies doubled again, and today women account for 29 percent of published scholarship. Both psychoanalytic critics and the icono-clasts of deconstruction found much that was fascinating in the novel, and interest in Hemingway expanded beyond an insular group of specialists. Spilka's prescient focus on Hemingway's androgynous impulses, and Bren-ner's psychoanalytic slant on the author's gender-bending relationships with his troubled father and strong-willed mother, once unusual points of view, were suddenly the order of the day.

The early 1980s had begun quietly for biography. Bernice Kert's *The Hemingway Women* and Norberto Fuentes' *Hemingway in Cuba* were the significant scholarly contributions of this period.[94] But in 1985, coincident with the rash of posthumous publication, an equivalent surge in Heming-way biographies began, prompted, perhaps, by an absorption of the recently opened papers and the relaxation of permissions (and scruples) attendant upon Mary Hemingway's departure from the scene.

Jeffrey Meyers' surly, demythologizing *Hemingway: A Biography* (1985) begins this trend, portraying the author's life as a rake's progress from "the confident genius of the twenties and swaggering hero of the thirties to the braggart of the forties and sad wreck of the late fifties."[95] Peter Griffin began what is projected to be a five-volume biography with *Along with Youth,* written in almost novelistic fashion, and accompanied by previously unpublished fragments from Hemingway's early fiction and letters.[96] Mi-chael Reynolds, too, began a five-volume biography, commencing with the highly regarded *The Young Hemingway* and *Hemingway: The Paris Years.*[97] Less thesis-driven and more meticulous in his research than other biographers of the 1980s, Reynolds may, when his work is completed, become the legitimate heir to Carlos Baker's mantle.

The most influential biography of the 1980s, however, was Kenneth Lynn's psychoanalytic, single-volume *Hemingway.*[98] Published the year af-ter *The Garden of Eden,* Lynn's book seized upon the idea advanced by Spilka in "Hemingway and Fauntleroy." Lynn interprets Hemingway's life and work exclusively in the light of the author's "androgyny" and "sexual confusion," which Lynn views as the result of Mrs. Hemingway's dressing the toddler Ernest in baby dresses identical to his older sister's. Public fas-cination with *The Garden of Eden* and Lynn's biography gained national attention for his "theory of androgyny." The baby clothes instantly became part of the Hemingway myth, and the "theory of androgyny" overtook the "wound theory" and notion of "code hero" Lynn had worked hard to debunk. Spilka's own book-length critical study, *Hemingway's Quarrel with Androgyny,* which places the idea of androgyny in its literary and cultural context and uses it in more complex ways to interpret Hemingway's fiction, did not appear until 1990, to be followed in 1994 by Robert Scholes and Nancy R. Comley's *Hemingway's Genders: Rereading the Hemingway Text.*[99]

By the late 1980s the market for exploitative biographies seemed sated, perhaps because some scholarly biographies were now more sensationalistic than their popular precursors. Acquaintance biographies fell off almost entirely as old age and death took their toll among Hemingway's cohorts; those that did appear are assisted (Denis Brian collected interviews with Hemingway acquaintances in *The True Gen;* James Nagel worked with World War I veteran Henry Villard on *Hemingway in Love and War: The Lost Diary of Agnes von Kurowsky*).[100] Family members, too, were relatively quiet, with the exception of son John in his *Misadventures of a Fly Fisherman.*[101]

The availability of manuscripts, posthumous publication, the debut of *The Garden of Eden,* the spate of scholarly biographies, and the overthrow of Philip Young's theories by Mark Spilka's and Kenneth Lynn's, all contributed to a single tendency: the return of scholars to familiar Hemingway texts for reassessment in the light of new ideas. This tendency was responsible for the general surge in Hemingway studies in the late 1980s, and affected the entire canon, but for some reason scholars seemed most compelled to revisit the short stories. The decade closed with Joseph M. Flora's *Ernest Hemingway: A Study of the Short Fiction,* Susan F. Beegel's *Hemingway's Neglected Short Fiction: New Perspectives,* Paul Smith's *A Reader's Guide to the Short Stories of Ernest Hemingway,* and Jackson Benson's *New Critical Approaches to the Short Stories of Ernest Hemingway.*[102]

And that, of course, brings us to the final and most obvious trend of a decade so lavish in scholarship – efforts designed to help Hemingwayans manipulate this wealth of material, including Earl Rovit and Gerry Brenner's *Ernest Hemingway,* Linda W. Wagner's *Ernest Hemingway: Six Decades of Criticism,* Kelli Larson's *Ernest Hemingway: A Reference Guide, 1974–1989,* and Albert J. DeFazio's biannual bibliographies for *The Hemingway Review.*[103]

It is too early to assess our own decade, but we can get out the crystal ball and make some predictions. The interest of widely known mainstream scholars of American literature, including Marjorie Perloff, Nina Baym, and Robert Scholes, suggests that Hemingway's place in the canon is more secure than ever.[104] A distinguished book chapter, "Disturbing Nurses and the Kindness of Sharks," by Nobel prize-winning African-American novelist Toni Morrison, may finally generate interest in multicultural interpretations of Hemingway's work.[105] A great deal of meat-and-potatoes critical and textual study remains to be done on *The Garden of Eden,* but by the end of the decade talk of "androgyny" will be old hat. With issues of gender taking center stage, the number of women in Hemingway studies will continue to grow, and perhaps by the year 2000 they will produce half of published scholarship.

It is harder to predict what new ideas might replace discussion of androgyny and gender as these issues grow stale, but perhaps Glen A. Love has the answer:

> Race, class, and gender are the words that we see and hear everywhere at our professional meetings and in our current publications. But curiously enough . . . the English profession has failed to respond in any significant way to the issue of the environment, the acknowledgment of our place within the natural world and our need to live heedfully within it, at peril of our very survival.[106]

Love suggests that critics may revise the canon to reflect a growing eco-consciousness, and that works such as *The Old Man and the Sea,* "which engages such issues profoundly," may become more widely taught. There are glimmerings that such a transformation may be underway in Hemingway studies: Margot Norris's "The Animal and Violence in Hemingway's *Death in the Afternoon,*" Anne E. Rowe's "The Last Wild Country," Love's own "Hemingway's Indian Virtues: An Ecological Consideration," and Susan Schmidt's "Ecological Renewal Images in 'Big Two-Hearted River': Jack Pines and Fisher King."[107]

Posthumous publication must, necessarily, abate, as materials are exhausted, but there will be at least a volume of Hemingway's World War II short stories, still largely unpublished, and perhaps publication of his "African book" from the disastrous safari of the 1950s. As Hemingway's cohorts wend their way to the grave, leaving their papers behind, a new volume of letters also seems likely.

Biography, too, ought to slow. It is difficult to imagine anyone wanting to write another single-volume biography after Baker, Meyers, Lynn, and, in 1992, James Mellow's excellent *Hemingway: A Life without Consequences.*[108] However, the significant women in Hemingway's life are claiming single-volume biographies. We have Carl Rollyson's 1990 *Nothing Ever Happens to the Brave: The Story of Martha Gellhorn* and Gioia DiLiberto's 1992 *Hadley.*[109] Biographies of Hemingway's second wife, Pauline Pfeiffer, and of his influential mother, Grace Hall Hemingway, seem both inevitable and necessary. And the multivolume biographers are not yet finished. Peter

Griffin, who published *Less Than a Treason* in 1990, owes us three more volumes; and Michael Reynolds, who produced *Hemingway: The American Homecoming* in 1992, owes us at least two more.[110]

It is also too early to tell what role the computer will play in the future of Hemingway studies. The enhancement and wider availability of scanning technology should assist textual studies, stylistic analyses, and finally, perhaps, the creation of scholarly editions. And, as the worldwide web of the Internet allows Hemingwayans around the world to communicate instantaneously with the click of a mouse, as on-line bibliography grows more complete, and electronic publication more prevalent, global appreciation of Hemingway's literary achievements can only intensify.

Ernest Hemingway was born in 1899, into a world with horsedrawn buggies, ragtime, and old growth forests; a world without airplanes, television, or women's suffrage. He committed suicide in 1961, the year the Berlin Wall was built, the Bay of Pigs debacle took place, the first intercontinental ballistic missile was launched, and Pete Seeger composed "Where Have All the Flowers Gone?" His critical reputation today is stronger than at any time since his death. He is widely read in a world where astronauts leave space shuttles to repair telescopes, seventy-five million Americans own computers, nations send delegates to international Earth Summits, and women and minorities, although still not in full possession of equal rights, have opportunities unheard of at either his birth or his death. Hemingway's critical reputation has already withstood the test of generations he set for himself: "Quite a lot of people remember and they tell their children and their children and their grandchildren remember. . . . And if it's good enough it lasts forever."

NOTES

Editor's Note: For the most important texts mentioned in this article, see the Selected Bibliography, which is also the work of Susan Beegel.

1. In Malcolm Cowley, "Portrait of Mister Papa," from *Life* (January 10, 1949), reprinted in *Ernest Hemingway: The Man and His Work* (1950), ed. John K. M. McCaffery (New York: Cooper Square, 1969), 56.

2. James D. Hart, *The Oxford Companion to American Literature*, 4th ed. (New York: Oxford University Press, 1965), 75–76.

3. *Publisher's Weekly* 180 (July 10, 1961): 49.

4. John Raeburn, *Fame Became of Him: Hemingway as Public Writer* (Bloomington: Indiana University Press, 1984), 143.

5. *Benét's Reader's Encyclopedia*, 3rd ed. (New York: Harper and Row, 1987), 393.

6. *Chicago American* (January 21, 1919), 3; *Toronto Daily Star* (July 30, 1924); Guy Hickok, *Brooklyn Daily Eagle* (March 4, 1924), 2F; *New York Herald Tribune* (November 17, 1933), 3; *New York Times* (August 4, 1944), 3; *New York Times* (March 15, 1946), 12.

7. Alajalov, "*Vanity Fair's* Own Paper Dolls. No. 5: Ernest Hemingway, America's Own Literary Cave Man; Hard-Drinking, Hard-Fighting, Hard-Loving – All for Art's Sake," *Vanity Fair* 42 (March 1934): 29; and Mary Hemingway, "Hamburger: Twelve Wonderful Ways with an Old Favorite," *Woman's Day* (January 1961): 34+.

8. *Hemingway: The Critical Heritage,* ed. Jeffrey Meyers (London, Boston, and Henley: Routledge and Kegan Paul, 1982), collects important reviews published during Hemingway's lifetime.

9. Hemingway to Wallace Meyer, February 21, 1952, in *Ernest Hemingway, Selected Letters: 1917–1961,* ed. Carlos Baker (New York: Charles Scribner's Sons, 1981), 751.

10. Princeton, N.J.: Princeton University Press, 1952; New York and Toronto: Rinehart, 1952; and New York: Farrar, Straus, and Young, 1954.

11. New York: Oxford University Press, 1959, and New York: Criterion Books, 1960.

12. Carlos Baker, *Ernest Hemingway: A Life Story* (New York: Charles Scribner's Sons, 1969), 504–5.

13. A. E. Hotchner, *Papa Hemingway: A Personal Memoir* (New York: Random House, 1966), 72.

14. In Baker, *A Life Story,* 528.

15. Norman Mailer, "First Advertisement for Myself" (1959), in *The Long Patrol: 25 Years of Writing from the Work of Norman Mailer,* ed. Robert F. Lucid (New York: World, 1971), 160.

16. Mary Hemingway, *How It Was* (New York: Alfred Knopf, 1976), 387.

17. P. 9.

18. *Saturday Review* 44 (July 1961) – Special Issue: Hemingway: A World View.

19. *Saturday Review* 44 (July 29, 1961): 20. Reprinted in Meyers 433–36.

20. *New Republic* 145 (July 24, 1961): 19–20, reprinted in Meyers 430–33.

21. *New Leader* 44 (August 14–21, 1961): 22–24; *Studies: An Irish Quarterly Review* 50 (Autumn 1961): 312–26; *Books Abroad* 36 (Winter 1962): 5–8.

22. (July 1, 1962): 1, 16.

23. This and other estimates of the amount of Hemingway scholarship produced during a given period are based on the annual *MLA International Bibliography of Books and Articles on the Modern Languages and Literatures,* the only bibliographic reference that follows Hemingway consistently throughout the thirty-year period covered in this essay.

24. Carlos Baker, *Hemingway: The Writer as Artist,* rev. ed. (Princeton: Princeton University Press, 1972), 187.

25. Lexington: University of Kentucky Press, 1961; New Haven: Yale University Press, 1963; New York: Twayne, 1963; Austin: University of Texas Press, 1965; Minneapolis: University of Minnesota Press, 1969.

26. Philip Young, *Ernest Hemingway: A Reconsideration* (University Park: Pennsylvania State University Press, 1966), 63.

27. Pittsburgh: University of Pittsburgh Press, 1963; New York: Thomas Y. Crowell, 1968; and Albuquerque: University of New Mexico Press, 1969.

28. *Hudson Review* 1 (1968): 104–11; *Tradition: A Journal of Orthodox Jewish Thought* 10.3 (Spring 1969), rptd. in *Modern Critical Interpretations: Ernest Hemingway's* The Sun Also Rises, ed. Harold Bloom (New Haven and New York: Chelsea House, 1987), 61–70; and *Yale Review* 58 (March 1969): 321–41.

29. Naomi M. Grant, "The Role of Women in the Fiction of Ernest Hemingway," *Dissertation Abstracts* 29:4456A.

30. Princeton: Princeton University Press, 1967.

31. *Twentieth Century Interpretations of* The Old Man and the Sea: *A Collection of Critical Essays* (Englewood Cliffs, N.J.: Prentice-Hall, 1968).

32. Baker, *The Writer as Artist,* 87; Francis Hackett, *Saturday Review of Literature* (August 6, 1949): 32–33; Edmund Wilson, "Hemingway: Gauge of Morale," *The Wound and the Bow* (1947), reprinted in McCaffery 255.

33. New York: Lancer, 1961; Los Angeles: Holloway House, 1962; New York: Paperback Library, 1962.

34. Cleveland: World, 1962, and Boston: Little, Brown, 1962.

35. New York: Random House, 1966. The Hotchner biography is often dismissed as apocryphal, but doctoral research by Albert J. DeFazio III has shown that it has a solid basis in Hemingway's correspondence with Hotchner, the text often paraphrasing Hemingway letters that Hotchner was forbidden to publish by the terms of the author's will.

36. Caldwell, Idaho: Caxton, 1968.

37. New York: Fleet, 1966.

38. New York: Hawthorn Books, 1965; and South Brunswick and New York: A. S. Barnes, 1969.

39. New York: Charles Scribner's Sons, 1969.

40. Baker, *The Writer as Artist,* 152.

41. Philip Young and Charles W. Mann, *The Hemingway Manuscripts: An Inventory* (University Park: Pennsylvania State University Press, 1969).

42. Chapel Hill: University of North Carolina Press, 1968.

43. American men were forced to register for the draft at age eighteen, but the minimum voting age for all elections was twenty-one.

44. Clifton Daniel, ed., *Chronicle of the Twentieth Century* (Mount Kisco, N.Y.: Chronicle, 1987), 1020.

45. Neil Young, "Ohio," copyright 1970.

46. *Men at War* (New York: Crown, 1942), xiii, xi.

47. Ibid., xi.

48. Ibid.

49. *DAI* 34:2621A and *DAI* 36:2818A–19A.

50. 1.3–4 (1976): 59–64; and 5.1 (Fall 1979): 2–10.

51. *DAI* 34:1282-A; and see MLA 1976 entry 10401.

52. *Fitzgerald-Hemingway Annual* 1972: 245–55; and *Linguistics in Literature* 1.2 (1976): 35–41.

53. *DAI* 35:3735A; *Lost Generation Journal* 3.2 (1974): 35–36; *Lost Generation Journal* 1.1 (1973): 16–19.

54. *Fitzgerald-Hemingway Annual* (1972): 273–80; and *Journal of the School of Languages* 3.2 (1975–76): 32–35.

55. *Journal of Popular Culture* 10.1 (Summer 1977): 203–14.

56. *Fitzgerald-Hemingway Annual* (1978): 307–12.

57. *Essays in Arts and Sciences* 8 (1979): 35–44.

58. *Arizona Quarterly* 26 (Winter 1970): 318–24.

59. New York: Farrar, Straus, & Giroux, 1972, and New York: McGraw-Hill, 1973; Princeton: Princeton University Press, 1975; East Lansing: Michigan State University Press, 1974, and Boston: G. K. Hall, 1977; Corvallis: Oregon State University Press, 1974, and Durham, N.C.: Duke University Press, 1975.

60. Young and Mann, *The Hemingway Manuscripts,* vii.

61. *Selected Letters,* 751.

62. Princeton: Princeton University Press, 1976, and University Park: Pennsylvania State University Press, 1979.

63. New York: David McKay, 1971; Garden City, N.Y.: Doubleday, 1972; and Sherman Oaks, Calif.: Banner Book International, 1977.

64. New York: Viking, 1973; New York: Crown, 1971; Oak Park, Ill.: The Historical Society of Oak Park and River Forest, 1973.

65. Washington D.C.: Microcard Editions, 1972.

66. New York: Alfred A. Knopf, 1976.

67. New York: Crown, 1975, and Boston: Houghton Mifflin, 1976.

68. New York: Viking, 1977.

69. Miami: E. A. Seemann, 1972, and New York: Dodd, Mead, 1973.

70. Washington, D.C.: NCR Microcards, 1971, and Pittsburgh: University of Pittsburgh Press, 1970.

71. Lincoln and London: University of Nebraska Press, 1979.

72. Irving Howe, in Meyers, *Critical Heritage,* 566; John Updike, in Meyers 562.

73. Wilson, in Meyers, *Critical Heritage,* 575; Theroux, in Meyers 584.

74. Updike, in Meyers, *Critical Heritage,* 563.

75. Rubin, in Meyers, *Critical Heritage,* 585.

76. New York: Charles Scribner's Sons, 1981.

77. In David Lehman, *Signs of the Times: Deconstruction and the Fall of Paul de Man* (New York: Simon and Schuster, 1992), 58.

78. Princeton: Princeton University Press, 1981, and New York: Garland, 1981.

79. London, Boston, and Henley: Routledge and Kegan Paul, 1982.

80. New York: Frederick Ungar, 1980, and Jackson: University of Mississippi Press, 1981.

81. *The Hemingway Review* 1.1 (Fall 1981): 27–32; and *Notes on Contemporary Literature* 16.5 (1986): 5–10.

82. *The Hemingway Review* 2.1 (Fall 1982): 68–69; and *Explicator* 42.4 (Summer 1984): 43–45.

83. *Commentary* 80.6 (December 1985): 56–59.

84. *College Literature* 7 (1980): 239–47; *Georgia Review* 35.1 (1981): 111–23; *The Hemingway Review* 3.2 (Spring 1984): 23–28; in *Ernest Hemingway's A Farewell to Arms,* ed. Harold Bloom (New York: Chelsea House, 1986), 131–48; Ann Arbor, Mich.: UMI Research Press, 47–73; *The Hemingway Review* 8.1 (Fall 1988): 2–12.

85. *The Hemingway Review* 3.2 (Spring 1984): 14–22; and *Dalhousie Review* 66.1–2 (Spring–Summer 1986): 181–87.

86. *College Literature* 8.1 (Winter 1981): 12–20.

87. Baton Rouge: Louisiana State University Press, 1982.

88. "Hemingway's Private War," *Commentary* 72.1 (July 1981): 24–33, reprinted in Kenneth S. Lynn, *The Air-Line to Seattle: Studies in Literary and Historical Writing about America* (Chicago: University of Chicago Press, 1983), 108–31.

89. Malcolm Cowley, "Hemingway's Wound – and Its Consequences for American Literature," *Georgia Review* 38.3 (Fall 1984): 670–72; Kenneth Lynn, "Reader's Forum," *Georgia Review* 38.3 (Fall 1984): 668–69; and Philip Young, "Reader's Forum," *Georgia Review* 38.3 (Fall 1984): 669–70.

90. In *American Novelists Revisited: Essays in Feminist Criticism,* ed. Fritz Fleishman (Boston: G. K. Hall, 1982; Columbus: Ohio State University Press, 1983).

91. In Kelli Larson, *Ernest Hemingway: A Reference Guide, 1974–1989* (Boston: G. K. Hall, 1991), 143; Brenner, *Concealments,* 13.

92. In Meyers, *Critical Heritage,* 172–80.

93. See William Kennedy's "The Last Olé," *New York Book Review* (June 9, 1985): 1, 32–33, 35 on *The Dangerous Summer;* Barbara Solomon's "Where's Papa? Scribner's *The Garden of Eden* Is Not the Novel Hemingway Wrote," *New Republic* 196 (March 9, 1986): 30–34; and my own grumblings about the not-so-complete *Complete Short Stories* in *Resources for American Literary Study* 18.1 (1992): 108–11.

94. New York and London: W. W. Norton, 1983, and Secaucus, N.J.: Lyle Stuart, 1984.

95. Dustjacket, New York: Harper and Row, 1985.

96. New York and Oxford: Oxford University Press, 1985.

97. New York and Oxford: Basil Blackwell, 1986, and New York and Oxford: Basil Blackwell, 1989.

98. New York: Simon and Schuster, 1987.

99. Lincoln and London: University of Nebraska Press, 1990; New Haven: Yale University Press, 1994.

100. New York: Grove Press, 1988, and Boston: Northeastern University Press, 1989.

101. Dallas, Tex.: Taylor, 1986.

102. Boston: Twayne, 1989; Ann Arbor: UMI, 1989; Boston: G. K. Hall, 1989; Durham, N.C.: Duke University Press, 1990.

103. Boston: Twayne, 1986; East Lansing: Michigan State University Press, 1987; and Boston: G. K. Hall, 1990.

104. " 'Ninety Percent Rotarian: Gertrude Stein's Hemingway,' " *American Literature* 62 (1990): 668–82; " 'Actually, I Felt Sorry for the Lion,' " in Benson, ed. *New Critical Approaches,* 112–20; with Nancy R. Comley, "Tribal Things: Hemingway's Erotics of Truth," *Novel* 25 (Spring 1992): 268–85.

105. Toni Morrison, *Playing in the Dark: Whiteness and the Literary Imagination* (Cambridge: Harvard University Press, 1992).

106. Glen A. Love, "Revaluing Nature: Toward an Ecological Criticism," in *Old West – New West: Centennial Essays,* ed. Barbara Howard Meldrum (Moscow: University of Idaho Press, 1993), 284.

107. In *Beasts of Modern Imagination* (Baltimore: Johns Hopkins University Press, 1985), 195–219; in *The Idea of Florida in American Literary Imagination* (Baton Rouge: Louisiana State University Press), 92–106; *Western American Literature* 22.3 (Fall 1987): 201–13; *The Hemingway Review* 9.2 (Spring 1990): 142–44.

108. Boston: Houghton Mifflin, 1992.

109. New York: St. Martin's, 1990, and New York: Ticknor and Fields, 1992.

110. New York: Oxford University Press, 1990, and Oxford: Basil Blackwell, 1992.

SELECTED BIBLIOGRAPHY

Works by Ernest Hemingway

BOOKS

Three Stories and Ten Poems. Paris: Contact, 1923; Columbia, S.C. and Bloomfield Hills, Mich.: Bruccoli Clark, 1977.

in our time. Paris: Three Mountains Press, 1924; Columbia, S.C. and Bloomfield Hills, Mich.: Bruccoli Clark, 1977.

In Our Time. New York: Boni and Liveright, 1925; rev. ed. New York: Charles Scribner's Sons, 1930.

The Torrents of Spring. New York: Charles Scribner's Sons, 1926; London: Jonathan Cape, 1933.

Today Is Friday. Englewood, N.J.: As Stable, 1926.

The Sun Also Rises. New York: Charles Scribner's Sons, 1926. *Fiesta.* London: Jonathan Cape, 1927.

Men without Women. New York: Charles Scribner's Sons, 1927; London: Jonathan Cape, 1928.

A Farewell to Arms. New York: Charles Scribner's Sons, 1929; London: Jonathan Cape, 1929.

Death in the Afternoon. New York and London: Charles Scribner's Sons, 1932; London: Jonathan Cape, 1932.

God Rest You Merry Gentlemen. New York: House of Books, 1933.

Winner Take Nothing. New York and London: Charles Scribner's Sons, 1933; London: Jonathan Cape, 1934.

Green Hills of Africa. New York and London: Charles Scribner's Sons, 1935; London: Jonathan Cape, 1936.

To Have and Have Not. New York: Charles Scribner's Sons, 1937; London: Jonathan Cape, 1937.

The Spanish Earth. Cleveland: J. B. Savage, 1938.

The Fifth Column and the First Forty-Nine Stories. New York: Charles Scribner's Sons, 1938; London: Jonathan Cape, 1939; republished as *The Short Stories of Ernest Hemingway.* New York: Charles Scribner's Sons, 1954.

The Fifth Column: A Play in Three Acts. New York: Charles Scribner's Sons, 1940; London: Jonathan Cape, 1968.

For Whom the Bell Tolls. New York: Charles Scribner's Sons, 1940; London: Jonathan Cape, 1941.

Across the River and into the Trees. London: Jonathan Cape, 1950; New York: Charles Scribner's Sons, 1950.

The Old Man and the Sea. New York: Charles Scribner's Sons, 1952; London: Jonathan Cape, 1952.

The Collected Poems, unauthorized edition. San Francisco, 1960.

Hemingway: The Wild Years. Ed. Gene Z. Hanrahan. New York: Dell, 1962.

A Moveable Feast. New York: Charles Scribner's Sons, 1964; London: Jonathan Cape, 1964.

Byline: Ernest Hemingway. Ed. William White. New York: Charles Scribner's Sons, 1967; London: Collins, 1968.

The Fifth Column and Four Stories of the Spanish Civil War. New York: Charles Scribner's Sons, 1969.

Ernest Hemingway, Cub Reporter: Kansas City Star Stories. Ed. Matthew J. Bruccoli. Pittsburgh: University of Pittsburgh Press, 1970.

Islands in the Stream. New York: Charles Scribner's Sons, 1970; London: Collins, 1970.

Ernest Hemingway's Apprenticeship: Oak Park, 1916–1917. Ed. Matthew J. Bruccoli. Washington, D.C.: Bruccoli Clark/NCR Microcard Editions, 1971.

The Nick Adams Stories. New York: Charles Scribner's Sons, 1972.

88 Poems. Ed. Nicholas Gerogiannis. New York and London: Harcourt Brace Jovanovich/Bruccoli Clark, 1979.

Complete Poems. Lincoln and London: University of Nebraska Press, 1983.

The Dangerous Summer. New York: Charles Scribner's Sons, 1985; London: Hamish Hamilton, 1985.

Dateline: Toronto. Ed. William White. New York: Charles Scribner's Sons, 1985.

The Garden of Eden. New York: Charles Scribner's Sons, 1986; London: Hamilton, 1987.

The Complete Short Stories of Ernest Hemingway: The Finca Vigía Edition. New York: Charles Scribner's Sons, 1987.

Matthew J. Bruccoli, ed. *The Sun Also Rises,* by Ernest Hemingway. Facsimile edition, 2 vols., Archives of Literary Documents Series. Detroit: Omnigraphics, 1990.

Cynthia Maziarka and Donald Vogel, Jr., eds. *Hemingway at Oak Park High.* Oak Park, Ill.: Oak Park and River Forest High School, 1993.

LETTERS

Ernest Hemingway: Selected Letters, 1917–1961. Ed. Carlos Baker. New York: Charles Scribner's Sons, 1981.

"The Finca Vigía Papers." Ed. Norberto Fuentes. *Hemingway in Cuba.* Secaucus, N.J.: Lyle Stuart, 1984, 307–416.

Hemingway in Love and War: The Lost Diary of Agnes von Kurowsky, Her Letters, and Correspondence of Ernest Hemingway. Ed. Henry S. Villard and James Nagel. Boston: Northeastern University Press, 1989.

COLLECTIONS

Viking Portable Hemingway. Ed. Malcolm Cowley. New York: Viking, 1944; abridged as *The Essential Hemingway.* London: Jonathan Cape, 1947.

The Hemingway Reader. Ed. Charles Poore. New York: Charles Scribner's Sons, 1953.

The Enduring Hemingway. Ed. Charles Scribner Jr. New York: Charles Scribner's
Sons, 1974.
Hemingway on Writing. Ed. Larry W. Phillips. New York: Charles Scribner's Sons,
1984; London: Granada, 1985.

PLAY PRODUCTION

The Fifth Column. Adapted by Benjamin Glazer, New York, Alvin Theater, March 6,
1940.

MOTION PICTURES

The Spanish Earth. Commentary written and spoken by Hemingway, Contemporary
Historians, 1937.
The Old Man and the Sea. Screenplay supervision and technical advice by Heming-
way, Warner Bros., 1958.

Selected Periodical Publications – Uncollected

FICTION

"A Divine Gesture." *Double Dealer* 3 (May 1922): 267–68.
"The Young Hemingway: Three Unpublished Short Stories." Ed. Peter Griffin. *New
York Times Sunday Magazine,* August 18, 1985, 14–23, 59, 61.
"[Philip Haines Was a Writer . . .]." Ed. Donald Junkins. *Hemingway Review* 9
(Spring 1990): 2–9.
"A Lack of Passion." Ed. Susan F. Beegel. *Hemingway Review* 9 (Spring 1990):
57–68.

NONFICTION

"Homage to Ezra." *This Quarter* 1 (Spring 1925): 221–25.
"Bullfighting, Sport and Industry." *Fortune* 1 (March 1930): 83–88, 139–46, 150.
"The Farm." *Cahiers d'Art* 9 (1934): 28–29.
"Who Murdered the Vets?" *New Masses* 16 (September 17, 1935): 9–10.
"On the American Dead in Spain." *New Masses* 30 (February 14, 1939): 3.
"Safari." *Look* 18 (January 26, 1954): 19–34.
"The Nobel Prize Speech." *Mark Twain Journal* 11 (Summer 1962): 10.
"African Journal." *Sports Illustrated* 35 (December 20, 1971): 5, 40–52, 57–66; 36
(January 3, 1972): 26–46; 37 (January 10, 1972): 22–30.
"The Art of the Short Story." *Paris Review* 23 (Spring 1981): 85–102.
"Hemingway's Spanish Civil War Dispatches." Ed. William Braasch Watson. *Hem-
ingway Review* 7 (Spring 1988): 4–92.

INTERVIEWS

Ross, Lillian. "How Do You Like it Now, Gentlemen?" *New Yorker* 26 (May 13,
1950): 40–51.

Plimpton, George. "An Interview with Ernest Hemingway." *Paris Review* 18 (Spring 1958): 85–108.
Betsky, Seymour, and Leslie Fiedler. "An Almost Imaginary Interview: Hemingway in Ketchum." *Partisan Review* 29 (Summer 1962): 395–405.
Bruccoli, Matthew J., ed. *Conversations with Ernest Hemingway.* Jackson: University of Mississippi Press, 1986.

PRINCIPAL MANUSCRIPT COLLECTIONS

Bancroft Library, University of California, Berkeley, Calif.
Carlos Baker Papers, Princeton University Library, Princeton, N.J.
Charles Scribner's Sons Archives, Princeton University Library, Princeton, N.J.
Ernest Hemingway Papers, John Fitzgerald Kennedy Library, Boston, Mass.
Humanities Research Center, University of Texas, Austin, Tex.
Lilly Library, Indiana University, Bloomington, Ind.
Monroe County Public Library, Key West, Fla.
University of Wisconsin Library, Milwaukee, Wis.

Works about Ernest Hemingway

BIBLIOGRAPHIES

Hanneman, Audre. *Ernest Hemingway: A Comprehensive Bibliography.* Princeton: Princeton University Press, 1967.
   Supplement to Ernest Hemingway: *A Comprehensive Bibliography.* Princeton: Princeton University Press, 1975.
Young, Philip, and Charles W. Mann. *The Hemingway Manuscripts: An Inventory.* University Park: Pennsylvania State University Press, 1969.
Benson, Jackson J. "A Comprehensive Checklist of Hemingway Short Fiction Criticism, Explication, and Commentary." *The Short Stories of Ernest Hemingway: Critical Essays.* Ed. Jackson J. Benson. Durham, N.C.: Duke University Press, 1975, 312–75.
Wagner, Linda Welshimer. *Ernest Hemingway: A Reference Guide.* Boston: G. K. Hall, 1977.
August, Jo, comp. *Catalog of the Ernest Hemingway Collection at the John F. Kennedy Library.* 2 vols. Boston: G. K. Hall, 1982.
Benson, Jackson J. "A Comprehensive Checklist of Hemingway Short Fiction Criticism, Explication, and Commentary, 1975–1989." *New Critical Approaches to the Short Stories of Ernest Hemingway.* Ed. Jackson J. Benson. Durham, N.C.: Duke University Press, 1990, 395–458.
Larson, Kelli A. *Ernest Hemingway: A Reference Guide, 1974–1989.* Boston: G. K. Hall, 1990.

OTHER REFERENCES

Brasch, James D., and Joseph Sigman, comps. *Hemingway's Library: A Composite Record.* New York: Garland, 1981.

Bruccoli, Matthew J., and C. E. Frazer Clark Jr., comps. *Hemingway at Auction, 1930–1973.* Detroit: Gale, 1973.

Fitch, Noel Riley. *Walks in Hemingway's Paris: A Guide to Paris for the Literary Traveler.* New York: St. Martin's, 1989.

Hays, Peter L., comp. *A Concordance to Hemingway's* In Our Time. Boston: G. K. Hall, 1990.

Leland, John. *A Guide to Hemingway's Paris.* Chapel Hill, N.C.: Algonquin Books of Chapel Hill, 1990.

Reynolds, Michael, comp. *Hemingway's Reading, 1910–1940.* Princeton: Princeton University Press, 1981.

PERIODICALS

Alderman, Taylor, and Kenneth Rosen, eds. *Hemingway notes.* Carlisle, Pa.: Dickinson College, 1971–74.

Bruccoli, Matthew J., and C. E. Frazer Clark, et al., eds. *Fitzgerald/Hemingway Annual.* Washington, D.C.: NCR Microcard Editions, 1969–74; Englewood, Colo.: Information Handling Services, 1975–76; Detroit: Gale, 1977–80.

Oliver, Charles S., ed. *Hemingway notes.* Ada: Ohio Northern University, 1979–81.

The Hemingway Review. Ada: Ohio Northern University, 1981–92.

The Hemingway Newsletter. Ada: Ohio Northern University, 1981–92.

The Hemingway Newsletter. Charlottesville, Va.: The Hemingway Society, 1992– .

Beegel, Susan F., ed. *The Hemingway Review.* Pensacola: University of West Florida and The Hemingway Society, 1992–93.

The Hemingway Review. Moscow: University of Idaho Press and The Hemingway Society, 1993– .

BIOGRAPHIES

Arnold, Lloyd. *Hemingway: High on the Wild.* New York: Grosset and Dunlap, 1968.

Baker, Carlos. *Ernest Hemingway: A Life Story.* New York: Charles Scribner's Sons, 1969.

Brian, Denis. *The True Gen: An Intimate Portrait of Hemingway by Those Who Knew Him.* New York: Grove, 1988.

Bruccoli, Matthew J. *Scott and Ernest: The Authority of Failure and the Authority of Success.* New York: Random House, 1978.

Burgess, Anthony. *Ernest Hemingway and His World.* New York: Charles Scribner's Sons, 1978.

Diliberto, Gioia. *Hadley.* New York: Ticknor and Fields, 1992.

Donaldson, Scott. *By Force of Will: The Life and Art of Ernest Hemingway.* New York: Viking, 1977.

Fuentes, Norberto. *Hemingway in Cuba.* Tr. Consuelo Corwin. Secaucus, N.J.: Lyle Stuart, 1984.

Gellhorn, Martha. *Travels with Myself and Another.* London: Allen Lane, 1978.

Griffin, Peter. *Along with Youth: Hemingway, The Early Years.* New York: Oxford University Press, 1985.

Less Than a Treason: Hemingway in Paris. New York: Oxford University Press, 1990.

Hardy, Richard E., and John G. Cull. *Hemingway: A Psychological Portrait.* New York: Irvington, 1988.

Hemingway, Gregory H. *Papa: A Personal Memoir.* Boston: Houghton Mifflin, 1976.

Hemingway, Jack. *Misadventures of a Fly Fisherman: My Life with and without Papa.* Dallas: Taylor, 1986.

Hemingway, Leicester. *My Brother, Ernest Hemingway.* Cleveland: World, 1961.

Hemingway, Mary Welsh. *How It Was.* New York: Alfred Knopf, 1976.

Hotchner, A. E. *Papa Hemingway: A Personal Memoir.* New York: Random House, 1966.

    Hemingway and His World. New York: Vendome, 1989.

Ivancich von Rex, Adriana. *La torre bianca.* Milan: Arnaldo Mondadori Editore, 1980.

Kert, Bernice. *The Hemingway Women.* New York: Norton, 1983.

Lynn, Kenneth S. *Hemingway.* New York: Simon and Schuster, 1987.

McLendon, James. *Papa: Hemingway in Key West.* Miami: Seeman, 1972.

Mellow, James R. *Hemingway: A Life without Consequences.* Boston: Houghton Mifflin, 1992.

Meyers, Jeffrey. *Hemingway: A Biography.* New York: Harper and Row, 1985.

Miller, Madelaine Hemingway. *Ernie: Hemingway's Sister "Sunny" Remembers.* New York: Crown, 1975.

Montgomery, Constance Cappel. *Hemingway in Michigan.* New York: Fleet, 1966.

Reynolds, Michael. *The Young Hemingway.* Oxford: Basil Blackwell, 1986.

    Hemingway: The Paris Years. Oxford: Basil Blackwell, 1989.

    Hemingway: The American Homecoming. Oxford: Basil Blackwell, 1992.

Rollyson, Carl. *Nothing Ever Happens to the Brave: The Story of Martha Gellhorn.* New York: St. Martin's, 1990.

Samuelson, Arnold. *With Hemingway: A Year in Key West and Cuba.* New York: Random House, 1984.

Sanford, Marcelline Hemingway. *At the Hemingways: A Family Portrait.* Boston: Atlantic/Little, Brown, 1962.

Sokoloff, Alice Hunt. *Hadley: The First Mrs. Hemingway.* New York: Dodd, Mead, 1973.

Criticism

BOOKS

Baker, Carlos. *Hemingway: The Writer as Artist.* Rev. ed. Princeton: Princeton University Press, 1972.

Baker, Sheridan. *Ernest Hemingway: An Introduction and Interpretation.* New York: Holt, Rinehart and Winston, 1967.

Beegel, Susan F. *Hemingway's Craft of Omission: Four Manuscript Examples.* Ann Arbor: UMI Research Press, 1988.

Benson, Jackson J. *Hemingway: The Writer's Art of Self-Defense.* Minneapolis: University of Minnesota, 1969.

Bredahl, A. Carl, Jr., and Susan Lynn Drake. *Hemingway's Green Hills of Africa as Evolutionary Narrative: Helix and Scimitar.* Lewiston, N.Y.: Edwin Mellen Press, 1990.

Broer, Lawrence R. *Hemingway's Spanish Tragedy.* Tuscaloosa: University of Alabama Press, 1973.

Brenner, Gerry. *Concealments in Hemingway's Works.* Columbus: Ohio State University Press, 1983.

The Old Man and the Sea: *Story of a Common Man.* Boston: Twayne, 1991.

Capellan, Angel. *Hemingway and the Hispanic World.* Ann Arbor: UMI Research Press, 1985.

Comley, Nancy R., and Robert Scholes. *Hemingway's Genders: Rereading the Hemingway Text.* New Haven: Yale University Press, 1994.

Cooper, Stephen. *The Politics of Ernest Hemingway.* Ann Arbor: UMI Research Press, 1987.

DeFalco, Joseph. *The Hero in Hemingway's Short Stories.* Pittsburgh: University of Pittsburgh Press, 1963.

Fenton, Charles A. *The Apprenticeship of Ernest Hemingway: The Early Years.* New York: Farrar, Straus, and Young, 1954.

Fleming, Robert E. *The Face in the Mirror: Hemingway's Writers.* Tuscaloosa: University of Alabama Press, 1994.

Flora, Joseph M. *Hemingway's Nick Adams.* Baton Rouge: Louisiana State University Press, 1982.

Friedrich, Otto. *An Inquiry into Madness "in our time."* New York: Simon and Schuster, 1976.

Gaggin, John. *Hemingway and Nineteenth-Century Aestheticism.* Ann Arbor: UMI Research Press, 1987.

Gladstein, Mimi. *The Indestructible Woman in the Works of Faulkner, Hemingway, and Steinbeck.* Ann Arbor: UMI Research Press, 1986.

Grebstein, Sheldon Norman. *Hemingway's Craft.* Carbondale: Southern Illinois University Press, 1973.

Grimes, Larry E. *The Religious Design of Hemingway's Early Fiction.* Ann Arbor: UMI Research Press, 1985.

Gurko, Leo. *Ernest Hemingway and the Pursuit of Heroism.* New York: Crowell, 1968.

Hays, Peter L. *Ernest Hemingway.* New York: Continuum, 1990.

Hovey, Richard B. *Hemingway: The Inward Terrain.* Seattle: University of Washington Press, 1973.

Johnston, Kenneth G. *The Tip of the Iceberg: Hemingway and the Short Story.* Greenwood, Fla.: Penkevill, 1987.

Joost, Nicholas. *Ernest Hemingway and the Little Magazines: The Paris Years.* Barre, Mass.: Barre Publishers, 1960.

Killinger, John. *Hemingway and the Dead Gods: A Study in Existentialism.* Lexington: University Press of Kentucky, 1960.

Kobler, J. F. *Ernest Hemingway: Journalist and Artist.* Ann Arbor: UMI Research Press, 1985.

Laurence, Frank M. *Hemingway and the Movies.* Jackson: University Press of Mississippi, 1981.

Lewis, Robert W. *Hemingway on Love.* Austin: University of Texas Press, 1965.

A Farewell to Arms: *The War of the Words.* Boston: Twayne, 1991.

Messent, Peter. *Ernest Hemingway.* London: Macmillan, 1992.

Morgan, Kathleen. *Tales Plainly Told: The Eyewitness Narratives of Hemingway and Homer.* Columbia, S.C.: Camden House, 1990.

Nahal, Chaman. *The Narrative Pattern in Hemingway's Fiction.* Rutherford, N.J.: Fairleigh Dickinson Press, 1971.

Nelson, Raymond S. *Hemingway: Expressionist Artist.* Ames: Iowa State University Press, 1979.

Oldsey, Bernard. *Hemingway's Hidden Craft: The Writing of* A Farewell to Arms. University Park: Pennsylvania State University Press, 1979.

Phillips, Gene D. *Hemingway and Film.* New York: Frederick Ungar, 1980.

Raeburn, John. *Fame Became of Him: Hemingway as Public Writer.* Bloomington: Indiana University Press, 1984.

Rao, E. Nageswara. *Ernest Hemingway: A Study of His Rhetoric.* Atlantic Highlands, N.J.: Humanities Press, 1983.

Reynolds, Michael. *Hemingway's First War: The Making of* A Farewell to Arms. Princeton: Princeton University Press, 1976.

The Sun Also Rises: *A Novel of the Twenties.* Boston: Twayne, 1988.

Rovit, Earl, and Gerry Brenner. *Ernest Hemingway.* Boston: Twayne, 1986.

Scholes, Robert, and Nancy R. Comley. *Hemingway's Genders: Rereading the Hemingway Text.* New Haven: Yale University Press, 1994.

Smith, Paul. *A Reader's Guide to the Short Stories of Ernest Hemingway.* Boston: G. K. Hall, 1989.

Spilka, Mark. *Hemingway's Quarrel with Androgyny.* Lincoln: University of Nebraska Press, 1990.

Stanton, Edward F. *Hemingway and Spain: A Pursuit.* Seattle and London: University of Washington Press, 1989.

Stephens, Robert O. *Hemingway's Nonfiction: The Public Voice.* Chapel Hill: University of North Carolina Press, 1968.

Stoltzfus, Ben. *Gide and Hemingway: Rebels against God.* Port Washington, N.Y.: Kennikat, 1978.

Svoboda, Frederic Joseph. *Hemingway's* The Sun Also Rises: *The Crafting of a Style.* Lawrence: University Press of Kansas, 1983.

Tetlow, Wendolyn. *Hemingway's* In Our Time: *Lyrical Dimensions.* Lewisburg: Bucknell University Press, 1992.

Unfried, Sarah P. *Man's Place in the Natural Order: A Study of Hemingway's Major Works.* New York: Gordon, 1976.

Waldhorn, Arthur. *A Reader's Guide to Ernest Hemingway.* New York: Farrar, Straus and Giroux, 1972.

Watts, Emily. *Ernest Hemingway and the Arts.* Urbana: University of Illinois Press, 1971.

Weber, Ronald. *Hemingway's Art of Non-Fiction.* New York: St. Martin's, 1990.

Whitlow, Roger. *Cassandra's Daughters: The Women in Hemingway.* Westport, Conn.: Greenwood, 1984.

Williams, Wirt. *The Tragic Art of Ernest Hemingway.* Baton Rouge: Louisiana State University Press, 1981.

Wilkinson, Meyer. *Hemingway and Turgenev: The Nature of Literary Influence.* Ann Arbor: UMI Research Press, 1986.

Workman, Brooke. *In Search of Ernest Hemingway: A Model for Teaching a Literature Seminar.* Urbana, Ill.: NCTE, 1979.

Wylder, Delbert. *Hemingway's Heroes.* Albuquerque: University of New Mexico Press, 1970.

Young, Philip. *Ernest Hemingway: A Reconsideration.* University Park: Pennsylvania State University Press, 1966.

Collections of Criticism

Astro, Richard, and Jackson J. Benson, eds. *Hemingway in Our Time.* Corvallis: Oregon State University Press, 1974.

Baker, Carlos, ed. *Critiques of Four Major Novels.* New York: Charles Scribner's Sons, 1962.

Hemingway and His Critics: An International Anthology. New York: Hill and Wang, 1961.

Beegel, Susan F., ed. *Hemingway's Neglected Short Fiction: New Perspectives.* Tuscaloosa: University of Alabama Press, 1992.

Benson, Jackson J., ed. *New Critical Approaches to the Short Stories of Ernest Hemingway.* Durham, N.C.: Duke University Press, 1990.

The Short Stories of Ernest Hemingway: Critical Essays. Durham, N.C.: Duke University Press, 1975.

Bloom, Harold, ed. *Modern Critical Interpretations: Ernest Hemingway's* A Farewell to Arms. New York: Chelsea House, 1987.

Modern Critical Interpretations: Ernest Hemingway's The Sun Also Rises. New York: Chelsea House, 1987.

Modern Critical Views: Ernest Hemingway. New York: Chelsea House, 1985.

Donaldson, Scott, ed. *New Essays on* A Farewell to Arms. Cambridge: Cambridge University Press, 1990.

Flora, Joseph M., ed. *Ernest Hemingway: A Study of the Short Fiction.* Boston: Twayne, 1989.

Gellens, Jay, ed. *Twentieth Century Interpretations of* A Farewell to Arms: *A Collection of Critical Essays.* Englewood Cliffs, N.J.: Prentice-Hall, 1970.

Graham, John, ed. *The Merrill Studies in* A Farewell to Arms. Columbus, Ohio: Merrill, 1971.

Grebstein, Sheldon Norman, ed. *The Merrill Studies in* For Whom the Bell Tolls. Columbus, Ohio: Merrill, 1971.

Howell, John M., ed. *Hemingway's African Stories: The Stories, Their Sources, Their Critics.* New York: Charles Scribner's Sons, 1969.

Josephs, Allen. For Whom the Bell Tolls: *Ernest Hemingway's Undiscovered Country.* New York: Twayne, 1994.

Jobes, Katherine T., ed. *Twentieth Century Interpretations of* The Old Man and the Sea. Englewood Cliffs, N.J.: Prentice-Hall, 1968.

Lee, A. Robert, ed. *Ernest Hemingway: New Critical Essays.* London and New York: Vision and Barnes and Noble, 1983.

Lewis, Robert W., ed. *Hemingway in Italy and Other Essays.* New York: Praeger, 1990.

McCaffery, John K. M., ed. *Ernest Hemingway: The Man and His Work*. New York: World, 1950.

Meyers, Jeffrey, ed. *Hemingway: The Critical Heritage*. London: Routledge and Kegan Paul, 1982.

Nagel, James, ed. *Ernest Hemingway: The Writer in Context*. Madison: University of Wisconsin Press, 1984.

Noble, Donald R., ed. *Hemingway: A Revaluation*. Troy, N.Y.: Whitston, 1983.

Oldsey, Bernard, ed. *Ernest Hemingway: The Papers of a Writer*. New York: Garland, 1981.

Oliver, Charles M., ed. *A Moving Picture Feast; the Filmgoer's Hemingway*. New York: Praeger, 1989.

Reynolds, Michael, ed. *Critical Essays on Ernest Hemingway's* In Our Time. Boston: G. K. Hall, 1983.

Rosen, Kenneth, ed. *Hemingway Repossessed*. Westport, Conn.: Praeger, 1994.

Sanderson, Rena, ed. *Blowing the Bridge: Essays on Hemingway and* For Whom the Bell Tolls. New York, Westport, and London: Greenwood, 1992.

Sarason, Bertram D., ed. *Hemingway and the Sun Set*. Washington, D.C.: NCR Microcard Editions, 1972.

Scafella, Frank, ed. *Hemingway: Essays of Reassessment*. Oxford: Oxford University Press, 1990.

Wagner, Linda Welshimer, ed. *Ernest Hemingway: Five Decades of Criticism*. East Lansing: Michigan State University Press, 1974.

Ernest Hemingway: Six Decades of Criticism. East Lansing: Michigan State University Press, 1987.

Wagner-Martin, Linda, ed. *New Essays on* The Sun Also Rises. Cambridge: Cambridge University Press, 1987.

Waldhorn, Arthur, ed. *Ernest Hemingway: A Collection of Criticism*. New York: McGraw-Hill, 1973.

Waldmeir, Joseph, and Kenneth Mareks, eds. *Up in Michigan: Proceedings of the First National Conference of the Hemingway Society*. Traverse City, Mich.: n.p., 1983.

Weeks, Robert P., ed. *Hemingway: A Collection of Critical Essays*. Englewood Cliffs, N.J.: Prentice-Hall, 1962.

White, William, ed. *The Merrill Studies in* The Sun Also Rises. Columbus, Ohio: Merrill, 1969.

Picture Books

Ernest Hemingway Rediscovered. Photographs by Roberto Herrera Sotolongo, text by Norberto Fuentes. New York: Charles Scribner's Sons, 1988.

Hemingway's Paris. Photographs and text compiled by Robert E. Gajdusek. New York: Charles Scribner's Sons, 1978.

Hemingway's Spain. Photographs by Loomis Dean, text by Barnaby Conrad. San Francisco: Chronicle, 1989.

Spanish civil war, 153–5
    Hemingway's writing on, 235–40
    and the North American Newspaper
        Alliance dispatches, 28–31
    short stories about, 236–7
Spanish Earth, The, 31, 154, 164, 225
Spengler, Oswald, 175
Spilka, Mark, 289, 291–2
Spofford, William, 282
Steffens, Lincoln, 160
Stein, Gertrude, 16, 22, 40, 41, 52n,
        57, 86n, 88, 174, 197–8, 214,
        270
    criticism of Hemingway, 183–4
    and experimentation in repetitive
        rhythm, 74
    in *For Whom the Bell Tolls*, 188
    and Grace Hemingway, 174
    and omission, 201
Stendahl, 112
Stephens, Robert O., 32–3, 279
Stetler, Charles, 281, 288
Stevens, Wallace, 264n
Stewart, Donald Ogden, 89, 200, 201
Stoneback, H. R., 264–5n, 266n
Strater, Mike, 227
stream of consciousness, 198, 210
success. *See* fame
suicide
    of Clarence Hemingway, 113, 182
    of famous artists, 14–15
    Hemingway's motives for, 14, 227,
        273
    in "Indian Camp," 62
    and psychic costs incurred by the
        writer, 11
Sun Also Rises, The, 57, 87–107, 199,
        224, 269
    autobiographical connections in,
        200–8, 215
    background of, 88, 89, 109, 200–1
    betrayal theme in, 95, 97, 98, 99,
        205
    bullfighting in, 229–32
    central problem of, 94–5
    characterization of Brett Ashley in,
        92–3, 95, 96, 99–100, 177–80

    characterization of Frances Clyne in,
        102–3
    characterization of Jake Barnes in,
        90, 91, 178, 179, 200–8
    as confessional, 90, 98
    early drafts of, 89–90, 91–2, 101–2,
        103, 104, 105, 200, 204, 205,
        213–14
    early titles of, 89, 231
    and the fiesta, 230–1
    Hemingway's treatment of Spain in,
        240
    influence of Paris on, 200–8
    influence on American lifestyle, 87
    and Jake's impotence, 178–9
    and the lost generation, 230–1
    as novel of character, 90
    political references in, 152
    and primitive purity, 179
    reception of, 90
    retrospective narration of, 90, 95
    reversal of gender roles in, 178–9
    rewriting of, 229
    Right Bank–Left Bank opposition
        pattern in, 203–5
    secondary female characters in,
        100–5
        Edna, 105
        Frances Clyne, 102–3, 205
        Georgette Hobin, 103–5
        Katherine Kirby, 100–1
    and shift in gender constructions,
        177–80
    as tragedy, 230–1
    and transformation in style, 87

Tender Is the Night, 140, 141
"textual perplexity" formula, 52n
Thomas, Norman, 159
Thoreau, David, 82
"Three-Day Blow, The," 47, 67–9
    and masculine behavior codes,
        67–9
Three Mountains Press, 58
"Three Shots," 46, 47–9
Three Stories and Ten Poems, 10, 42,
        88, 199